Advances in Information Security

Volume 70

Series editor
Sushil Jajodia, George Mason University, Fairfax, VA, USA

More information about this series at http://www.springer.com/series/5576

Ali Dehghantanha • Mauro Conti
Tooska Dargahi

Editors

Cyber Threat Intelligence

Editors
Ali Dehghantanha
Department of Computer Science
University of Sheffield
Sheffield, UK

Mauro Conti
Department of Mathematics
University of Padua
Padua, Italy

Tooska Dargahi
Department of Computer Science
University of Salford
Manchester, UK

ISSN 1568-2633
Advances in Information Security
ISBN 978-3-030-08891-0   ISBN 978-3-319-73951-9   (eBook)
https://doi.org/10.1007/978-3-319-73951-9

Printed on acid-free paper

This Springer imprint is published by the registered company Springer International Publishing AG part of Springer Nature.
The registered company address is: Gewerbestrasse 11, 6330 Cham, Switzerland

Contents

Cyber Threat Intelligence: Challenges and Opportunities

Mauro Conti, Tooska Dargahi, and Ali Dehghantanha

Abstract The ever increasing number of cyber attacks requires the cyber security and forensic specialists to detect, analyze and defend against the cyber threats in almost real-time. In practice, timely dealing with such a large number of attacks is not possible without deeply perusing the attack features and taking corresponding intelligent defensive actions—this in essence defines cyber threat intelligence notion. However, such an intelligence would not be possible without the aid of artificial intelligence, machine learning and advanced data mining techniques to collect, analyse, and interpret cyber attack evidences. In this introductory chapter we first discuss the notion of cyber threat intelligence and its main challenges and opportunities, and then briefly introduce the chapters of the book which either address the identified challenges or present opportunistic solutions to provide threat intelligence.

Keywords Cyber threat intelligence · Indicators of attack · Indicators of compromise · Artificial intelligence

1 Introduction

In the era of digital information technology and connected devices, the most challenging issue is ensuring the security and privacy of the individuals' and organizations' data. During the recent years, there has been a significant increase in the

M. Conti
University of Padua, Padua, Italy
e-mail: conti@math.unipd.it

T. Dargahi (✉)
Department of Computer Science, University of Salford, Manchester, UK
e-mail: t.dargahi@salford.ac.uk

A. Dehghantanha
Department of Computer Science, University of Sheffield, Sheffield, UK
e-mail: A.Dehghantanha@sheffield.ac.uk

© Springer International Publishing AG, part of Springer Nature 2018
A. Dehghantanha et al. (eds.), *Cyber Threat Intelligence*, Advances in Information Security 70, https://doi.org/10.1007/978-3-319-73951-9_1

1

number and variety of cyber attacks and malware samples which make it extremely difficult for security analysts and forensic investigators to detect and defend against such security attacks. In order to cope with this problem, researchers introduced the notion of *"Threat Intelligence"*, which refers to *"the set of data collected, assessed and applied regarding security threats, threat actors, exploits, malware, vulnerabilities and compromise indicators"* [14]. In fact, Cyber Threat Intelligence (CTI) emerged in order to help security practitioners in recognizing the indicators of cyber attacks, extracting information about the attack methods, and consequently responding to the attack accurately and in a timely manner. Here an important challenge would be: How to provide such an intelligence? When a significant amount of data is collected from or generated by different security monitoring solutions, intelligent big-data analytical techniques are necessary to mine, interpret and extract knowledge out of the collected data. In this regard, several concerns come along and introduce new challenges to the filed, which we discuss in the following.

1.1 Cyber Threat Intelligence Challenges

As a matter of fact, cybercriminals adopt several methods to attack a victim in order to (1) steal victim's sensitive personal information (e.g., financial information); or (2) access and take control of the victim's machine to perform further malicious activities, such as delivering malware (in case of botnet), locking/encrypting victim machine (in case of ransomware). Though, different cyber attacks seem to follow different methods of infection, in essence they have more or less similar life cycle: starting from victim reconnaissance to performing malicious activities on the victim machine/network.

1.1.1 Attack Vector Reconnaissance

An important challenge in defending against cyber attacks, is recognizing the point of attacks and the system vulnerabilities that could be exploited by the cybercriminals. Along with the common methods that have always been used to deceive victims (e.g., phishing [16]) in performing the actions that the attackers desire, during the recent years, attackers have used smarter and more innovative methods for attacking victims. These methods are ranging from delivering a malicious software (malware) in an unexpected format (e.g., Word documents or PDF files) to the victim machine [6], to exploiting 0-day vulnerabilities,[1] and trespassing anonymous communications in order to contact threat actors [8]. Some examples of such advanced attacks are the new families of Ransomware that have worm-like

---

[1] An application vulnerability that is undisclosed and could be exploited by the attackers to access the victim's machine [12].

behaviours, which have infected tens of hundreds of individuals, organizations and critical systems. These advancements in attack methods make the recognition of the attacker and attack's point of arrival an extremely challenging issue.

1.1.2 Attack Indicator Reconnaissance

Another important issue regarding the emerging cyber attacks is the fact that cybercriminals use advanced anti-forensics and evasion methods in their malicious code, which makes the usual security assessment techniques, e.g., CVSS (Common Vulnerability Scoring System), or static malware and traffic analysis less efficient [13, 15]. Moreover, the new networking paradigms, such as software-defined networking (SDN), Internet of Things (IoT), and cloud computing, and their widely adoption by organizations (e.g., using cloud resources for their big-data storage and processing) call for modern techniques in forensic investigation of exchanged and stored data [2, 7, 10, 17].

1.2 Cyber Threat Intelligence Opportunities

In order to address the challenges explained in the previous section, the emerging field of cyber threat intelligence considers the application of artificial intelligence and machine learning techniques to perceive, reason, learn and act intelligently against advanced cyber attacks. During the recent years, researchers have taken different artificial intelligence techniques into consideration in order to provide the security professionals with a means of recognizing cyber threat indicators. In particular, there is an increasing trend in the usage of Machine Learning (ML) and data mining techniques due to their proved efficiency in malware analysis (in both static and dynamic analysis), as well as network anomaly detection [1, 3–5, 9, 15]. Along with the methods that the cyber defenders could use in order to prevent or detect cyber attacks, there are other mechanisms that could be adopted in order to deceive the attackers, such as using honeypots. In such mechanisms, security specialists provide fake information or resources that seem to be legitimate to attract attackers, while at the same time they monitor the attackers' activities and proactively detect the attack [11]. Totally, a combination of these methods would be required to provide up-to-date information for security practitioners and analysts.

2 A Brief Review of the Book Chapters

This book provides an up-to-date and advanced knowledge, from both academia and industry, in cyber threat intelligence. In particular, in this book we provide wider knowledge of the field with specific focus on the cyber attack methods and processes, as well as combination of tools and techniques to perceive, reason, learn and act on a wide range of data collected from different cyber security and forensics solutions.

The remainder of the book is structured as follows. The first six chapters discuss, in details, how the adoption of artificial intelligence would advance the cyber threat intelligence in several contexts, i.e., in static malware analysis (chapter "Machine Learning Aided Static Malware Analysis: A Survey and Tutorial"), network anomaly detection (chapter "Application of Machine Learning Techniques to Detecting Anomalies in Communication Networks: Datasets and Feature Selection Algorithms" and "Application of Machine Learning Techniques to Detecting Anomalies in Communication Networks: Classification Algorithms"), Ransomware detection (chapter "Leveraging Machine Learning Techniques for Windows Ransomware Network Traffic Detection"and "Leveraging Support Vector Machine for Opcode Density Based Detection of Crypto-Ransomware"), and Botnet detection (chapter "BoTShark : A Deep Learning Approach for Botnet Traffic Detection"). The next chapter (chapter "A Practical Analysis of the Rise in Mobile Phishing") presents an investigative analysis of mobile-specific phishing methods and the results of a case study by PayPal. Chapter "PDF-Malware Detection: A Survey and Taxonomy of Current Techniques" reviews several methods of malicious payload delivery through PDF files and provides a taxonomy of malicious PDF detection methods. Chapter "Adaptive Traffic Fingerprinting for Darknet Threat Intelligence" presents a traffic fingerprinting algorithm for Darknet threat intelligence, which in essence serves as an adaptive traffic association and BGP interception algorithm against Tor networks. Chapter "A Model for Android and iOS Applications Risk Calculation: CVSS Analysis and Enhancement Using Case-Control Studies" investigates the effectiveness of existing CVSS evaluation results and proposes a model for CVSS analysis suggesting improvements to the calculation of CVSS scores (to be used for Android and iOS applications). Chapter "A Honeypot Proxy Framework for Deceiving Attackers with Fabricated Content" studies the attributes of an effective fake content generator to be used to deceive cyber attackers, and presents an implementation design for an efficient honeypot proxy framework. Chapter "Investigating the Possibility of Data Leakage in Time of Live VM Migration" discusses possible attacks to the memory data of VMs (Virtual Machines) during live migration in the cloud environment and proposes a secure live VM migration. Chapter "Forensics Investigation of OpenFlow-Based SDN Platforms" introduces a forensic investigation framework for SDN, validating its efficiency considering two use-case scenarios. Finally, the last two chapters warp up the book by assessing and reviewing the state-of-the-art in mobile forensics (chapter "Mobile Forensics: A Bibliometric Analysis") and cloud forensics (chapter "Emerging from The Cloud: A Bibliometric Analysis of Cloud Forensics Studies").

Acknowledgements We would like to sincerely thank all the authors and reviewers, as well as Springer editorial office for their effort towards the success of this book.

References

1. Alhawi, O.M.K., Baldwin, J., Dehghantanha, A.: Leveraging machine learning techniques for windows ransomware network traffic detection. In: M. Conti, A. Dehghantanha, T. Dargahi (eds.) Cyber Threat Intelligence, chap. 5. Springer - Advances in Information Security series (2018, in press)
2. Baldwin, J., Alhawi, O.M.K., Shaughnessy, S., Akinbi, A., Dehghantanha, A.: Emerging from The Cloud: a Bibliometric Analysis of Cloud Forensics Studies. In: M. Conti, A. Dehghantanha, T. Dargahi (eds.) Cyber Threat Intelligence, chap. 16, p. in press. Springer - Advances in Information Security series (2018)
3. Baldwin, J., Dehghantanha, A.: Leveraging support vector machine for opcode density based detection of crypto-ransomware. In: M. Conti, A. Dehghantanha, T. Dargahi (eds.) Cyber Threat Intelligence, chap. 6, p. in press. Springer - Advances in Information Security series (2018)
4. Ding, Q., Li, Z., Haeri, S., Trajković, L.: Application of machine learning techniques to detecting anomalies in communication networks: Classification algorithms. In: M. Conti, A. Dehghantanha, T. Dargahi (eds.) Cyber Threat Intelligence, chap. 4, p. in press. Springer - Advances in Information Security series (2018)
5. Ding, Q., Li, Z., Haeri, S., Trajković, L.: Application of machine learning techniques to detecting anomalies in communication networks: Datasets and feature selection algorithms. In: M. Conti, A. Dehghantanha, T. Dargahi (eds.) Cyber Threat Intelligence, chap. 3, p. in press. Springer - Advances in Information Security series (2018)
6. Elingiusti, M., Aniello, L., Querzoni, L., Baldoni, R.: PDF-malware detection: a survey and taxonomy of current techniques. In: M. Conti, A. Dehghantanha, T. Dargahi (eds.) Cyber Threat Intelligence, chap. 9, p. in press. Springer - Advances in Information Security series (2018)
7. Gill, J., Okere, I., HaddadPajouh, H., Dehghantanha, A.: Mobile Forensics: A Bibliometric Analysis. In: M. Conti, A. Dehghantanha, T. Dargahi (eds.) Cyber Threat Intelligence, chap. 15, p. in press. Springer - Advances in Information Security series (2018)
8. Haughey, H., Epiphaniou, G., Al-Khateeb, H., Dehghantanha, A.: Adaptive Traffic Fingerprinting for Darknet Threat Intelligence. In: M. Conti, A. Dehghantanha, T. Dargahi (eds.) Cyber Threat Intelligence, chap. 10, p. in press. Springer - Advances in Information Security series (2018)
9. Homayoun, S., Ahmadzadeh, M., Hashemi, S., Dehghantanha, A., Khayami, R.: BoTShark: A deep learning approach for botnet traffic detection. In: M. Conti, A. Dehghantanha, T. Dargahi (eds.) Cyber Threat Intelligence, chap. 7, p. in press. Springer - Advances in Information Security series (2018)
10. Pandya, M.K., Homayoun, S., Dehghantanha, A.: Forensics Investigation of OpenFlow-Based SDN Platforms. In: M. Conti, A. Dehghantanha, T. Dargahi (eds.) Cyber Threat Intelligence, chap. 14, p. in press. Springer - Advances in Information Security series (2018)
11. Papalitsas, J., Rauti, S., Tammi, J., Leppänen, V.: A honeypot proxy framework for deceiving attackers with fabricated content. In: M. Conti, A. Dehghantanha, T. Dargahi (eds.) Cyber Threat Intelligence, chap. 12, p. in press. Springer - Advances in Information Security series (2018)
12. Park, R.: Guide to zero-day exploits (2015). URL https://www.symantec.com/connect/blogs/guide-zero-day-exploits
13. Petraityte, M., Dehghantanha, A., Epiphaniou, G.: A Model for Android and iOS Applications Risk Calculation: CVSS Analysis and Enhancement Using Case-Control Studies. In: M. Conti, A. Dehghantanha, T. Dargahi (eds.) Cyber Threat Intelligence, chap. 11, p. in press. Springer - Advances in Information Security series (2018)

14. Shackleford, D.: Who's using cyberthreat intelligence and how? – a SANS survey (2015). URL https://www.sans.org/reading-room/whitepapers/analyst/cyberthreat-intelligence-how-35767
15. Shalaginov, A., Banin, S., Dehghantanha, A., Franke, K.: Machine learning aided static malware analysis: A survey and tutorial. In: M. Conti, A. Dehghantanha, T. Dargahi (eds.) Cyber Threat Intelligence, chap. 2, p. in press. Springer - Advances in Information Security series (2018)
16. Wardman, B., Weideman, M., Burgis, J., Harris, N., Butler, B., Pratt, N.: A practical analysis of the rise in mobile phishing. In: M. Conti, A. Dehghantanha, T. Dargahi (eds.) Cyber Threat Intelligence, chap. 8, p. in press. Springer - Advances in Information Security series (2018)
17. Yasmin, R., Memarian, M.R., Hosseinzadeh, S., Conti, M., Leppänen, V.: Investigating the possibility of data leakage in time of live VM migration. In: M. Conti, A. Dehghantanha, T. Dargahi (eds.) Cyber Threat Intelligence, chap. 13, p. in press. Springer - Advances in Information Security series (2018)

Machine Learning Aided Static Malware Analysis: A Survey and Tutorial

Andrii Shalaginov, Sergii Banin, Ali Dehghantanha, and Katrin Franke

Abstract Malware analysis and detection techniques have been evolving during the last decade as a reflection to development of different malware techniques to evade network-based and host-based security protections. The fast growth in variety and number of malware species made it very difficult for forensics investigators to provide an on time response. Therefore, Machine Learning (ML) aided malware analysis became a necessity to automate different aspects of static and dynamic malware investigation. We believe that machine learning aided static analysis can be used as a methodological approach in technical Cyber Threats Intelligence (CTI) rather than resource-consuming dynamic malware analysis that has been thoroughly studied before. In this paper, we address this research gap by conducting an in-depth survey of different machine learning methods for classification of static characteristics of 32-bit malicious Portable Executable (PE32) Windows files and develop taxonomy for better understanding of these techniques. Afterwards, we offer a tutorial on how different machine learning techniques can be utilized in extraction and analysis of a variety of static characteristic of PE binaries and evaluate accuracy and practical generalization of these techniques. Finally, the results of experimental study of all the method using common data was given to demonstrate the accuracy and complexity. This paper may serve as a stepping stone for future researchers in cross-disciplinary field of machine learning aided malware forensics.

Keywords Machine learning · Malware · Static analysis · Artificial intelligence

A. Shalaginov · S. Banin · K. Franke
Norwegian Information Security Laboratory, Center for Cyber- and Information Security,
Norwegian University of Science and Technology, Gjøvik, Norway
e-mail: andrii.shalaginov@ntnu.no; sergii.banin@ntnu.no; katrin.franke@ntnu.no

A. Dehghantanha (✉)
Department of Computer Science, University of Sheffield, Sheffield, UK
e-mail: A.Dehghantanha@sheffield.ac.uk

© Springer International Publishing AG, part of Springer Nature 2018   7
A. Dehghantanha et al. (eds.), *Cyber Threat Intelligence*, Advances in Information
Security 70, https://doi.org/10.1007/978-3-319-73951-9_2

1 Introduction

Stealing users' personal and private information has been always among top interests of malicious programs [8]. Platforms which are widely used by normal users have always been best targets for malware developers [9].

Attackers have leveraged malware to target personal computers [22], mobile devices [61], cloud storage systems [13], Supervisory Control and Data Acquisition Systems (SCADA) [12], Internet of Things (IoT) network [81] and even big data platforms [67].

Forensics examiners and incident handlers on the other side have developed different techniques for detection of compromised systems, removal of detected malicious programs [14, 23], network traffic [63], and even log analysis [69]. Different models have been suggested for detection, correlation and analyses of cyber threats [20] (on a range of mobile devices [43] and mobile applications [45], cloud applications [11], cloud infrastructure [46] and Internet of Things networks [47]). Windows users are still comprising majority of Internet users hence, it is not surprising to see Windows as the most adopted PC Operating System (OS) on top of the list of malware targeted platforms [73]. In response, lots of efforts have been made to secure Windows platform such as educating users [25, 54], embedding an anti-virus software [40], deploying anti-malware and anti-exploitation tools [52, 53], and limiting users applications privilege [41].

In spite of all security enhancements, many malware are still successfully compromising Windows machines [36, 73] and malware is still ranked as an important threat to Windows platforms [33]. As result, many security professionals are still required to spend a lot of time on analyzing different malware species [10]. This is a logical step since malware analysis plays a crucial role in Cyber Threats Intelligence (CTI). There has been proposed a portal to facilitate CTI and malware analysis through interactive collaboration and information fusion [56].

There are two major approaches for malware analysis namely *static* (code) and *dynamic* (behavioral) malware analysis [8, 16]. In dynamic malware analysis, samples are executed and their run time behavior such as transmitted network traffic, the length of execution, changes that are made in the file system, etc. are used to understand the malware behavior and create indications of compromise for malware detection [16]. However, dynamic analysis techniques can be easily evaded by malware that are aware of execution conditions and computing environment [34]. Dynamic malware analysis techniques can only provide a snapshot view of the malware behavior and hence very limited in analysis of Polymorph or Metamorph species [44]. Moreover, dynamic malware analysis techniques are quite resource hungry which limits their enterprise deployment [37].

In static malware analysis, the analyst is reversing the malware code to achieve a deeper understanding of the malware possible activities [28]. Static analysis relies on extraction of a variety of characteristics from the binary file such that function calls, header sections, etc. [83]. Such characteristics may reveal indicators of malicious activity that are going to be used in CTI [57]. However, static analysis is quite a slow process and requires a lot of human interpretation and hence [8].

Static analysis of PE32 is a many-sided challenge that was studied by different authors. Static malware analysis also was used before for discovering interconnections in malware species for improved Cyber Threat Intelligence [42, 66]. As 32-bit malware are still capable of infecting 64-bit platforms and considering there are still many 32-bit Windows OS it is not surprising that still majority of Windows malware are 32-bit Portable Executable files [8]. To authors knowledge there has not been a comparative study of ML-based static malware using a single dataset which produces comparable results. We believe that utilization of ML-aided automated analysis can speed up intelligent malware analysis process and reduce human interaction required for binaries processing. Therefore, there is a need for thorough review of the relevant scientific contributions and offer a taxonomy for automated static malware analysis.

The remainder of this paper is organized as follows. We first offer a comprehensive review of existing literature in machine learning aided static malware analysis. We believe this survey paves the way for further research in application of machine learning in static malware analysis and calls for further development in this field. Then, taxonomy of feature construction methods for variety of static characteristics and corresponding ML classification methods is offered. Afterwards, we offer a tutorial that applies variety of set of machine learning techniques and compares their performance. The tutorial findings provide a clear picture of pros and cons of ML-aided static malware analysis techniques. To equally compare all the methods we used one benign and two malware datasets to evaluate all of the studied methods. This important part complements the paper due to the fact that most of the surveyed works used own collections, sometimes not available for public access or not published at all. Therefore, experimental study showed performance comparison and other practical aspects of ML-aided malware analysis. Section 4 gives an insight into a practical routine that we used to establish our experimental setup. Analysis of results and findings are given in Sect. 5. Finally, the paper is concluded and several future works are suggested in Sect. 6.

2 An Overview of Machine Learning-Aided Static Malware Detection

This section provides an analysis of detectable static properties of 32 bit PE malware followed by detailed description of different machine learning techniques to develop a taxonomy of machine learning techniques for static malware analysis.

2.1 Static Characteristics of PE Files

PE file format was introduced in Windows 3.1 as PE32 and further developed as PE32+ format for 64 bit Windows Operating Systems. PE files contain a Common Object File Format (COFF) header, standard COFF fields such as header, section table, data directories and Import Address Table (IAT). Beside the PE header fields a number of other static features can be extracted from a binary executable such as strings, entropy and size of various sections.

To be able to apply Machine Learning PE32 files static characteristics should be converted into a machine-understandable features. There exist different types of features depending on the nature of their values such that *numerical* that describes a quantitative measure (can be integer, real or binary value) or *nominal* that describes finite set of categories or labels. An example of the *numerical* feature is CPU (in %) or RAM (in Megabytes) usage, while *nominal* can be a file type (like *.dll* or *.exe*) or Application Program Interface (API) function call (like $write()$ or $read()$).

1. *n-grams of byte sequences* is a well-known method of feature construction utilizing sequences of bytes from binary files to create features. Many tools have been developed for this purpose such as *hexdump* [39] created 4-grams from byte sequences of PE32 files. The features are collected by sliding window of n bytes. This resulted in 200 millions of features using 10-grams for about two thousands files in overall. Moreover, feature selection (FS) was applied to select 500 most valuable features based on Information Gain metric. Achieved accuracy on malware detection was up to 97% using such features. Another work on byte n-grams [51] described usage of 100–500 selected n-grams yet on a set of 250 malicious and 250 benign samples. Similar approach [31] was used with $10, \ldots, 10,000$ best n-grams for $n = 1, \ldots, 10$. Additionally, ML methods such that Naive Bayes, C4.5, k-NN and others were investigated to evaluate their applicability and accuracy. Finally, a range of 1–8 n-grams [27] can result in 500 best selected n-grams that are used later to train AdaBoost and Random Forests in addition to previously mentioned works.

2. *Opcode sequences* or operation codes are set of consecutive low level machine abstractions used to perform various CPU operations. As it was shown [62] such features can be used to train Machine Learning methods for successful classification of the malware samples. However, there should be a balance between the size of the feature set and the length of n-gram opcode sequence. n-Grams with the size of 4 and 5 result in highest classification accuracy as unknown malware samples could be unveiled on a collection of 17,000 malware and 1000 benign files with a classification accuracy up to 94% [58]. Bragen [6] explored reliability of malware analysis using sequences of opcodes based on the 992 PE-files malware and benign samples. During the experiments, about 50 millions of opcodes were extracted. 1-gram- and 2-gram-based features showed good computational results and accuracy. Wang et al. [79] presented how the 2-tuple opcode sequences can be used in combination with density clustering to detect malicious or benign files.

3. *API calls* are the function calls used by a program to execute specific functionality. We have to distinguish between System API calls that are available through standard system DLLs and User API calls provided by user installed software. These are designed to perform a pre-defined task during invocation. Suspicious API calls, anti-VM and anti-debugger hooks and calls can be extracted by PE analysers such as PEframe [4]. Zabidi et al. [83] studied 23 malware samples and found that some of the API calls are present only in malwares rather than benign software. Function calls may compose in graphs to represent PE32 header features as nodes, edges and subgraphs [84]. This work shows that ML methods achieve accuracy of 96% on 24 features extracted after analysis of 1037 malware and 2072 benign executables. Further, in [71] 20,682 API calls were extracted using PE parser for 1593 malicious and benign samples. Such large number of extracted features can help to create linearly separable model that is crucial for many ML methods as Support Vector Machines (SVM) or single-layer Neural Networks. Another work by [55] described how API sequences can be analysed in analogy with byte n-grams and opcode n-grams to extract corresponding features to classify malware and benign files. Also in this work, an array of API calls from IAT (PE32 header filed) was processed by Fisher score to select relevant features after analysis of more than 34 k samples.

4. *PE header* represents a collection of meta data related to a Portable Executable file. Basic features that can be extracted from PE32 header are *Size of Header*, *Size of Uninitialized Data*, *Size of Stack Reserve*, which may indicate if a binary file is malicious or benign [15]. The work [76] utilized Decision Trees to analyse PE header structural information for describing malicious and benign files. Ugarte-Pedrero et al. [77] used 125 raw header characteristics, 31 section characteristics, 29 section characteristics to detect unknown malware in a semi-supervised approach. Another work [80] used a dataset containing 7863 malware samples from Vx Heaven web site in addition to 1908 benign files to develop a SVM based malware detection model with accuracy of 98%. Markel and Bilzor [38] used F-score as a performance metric to analyse PE32 header features of 164,802 malicious and benign samples. Also [29] presented research of two novel methods related to PE32 string-based classier that do not require additional extraction of structural or meta-data information from the binary files. Moreover, [84] described application of 24 features along with API calls for classification of malware and benign samples from VxHeaven and Windows XP SP3 respectively. Further, ensemble of features was explored [59], where authors used in total 209 features including structural and raw data from PE32 file header. Further, Le-Khac et al. [35] focused on Control Flow Change over first 256 addresses to construct n-gram features.

In addition to study of specific features used for malware detection, we analyzed articles devoted to application of ML for static malware analysis published between 2000 and 2016, which covers the timeline of Windows NT family that are still in use as depicted in Fig. 1. We can see that the number of papers that are relevant

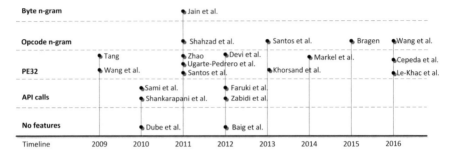

Fig. 1 Timeline of works since 2009 that involved static analysis of Portable Executable files using method characteristics using also ML method for binary malware classification

to our study is growing from 2009 and later, which can be justified on the basis of increase in the number of Windows users (potential targets) and corresponding malware families.

Challenges Despite the fact that some of the feature construction techniques reflected promising precision of 90+ % in differentiation between malicious and benign executables, there are still no best static characteristic that guarantee 100% accuracy of malware detection. This can be explained by the fact that malware are using obfuscation and encryption techniques to subvert detection mechanisms. In addition, more accurate approaches such as bytes N-GRAMS are quite resource intensive and hardly practical in the real world.

2.2 Machine Learning Methods Used for Static-Based Malware Detection

2.2.1 Statistical Methods

Exploring large amounts of binary files consists of statistical features may be simplified using so called frequencies or likelihood of features values. These methods are made to provide prediction about the binary executable class based on statistics of different static characteristics (either automatically or manually collected) which are applicable to malware analysis too as describe by Shabtai et al. [60]. To process such data, extract new or make predictions the following set of statistical methods can be used:

Naive Bayes is a simple probabilistic classifier, which is based on Bayesian theorem with naive assumptions about independence in correlation of different features. The Bayes Rule can be explained as a following conditional independences of features values with respect to a class:

$$P(C_k|V) = P(C_k)\frac{P(V|C_k)}{P(V)} \tag{1}$$

where $P(C_k)$ is a prior probability of class $C_k, k = 1, \ldots, m_0$ which is calculated from collected statistics according to description of variables provided by Kononenko et al. [32]. This method is considered to tackle just binary classification problem (benign against malicious) since it was originally designed as multinomial classifier. $V = \langle v_1, \ldots, v_a \rangle$ is the vector of attributes values that belongs to a sample. In case of Naive Bayes *input* values should be symbolical, for example strings, opcodes, instruction n-grams etc. $P(V)$ is the prior probability of a sample described with vector V. Having training data set and given vector V we count how many samples contain equal values of attributes (e.g. based on the number of sections or given opcode sequence). It is important to mention that V have not to be of length of full attribute vector and can contain only one attribute value. $P(V|C_k)$ is the conditional probability of a sample described with V given the class C_k. And $P(C_k|V)$ conditional probability of class C_k with V. Based on simple probability theory we can describe conditional independence of attribute values v_i given the class C_k:

$$P(V|C_k) = P(v_1 \wedge \ldots \wedge v_a|C_k) = \prod_{i=1}^{a} P(v_i|C_k) \tag{2}$$

Dropping the mathematical operations we get final version of Eq. (1):

$$P(C_k|V) = P(C_k) \prod_{i=1}^{a} \frac{P(C_k|v_i)}{P(C_k)} \tag{3}$$

So, the task of this machine learning algorithm is to calculate conditional and unconditional probabilities as described in Eq. (3) using a training dataset. To be more specific, the Algorithm 1 pseudo code shows the calculation of the conditional probability.

So, we can see from Eq. (1) that given *output* is as a probability that a questioned software sample belongs to one or another class. Therefore, the classification decision will be made by finding a maximal value from set of corresponding class likelihoods. Equation (4) provides formula that assigns class label to the *output*:

$$\hat{y} = \underset{k \in \{1, \ldots, K\}}{\mathrm{argmax}} \; P(C_k) P(V|C_k). \tag{4}$$

Bayesian Networks is a probabilistic directed acyclic graphical model (sometimes also named as Bayesian Belief Networks), which shows conditional dependencies using directed acyclic graph. Network can be used to detect "*update knowledge of the state of a subset of variables when other variables (the evidence variables) are observed*" [32]. Bayesian Networks are used in many cases of classification and information retrieval (such as semantic search). The method's routine can be described as following. If edge goes from vertex A to vertex B, then A is a parent of B, and B is an ancestor of A. If from A there is oriented path

---

Algorithm 1 Calculating $P(C_k|V)$—conditional probability of class C_k with V

1: *Sample* structure with class label and attribute values
2: $S \leftarrow$ array of training Samples
3: $V \leftarrow$ array of attribute values
4: $C_k \leftarrow$ class number
5: $P\_C_k = 0$
6: **function** $get\_P\_C_k(ClassNumber, Samples)$
7:      $output = 0$
8:      **for all** sample from Samples **do**
9:          **if** $sample.getClass() == ClassNumber$ **then**
10:              $output += \frac{1}{size[Samples]}$
11:          **end if**
12:      **end for**
13:      return $output$
14: **end function**
15: **function** $get\_P\_C_k\_v_i(ClassNumber, v, i, Samples)$
16:      $output = 0$
17:      **for all** sample from Samples **do**
18:          **if** $sample.getClass() == ClassNumber$ AND $sample.getAttribute(i) == v$
         then
19:              $output += \frac{1}{size[Samples]}$
20:          **end if**
21:      **end for**
22:      return $output$
23: **end function**
24: $P(C_k|V = 0)$
25: $prod = 1$
26: i=0
27: **for all** $v \, from \, V$ **do**
28:      $prod* = \frac{get\_P\_C_k\_v_i(ClassNumber, v, i, Samples)}{get\_P\_C_k(ClassNumber, Samples)}$
29:      $i += 1$
30: **end for**
31: $P(C_k|V) = prod * get\_P\_C_k(ClassNumber, Samples))$

---

to another vertex B exists then B is ancestor of A, and A is a predecessor of B. Let's designate set of parent vertexes of vertex V_i as $parents(V_i) = PA_i$. Direct acyclic graph is called Bayesian Network for probability distribution $P(v)$ given for set of random variables V if each vertex of graph has matched with random variable from V. And edge of a graph fits next condition: every variable v_i from V must be conditionally independent from all vertexes that are not its ancestors if all its direct parents PA_i are initialized in graph G:

$$\forall V_i \in V \Rightarrow P(v_i|pa_i, s) = P(v_i|pa_i) \tag{5}$$

where v_i is a value of V_i, S—set of all vertexes that are not ancestors of V_i, s—configuration of S, pa_i—configuration of PA_i. Then full general distribution of the values in vertexes could be written as product of local distributions, similarly to Naive Bayes rules:

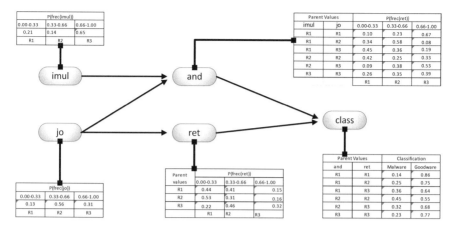

Fig. 2 Bayesian network suitable for malware classification [58]

$$P(V_1, \ldots, V_n) = \prod_{i=1}^{n} P(V_i \mid \text{parents}(V_i)) \qquad (6)$$

Bayesian Belief Networks can be used for classification [32], thus can be applied for malware detection and classification as well [58]. To make Bayesian Network capable of classification it should contain classes as parent nodes which don't have parents themselves. Figure 2 shows an example of such Bayesian network.

2.2.2 Rule Based

Rule based algorithms are used for generating crisp or inexact rules in different Machine Learning approaches [32]. The main advantage of having logic rules involved in malware classification is that logical rules that operate with statements like *equal, grater then, less or equal to* can be executed on the hardware level which significantly increases the speed of decision making.

C4.5 is specially proposed by Quinlan [50] to construct decision trees. These trees can be used for classification and especially for malware detection [75]. The process of trees training includes processing of previously classified dataset and on each step looks for an attribute that divides set of samples into subsets with the best information gain. C4.5 has several benefits in compare with other decision tree building algorithms:

- Works not only with discrete but with continuous attributes as well. For continuous attributes it creates threshold tp compares values against [49].
- Take into account missing attributes values.
- Works with attributes with different costs.

Algorithm 2 Decision tree making algorithm

1: $S = s_1, s_2, \ldots$ labelled training dataset of classified data
2: $x_{1i}, x_{2i}, \ldots, x_{pi}$ - p-dimensional vector of attributes of each sample s_i form S
3: Check for base cases
4: **for all** attributes x **do**
5:     Find the normalized gain ratio from splitting set of sample on x
6: **end for**
7: Let x_{best} be the attribute with the highest normalized information gain.
8: Create decision *node* that splits on x_{best}
9: Repeat on the subsets created by splitting with x_{best}. Newly gained nodes add as *children* of
   current *node*.

- Perform automate tree pruning by going backward through the tree and removing useless branches with leaf nodes.

Algorithm 2 shows a simplified version of decision tree building algorithm.

Neuro-Fuzzy is a hybrid models that ensembles neural networks and fuzzy logic to create human-like linguistic rules using the power of neural networks. Neural network also known as artificial neural network is a network of simple elements which are based on the model of perceptron [65]. Perceptron implements previously chosen activation functions which take input signals and their weights and produces an output, usually in the range of $[0, 1]$ or $[-1, 1]$. The network can be trained to perform classification of complex and high-dimensional data. Neural Networks are widely used for classification and pattern recognition tasks, thus for malware analysis [72]. The problem is that solutions gained by Neural Networks are usually impossible to interpret because of complexity of internal structure and increased weights on the edges. This stimulates usage of Fuzzy Logic techniques, where generated rules are made in human-like easy-interpretable format: *IF X > 3 AND X < 5 THEN Y = 7*.

Basic idea of Neuro-Fuzzy (NF) model is a fuzzy system that is trained with a learning algorithm similar to one from neural networks theory. NF system can be represented as a neural network which takes input variables and produces output variables while connection weights are represented as encoded fuzzy sets. Thus at any stage (like prior to, in process of and after training) NF can be represented as a set of fuzzy rules. Self-Organising (Kohonen) maps [30] is the most common techniques of combining Neuro and Fuzzy approaches. Shalaginov et al. [64] showed the possibility of malware detection using specially-tuned Neuro-Fuzzy technique on a small dataset. Further, NF showed good performance on large-scale binary problem of network traffic analysis [63]. This method has also proven its efficiency on a set of multinomial classification problems. In particular, it is useful when we are talking about distinguishing not only "malware" or "goodware" but also detecting specific type of "malware" [68]. Therefore, it has been improved for the multinational classification of malware types and families by Shalaginov et al. [70].

2.2.3 Distance Based

This set of methods is used for classification based on predefined distance measure. Data for distance-based methods should be carefully prepared, because computational complexity grows significantly with space dimensionality (number of features) and number of training samples. Thus there is a need for proper feature selection as well as sometimes for data normalization.

k-Nearest Neighbours or k-NN is classification and regression method. k-NN does not need special preparation of the dataset or actual "training" as the algorithm is ready for classification right after labelling the dataset. The algorithm takes a sample that is need to be classified and calculates distances to samples from training dataset, then it selects k nearest neighbours (with shortest distances) and makes decision based on class of this k nearest neighbours. Sometimes it makes decision just on the majority of classes in this k neighbours selection, while in other cases there is weights involved in process of making decision. When k-NN is used for malware classification and detection there is a need for careful feature selection as well as a methodology for dealing with outliers and highly mixed data, when training samples cannot create distinguishable clusters [58].

Support Vector Machine or SVM is a supervised learning method. It constructs one or several hyperplanes to divide dataset for classification. Hyperplane is constructed to maximize distance from it to the nearest data points. Sometimes kernel transformation is used to simplify hyperplanes. Building a hyperplane is usually turned into two-class problem (one vs one, one vs many) and involves quadratic programming. Let's have linearly separable data (as shown in Fig. 3)

Fig. 3 Maximum margin hyperplane for two class problem [32]

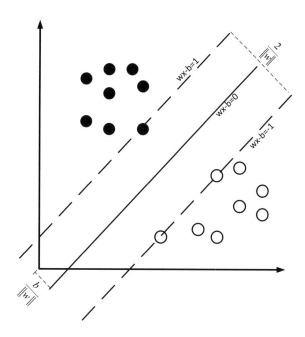

which can be represented as $\mathscr{D} = \{(\mathbf{x}_i, y_i) \mid \mathbf{x}_i \in \mathbb{R}^p, \ y_i \in \{-1, 1\}\}_{i=1}^n$. Where y_i is 1 or -1 depending on class of point x_i. Each x_i is p-dimensional vector (not always normalised). The task is to find hyperplane with maximum margin that divides dataset on points with $y_i = 1$ and $y_i = -1$: $w \cdot x - b = 0$. Where w is a normal vector to a hyperplane [21]. If dataset is linearly separable we can build two hyperplanes $w \cdot x - b = 1$ and $w \cdot x - b = -1$ between which there will be no (or in case of soft margin maximal allowed number) points. Distance between them (margin) is $\frac{2}{\|w\|}$, so to maximize margin we need to minimize $\|w\|$ and to find parameters of hyperplane we need to introduce Lagrangian multipliers α and solve Eq. (7) with quadratic programming techniques.

$$\arg\min_{\mathbf{w},b} \max_{\alpha \geq 0} \left\{ \frac{1}{2}\|\mathbf{w}\|^2 - \sum_{i=1}^n \alpha_i [y_i(\mathbf{w} \cdot \mathbf{x_i} - b) - 1] \right\} \tag{7}$$

Sometimes there is a need to allow an algorithm to work with misclassified data hence leaving some points inside the margin based on the degree of misclassification ξ. So Eq. (3) turns into Eq. (8).

$$\arg\min_{\mathbf{w},\xi,b} \max_{\alpha,\beta} \left\{ \frac{1}{2}\|\mathbf{w}\|^2 + C\sum_{i=1}^n \xi_i - \sum_{i=1}^n \alpha_i[y_i(\mathbf{w} \cdot \mathbf{x_i} - b) - 1 + \xi_i] - \sum_{i=1}^n \beta_i \xi_i \right\}$$

$$with \ \alpha_i, \beta_i \geq 0 \tag{8}$$

Also the data might be linearly separated, so there is a need for kernel trick. The basic idea is to substitute every *dot product* with non-linear kernel function. Kernel function can be chosen depending on situation and can be polynomial, Gaussian, hyperbolic etc. SVM is a very powerful technique which can give good accuracy if properly used, so it often used in malware detection studies as shown by Ye et al. [82].

2.2.4 Neural Networks

Neural Network is based on the model of perceptron which has predefined activation function. In the process of training weights of the links between neurons are trained to fit train data set with minimum error with use of back propagation. Artificial Neural network (ANN) consists of input layer, hidden layer (layers) and output layer as it is shown on Fig. 4.

The input layer takes normalized data, while hidden output layer produces activation output using neuron's weighted input and activation function. Activation function is a basic property of neuron that takes input values given on the input edges, multiply them by weights of these edges and produces output usually in a range of $[0,1]$ or $[-1,1]$. Output layer is needed to present results and then interpret them. Training of ANN starts with random initialization of weights for all edges.

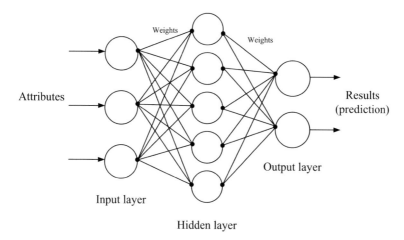

Fig. 4 Artificial neural network [32]

Algorithm 3 ANN training

1: $S = s_1, s_2, \ldots$ labeled training dataset of classified data
2: $x_{1i}, x_{2i}, \ldots, x_{pi}$ - p-dimensional vector of attributes of each sample s_i form S
3: N number of training cycles
4: L_{rate} learning rate
5: Random weight initialization
6: **for all** training cycles N **do**
7:     **for all** samples S **do**
8:         give features x_i as input to the ANN
9:         compare class of s_i with gained output of ANN
10:         calculate error
11:         using back-propagation tune weights inside the ANN with L_{rate}
12:     **end for**
13:     reduce L_{rate}
14: **end for**

Then feature vector of each sample is used as an input. Afterwards, result gained on the output layer is compared to the real answers. Any errors are calculated and using back-propagation all weights are tuned. Training can continue until reaching desired number of training cycles or accuracy. Learning process of ANN can be presented as shown in the Algorithm 3. Artificial Neural networks can be applied for complex models in high-dimensional spaces. This is why it often used for malware research [72].

2.2.5 Open Source and Freely Available ML Tools

Today machine learning is widely used in many areas of research with many publicly available tools (Software products, libraries etc.).

Weka or Waikato Environment for Knowledge Analysis is a popular, free, cross platform and open source tool for machine learning. It supports many of popular ML methods with possibility of fine tuning of the parameters and final results analysis. It provides many features such as splitting dataset and graphical representation of the results. Weka results are saved in .arff file which is specially prepared CSV file with header. It suffers from couple of issues including no support for multi-thread computations and poor memory utilization especially with big datasets.

Python weka wrapper is the package which allows using power of Weka through Python programs. It uses javabridge to link Java-based Weka libraries to python. It provides the same functionality as Weka, but provides more automation capacities.

LIBSVM and LIBLINEAR are open source ML libraries written in C++ supporting kernelized SVMs for linear, classification and regression analysis. Bindings for Java, Mathlab and R are also present. It uses space-separated files as input, where zero values need not to be mentioned.

RapidMiner is machine learning and data mining tool with a user friendly GUI and support for a lot of ML and data mining algorithms.

Dlib is a free and cross-platform C++ toolkit which supports different -machine learning algorithms and allows multi-threading and utilization of Python APIs.

2.2.6   Feature Selection and Construction Process

Next important step after the characteristics extraction is so-called Feature Selection process [32]. Feature Selection is a set of methods that focus on elimination of irrelevant or redundant features that are not influential for malware classification. This is important since the number of characteristics can be extremely large, while only a few can actually be used to differentiate malware and benign applications with a high degree of confidence. The most common feature selection methods are *Information Gain, a*nd *Correlation-based Feature Subset Selection (CFS)* [24]. The final goal of Feature Selection is to simplify the process of knowledge transfer from data to a reusable classification model.

2.3   Taxonomy of Malware Static Analysis Using Machine Learning

Our extensive literature study as reflected in Table 1 resulted to proposing a taxonomy for malware static analysis using machine learning as shown in Fig. 5. Our taxonomy depicts the most common methods for analysis of static characteristics, extracting and selecting features and utilizing machine learning classification techniques. Statistical Pattern Recognition process [26] was used as the basis for our taxonomy modelling.

To get a clear picture on application domain of each machine learning and feature selection method we analysed reported performance as shown in Fig. 6. Majority

Table 1 Analysis of ML methods applicability for different types of static characteristics

Year	Authors	Dataset	Features	FS	ML
PE32 header					
2016	Cepeda et al. [7]	7630 malware and 1.818 goodware	57 features from VirisTotal	ChiSqSelector with 9 features finally	SVM, RF, NN
2016	Le-Khac et al. [35]	Malicious: 94 ; benign: 620	Control flow change and 2–6 n-grams	–	Naive Bayes
2014	Markel et al. [38]	Malicious: 122,799, benign: 42,003	46 features use python 'pefile'	–	Naive Bayes, logistic regression, classification and regression tree (CART)
2013	Khorsand et al. [29]	Benign: 850 "EXE" and 750 "DLL"; malware: 1600 from VX heavens	Eliminated	–	Prediction by partial matching
2012	Devi et al. [15]	4075 PE files: 2954 malicious and 1121 Windows XP SP2 benign	2 + 5 features	–	BayesNet, k-NN, SVM, AdaBoostM1, decision table, C4.5, random forest, random tree
2011	Zhao [84]	3109 PE: 1037 viruses from Vx heavens and 2072 benign executable on Win XP Sp3	24 features from PE files using control flow graph-based on nodes		Random forest, decision tree, bagging, C4.5
2011	Ugarte-Pedrero et al. [77]	500 benign from WinXP and 500 non-packed from Vx heaven; 500 packed + 500 Zeus	166 structure features of PE file	InfoGain	Learning with local and global consistency; random forest
2011	Santos et al. [59]	500 benign and 500 malicious from VxHeavens, also packed and not packed	209 structural features	InfoGain	Collective forest
2009	Tang [76]	361 executables and 449 normal trojan files	PE header structural features	–	Decision tree
2009	Wang et al. [80]	Benign: 1908, malicious: 7863	143 PE header entries	InfoGain, gain ratio	SVM

(continued)

Table 1 (continued)

Year	Authors	Dataset	Features	FS	ML
Bytes n-gram sequences					
2011	Jain et al. [27]	1018 malware and 1120 benign samples	1–8 byte, n-gram, best n-gram by documentwise frequency	–	NB, iBK, J48, AdaBoost1, random forest
2007	Masud et al. [39]	1st set—1435 executables: 597 of which are benign and 838 are malicious. 2nd set—2452 executables: 1370 benign and 1082 malicious	500 best n-grams	InfoGain	SVM
2006	Reddy et al. [51]	250 malware vs 250 benign	100–500 best n-gram	Document frequency, InfoGain	NB, iBK, decision tree
2004	Kolter et al. [31]	1971 benign, 1651 malicious from Vx heaven	500 best n-grams	InfoGain	Naive Bayes, SVM, C4.5
Opcode n-gram sequences					
2016	Wang et al. [79]	11,665 malware and 1000 benign samples	2-tuple opcode sequences	Information entropy	Density clustering
2015	Bragen [6]	992 malwares, 771 benign from Windows Vista	1–4 n-gram opcode with vocabulary 530–714,390	Cfs, Chi-sqaured, InfoGain, ReliefF, SymUncert.	Random forest, C4.5, Naive Bayes, Bayes Net, Baggin, ANN, SOM, k-nn
2013	Santos et al. [58]	13,189 malware vs 13,000 benign	Top 1000 features	InfoGain	Random forest, J48, k-nearest neighbours, Bayesian networks, SVM
2011	Shahzad et al. [62]	Benign: 300, malicious: 300 on Windows XP	Vocabulary of 1413 with n-gram=4	tf-idf	ZeroR, ripper, C4.5, SVM, Naive Bayes, k-nn

API calls				
2012	Zabidi et al. [83]	API calls, debugger features, VM features	–	–
2012	Faruki et al. [19]	1–4 API call-gram	–	Random forest, SVM, ANN, C4.5, Naive Bayes
2010	Shankarapani et al. [71]	API calls sequence	–	SVM
2010	Sami et al. [55]	API calls	Fisher score	Random forest, C4.5, Naive Bayes
No features/not described				
2012	Baig et al. [5]	File entropy	–	–
2010	Dube et al. [17]	From 32 bit files	–	Decision tree

Additional data column (samples):

Zabidi et al. [83]	23 malware and 1 benign
Faruki et al. [19]	3234 benign, 3256 malware
Shankarapani et al. [71]	1593 PE files:875 benign and 715 malicious
Sami et al. [55]	34,820 PE: 31,869 malicious and 2951 benign from Windows
Baig et al. [5]	200 packed PE and 200 unpacked from Windows 7, Windows 2003 Server
Dube et al. [17]	40,498 samples: 25,974 malware, 14,524 benign

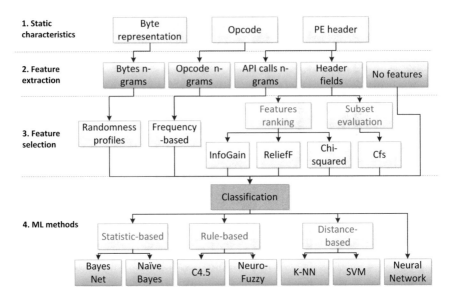

Fig. 5 Taxonomy of common malware detection process based on static characteristics and machine learning

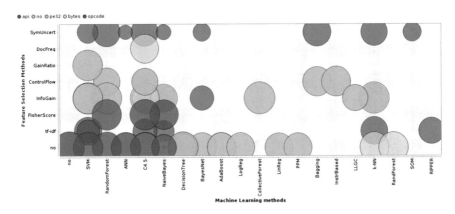

Fig. 6 Comparison of accuracy of various static characteristics with respect to feature selection and machine learning methods. Colour of the bubbles shows used characteristics for detection, while size of the bubble denotes achieved accuracy

of researchers were using byte n-gram, opcode n-gram and PE32 header fields for static analysis while C4.5, SVM or k-NN methods were mainly used for malware detection. Information Gain is the prevalent method to define malware attributes. Also we can see that n-gram-based method tend to use corresponding set of feature selection like tf-idf and Symmetric Uncertainty that are more relevant for large number of similar sequences. On the other hand, PE32 header-based features tend to provide higher entropies for classification and therefore Control-Flow graph-based and Gain Ratio are more suitable for this task.

To conclude, one can say that majority of authors either extract features that offers good classification accuracy, or use conventional methods like Information Gain. However, n-gram based characteristics need other FS approaches to eliminate irrelevant features. Rule-based ML is the most commonly used classification method along with SVM. Forest-based method tends to be more applicable for PE32 header-based features. Also ANN is not commonly-used technique. While most of the works achieved accuracies of 80–100%, some Bayes-based methods offered much lower accuracy even down to 50% only.

3 Approaches for Malware Feature Construction

Similar the previous works, following four sets of static properties are suggested for feature classification in this paper:

PE32 header features characterize the PE32 header information using the *PEframe* tools [77]. Following numerical features will be used in our experiments:

- *ShortInfo_Directories* describes 16 possible data directories available in PE file. The most commonly used are "Import", "Export", "Resource", "Debug", "Relocation".
- *ShortInfo_Xor* indicates detected XOR obfuscation.
- *ShortInfo_DLL* is a binary flag of whether a file is executable or dynamically-linked library.
- *ShortInfo_FileSize* measures size of a binary file in bytes.
- *ShortInfo_Detected* shows present techniques used to evade the detection by anti-viruses like hooks to disable execution in virtualized environment or suspicious API calls.
- *ShortInfo_Sections* is a number of subsections available in the header.
- *DigitalSignature* contains information about the digital signatture that can be present in a file
- *Packer* describes used packer detected by *PEframe*
- *AntiDebug* gives insight into the techniques used to prevent debugging process.
- *AntiVM* is included to prevent the execution in a virtualize environment.
- *SuspiciousAPI* indicates functions calls that are labelled by *PEframe* as suspicious.
- *SuspiciousSections* contains information about suspicious sections like ".rsrc \u0000 \u0000 \u0000"
- *Url* is a number of different url addresses found in the binary file.

Byte n-Gram n-Gram is a sequence of some items (with minimum length of 1) that are predefined as minimal parts of the object expressed in Bytes. By having the file represented as a sequence of bytes we can construct 1-gram, 2-gram, 3-gram etc. n-Grams of bytes, or byte n-grams are widely used as features for machine learning and static malware analysis [27, 51].

Reddy et al. [51] used n-grams of size 2, 3 and 4 with combination of SVM, Instance-based learner and Decision Tree algorithms to distinguish between malicious and benign executables. After extracting n-grams they used class-wise document frequency as a feature selection measure and showed that class-wise document frequency is performing better than Information Gain as a feature selection measure. Jain et al. [27] used n-grams in range of 1–8 as features and Naive Bayes, Instance Based Learner and AdaBoost1 [3] as machine learning algorithms for malware classification and reported byte 3-grams as the best technique.

Opcode n-gram represent a set of instructions that will be performed on the CPU when binary is executed. These instructions are called operational codes or **opcodes**. To extract opcodes from executable we need to perform disassembly procedure. After this opcodes will be represented as short instructions names such as *POP, PUSH, MOV, ADD, SUB* etc. Santos et al. [58] described a method to distinguish between malicious and benign executables or detecting different malware families using opcode sequences of length 1–4 using Random Forest, J48, k-Nearest Neighbours, Bayesian Networks and Support Vector Machine algorithms [3].

API calls is a set of tools and routines that help to develop a program using existent functionality of an operating system. Since most of the malware samples are platform dependent it is very much likely that their developers have use APIs as well. Therefore, analysing API calls usage among benign and malicious software can help to find malware-specific API calls and therefore are suitable to be used as a feature for machine learning algorithms. For example, [71] successfully used Support Vector Machines with frequency of API calls for malware classification. [78] provided a methodology for classification of malicious and benign executables using API calls and n-grams with n from 1 to 4 and achieved accuracy of 97.23% for 1-gram features. [19] used so-called API call-gram model with sequence length ranging from 1 to 4 and reached accuracy of 97.7% was achieved by training with 3-grams. In our experiments we are going to use 1 and 2 n-grams as features generated from API calls.

4   Experimental Design

All experiments were conducted on a dedicated Virtual machine (VM) on Ubuntu 14.04 server running on Xen 4.4. The server had an Intel(R) Core(TM) i7-3820 CPU @ 3.60 GHz with 4 cores (8 threads), out of which 2 cores (4 threads) were provided to the VM. Disk space is allocated on the SSD RAID storage based on Samsung 845DC. Installed server memory was Kingston PC-1600 RAM, out of which 8 GB was available for the VM. Operating system was an Ubuntu 14.04 64 bit running on ae dedicated VM together with all default tools and utilities available in the OS's repository. Files pre-processing were performed using *bash* scripts due to native support in Linux OS. To store extracted features we utilised MySQL 5.5 database engine together with Python v 2.7.6 and PHP v 5.5.9 connectors.

For the experiments we used a set of benign and malicious samples. To authors knowledge there have not been published any large BENIGN SOFTWARE REFERENCE DATASETS, so we have to create our own set of benign files. Since the focus of the paper is mainly on PE32 Windows executables, we decided to extract corresponding known-to-be-good files from different versions of MS Windows, including different software and multimedia programs installations that are available. The OSes that we processed were 32 bit versions of Windows XP, Windows 7, Windows 8.1 and Windows 10. Following two Windows malware datasets were used in our research:

1. VX HEAVEN [2] dedicated to distribute information about the computer viruses and contains 271,092 sorted samples dating back from 1999.
2. VIRUS SHARE [1] represent sharing resource that offers 29,119,178 malware samples and accessible through VirusShare tracker as of 12th of July, 2017. We utilized following two archives: *VirusShare_00000.zip* created on 2012-06-15 00:39:38 with a size of 13.56 GB and *VirusShare_00207.zip* created on 2015-12-16 22:56:17 with a size of 13.91 GB, all together contained 131,072 unique, uncategorised and unsorted malware samples. They will be referred further as *malware_000* and *malware_207*.

To be able to perform experiments on the dataset, we have to filter out irrelevant samples (not specific PE32 and not executables), which are out of scope in this paper. However, processing of more than 100k samples put limitations and require non-trivial approaches to handle such amount of files. We discovered that common ways of working with files in directory such that simple *ls* and *mv* in *bash* take unreasonable amount of time to execute. Also there is no way to distinguish files by extension like *.dll* or *.exe* since the names are just *md5* sums. So, following filtering steps were performed:

1. Heap of unfiltered malware and benign files were placed into two directories "malware/" and "benign/".
2. To eliminate duplicates, we renamed all the files to their MD5 sums.
3. PE32 files were detected in each folder using *file* Linux command:

```
\$ file 000000b4dccfbaa5bd981af2c1bbf59a
000000b4dccfbaa5bd981af2c1bbf59a: PE32 executable (
    DLL) (GUI) Intel 80386, for MS Windows
```

4. All PE32 files from current directory that meet our requirement were scrapped and move to a dedicated one:

```
#!/bin/sh
cd ../windows1;
counter=0;
for i in *; do
counter=$((counter+1));
echo "$counter";
VAR="file $i | grep PE32 " ;
```

```
VAR1=$( eval  "$VAR" )  ;
len1 =${ #VAR1 };
if  [ −n "$VAR1" ] && [ "$len1" −gt "1" ] ;
then
 echo "$VAR1" | awk '{ print $1 }' | awk '{ gsub (/:$/,""
     ); print $1 "␣../windows/PE/" $1 }'| xargs mv −f ;
else
 echo "other";
 file $i | awk '{ print $1 }' | awk '{ gsub (/:$/,"");
     print $1 "␣../windows/other/" $1 }' | xargs mv −f
     ;
 fi
done
```

5. We further can see a variety of PE32 modifications for 32bit architecture:

PE32 executable (GUI) Intel 80386, for MS Windows
PE32 executable (DLL) (GUI) Intel 80386, for MS
    Windows
PE32 executable (GUI) Intel 80386, for MS Windows,
    UPX compressed

Following our purpose to concentrate on 32bit architecture, only PE32 are filtered out from all possible variants of PE32 files shown about.
6. After extracting a target group of benign and malicious PE32 files, multiple rounds of feature extraction are performed according to methods used in the literature.
7. Finally, we insert extracted features into the corresponding MySQL database to ease the handling, feature selection and machine learning processes respectively.

After collecting all possible files and performing the pre-processing phase, we ended up with the sets represented in Table 2.

Further, feature construction and extraction routine from PE files was performed using several tools as follows:

1. PEFRAME [4] is an open source tool specifically designed for static analysis of PE malware. It extracts various information from PE header ranging from packers to anti debug and anti vm tricks.

Table 2 Characteristics of the dataset collected and used for our experiments after filtering PE files

Dataset	Number of files	Size
Benign	16,632	7.4 GB
Malware_000	58,023	14.0 GB
Malware_207	41,899	16.0 GB

2. HEXDUMP is a standard Linux command line tool which is used to display a file in specific format like ASCII or one-byte octal.
3. OBJDUMP is a standard Linux command line too to detect applications instructions, consumed memory addresses, etc.

5 Results and Discussions

Before testing different ML techniques for malware detection it is important to show that our datasets actually represent the real-world distribution of the malware and goodware. Comparison of "Compile Time" field of PE32 header can be utilized for this purpose. Figure 7 represents log-scale histogram of the compilation time for our benign dataset. Taking into consideration the Windows OS timeline we found a harmony between our benign dataset applications compile time and development of Microsoft Windows operating systems. To start with, **Windows 3.1** was originally released on April 6, 1992 and our plot of benign applications indicates the biggest spike in early 1992. Later on in 1990th, **Windows 95** was due on 24 August 1995, while next **Windows 98** was announced on 25 June 1998. Further, 2000th marked release of **Windows XP** on October 25, 2001. Next phases on the plot correspond to the release of **Windows Vista** on 30th January 2007 and **Windows 7** on 22nd October 2009. Next popular version (Windows 8) appeared on 26th October 2012 and the latest major spike in the end of 2014 corresponds to the release of **Windows 10** on 29th July 2015.

Further, compilation time distribution for the first malware dataset *malware_000* is given in Fig. 8. We can clearly see that release of newer Windows version is always followed by an increase of cumulative distribution of malware samples in following 6–12 month. It can be seen that the release of 32bit Windows 3.1 cause

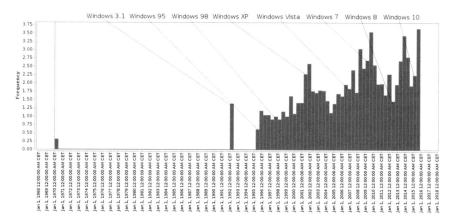

Fig. 7 Log-scale histogram of compilation times for *benign* dataset

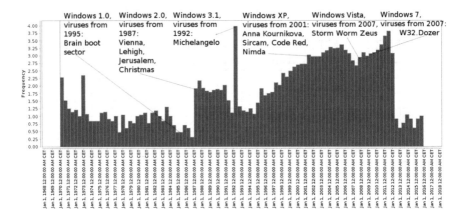

Fig. 8 Log-scale histogram of compilation times for *malware_000* dataset

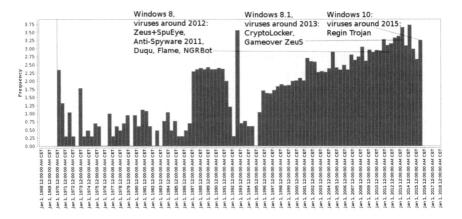

Fig. 9 Log-scale histogram of compilation times for *malware_207* dataset

a spike in a number of malware. After this the number of malware compiled each year is constantly growing. Then, another increase can be observed in second half of the 2001 which corresponds to the release of the Windows XP and so on.

Considering the fact that MS DOS was released in 1981 it makes compilation times before this day look like fake or just obfuscated intentionally. On the other hand the dataset *malware_000* cannot have dates later than June 2012. Therefore, malware with compilation time prior to 1981 or later than Jan 2012 are tampered (Fig. 9).

5.1 Accuracy of ML-Aided Malware Detection Using Static Characteristics

This part presents results of apply Naive Bayes, BayesNet, C4.5, k-NN, SVM, ANN and NF machine learning algorithms against static features of our dataset namely PE32 header, Bytes n-gram, Opcode n-gram, and API calls n-gram.

5.1.1 PE32 Header

PE32 header is one of the most important features relevant to threat intelligence of PE32 applications. We performed feature selection using *Cfs* and *InfoGain* methods with fivefold cross-validation as presented in Table 3.

We can clearly see that the features from the *Short Info* section in PE32 headers can be used as a stand-alone malware indicators, including different epochs. Number of directories in this section as well as file size and flag of EXE or DLL have bigger merits in comparison to other features. To contrary, *Anti Debug* and *Suspicious*

Table 3 Feature selection on PE32 features

Benign vs Malware_000		Benign vs Malware_207		Malware_000 vs Malware_207	
Information gain					
Merit	Attribute	Merit	Attribute	Merit	Attribute
0.377	**ShortInfo_Directories**	0.369	**ShortInfo_DLL**	0.131	**ShortInfo_FileSize**
0.278	**ShortInfo_DLL**	0.252	**ShortInfo_Directories**	0.094	ShortInfo_Detected
0.118	**AntiDebug**	0.142	**ShortInfo_FileSize**	0.064	SuspiciousAPI
0.099	Packer	0.105	**SuspiciousSections**	0.044	ShortInfo_Directories
0.088	SuspiciousSections	0.101	**SuspiciousAPI**	0.036	Packer
0.082	ShortInfo_Xor	0.089	AntiDebug	0.028	AntiDebug
0.076	SuspiciousAPI	0.084	ShortInfo_Detected	0.017	SuspiciousSections
0.045	ShortInfo_FileSize	0.054	ShortInfo_Xor	0.016	Url
0.034	ShortInfo_Detected	0.050	Packer	0.015	AntiVM
0.022	Url	0.036	Url	0.012	ShortInfo_Xor
0.004	AntiVM	0.002	AntiVM	0.002	ShortInfo_DLL
0	ShortInfo_Sections	0	ShortInfo_Sections	0	ShortInfo_Sections
0	DigitalSignature	0	DigitalSignature	0	DigitalSignature
Cfs					
Attribute		Attribute		Attribute	
ShortInfo_Directories		ShortInfo_Directories		ShortInfo_Directories	
ShortInfo_Xor		ShortInfo_Xor		ShortInfo_FileSize	
ShortInfo_DLL		ShortInfo_DLL		ShortInfo_Detected	
ShortInfo_Detected				Packer	
Url					

Bold font denotes selected features according to *InfoGain* method

Table 4 Comparative classification accuracy based on features from PE32 header, in %

Dataset	Naive Bayes	BayesNet	C4.5	k-NN	SVM	ANN	NF
All features							
Bn vs Ml_000	90.29	91.42	**97.63**	97.30	87.75	95.08	92.46
Bn vs Ml_207	88.27	91.21	**96.43**	95.99	84.88	93.24	89.03
Ml_000 vs Ml_207	63.41	71.59	**82.45**	82.11	73.77	69.99	69.01
Information gain							
Bn vs Ml_000	88.32	89.17	**94.09**	94.01	94.09	93.51	87.53
Bn vs Ml_207	87.25	90.39	**95.06**	94.58	84.55	92.37	87.88
Ml_000 vs Ml_207	58.26	67.05	67.77	**70.70**	69.46	63.19	51.31
Cfs							
Bn vs Ml_000	89.35	90.89	**95.39**	95.38	95.16	93.69	85.85
Bn vs Ml_207	86.88	89.67	91.61	**91.68**	91.68	91.68	81.91
Ml_000 vs Ml_207	67.45	70.95	76.98	**76.92**	72.15	68.18	67.06

Bn, Ml_000 and Ml_207 are benign and two malaware datasets respectively
Items in bold reflecting highest achieved accuracy

API sections from *PEframe* cannot classify a binary file. Finally, we can say that digital signature and *Anti VM* files in PE32 headers are almost irrelevant in malware detection. Further, we performed exploration of selected ML methods that can be used with selected features. By extracting corresponding numerical features mentioned earlier, we were able to achieve classification accuracy levels presented in Table 4. Table 3 presents also accuracy of ML method after performing feature selection. Here we used whole sub-sets defined by *Cfs* method and features with merit of ≥ 0.1 detected by *InfoGain*.

Malware and goodware can be easily classified using full set as well as sub-set of features. One can notice that ANN and C4.5 performed much better than other methods. It can be also seen that the high quality of these features made them very appropriate to differentiate between the *benign* and *malware_000* dataset. Further, we can see that the two datasets *malware_000* and *malware_207* are similar and extracted features do not provide a high classification accuracy. Neural Network was used with three hidden layers making it a non-linear model and experiments were performed using fivefold cross-validation technique.

5.1.2 Bytes n-Gram

Bytes n-gram is a very popular method for static analysis of binary executables. This method has one significant benefit: in order to perform analysis there is no need of previous knowledge about file type and internal structure since we use its raw (binary) form. For feature construction we used random profiles that were first presented by Ebringer et al. [18] called *fixed sample count* (see Fig. 10), which generates fixed number of random profiles regardless of the file size and *sliding window algorithm*. In this method each file is represented in a hexadecimal format

Fig. 10 Sliding window algorithm [18]

Generate randomness measurements for a file, output proportional to file length

INPUT: An array of bytes $b_1, \ldots, b_n$, a window size w and a skip size a.

OUTPUT: An array of $\left\lceil \dfrac{n-w}{a} \right\rceil$ samples of the randomness, ranging from 0.0 to 1.0.

1. Construct the Huffman tree for the input bytes.

2. Construct an array $e_1, \ldots, e_{256}$ containing the encoding length for each of the input bytes.

3. For i from 1 to $\left\lceil \dfrac{n-w}{a} \right\rceil$, do the following:

    a) $r_i \leftarrow \sum_{j=a(i-1)+1}^{a(i-1)+w+1} e_j$

4. Rescale r_i between 0.0 and 1.0, where $\min(r_i) = 0.0$ and $\max(r_i) = 1.0$.

Table 5 Classification accuracy based on features from bytes n-gram randomness profiles, in %

Dataset	Naive Bayes	BayesNet	C4.5	k-NN	SVM	ANN	NF
All features							
Bn vs Ml_000	69.9	60.4	76.9	75.6	78.3	78.3	74.8
Bn vs Ml_207	70.3	68.2	75.8	75.6	72.1	71.6	68.2
Ml_000 vs Ml_207	50.1	64.0	68.1	64.7	58.1	60.1	58.2

and frequencies of each byte are counted to build a Huffman tree for each file. Then using window of fixed size and moving it on fixed skip size the randomness profile of each window is calculated. A Randomness profile is sum of Huffman code length of each byte in a single window. The lower the randomness in a particular window the bigger will be the randomness of that profile.

We chose 32 bytes as the most promising sliding window size [18, 48, 74] and due to big variety of file sizes in our dataset, we chose 30 best features (or *pruning size* in terminology from [18]) which are the areas of biggest randomness (the most unique parts) in their original order. This features was fed into different machine learning algorithms as shown in Table 5. Our results indicate that the accuracy of this technique is not that high as it was originally developed to preserve local details of a file ([18])while the size of file affects localness a lot. In our case file sizes vary from around 0.5 Kb to 53.7 Mb which adversely affect the results. Despite worse results it is still easier to distinguish between benign executables and malware than between malware from different time slices. Also we can see that ANN is better in *Benign vs Malware_000* dataset, C4.5 in *Benign vs Malware_207* and *Malware_000 vs Malware_207* datasets.

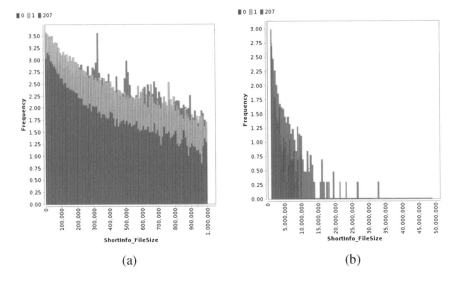

Fig. 11 Distribution of file size values in bytes for three classes. (**a**) Less than 1M. (**b**) Bigger than 1M

Also it should be noted that we did not use feature selection methods as in the case of PE32 header features. Both Information gain and Cfs are not efficient due to the similarity of features and equivalence in importance for classification process. For the first dataset the Information Gain was in the range of 0.0473–0.0672 while for the second dataset it was in the range of 0.0672–0.1304 and for the last it was 0.0499–0.0725. Moreover, Cfs produces best feature subset nearly equal to full set. Therefore, we decided to use all features as there is no subset that could possibly be better than original one (Fig. 11).

5.1.3 Opcode n-Gram

Opcode n-gram consists of assembly instructions which construct the executable file. The main limitation of this method is that in order to gain opcodes we need disassemble an application which sometimes fails to give correct opcodes due to different anti-disassembly and packing techniques used in executables hence we filtered out this kind of files from our dataset. We extracted 100 most common 3- and 4-grams from each of three file sets in our dataset. Then we extracted a set of 200 most common n-grams—which are called feature n-grams—to build a presence vector where value 1 was assigned if a certain n-gram from feature n-grams is present in top 100 most used n-grams of the file. Table 6 represents results of feature selection performed on the dataset with 3-grams. As can be seen the first two pair of datasets have a lot of common n-grams, while selected n-grams for the third pair of dataset is totally different. For Information Gain the threshold of 0.1 was used for both benign and malware datasets, while for the last set we used InfoGain of 0.02.

Table 6 Feature selection on 3-gram opcode features

Benign vs Malware_000		Benign vs Malware_207		Malware_000 vs Malware_207	
Information gain					
Merit	Attribute	Merit	Attribute	Merit	Attribute
0.302483	**int3movpush**	0.298812	**int3movpush**	0.042229	pushlcallpushl
0.283229	**int3int3mov**	0.279371	**int3int3mov**	0.039779	movtestjne
0.266485	**popretint3**	0.227489	**popretint3**	0.037087	callpushlcall
0.236949	**retint3int3**	0.202162	**retint3int3**	0.031045	pushpushlcall
0.191866	**jmpint3int3**	0.193938	**jmpint3int3**		
0.134709	callmovtest	0.108580	retpushmov		
0.133258	movtestje				
0.115976	callmovpop				
0.114482	testjemov				
0.101328	poppopret				
0.100371	movtestjne				
Cfs					
Attribute		Attribute		Attribute	
movtestje		movmovadd		pushpushlcall	
callmovtest		retpushmov		movtestjne	
callmovpop		xormovmov		movmovjmp	
retint3int3		**callmovtest**		jecmpje	
popretint3		**popretint3**		cmpjepush	
pushmovadd		**pushmovadd**		pushleacall	
int3int3mov		**int3int3mov**		callpopret	
callmovjmp		**callmovjmp**		leaveretpush	
jmpint3int3		**jmpint3int3**		pushmovadd	
int3movpush		**int3movpush**		pushcalllea	
				callpushlcall	
				callmovlea	
				pushlcallpushl	
				movmovmovl	
				calljmpmov	

Bold font denotes features that present in both datasets that include benign samples

These data were passed to machine learning algorithms and results are shown in Tables 7 and 9. As can be seen C4.5 performed well and had the highest accuracy almost in all experiments. Also feature selection significantly reduced the number of n-grams from 200 down to 10–15, while overall accuracy on all methods did not dropped significantly. In fact, Naive Bayes performed even better that can be justified by reduced complexity of the probabilistic model. Also NF showed much better accuracy in comparison to other methods when using all features to distinguish between two malware datasets which can be linked to non-linear correlation in the data that are circumscribed in the Gaussian fuzzy patches.

Table 7 Classification accuracy based on features from opcode 3-gram, in %

Dataset	Naive Bayes	BayesNet	C4.5	k-NN	SVM	ANN	NF
All features							
Bn vs Ml_000	83.51	83.52	**95.53**	93.82	94.43	94.51	95.28
Bn vs Ml_207	84.52	84.52	**93.93**	91.84	92.32	92.44	93.20
Mn_000 vs Ml_207	63.73	63.73	81.21	78.64	75.42	76.64	**83.13**
Information gain							
Bn vs Ml_000	86.74	86.94	90.41	**90.45**	89.98	90.26	84.45
Bn vs Ml_207	86.22	86.22	86.22	86.22	87.46	**87.48**	83.36
Mn_000 vs Ml_207	63.19	62.55	71.19	**71.89**	69.54	67.36	69.14
Cfs							
Bn vs Ml_000	87.79	88.66	91.15	**91.22**	90.90	90.82	85.31
Bn vs Ml_207	86.24	86.33	**89.92**	89.73	89.17	89.34	81.58
Mn_000 vs Ml_207	86.24	86.33	**89.92**	89.73	89.17	89.34	69.25

Items in bold reflecting highest achieved accuracy

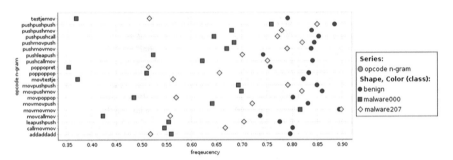

Fig. 12 Distribution of the frequencies of top 20 opcode 3-grams from benign set in comparison to both malicious datasets

Further, we investigated if there is any correlation between n-grams in files that belong to both benign and malicious classes. We extracted relative frequency of each n-gram according to the following formula $h_{n-gram} = \frac{N_{files \in n-gram}^{Class}}{N_{files}^{Class}}$, where $N_{files \in n-gram}^{Class}$ indicates number of files in class that has n-gram and N_{files}^{Class} is a total number of files in this class. The results for 3-gram is depicted in Fig. 12. As a reference we took top 20 most frequent n-grams from benign class and found frequency of the corresponding n-grams from both malware datasets. It can be seen that the frequency does not differ fundamentally, yet n-grams for both malicious classes tend to have very close numbers in comparison to benign files. Moreover, there is a clear dependency between both malicious classes. We also can notice that most of the features selected from two datasets that includes benign samples are same. This highlights reliability of the selected 4-grams and generalization of this method for malware detection.

Additionally, we studied 4-gram features and extracted 200 features as shown in Table 8. Similar to the 3-grams features selected in the Table 6 one can see that two

Table 8 Feature selection on 4-gram opcode features

Benign vs Malware_000		Benign vs Malware_207		Malware_000 vs Malware_207	
Information gain					
Merit	Attribute	Merit	Attribute	Merit	Attribute
0.303209	**int3int3movpush**	0.295427	**int3int3movpush**	0.047452	pushlcallpushlcall
0.295280	**int3movpushmov**	0.286378	**int3movpushmov**	0.045860	movpoppopret
0.285608	**int3int3int3mov**	0.266966	**int3int3int3mov**	0.044750	jepushcallpop
0.258733	**popretint3int3**	0.229431	**jmpint3int3int3**	0.044573	callpushlcallpushl
0.241215	**poppopretint3**	0.224318	**poppopretint3**	0.038822	cmpjepushcall
0.233205	**jmpint3int3int3**	0.210289	**popretint3int3**	0.035731	pushcallpopret
0.220679	**retint3int3int3**	0.170367	**retint3int3int3**	0.030460	pushcallpopmov
0.185178	**movpopretint3**	0.148442	**movpopretint3**	0.028564	movcmpjepush
0.151337	**movpushmovsub**	0.116760	**movpushmovsub**	0.025813	cmpjecmpje
0.125703	pushcallmovtest	0.103841	**movpushmovpush**	0.024372	leaveretpushmov
0.104993	**movpushmovpush**	0.102730	**movpushmovmov**	0.023374	pushpushpushlcall
0.104416	**movpushmovmov**			0.022312	pushcallpoppop
				0.021929	movtestjepush
				0.020003	pushpushleapush
Cfs					
attribute		attribute		attribute	
incaddincadd		addaddaddadd		leaveretpushmov	
movpushmovsub		movmovpushpush		callmovtestje	
jmpmovmovmov		**movpushmovsub**		jepushcallpop	
pushcallmovtest		**pushcallmovtest**		pushlcallpushlcall	
int3int3int3mov		**int3int3int3mov**		pushpushpushlea	
movpoppopret		movxormovmov		jecmpjecmp	
jmpint3int3int3		pushlcallpushlcall		movpoppopret	
movpopretint3		**jmpint3int3int3**		pushcallmovpush	
int3int3movpush		movpopretint3		pushmovmovcall	
int3movpushmov		**int3int3movpush**		movpopretint3	
poppopretint3		**int3movpushmov**		cmpjepushcall	
addpushpushpush		**poppopretint3**		movleamovmov	
pushpushcalllea				movmovjmpmov	
				pushpushcalllea	
				retnopnopnop	
				movaddpushpush	
				subpushpushpush	

Bold font denotes features that present in both datasets that include benign samples

first pairs of datasets have a lot of common features, while the last one provides a significantly different set. As in case with 3-grams we used Information Gain with threshold of 0.1 for both benign and the first malware dataset, while for the last malware set we used InfoGain of 0.02, which looks reasonable with respect to number of selected' features.

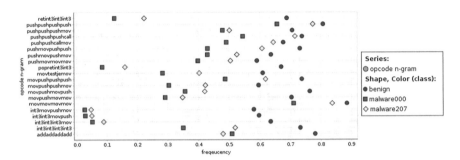

Fig. 13 Distribution of the frequencies of top 20 opcode 4-grams from benign set in comparison to both malicious datasets

Table 9 Classification accuracy based on features from opcode 4-gram, in %

Dataset	Naive Bayes	BayesNet	C4.5	k-NN	SVM	ANN	NF
All features							
Bn vs Ml_000	86.92	86.92	95.31	93.73	94.28	94.23	**95.54**
Bn vs Ml_207	86.84	86.84	93.33	91.71	92.03	92.04	**93.75**
Ml_000 vs Ml_207	64.90	64.90	**81.58**	78.98	74.98	75.77	78.80
Information gain							
Bn vs Ml_000	87.79	87.89	**91.48**	91.45	91.31	90.84	85.74
Bn vs Ml_207	84.64	84.57	**87.84**	87.83	87.25	87.70	48.67
Mn_000 vs Ml_207	62.73	63.20	69.96	**70.25**	68.40	67.24	68.90
Cfs							
Bn vs Ml_000	89.63	89.63	91.51	**91.52**	91.52	90.76	84.95
Bn vs Ml_207	86.41	86.64	89.36	**89.48**	89.16	89.12	81.13
Mn_000 vs Ml_207	66.28	66.17	72.00	**72.27**	68.96	69.17	69.32

Items in bold reflecting highest achieved accuracy

The classification performance is given in Fig. 9. As can be seen, 3-grams can show a bit better result than 4-grams in case of distinguishing between benign and malware_000 or Benign and malware_207 with C4.5 classifier. At the same time 4-grams are better in order to distinguish between two malware datasets with C4.5 classifier. We can conclude that results are quite good, and can be used for malware detection. In our opinion results can be improved by extracting more features and usage of relative frequencies rather than pure vectors.

In contrary to 3-grams we can see that the histograms of 4-grams have fundamental differences when it comes to malicious and benign sets as it is depicted in Fig. 13. We can see that the frequencies correspond to malware_000 and malware_207 datasets are nearly similar and are far from the frequencies detected for the benign class. Moreover, there is a clear and strong correlation between two malware datasets. So, we can conclude that in case of probabilistic-based models like Bayes Network and Naive Bayes the classification could be a bit better due to differences in likelihood of appearance, which can be also found in Tables 7 and 9.

Table 10 Classification accuracy based on API call 1-gram features, %

Dataset	Naive Bayes	BayesNet	C4.5	k-NN	SVM	ANN	NF
All features							
Bn vs Ml_000	90.79	90.79	93.39	93.47	**93.51**	93.43	82.44
Bn vs Ml_207	87.18	87.18	90.94	91.03	**91.37**	91.23	81.28
Ml_000 vs Ml_207	66.19	66.2	**78.44**	77.09	73.33	72.77	73.55

Items in bold reflecting highest achieved accuracy

Table 11 Classification accuracy based on API call 2-gram features, %

Dataset	Naive Bayes	BayesNet	C4.5	k-NN	SVM	ANN	NF
All features							
Bn vs Ml_000	86.54	86.55	90.88	91.53	**91.96**	91.85	75.24
Bn vs Ml_207	81.94	81.91	87.84	**88.82**	88.31	87.81	83.61
Ml_000 vs Ml_207	62.31	62.31	**73.69**	73.17	70.27	69.45	70.08

Items in bold reflecting highest achieved accuracy

5.1.4 API Call n-Grams

API calls n-grams is the combination of specific operations invoked by the process in order to use functionalities of an operation system. In this study we used *peframe* to extract API calls from PE32 files. The bigger the n-gram size is the lower accuracy is possible to gain. The reason for this is that single API calls and their n-grams are far fewer in comparison with for example opcode n-grams. After extraction of API calls, we combined them into 1- and 2-grams. For each task we selected 100 most frequent features in a particular class and combined them into 200-feature vectors. Tables 10 and 11 presents results of machine learning evaluation on API call n-grams data.

As we can see ANN, k-NN and C4.5 are the best classifiers similar to previous results. It is also more difficult to distinguish between files from *malware_000* and *malware_207*. We gained quite high accuracy, but it is still lower than in related studies. It could be explained by the size of datasets: other studies datasets usually consist of several hundreds or thousands of files while our dataset has more than 110,000 files. After analysing feature selection results we decided not to include them in the results section since most of the features are similar in terms of distinguishing between malware and goodware. It means that there is large number of unique API calls that can be found once or twice in a file in contrary to the byte or opcode n-gram.

We also studied the difference between frequencies distributions of API calls. Figure 14 sketches extracted API 1-grams from three datasets. One can see that there is a significant spread between numbers of occurrences in benign class in contrary to both malicious datasets. On the other hand, results for both malware datasets are similar, which indicates statistical significance of extracted features. It is important ho highlight that the largest scatter are in frequencies for *memset()*, *malloc()* and *free()* API calls. On the other hand, malicious programs tend to use

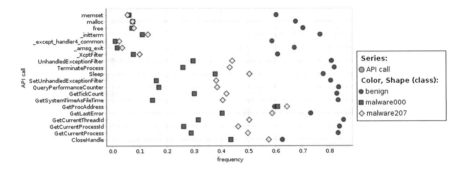

Fig. 14 Frequencies of 20 most frequent API 1-grams for three different datasets

GetProcAddress() function more often for retrieving the address of any function from dynamic-link libraries in the system.

6 Conclusion

In this paper we presented a survey on applications of machine learning techniques for static analysis of PE32 Windows malware. First, we elaborated on different methods for extracting static characteristics of the executable files. Second, an overview of different machine learning methods utilized for classification of static characteristics of PE32 files was given. In addition, we offered a taxonomy of malware static features and corresponding ML methods. Finally, we provided a tutorial on how to apply different ML methods on benign and malware dataset for classification. We found that C4.5 and k-NN in most cases perform better than other methods, while SVM and ANN on some feature sets showed good performance. On the other hand Bayes Network and Naive Bayes have poor performance compared to other ML methods. This can be explained by negligibly low probabilities which present in a large number of features such as opcode and bytes n-grams. So, it can see that static-analysis using ML is a fast and reliable mechanism to classify malicious and benign samples considering different characteristic of PE32 executables. Machine Learning- aided static malware analysis can be used as part of Cyber Threat Intelligence (CTI) activities to automate detection of indications of compromise from static features of PE32 Windows files.

References

1. Virusshare.com. http://virusshare.com/. accessed: 15.10.2015.
2. Vx heaven. http://vxheaven.org/. accessed: 25.10.2015.
3. Weka 3: Data mining software in java. http://www.cs.waikato.ac.nz/ml/weka/. accessed: 10.09.2015.

4. Gianni Amato. Peframe. https://github.com/guelfoweb/peframe. accessed: 20.10.2015.
5. M. Baig, P. Zavarsky, R. Ruhl, and D. Lindskog. The study of evasion of packed pe from static detection. In *Internet Security (WorldCIS), 2012 World Congress on*, pages 99–104, June 2012.
6. Simen Rune Bragen. Malware detection through opcode sequence analysis using machine learning. Master's thesis, Gjøvik University College, 2015.
7. C. Cepeda, D. L. C. Tien, and P. Ordóñez. Feature selection and improving classification performance for malware detection. In *2016 IEEE International Conferences on Big Data and Cloud Computing (BDCloud), Social Computing and Networking (SocialCom), Sustainable Computing and Communications (SustainCom) (BDCloud-SocialCom-SustainCom)*, pages 560–566, Oct 2016.
8. Mohsen Damshenas, Ali Dehghantanha, and Ramlan Mahmoud. A survey on malware propagation, analysis, and detection. *International Journal of Cyber-Security and Digital Forensics (IJCSDF)*, 2(4):10–29, 2013.
9. F. Daryabar, A. Dehghantanha, and N. I. Udzir. Investigation of bypassing malware defences and malware detections. In *2011 7th International Conference on Information Assurance and Security (IAS)*, pages 173–178, Dec 2011.
10. Farid Daryabar, Ali Dehghantanha, and Hoorang Ghasem Broujerdi. Investigation of malware defence and detection techniques. *International Journal of Digital Information and Wireless Communications (IJDIWC)*, 1(3):645–650, 2011.
11. Farid Daryabar, Ali Dehghantanha, Brett Eterovic-Soric, and Kim-Kwang Raymond Choo. Forensic investigation of onedrive, box, googledrive and dropbox applications on android and ios devices. *Australian Journal of Forensic Sciences*, 48(6):615–642, 2016.
12. Farid Daryabar, Ali Dehghantanha, Nur Izura Udzir, Solahuddin bin Shamsuddin, et al. Towards secure model for scada systems. In *Cyber Security, Cyber Warfare and Digital Forensic (CyberSec), 2012 International Conference on*, pages 60–64. IEEE, 2012.
13. Farid Daryabar, Ali Dehghantanha, Nur Izura Udzir, et al. A review on impacts of cloud computing on digital forensics. *International Journal of Cyber-Security and Digital Forensics (IJCSDF)*, 2(2):77–94, 2013.
14. Ali Dehghantanha and Katrin Franke. Privacy-respecting digital investigation. In *Privacy, Security and Trust (PST), 2014 Twelfth Annual International Conference on*, pages 129–138. IEEE, 2014.
15. Dhruwajita Devi and Sukumar Nandi. Detection of packed malware. In *Proceedings of the First International Conference on Security of Internet of Things*, SecurIT '12, pages 22–26, New York, NY, USA, 2012. ACM.
16. Dennis Distler and Charles Hornat. Malware analysis: An introduction. *Sans Reading Room*, 2007.
17. T. Dube, R. Raines, G. Peterson, K. Bauer, M. Grimaila, and S. Rogers. Malware type recognition and cyber situational awareness. In *Social Computing (SocialCom), 2010 IEEE Second International Conference on*, pages 938–943, Aug 2010.
18. Tim Ebringer, Li Sun, and Serdar Boztas. A fast randomness test that preserves local detail. *Virus Bulletin*, 2008, 2008.
19. Parvez Faruki, Vijay Laxmi, M. S. Gaur, and P. Vinod. Mining control flow graph as api call-grams to detect portable executable malware. In *Proceedings of the Fifth International Conference on Security of Information and Networks*, SIN '12, pages 130–137, New York, NY, USA, 2012. ACM.
20. Anders Flaglien, Katrin Franke, and Andre Arnes. Identifying malware using cross-evidence correlation. In *IFIP International Conference on Digital Forensics*, pages 169–182. Springer Berlin Heidelberg, 2011.
21. Tristan Fletcher. Support vector machines explained. *[Online]*. http://sutikno.blog.undip.ac.id/files/2011/11/SVM-Explained.pdf.*[Accessed 06 06 2013]*, 2009.
22. Katrin Franke, Erik Hjelmås, and Stephen D Wolthusen. Advancing digital forensics. In *IFIP World Conference on Information Security Education*, pages 288–295. Springer Berlin Heidelberg, 2009.

23. Katrin Franke and Sargur N Srihari. Computational forensics: Towards hybrid-intelligent crime investigation. In *Information Assurance and Security, 2007. IAS 2007. Third International Symposium on*, pages 383–386. IEEE, 2007.
24. Mark A Hall and Lloyd A Smith. Practical feature subset selection for machine learning. *Proceedings of the 21st Australasian Computer Science Conference ACSC'98*, 1998.
25. Chris Hoffman. How to keep your pc secure when microsoft ends windows xp support. http://www.pcworld.com/article/2102606/how-to-keep-your-pc-secure-when-microsoft-ends-windows-xp-support.html. accessed: 18.04.2016.
26. Anil K Jain, Robert PW Duin, and Jianchang Mao. Statistical pattern recognition: A review. *Pattern Analysis and Machine Intelligence, IEEE Transactions on*, 22(1):4–37, 2000.
27. Sachin Jain and Yogesh Kumar Meena. Byte level n–gram analysis for malware detection. In *Computer Networks and Intelligent Computing*, pages 51–59. Springer, 2011.
28. Kris Kendall and Chad McMillan. Practical malware analysis. In *Black Hat Conference, USA*, 2007.
29. Z. Khorsand and A. Hamzeh. A novel compression-based approach for malware detection using pe header. In *Information and Knowledge Technology (IKT), 2013 5th Conference on*, pages 127–133, May 2013.
30. Teuvo Kohonen and Timo Honkela. Kohonen network. *Scholarpedia*, 2(1):1568, 2007.
31. Jeremy Z. Kolter and Marcus A. Maloof. Learning to detect malicious executables in the wild. In *Proceedings of the Tenth ACM SIGKDD International Conference on Knowledge Discovery and Data Mining*, KDD '04, pages 470–478, New York, NY, USA, 2004. ACM.
32. Igor Kononenko and Matjaž Kukar. *Machine learning and data mining: introduction to principles and algorithms*. Horwood Publishing, 2007.
33. S. Kumar, M. Azad, O. Gomez, and R. Valdez. Can microsoft's service pack2 (sp2) security software prevent smurf attacks? In *Advanced Int'l Conference on Telecommunications and Int'l Conference on Internet and Web Applications and Services (AICT-ICIW'06)*, pages 89–89, Feb 2006.
34. Lastline. The threat of evasive malware. white paper, Lastline Labs, https://www.lastline.com/papers/evasive_threats.pdf, February 2013. accessed: 29.10.2015.
35. N. A. Le-Khac and A. Linke. Control flow change in assembly as a classifier in malware analysis. In *2016 4th International Symposium on Digital Forensic and Security (ISDFS)*, pages 38–43, April 2016.
36. Woody Leonhard. Atms will still run windows xp – but a bigger shift in security looms. http://www.infoworld.com/article/2610392/microsoft-windows/atms-will-still-run-windows-xp----but-a-bigger-shift-in-security-looms.html, March 2014. accessed: 09.11.2015.
37. R. J. Mangialardo and J. C. Duarte. Integrating static and dynamic malware analysis using machine learning. *IEEE Latin America Transactions*, 13(9):3080–3087, Sept 2015.
38. Z. Markel and M. Bilzor. Building a machine learning classifier for malware detection. In *Anti-malware Testing Research (WATeR), 2014 Second Workshop on*, pages 1–4, Oct 2014.
39. M.M. Masud, L. Khan, and B. Thuraisingham. A hybrid model to detect malicious executables. In *Communications, 2007. ICC '07. IEEE International Conference on*, pages 1443–1448, June 2007.
40. Microsoft. Microsoft security essentials. http://windows.microsoft.com/en-us/windows/security-essentials-download. accessed: 18.04.2016.
41. Microsoft. Set application-specific access permissions. https://technet.microsoft.com/en-us/library/cc731858%28v=ws.11%29.aspx. accessed: 30.05.2016.
42. C. Miles, A. Lakhotia, C. LeDoux, A. Newsom, and V. Notani. Virusbattle: State-of-the-art malware analysis for better cyber threat intelligence. In *2014 7th International Symposium on Resilient Control Systems (ISRCS)*, pages 1–6, Aug 2014.
43. Nikola Milosevic, Ali Dehghantanha, and Kim-Kwang Raymond Choo. Machine learning aided android malware classification. *Computers & Electrical Engineering*, 2017.
44. S. Naval, V. Laxmi, M. Rajarajan, M. S. Gaur, and M. Conti. Employing program semantics for malware detection. *IEEE Transactions on Information Forensics and Security*, 10(12):2591–2604, Dec 2015.

45. Farhood Norouzizadeh Dezfouli, Ali Dehghantanha, Brett Eterovic-Soric, and Kim-Kwang Raymond Choo. Investigating social networking applications on smartphones detecting facebook, twitter, linkedin and google+ artefacts on android and ios platforms. *Australian journal of forensic sciences*, 48(4):469–488, 2016.
46. Opeyemi Osanaiye, Haibin Cai, Kim-Kwang Raymond Choo, Ali Dehghantanha, Zheng Xu, and Mqhele Dlodlo. Ensemble-based multi-filter feature selection method for ddos detection in cloud computing. *EURASIP Journal on Wireless Communications and Networking*, 2016(1):130, 2016.
47. Hamed Haddad Pajouh, Reza Javidan, Raouf Khayami, Dehghantanha Ali, and Kim-Kwang Raymond Choo. A two-layer dimension reduction and two-tier classification model for anomaly-based intrusion detection in iot backbone networks. *IEEE Transactions on Emerging Topics in Computing*, 2016.
48. Shuhui Qi, Ming Xu, and Ning Zheng. A malware variant detection method based on byte randomness test. *Journal of Computers*, 8(10):2469–2477, 2013.
49. J. Ross Quinlan. Improved use of continuous attributes in c4. 5. *Journal of artificial intelligence research*, pages 77–90, 1996.
50. RC Quinlan. 4.5: Programs for machine learning morgan kaufmann publishers inc. *San Francisco, USA*, 1993.
51. D Krishna Sandeep Reddy and Arun K Pujari. N-gram analysis for computer virus detection. *Journal in Computer Virology*, 2(3):231–239, 2006.
52. Seth Rosenblatt. Malwarebytes: With anti-exploit, we'll stop the worst attacks on pcs. http://www.cnet.com/news/malwarebytes-finally-unveils-freeware-exploit-killer/. accessed: 30.05.2016.
53. Neil J. Rubenking. The best antivirus utilities for 2016. http://uk.pcmag.com/antivirus-reviews/8141/guide/the-best-antivirus-utilities-for-2016. accessed: 30.05.2016.
54. Paul Rubens. 10 ways to keep windows xp machines secure. http://www.cio.com/article/2376575/windows-xp/10-ways-to-keep-windows-xp-machines-secure.html. accessed: 18.04.2016.
55. Ashkan Sami, Babak Yadegari, Hossein Rahimi, Naser Peiravian, Sattar Hashemi, and Ali Hamze. Malware detection based on mining api calls. In *Proceedings of the 2010 ACM Symposium on Applied Computing*, SAC '10, pages 1020–1025, New York, NY, USA, 2010. ACM.
56. S. Samtani, K. Chinn, C. Larson, and H. Chen. Azsecure hacker assets portal: Cyber threat intelligence and malware analysis. In *2016 IEEE Conference on Intelligence and Security Informatics (ISI)*, pages 19–24, Sept 2016.
57. SANS. Who's using cyberthreat intelligence and how? https://www.sans.org/reading-room/whitepapers/analyst/cyberthreat-intelligence-how-35767. accessed: 01.03.2017.
58. Igor Santos, Felix Brezo, Xabier Ugarte-Pedrero, and Pablo G Bringas. Opcode sequences as representation of executables for data-mining-based unknown malware detection. *Information Sciences*, 231:64–82, 2013.
59. Igor Santos, Xabier Ugarte-Pedrero, Borja Sanz, Carlos Laorden, and Pablo G. Bringas. Collective classification for packed executable identification. In *Proceedings of the 8th Annual Collaboration, Electronic Messaging, Anti-Abuse and Spam Conference*, CEAS '11, pages 23–30, New York, NY, USA, 2011. ACM.
60. Asaf Shabtai, Yuval Fledel, and Yuval Elovici. Automated static code analysis for classifying android applications using machine learning. In *Computational Intelligence and Security (CIS), 2010 International Conference on*, pages 329–333. IEEE, 2010.
61. Kaveh Shaerpour, Ali Dehghantanha, and Ramlan Mahmod. Trends in android malware detection. *The Journal of Digital Forensics, Security and Law: JDFSL*, 8(3):21, 2013.
62. R.K. Shahzad, N. Lavesson, and H. Johnson. Accurate adware detection using opcode sequence extraction. In *Availability, Reliability and Security (ARES), 2011 Sixth International Conference on*, pages 189–195, Aug 2011.

63. Andrii Shalaginov and Katrin Franke. Automated generation of fuzzy rules from large-scale network traffic analysis in digital forensics investigations. In *7th International Conference on Soft Computing and Pattern Recognition (SoCPaR 2015)*. IEEE, 2015.
64. Andrii Shalaginov and Katrin Franke. A new method for an optimal som size determination in neuro-fuzzy for the digital forensics applications. In *Advances in Computational Intelligence*, pages 549–563. Springer International Publishing, 2015.
65. Andrii Shalaginov and Katrin Franke. A new method of fuzzy patches construction in neuro-fuzzy for malware detection. In *IFSA-EUSFLAT*. Atlantis Press, 2015.
66. Andrii Shalaginov and Katrin Franke. Automated intelligent multinomial classification of malware species using dynamic behavioural analysis. In *IEEE Privacy, Security and Trust 2016*, 2016.
67. Andrii Shalaginov and Katrin Franke. Big data analytics by automated generation of fuzzy rules for network forensics readiness. *Applied Soft Computing*, 2016.
68. Andrii Shalaginov and Katrin Franke. *Towards Improvement of Multinomial Classification Accuracy of Neuro-Fuzzy for Digital Forensics Applications*, pages 199–210. Springer International Publishing, Cham, 2016.
69. Andrii Shalaginov, Katrin Franke, and Xiongwei Huang. Malware beaconing detection by mining large-scale dns logs for targeted attack identification. In *18th International Conference on Computational Intelligence in Security Information Systems*. WASET, 2016.
70. Andrii Shalaginov, Lars Strande Grini, and Katrin Franke. Understanding neuro-fuzzy on a class of multinomial malware detection problems. In *IEEE International Joint Conference on Neural Networks (IJCNN 2016)*, Jul 2016.
71. M. Shankarapani, K. Kancherla, S. Ramammoorthy, R. Movva, and S. Mukkamala. Kernel machines for malware classification and similarity analysis. In *Neural Networks (IJCNN), The 2010 International Joint Conference on*, pages 1–6, July 2010.
72. Muazzam Ahmed Siddiqui. *Data mining methods for malware detection*. ProQuest, 2008.
73. Holly Stewart. Infection rates and end of support for windows xp. https://blogs.technet. microsoft.com/mmpc/2013/10/29/infection-rates-and-end-of-support-for-windows-xp/. accessed: 01.04.2016.
74. Li Sun, Steven Versteeg, Serdar Boztaş, and Trevor Yann. Pattern recognition techniques for the classification of malware packers. In *Information security and privacy*, pages 370–390. Springer, 2010.
75. S Momina Tabish, M Zubair Shafiq, and Muddassar Farooq. Malware detection using statistical analysis of byte-level file content. In *Proceedings of the ACM SIGKDD Workshop on CyberSecurity and Intelligence Informatics*, pages 23–31. ACM, 2009.
76. Shugang Tang. The detection of trojan horse based on the data mining. In *Fuzzy Systems and Knowledge Discovery, 2009. FSKD '09. Sixth International Conference on*, volume 1, pages 311–314, Aug 2009.
77. X. Ugarte-Pedrero, I. Santos, P.G. Bringas, M. Gastesi, and J.M. Esparza. Semi-supervised learning for packed executable detection. In *Network and System Security (NSS), 2011 5th International Conference on*, pages 342–346, Sept 2011.
78. R Veeramani and Nitin Rai. Windows api based malware detection and framework analysis. In *International conference on networks and cyber security*, volume 25, 2012.
79. C. Wang, Z. Qin, J. Zhang, and H. Yin. A malware variants detection methodology with an opcode based feature method and a fast density based clustering algorithm. In *2016 12th International Conference on Natural Computation, Fuzzy Systems and Knowledge Discovery (ICNC-FSKD)*, pages 481–487, Aug 2016.
80. Tzu-Yen Wang, Chin-Hsiung Wu, and Chu-Cheng Hsieh. Detecting unknown malicious executables using portable executable headers. In *INC, IMS and IDC, 2009. NCM '09. Fifth International Joint Conference on*, pages 278–284, Aug 2009.

81. Steve Watson and Ali Dehghantanha. Digital forensics: the missing piece of the internet of things promise. *Computer Fraud & Security*, 2016(6):5–8, 2016.
82. Yanfang Ye, Dingding Wang, Tao Li, Dongyi Ye, and Qingshan Jiang. An intelligent pe-malware detection system based on association mining. *Journal in computer virology*, 4(4):323–334, 2008.
83. M.N.A. Zabidi, M.A. Maarof, and A. Zainal. Malware analysis with multiple features. In *Computer Modelling and Simulation (UKSim), 2012 UKSim 14th International Conference on*, pages 231–235, March 2012.
84. Zongqu Zhao. A virus detection scheme based on features of control flow graph. In *Artificial Intelligence, Management Science and Electronic Commerce (AIMSEC), 2011 2nd International Conference on*, pages 943–947, Aug 2011.

Application of Machine Learning Techniques to Detecting Anomalies in Communication Networks: Datasets and Feature Selection Algorithms

Qingye Ding, Zhida Li, Soroush Haeri, and Ljiljana Trajković

Abstract Detecting, analyzing, and defending against cyber threats is an important topic in cyber security. Applying machine learning techniques to detect such threats has received considerable attention in research literature. Anomalies of Border Gateway Protocol (BGP) affect network operations and their detection is of interest to researchers and practitioners. In this Chapter, we describe main properties of the protocol and datasets that contain BGP records collected from various public and private domain repositories such as Route Views, Réseaux IP Européens (RIPE), and BCNET. We employ various feature selection algorithms to extract the most relevant features that are later used to classify BGP anomalies.

Keywords Routing anomalies · Border Gateway Protocol · Feature extraction · Feature selection · Machine learning techniques

1 Introduction

The Internet is a critical asset of information and communication technology. Cyber attacks and threats significantly impact the Internet performance. Hence, detecting such network anomalies is of great interest to researchers and practitioners. In this Chapter, we describe BGP, datasets used to detect anomalies, feature extraction process, and various feature selection algorithms. We consider BGP update messages because they contain information about the protocol status and configurations. BGP update messages are extracted from the collected data during the time periods when the Internet experienced known anomalies. BGP features are extracted and selected in order to improve the classification results. The classifiers are then used in Chapter 4 to detect anomalies and to compare classification results.

Q. Ding · Z. Li · S. Haeri · L. Trajković (✉)
Simon Fraser University, Vancouver, BC, Canada
e-mail: qingyed@sfu.ca; zhidal@sfu.ca; shaeri@sfu.ca; ljilja@cs.sfu.ca

© Springer International Publishing AG, part of Springer Nature 2018   47
A. Dehghantanha et al. (eds.), *Cyber Threat Intelligence*, Advances in Information
Security 70, https://doi.org/10.1007/978-3-319-73951-9_3

We extract *AS-path* and *volume* features from the BGP datasets [1, 9, 11]. Subsets of features are then selected using various feature selection algorithms to reduce the dimensionality of the dataset matrix while preserving their physical meaning. The employed algorithms belong to the category of filter methods where feature selection is independent of the underlying learning algorithm [28]. For feature selection, we employ: Fisher [35], minimum redundancy maximum relevance (mRMR) [40] (including mutual information difference (MID), mutual information quotient (MIQ), and mutual information base (MIBASE)), odds ratio (OR), extended/weighted/multi-class odds ratio (EOR/WOR/MOR), class discriminating measure (CDM) [21], and decision tree [42].

In this survey, we have revised our previous research findings and results by carefully processing the considered datasets, selecting better parameters for various techniques, and reevaluating past performance results. We revised previously reported performance results [16, 24] for feature selection algorithms (Fisher, MID, MIQ, MIBASE, OR, EOR, WOR, MOR, and CDM). Other approaches include using fuzzy rough sets for feature selection [34]. Fuzzy sets and rough sets [38, 43] have greatly affected the way we compute with imperfect information. Fuzzy rough sets deal with the approximation of fuzzy sets in an approximation space [52]. Even though the classification accuracy usually improves by performing feature reduction using fuzzy rough sets, the computational complexity of the algorithm remains rather high. Hence, this approach is unsuitable in cases with large number of samples and attributes. In comparison, the decision tree algorithm is faster and may achieve acceptable classification accuracy.

This Chapter is organized as follows. We first briefly described BGP, the effect of network anomalies, and approaches for their detection. In Sect. 2, we provide details of various BGP anomalies that we have considered in our previous work and in this survey. The description of the datasets and data processing is introduced in Sect. 3. Various approaches for feature extractions are described in Sect. 4 while feature selection algorithms are described in Sect. 5. We conclude with Sect. 6. List of relevant references is also provided.

1.1 Border Gateway Protocol (BGP)

BGP [44] is a routing protocol that plays an essential role in forwarding Internet Protocol (IP) traffic between the source and the destination Autonomous Systems (ASes). An AS is a collection of BGP peers managed by a single administrative domain [51]. It consists of one or more networks that possess uniform routing policies while operating independently. Internet operations such as connectivity and data packet delivery are facilitated by various ASes.

The main function of BGP is to select the best routes between ASes based on network policies enforced by network administrators. Routing algorithms determine the route that a data packet takes while traversing the Internet. They exchange reachability information about possible destinations. BGP is an upgrade of the

Exterior Gateway Protocol (EGP) [45]. It is an interdomain routing protocol used for routing packets in networks consisting of a large number of ASs. BGP version 4 allows Classless Interdomain Routing (CIDR), aggregation of routes, incremental additions, better filtering options, and it has the ability to set routing policies. BGP employs the path vector protocol, which is a modified version of the distance vector protocol [30]. It is a standard for the exchange of information among the Internet Service Providers (ISPs).

BGP relies on the Transport Control Protocol (TCP) to establish a connection (port 179) between the routers. A BGP router establishes a TCP connection with its peers that reside in different ASes. Because of their size, BGP routing tables are exchanged once between the peering routers when they first connect. BGP allows ASes to exchange reachability information with peering ASes to transmit information about the availability of routes within an AS. Based on the exchanged information and routing policies, it determines the most appropriate path to destination. BGP allows each subnet to announce its existence to the Internet and to publish its reachability information. Hence, all sub-networks are inter-connected and are known to the Internet.

BGP is an incremental protocol that sends updates only if there are reachability or topology changes within the network. Afterwards, only updates regarding new prefixes or withdrawals of the existing prefixes are exchanged. BGP routers exchange four types of messages: *open, update, keep-alive,* and *notification* [45]. The *open* message that contains basic information such as router identifier, BGP version, and the AS number is used to open a peering session. Routers exchange all known routes using the *update* message after the BGP session is established and when there is a change of BGP routes in the routing tables. *Keep-alive* messages are exchanged between peers during inactivity periods to ensure that the connections still exist. The *notification* message closes a peering session if there is a disagreement in the configuration parameters. A sample of a BGP *update* message is shown in Table 1. It contains two Network Layer Reachability Information (NLRI) announcements, which share attributes such as the *AS-path.* The *AS-path* attribute in the BGP update message indicates the path that a BGP packet traverses among AS peers. The *AS-path* attribute enables BGP to route packets via the best path.

Propagation of the BGP routing information is susceptible to various anomalous events such as worms, malicious attacks, power outages, blackouts, and misconfigurations of BGP routers. BGP anomalies are caused by changes in network topologies, updated AS policies, or router misconfigurations. They affect the Internet servers and hosts and are manifested by anomalous traffic behavior. Anomalous events in communication networks cause traffic behavior to deviate from its usual profile. These events may spread false routing information throughout the Internet by either dropping packets or directing traffic through unauthorized ASes and, hence, risking eavesdropping. Large-scale power outages may affect ISPs due to unreliable power backup. They could also cause network equipment failures leaving affected networks isolated and their service disrupted. Configuration errors in BGP routers also induce anomalous routing behavior. Routing table leak and prefix hijack [10] events are examples of BGP configuration errors that may lead

Table 1 Sample of a BGP update message

Field	Value
Time	2003 1 24 00:39:53
Type	BGP4MP/BGP4MP_MESSAGE AFI_IP
From	192.65.184.3
To	193.0.4.28
BGP packet type	Update
Origin	IGP
AS-path	513 3320 7176 15570 7246 7246 7246
	7246 7246 7246 7246 7246 7246
Next-hop	192.65.184.3
Announced NLRI prefix	198.155.189.0/24
Announced NLRI prefix	198.155.241.0/24

IGP: Interior Gateway Protocol, NLRI: Network Layer Reachability Information

to large-scale disconnections in the Internet. A routing table leak occurs when an AS such as an ISP announces a prefix from its Route Information Base (RIB) that violates previously agreed upon routing policy. A prefix hijack is the consequence of an AS originating a prefix that it does not own.

1.2 Approaches for Detecting Network Anomalies

Detailed comparison of various network intrusion techniques has been reported in the literature [18]. Demands for Internet services have been steadily increasing and anomalous events and their effects have dire economic consequences. Determining the anomalous events and their causes is an important step in assessing loss of data by anomalous routing. Hence, it is important to classify these anomalous events and prevent their effects on BGP.

Anomaly detection techniques have been applied in communication networks [14]. These techniques are employed to detect BGP anomalies such as intrusion attacks, worms, and distributed denial of service attacks (DDoS) [32, 39] that frequently affect the Internet and its applications. BGP data have been analyzed to identify anomalous events and design tools that have been used in anomaly predictions. Network anomalies are detected by analyzing collected traffic data and generating various classification models. A variety of techniques have been proposed to detect BGP anomalies.

Early approaches include developing traffic models using statistical signal processing techniques where a baseline profile of network regular operation is developed based on a parametric model of traffic behavior and a large collection of traffic samples to account for regular (anomaly-free) cases [27]. Anomalies may then be detected as sudden changes in the mean values of variables describing the baseline model. However, it is infeasible to acquire datasets that include all possible cases. In a network with quasi-stationary traffic, statistical signal processing methods have been employed to detect anomalies as correlated abrupt changes in network traffic [47].

The main focus of approaches also proposed in the past is developing models for classification of anomalies. The accuracy of a classifier depends on the extracted features, combination of selected features, and underlying models. Recent research reports describe a number of applicable classification techniques. One of the most common approaches is based on a statistical pattern recognition model implemented as an anomaly classifier and detector [23]. Its main disadvantage is the difficulty in estimating distributions of higher dimensions. For example, a Bayesian detection algorithm was designed to identify unexpected route mis-configurations as statistical anomalies [17]. An instance-learning framework also employed wavelets to systematically identify anomalous BGP route advertisements [53]. Other proposed techniques are rule-based methods that have been employed for detecting anomalous BGP events. An example is the Internet Routing Forensics (IRF) that was applied to classify anomaly events [33]. However, rule-based techniques are not adaptable learning mechanisms. They are slow, have high degree of computational complexity, and require a priority knowledge of network conditions.

We view anomaly detection as a classification problem of assigning an "anomaly" or "regular" label to a data point. There are numerous machine learning methods that address these classification tasks. However, redundancies in the collected data may affect the performance of classification methods. Feature extraction and selection are used to select a subset of features from the original feature space and, thus, to reduce redundancy among features that leads to improving the classification accuracy. Feature extraction methods such as principal component analysis project the original data points onto a lower dimensional space. However, features transformed by feature extraction lose their original physical meaning. We extract BGP features based on the attributes of BGP update messages in order to achieve reliable classification results. Recent trends in designing BGP anomaly detection systems rely more frequently on machine learning techniques. Known classifiers are tested for their ability to detect network anomalies in datasets that include known BGP anomalies. In this survey, we described several machine learning techniques that we have used in the past for classification due to their superior performance compared to earlier approaches.

2 Examples of BGP Anomalies

Anomalous events considered in this Chapter are worms, power outages, and BGP router configuration errors. They are manifested by sharp and sustained increases in the number of announcement or withdrawal messages exchanged by BGP routers. *Volume* and *AS-path* features are collected over 1-min time intervals during 5-day periods for well known anomalous Internet events. While the available datasets

Table 2 Examples of known BGP Internet worms

Dataset	Class	Date		Duration (min)
		Beginning of the event	End of the event	
Slammer	Anomaly	25.01.2003 at 5:31 GMT	25.01.2003 at 19:59 GMT	869
Nimda	Anomaly	18.09.2001 at 13:19 GMT	20.09.2001 at 23:59 GMT	3,521
Code Red I	Anomaly	19.07.2001 at 13:20 GMT	19.07.2001 at 23:19 GMT	600

Table 3 Datasets of the Internet anomalous events

Event	Date	RRC	Peers
Moscow power blackout	May 2005	RIS 05	AS 1853, AS 12793, AS 13237
AS 9121 routing table leak	Dec. 2004	RIS 05	AS 1853, AS 12793, AS 13237
AS 3561 improper filtering	Apr. 2001	RIS 03	AS 3257, AS 3333, AS 286
Panix domain hijack	Jan. 2006	Route Views	AS 12956, AS 6762, AS 6939, AS 3549
AS-path error	Oct. 2001	RIS 03	AS 3257, AS 3333, AS 6762, AS 9057
AS 3356/AS 714 de-peering	Oct. 2005	RIS 01	AS 13237, AS 8342, AS 5511, AS 16034

contain data over much longer periods of time, we have selected for our analysis a 5-day period to minimize storage and computational requirements. Furthermore, selecting longer periods of regular data would make datasets ever more unbalanced. Several methods that we surveyed offer better performance when dealing with balanced datasets. Details including dates of the events, remote route collectors (RRC) that acquired data using Routing Information Service (RIS), and observed peers are given in Tables 2 and 3. For example, Slammer event occurred on January 25, 2003 and lasted almost 16 hours. Hence, BGP update messages collected between January 23, 2003 and January 27, 2003 are selected as samples for feature extraction.

The Structured Query Language (SQL) Slammer worm attacked Microsoft SQL servers on January 25, 2003 [12]. It generated random IP addresses and replicates itself by sending 376 bytes of code to those IP addresses. As a result, the update messages consumed most of the routers' bandwidth, which in turn slowed down the routers and, in some cases, caused the routers to crash. The Nimda worm [8] was released on September 18, 2001. It propagated fast through email messages, web browsers, and file systems. Viewing the email message triggered the worm payload. The worm modified the content of the web document file in the infected hosts and copied itself in local host directories. The Code Red I worm attacked web servers on July 19, 2001 [3]. The worm affected approximately half a million IP addresses a day. It took advantage of vulnerability in the Internet Information Services (IIS) indexing software. It triggered a buffer overflow in the infected hosts by writing to the buffers without checking their limits.

We consider BGP anomalous events such as Slammer [12], Nimda [8], Code Red I [3], AS 9121 routing table leak [41], Moscow power blackout, AS 3561 improper filtering, Panix domain hijack, AS path error, and AS 3356/AS 714 de-peering [54].

Slammer [12] Microsoft SQL servers were infected through a small piece of code that generated IP addresses at random. Furthermore, code replicated itself by infecting new machines through randomly generated targets. If the destination IP address was a Microsoft SQL server or a user's PC with the Microsoft SQL Server Data Engine (MSDE) installed, the server became infected and began infecting other servers. The number of infected machines doubled approximately every 9 s. Single infected machines have reported additional traffic of 50 Mb/s [13] as a consequence of increased generation of update messages.

Nimda [8] Nimda exploited vulnerabilities in the Microsoft Internet Information Services (IIS) web servers for the Internet Explorer 5. It used three methods for propagation: email, network shares, and the web. The worm propagated by sending an infected attachment that was automatically downloaded after viewing email. A user could also download it from the website or access an infected file through the network.

Code Red I [3] Although the Code Red I worm attacked Microsoft IIS web servers earlier, the peak of infected computers was observed on July 19, 2001. The worm replicated itself by exploiting weakness of the IIS servers and, unlike the Slammer worm, Code Red I searched for vulnerable servers to infect. Rate of infection was doubling every 37 min.

Records of three BGP anomalies along with regular RIPE traffic are shown in Fig. 1. The effect of Slammer worm on *volume* and *AS-path* features is shown in Fig. 2.

Moscow Power Blackout The blackout occurred on May 25, 2005 and lasted several hours. The Moscow Internet exchange was shut down during the power outage. Routing instabilities were observed due to loss of connectivity of some ISPs peering at this exchange. This effect was apparent at the RIS remote route collector in Vienna (rrc05) through a surge in announcement messages arriving from peer AS 12793, as shown in Fig. 3. Hence, volume of announcements was one of the features used to detect the anomaly.

AS 9121 Routing Table Leak It occurred on December 24, 2004 when AS 9121 announced to peers that it could be used to reach almost 70% of all prefixes (over 106,000). As a consequence, numerous networks had either misdirected or lost their traffic. The AS 9121 started announcing prefixes to peers around 9:20 GMT and the event lasted until shortly after 10:00 GMT. It continued to announce bad prefixes throughout the day. The announcement rate reached the second peak at 19:47 GMT.

AS 3561 Improper Filtering This was a BGP mis-configuration error that occurred on April 6, 2001. AS 3561 allowed improper route announcements from its downstream customers, which created connectivity disruptions. Surge of announcement messages originating from peer AS 3257 was observed at the RIS rrc03.

Panix Domain Hijack Panix, the oldest commercial ISP in New York state, was hijacked on January 22, 2006. Its services were unreachable from the greater part

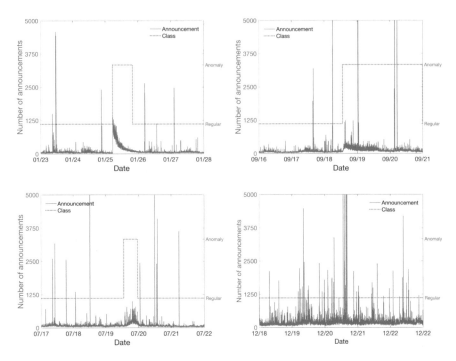

Fig. 1 Number of BGP announcements in Slammer (top left), Nimda (top right), Code Red I (bottom left), and regular RIPE (bottom right) traffic

of the Internet. Con Edison (AS 27506) advertised routes that it did not own at the time. Panix was previously a customer of Con Edison, which was once authorized to offer advertised routes. Even though AS 27506 originated improper routes, major downstream ISPs did not properly configure filters and propagated those routes, leading to excess number of update messages.

AS-path Error The AS-path error occurred on October 7, 2001. It was caused by an abnormal AS-path (AS 3300, AS 64603, AS 2008) that contained private AS 64603 that should not have been included in the path. At the time, AS 3300 and AS 2008 belonged to INFONET Europe and INFONET USA, respectively. The path was distributed to the network via mis-configured routers and caused the leak of the private AS numbers. Shown in Fig. 4, is the increase of incomplete packets around 20:00 GMT, peaking around 21:00 GMT, and slowly decreasing during the following 4 hours.

De-Peering The AS 3356/AS 714 De-Peering event occurred on October 5, 2005. Even though the Level 3 Communications (AS 3356) notified the Cogent Communications (AS 714) 2 months in advance of de-peering, the event created reachability problems for many Internet locations. Mostly affected were single-homed customers of Cogent (approximately 2,300 prefixes) and Level 3 Communications (approximately 5,000 prefixes). De-Peering resulted in partitioning of approximately 4% of prefixes in the global routing table.

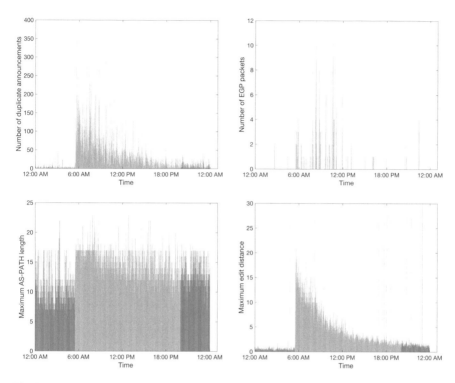

Fig. 2 BGP announcements during the Slammer worm attack: number of duplicate announce-ments (top left), number of EGP packets (top right), maximum AS-path length (bottom left), and maximum AS-path edit distance (bottom right)

3 Analyzed BGP Datasets

The Internet routing data used in this chapter to detect BGP anomalies are acquired from projects that provide valuable information to networking research: the Route Views project [11] at the University of Oregon, USA and the Routing Information Service (RIS) project initiated in 2001 by the Réseaux IP Européens (RIPE) Net-work Coordination Centre (NCC) [9]. Both projects collect and store chronological routing data that offer a unique view of the Internet topology. The Route Views and RIPE BGP update messages are publicly available to the research community. The regular BCNET dataset is collected at the BCNET location in Vancouver, British Columbia, Canada [25, 31]. We use BGP update messages that originated from AS 513 (route collector rrc04) member of the CERN Internet Exchange Point (CIXP). Only data collected during the periods of Internet anomalies are considered.

The Route Views project collects BGP routing tables from multiple geographi-cally distributed BGP Cisco routers and Zebra servers every 2 hours. At the time of BGP anomalies considered in this study, two Cisco routers and two Zebra servers were located at the University of Oregon, USA. The remaining five Zebra servers are

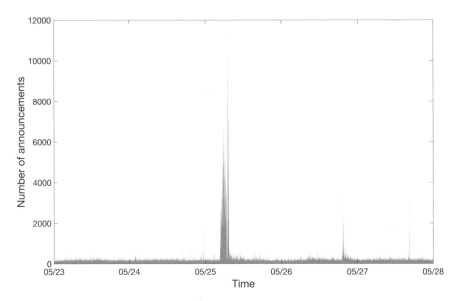

Fig. 3 Surge of announcement messages at the AS 12793 peer during the Moscow Power blackout

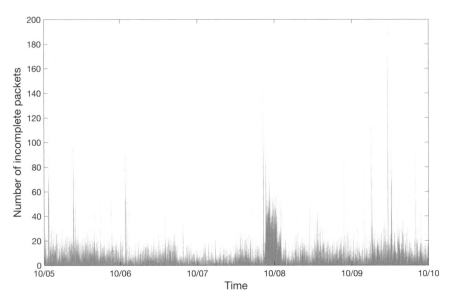

Fig. 4 Surge of incomplete packets at the AS 6762 peer during the AS-path error

located at Equinix-USA, ISC-USA, KIXP-Kenya, LINX-Great Britain, and DIXIE-Japan [11]. Most participating ASes in the Route Views project are located in North America.

The RIPE NCC began collecting and storing Internet routing data in 2001 through the RIS project [9]. The data were exported every 15 min until July 2003. The interval between consecutive exports was later decreased to 5 min. BGP update messages are collected by the RRCs and stored in the multi-threaded routing toolkit (MRT) binary format [7]. The Internet Engineering Task Force (IETF) [4] introduced MRT to export routing protocol messages, state changes, and content of the routing information base (RIB). We transformed BGP update messages from MRT into ASCII format by using libBGPdump library [5] on a Linux platform. LibBGPdump is a C library maintained by the RIPE NCC and it is used to analyze dump files, which are in MRT format.

We use data from the Route Views and RIPE projects data collectors. Only data collected during the periods of Internet anomalies are considered. BGP update messages originated from RIS route collectors: rrc01 (LINX, London), rcc03 (AMS-IX, Amsterdam), rrc04 (CIXP, Geneva), and rrc05 (VIX, Vienna).

3.1 Processing of Collected Data

BGP update messages are collected during the time period when the Internet experienced anomalies. Datasets are concatenated to increase the size of training datasets and thus improve the classification results. Anomaly datasets and their concatenations used for training and testing are shown in Table 4.

We consider a 5-day period for each anomaly: the days of the attack (anomalous data points) and 2 days prior and 2 days after the attack (regular data points). The exception is Nimda dataset where the anomaly lasted longer than 2 days and, hence, we only use 2 days prior to the event as regular data points. Datasets consist of $14,400$ ($2 \times 7,200$) data points represented by $14,400 \times 37$ and $14,400 \times 10$ matrices that correspond to 37 and 10 features, respectively. In some cases choosing 15 features was suitable for detecting anomalous events [22] leading to the feature matrices of dimension $7,200 \times 15$. In addition to anomalous test datasets, we also use regular datasets collected from RIPE [9] and BCNET [1]. Details of the three anomalies are listed in Table 5.

Table 4 Training and test datasets

Training dataset	Anomalies	Test dataset
1	Slammer and Nimda	Code Red I
2	Slammer and Code Red I	Nimda
3	Nimda and Code Red I	Slammer
4	Slammer	Nimda and Code Red I
5	Nimda	Slammer and Code Red I
6	Code Red I	Slammer and Nimda
7	Slammer, Nimda, and Code Red I	RIPE or BCNET

Table 5 Duration of analyzed BGP events

	Anomaly (min)	Regular (min)
Slammer	869	6,331
Nimda	3,521	3,679
Code Red I	600	6,600

Table 6 List of features extracted from BGP *update* messages

Feature	Name	Category
1	Number of announcements	*volume*
2	Number of withdrawals	*volume*
3	Number of announced NLRI prefixes	*volume*
4	Number of withdrawn NLRI prefixes	*volume*
5	Average *AS-path* length	*AS-path*
6	Maximum *AS-path* length	*AS-path*
7	Average unique *AS-path* length	*AS-path*
8	Number of duplicate announcements	*volume*
9	Number of duplicate withdrawals	*volume*
10	Number of implicit withdrawals	*volume*
11	Average edit distance	*AS-path*
12	Maximum edit distance	*AS-path*
13	Inter-arrival time	*volume*
14–24	Maximum edit distance $= n$, where $n = (7, \ldots, 17)$	*AS-path*
25–33	Maximum *AS-path* length $= n$, where $n = (7, \ldots, 15)$	*AS-path*
34	Number of Interior Gateway Protocol (IGP) packets	*volume*
35	Number of Exterior Gateway Protocol (EGP) packets	*volume*
36	Number of incomplete packets	*volume*
37	Packet size (B)	*volume*

4   Extraction of Features from BGP Update Messages

Feature extraction and selection are the first steps in the classification process. We developed a tool (written in C#) [15] to parse the ASCII files and extract statistics of the desired features. The *AS-path* is a BGP update message attribute that enables the protocol to select the best path for routing packets. It indicates a path that a packet may traverse to reach its destination. If a feature is derived from the *AS-path* attribute, it is categorized as an *AS-path* feature. Otherwise, it is categorized as a *volume* feature. There are three types of features: continuous, categorical, and binary. We extracted *AS-path* and *volume* features shown in Table 6 [15].

Definitions of the extracted features are listed in Table 7. BGP update messages are either announcement or withdrawal messages for the NLRI prefixes. The NLRI prefixes that have identical BGP attributes are encapsulated and sent in one BGP packet [37]. Hence, a BGP packet may contain more than one announced or withdrawn NLRI prefix. The average and the maximum number of AS peers are used for calculating *AS-path* lengths. Duplicate announcements are the BGP update packets

Table 7 Definition of *volume* and *AS-path* features extracted from BGP *update* messages

Feature	Name	Definition
1	Number of announcements	Routes available for delivery of data
2	Number of withdrawals	Routes no longer reachable
3/4	Number of announced/withdrawn NLRI prefixes	BGP update messages that have type field set to announcement/withdrawal
5/6/7	Average/maximum/average unique *AS-path* length	Various *AS-path* lengths
8/9	Number of duplicate announcements/withdrawals	Duplicate BGP update messages with type field set to announcement/withdrawal
10	Number of implicit withdrawals	BGP update messages with type field set to announcement and different *AS-path* attribute for already announced NLRI prefixes
11/12	Average/maximum edit distance	Average/maximum of edit distances of messages
34/35/36	Number of IGP, EGP or, incomplete packets	BGP update messages generated by IGP, EGP, or unknown sources

Table 8 Example of BGP features

Time	Definition	BGP update type	NLRI	AS-path
t_0	Announcement	Announcement	199.60.12.130	13455 614
t_1	Withdrawal	Withdrawal	199.60.12.130	13455 614
t_2	Duplicate announcement	Announcement	199.60.12.130	13455 614
t_3	Implicit withdrawal	Announcement	199.60.12.130	16180 614
t_4	Duplicate withdrawal	Withdrawal	199.60.12.130	13455 614

that have identical NLRI prefixes and the *AS-path* attributes. Implicit withdrawals are the BGP announcements with different *AS-paths* for already announced NLRI prefixes [48]. The edit distance between two *AS-path* attributes is the minimum number of deletions, insertions, or substitutions that need to be executed to match the two attributes [23]. For example, the edit distance between *AS-path* 513 940 and *AS-path* 513 4567 1318 is two because one insertion and one substitution are sufficient to match the two *AS-paths*. The maximum *AS-path* length and the maximum edit distance are used to count Features 14–33. We also consider Features 34, 35, and 36 based on distinct values of the origin attribute that specifies the origin of a BGP update packet and may assume three values: IGP, EGP, and incomplete. Even though the EGP protocol is the predecessor of BGP, EGP packets still appear in traffic traces containing BGP updates messages. Under a worm attack, BGP traces contain large volume of EGP packets. Furthermore, incomplete update messages imply that the announced NLRI prefixes are generated from unknown sources. They usually originate from BGP redistribution configurations [37]. Examples are shown in Table 8 while various distributions are shown in Figs. 5 and 6.

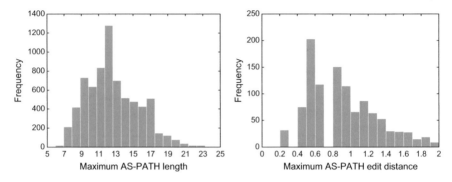

Fig. 5 Distributions of the maximum *AS-path* length (left) and the maximum edit distance (right) collected during the Slammer worm

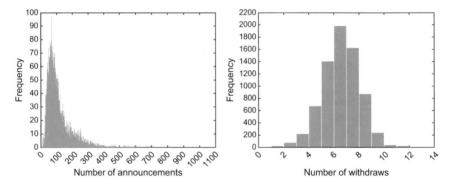

Fig. 6 Distribution of the number of BGP announcements (left) and withdrawals (right) for the Code Red I worm

Performance of the BGP protocol is based on trust among BGP peers because they assume that the interchanged announcements are accurate and reliable. This trust relationship is vulnerable during BGP anomalies. For example, during BGP hijacks, a BGP peer may announce unauthorized prefixes that indicate to other peers that it is the originating peer. These false announcements propagate across the Internet to other BGP peers and, hence, affect the number of BGP announcements (updates and withdrawals) worldwide. This storm of BGP announcements affects the quantity of *volume* features. For example, we have observed that 65% of the influential features are *volume* features. They proved to be more relevant to the anomaly class than the *AS-path* features, which confirms the known consequence of BGP anomalies on the volume of announcements. Hence, using BGP *volume* features is a feasible approach for detecting BGP anomalies and possible worm attacks in communication networks.

The top selected *AS-path* features appear on the boundaries of the distributions. This indicates that during BGP anomalies, the edit distance and *AS-path* length of the BGP announcements tend to have a very high or a very low value and, hence, large variance. This implies that during an anomaly attack, *AS-path* features are the distribution outliers. For example, approximately 58% of the *AS-path* features are larger than the distribution mean. Large length of the *AS-path* BGP attribute implies that the packet is routed via a longer path to its destination, which causes large routing delays during BGP anomalies. In a similar case, very short lengths of *AS-path* attributes occur during BGP hijacks when the new (false) originator usually gains a preferred or shorter path to the destination [10].

5   Review of Feature Selection Algorithms

Machine learning models classify data points using a feature matrix. The rows correspond to the data points while the columns correspond to the features. Even though machine learning provides general models to classify anomalies, it may easily misclassify test data points due to the redundancy or noise contained in datasets. By providing a sufficient number of relevant features, machine learning models overcome this deficiency and may help design a generalized model to classify data with small error rates [28, 29]. Performance of anomaly classifiers is closely related to feature selection algorithms [20].

Feature selection is used to pre-process data prior to applying machine learning algorithms for classification. Selecting appropriate combination of features is essential for an accurate classification. For example, the scatterings of anomalous and regular classes for Feature 9 (*volume*) vs. Feature 1 (*volume*) and vs. Feature 6 (*AS-path*) are shown in Fig. 7 (left) and (right), respectively. The graphs indicate spatial separation of features. While selecting Feature 9 and Feature 1 may lead to a feasible classification based on visible clusters, using only Feature 9 and Feature 6 would lead to poor classification.

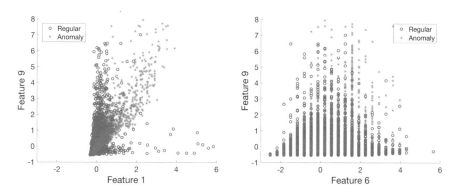

Fig. 7 Scattered graph of Feature 9 vs. Feature 1 (left) and vs. Feature 6 (right) extracted from the BCNET traffic. Feature values are normalized to have zero mean and unit variance. Shown are two traffic classes: regular (open circle) and anomaly (asterisk)

Feature selection follows a feature extraction process and it is used to decrease dimension of the dataset matrix by selecting a subset of original features to create a new matrix according to certain criteria. The number of features is reduced by removing irrelevant, redundant, and noisy features [36]. Feature selection reduces overfitting by minimizing the redundancies in data, improves modeling accuracy, and decreases training time. It also reduces computational complexity and memory usage. Performance of classification algorithms may also be improved by using pre-selection of features that are most relevant to the classification task. We select the top ten features while dismissing weak and distorted features. We employ Fisher [26, 35, 49], mRMR [40] (including MID, MIQ, and MIBASE), OR (including EOR, WOR, MOR, and CDM) [21], and Decision Tree [42] feature selection algorithms to select relevant features from BGP datasets.

Each sample is a point in n-dimensional space, where kth dimension is a column vector $\mathbf{X}_k$ representing one feature. For example, $\mathbf{X}_1$ is a column vector representing 7,200 announcements in each sampling window of 1 min.

5.1   Fisher Algorithm

The Fisher feature selection algorithm [26, 35, 49] computes the score Φ_k for the kth feature as a ratio of inter-class separation and intra-class variance. Features with higher inter-class separation and lower intra-class variance have higher Fisher scores. If there are N_a^k anomalous samples and N_r^k regular samples of the kth feature, the mean values m_a^k of anomalous samples and m_r^k of regular samples are calculated as:

$$m_a^k = \frac{1}{N_a^k} \sum_{i \in \mathbf{a}_k} x_{ik}$$

$$m_r^k = \frac{1}{N_r^k} \sum_{i \in \mathbf{r}_k} x_{ik}, \tag{1}$$

where $\mathbf{a}_k$ and $\mathbf{r}_k$ are the sets of anomalous and regular samples for the kth feature, respectively. The Fisher score for the kth feature is calculated as:

$$\Phi_k = \frac{\left|\left(m_a^k\right)^2 - \left(m_r^k\right)^2\right|}{\frac{1}{N_a^k} \sum_{i \in \mathbf{a}_k} \left(x_{ik} - m_a^k\right)^2 + \frac{1}{N_r^k} \sum_{i \in \mathbf{r}_k} \left(x_{ik} - m_r^k\right)^2}. \tag{2}$$

Table 9 The top ten features selected using the Fisher feature selection algorithm and Dataset 2 (two-way classification)

Feature	9	10	8	3	6	11	1	34	36	2
Fisher score	0.2280	0.1665	0.0794	0.0656	0.0614	0.0610	0.0528	0.0526	0.0499	0.0336

Table 10 The top ten features selected using the Fisher feature selection algorithm and Dataset 7 (four-way classification)

Feature	9	10	6	11	8	36	3	37	1	34
Fisher score	0.1259	0.0502	0.0414	0.0409	0.0281	0.0271	0.0240	0.0239	0.0210	0.0203

Examples of features selected using the Fisher algorithm applied to various training datasets are shown in Tables 9 and 10.

5.2 Minimum Redundancy Maximum Relevance (mRMR) Algorithms

The mRMR algorithm [6, 40] relies on information theory for feature selection. It selects a subset of features that contains more information about the target class while having less pairwise mutual information. A subset of features $S = \{\mathbf{X_1}, \ldots, \mathbf{X_k}, \ldots\}$ with $|S|$ elements has the minimum redundancy if it minimizes:

$$\mathscr{W} = \frac{1}{|S|^2} \sum_{\mathbf{X}_k, \mathbf{X}_l \in S} \mathscr{I}(\mathbf{X}_k, \mathbf{X}_l). \tag{3}$$

It has maximum relevance to the classification task if it maximizes:

$$\mathscr{V} = \frac{1}{|S|} \sum_{\mathbf{X}_k \in S} \mathscr{I}(\mathbf{X}_k, \mathbf{C}), \tag{4}$$

where $\mathbf{C}$ is a class vector and $\mathscr{I}$ denotes the mutual information function calculated as:

$$\mathscr{I}(\mathbf{X}_k, \mathbf{X}_l) = \sum_{k,l} p(\mathbf{X}_k, \mathbf{X}_l) log \frac{p(\mathbf{X}_k, \mathbf{X}_l)}{p(\mathbf{X}_k)p(\mathbf{X}_l)}. \tag{5}$$

The mRMR algorithm offers three variants for feature selection: Mutual Information Difference (MID), Mutual Information Quotient (MIQ), and Mutual Information Base (MIBASE). MID and MIQ select the best features based on $\max_{S \subset \Omega}[\mathscr{V} - \mathscr{W}]$ and $\max_{S \subset \Omega}[\mathscr{V} / \mathscr{W}]$, respectively, where Ω is the set of all features.

Table 11 The top ten features selected using the mRMR feature selection algorithms and Dataset 2 (two-way classification)

mRMR					
MID		MIQ		MIBASE	
Feature	Score	Feature	Score	Feature	Score
34	0.0554	34	0.0554	34	0.0554
10	0.0117	10	0.7527	1	0.0545
20	0.0047	8	0.6583	8	0.0469
25	0.0014	20	0.5014	10	0.0469
24	0.0012	4	0.4937	3	0.0421
23	0.0008	36	0.4095	9	0.0411
4	0.0007	1	0.3720	36	0.0377
8	0.0007	9	0.3260	4	0.0367
22	0.0006	3	0.2824	6	0.0205
21	0.0005	6	0.2809	11	0.0201

Table 12 The top ten features selected using the mRMR feature selection algorithms and Dataset 7 (four-way classification)

mRMR					
MID		MIQ		MIBASE	
Feature	Score	Feature	Score	Feature	Score
9	0.0407	9	0.0407	9	0.0407
20	0.0030	34	0.4797	1	0.0308
36	0.0024	36	0.3790	34	0.0305
34	0.0024	10	0.3730	36	0.0305
22	0.0017	5	0.3333	3	0.0234
21	0.0017	8	0.3322	8	0.0225
5	0.0003	1	0.3156	10	0.0200
10	0.0003	6	0.2920	6	0.0179
29	0.0002	37	0.2387	11	0.0177
23	0.0000	3	0.2299	37	0.0175

The top ten features selected by mRMR from various datasets are shown in Tables 11 and 12. They are used for two-way and four-way classifications. Selected features shown in Table 11 are generated by using Dataset 2 (Table 4) and are intended for two-way classification. Features shown in Table 12 are generated by using Dataset 7 (Table 4) and are used for four-way classification.

5.3 Odds Ratio Algorithms

The odds ratio (OR) algorithm and its variants perform well when selecting features to be used in binary classification using naive Bayes models. In case of a binary classification with two target classes c and $\bar{c}$, the odds ratio for a feature $\mathbf{X}_k$ is calculated as:

$$OR(\mathbf{X}_k) = \log \frac{\Pr(\mathbf{X}_k|c)\big(1 - \Pr(\mathbf{X}_k|\bar{c})\big)}{\Pr(\mathbf{X}_k|\bar{c})\big(1 - \Pr(\mathbf{X}_k|c)\big)}, \tag{6}$$

where $\Pr(\mathbf{X}_k|c)$ and $\Pr(\mathbf{X}_k|\bar{c})$ are the probabilities of feature $\mathbf{X}_k$ being in classes c and $\bar{c}$, respectively.

The extended odds ratio (EOR), weighted odds ratio (WOR), multi-class odds ratio (MOR), and class discriminating measure (CDM) are variants that enable multi-class feature selections in case of $\gamma = \{c_1, c_2, \ldots, c_J\}$ classes:

$$EOR(\mathbf{X}_k) = \sum_{j=1}^{J} \log \frac{\Pr(\mathbf{X}_k|c_j)\big(1 - \Pr(\mathbf{X}_k|\bar{c}_j)\big)}{\Pr(\mathbf{X}_k|\bar{c}_j)\big(1 - \Pr(\mathbf{X}_k|c_j)\big)}$$

$$WOR(\mathbf{X}_k) = \sum_{j=1}^{J} \Pr(c_j) \times \log \frac{\Pr(\mathbf{X}_k|c_j)\big(1 - \Pr(\mathbf{X}_k|\bar{c}_j)\big)}{\Pr(\mathbf{X}_k|\bar{c}_j)\big(1 - \Pr(\mathbf{X}_k|c_j)\big)}$$

$$MOR(\mathbf{X}_k) = \sum_{j=1}^{J} \left| \log \frac{\Pr(\mathbf{X}_k|c_j)\big(1 - \Pr(\mathbf{X}_k|\bar{c}_j)\big)}{\Pr(\mathbf{X}_k|\bar{c}_j)\big(1 - \Pr(\mathbf{X}_k|c_j)\big)} \right|$$

$$CDM(\mathbf{X}_k) = \sum_{j=1}^{J} \left| \log \frac{\Pr(\mathbf{X}_k|c_j)}{\Pr(\mathbf{X}_k|\bar{c}_j)} \right|, \tag{7}$$

where $\Pr(\mathbf{X}_k|c_j)$ is the conditional probability of $\mathbf{X}_k$ given the class c_j and $\Pr(c_j)$ is the probability of occurrence of the class j. The OR algorithm is extended by calculating $\Pr(\mathbf{X}_k|c_j)$ for continuous features. If the sample points are independent and identically distributed, (6) is written as:

$$OR(\mathbf{X}_k) = \sum_{i=1}^{|\mathbf{X}_k|} \log \frac{\Pr(X_{ik} = x_{ik}|c)\big(1 - \Pr(X_{ik} = x_{ik}|\bar{c})\big)}{\Pr(X_{ik} = x_{ik}|\bar{c})\big(1 - \Pr(X_{ik} = x_{ik}|c)\big)}, \tag{8}$$

where $|\mathbf{X}_k|$ denote the size of the kth feature vector, X_{ik} is the ith element of the kth feature vector, and x_{ik} is realization of the random variable X_{ik}. Other variants of the OR feature selection algorithm are extended to continuous cases in a similar manner. The top ten selected features used for two-way and four-way classifications are shown in Tables 13 and 14, respectively.

5.4 Decision Tree Algorithm

The decision tree approach is commonly used in data mining to predict the class label based on several input variables. A classification tree is a directed tree where the root is the source sample set and each internal (non-leaf) node is labeled with an input feature. The tree branches are prediction outcomes that are labeled with possible feature values while each leaf node is labeled with a class or a class probability distribution [50]. A top-down approach is commonly used for

Table 13 The top ten features selected using the OR feature selection algorithms and Dataset 2 (two-way classification)

Odds Ratio variants							
OR		WOR		MOR		CDM	
Feature	Score $\times 10^4$	Feature	Score $\times 10^4$	Feature	Score $\times 10^5$	Feature	Score $\times 10^5$
13	−2.7046	12	3.9676	12	1.0789	12	1.0713
7	−2.8051	1	3.4121	34	0.9214	34	0.9199
5	−2.8064	34	3.4095	1	0.9213	1	0.9198
29	−2.8774	3	3.3482	3	0.8908	3	0.8885
15	−2.8777	4	3.3468	4	0.8775	4	0.8702
28	−2.9136	23	2.9348	9	0.7406	9	0.7224
14	−2.9137	24	2.7628	36	0.7264	36	0.7201
6	−2.9190	22	2.7051	37	0.7229	37	0.7192
11	−2.9248	21	2.6662	23	0.7208	2	0.7145
30	−2.9288	20	2.5821	2	0.6782	8	0.6624

Table 14 The top ten features selected using the OR feature selection algorithms and Dataset 7 (four-way classification)

Odds Ratio variants							
EOR		WOR		MOR		CDM	
Feature	Score $\times 10^5$	Feature	Score $\times 10^4$	Feature	Score $\times 10^5$	Feature	Score $\times 10^5$
3	−1.5496	12	1.7791	12	3.0894	12	3.0700
13	−1.5681	1	1.3293	34	2.5964	34	2.5924
9	−1.6063	34	1.3273	1	2.5723	1	2.5688
11	−1.6184	4	1.1140	4	2.5252	4	2.5190
6	−1.6184	36	1.0763	36	2.4617	36	2.4422
37	−1.6191	2	1.0140	2	2.3024	2	2.2300
5	−1.6499	23	0.8669	23	2.2832	8	2.2068
7	−1.6522	24	0.8529	24	2.2733	9	2.1357
29	−1.6783	21	0.8508	21	2.2696	10	2.1168
15	−1.6784	20	0.8504	22	2.2696	3	2.0848

constructing decision trees. At each step, an appropriate variable is chosen to best split the set of items. A quality measure is the homogeneity of the target variable within subsets and it is applied to each candidate subset. The combined results measure the split quality [19, 46].

The C5 [2] software tool is used to generate decision tree for both feature selections and anomaly classifications. The C5 decision tree algorithm relies on the information gain measure. The continuous attribute values are discretized and the most important features are iteratively used to split the sample space until a certain portion of samples associated with the leaf node has the same value as the target attribute. For each training dataset, a set of rules used for classification is extracted from the constructed decision tree.

Table 15 Selected features using the decision tree algorithm

Training dataset	Selected features
Dataset 1	1–21, 23–29, 34–37
Dataset 2	1–22, 24–29, 34–37
Dataset 3	1–29, 34–37

We apply the decision tree algorithm for feature selection to form the training datasets shown in Table 4. These datasets are also used in the classification stage. The selected features are shown in Table 15. Based on the outcome of the decision tree algorithm, some features are removed in the constructed trees. Fewer features are selected either based on the number of leaf nodes with the largest correct classified samples or based on the number of rules with maximum sample coverage. The features that appear in the selected rules are considered to be important and, therefore, are preserved.

6 Conclusion

Detecting network anomalies and intrusions are crucial in fighting cyber attacks and insuring cyber security to service providers and network customers. Machine learning techniques are one of the most promising approaches for detecting network anomalies and have been employed in analyzing BGP behavior. In this chapter, we introduce BGP datasets, investigate BGP anomalies, and describe various feature selection techniques. Datasets used in these experiments are examples of known anomalies that proved useful for developing anomaly detection models. We have processed and extracted features from known BGP anomalies such as Slammer, Nimda, and Code Red I worms as well as the Moscow power blackout, AS 9121 routing table leak, Panix hijack, and AS-path error datasets. Various feature selection and attribute reduction algorithms are used to select a subset of features important for classification. After the feature selection process, extracted features are used as input to machine learning classification algorithms described in the follow-up Chapter.

Acknowledgements We thank Yan Li, Hong-Jie Xing, Qiang Hua, and Xi-Zhao Wang from Hebei University, Marijana Ćosović from University of East Sarajevo, and Prerna Batta from Simon Fraser University for their helpful contributions in earlier publications related to this project.

References

1. (Mar. 2018) BCNET. [Online]. Available: http://www.bc.net.
2. (Mar. 2018) Data Mining Tools See5 and C5.0. [Online]. Available: http://www.rulequest. com/see5-info.html.

3. (Mar. 2018) Sans Institute. The mechanisms and effects of the Code Red worm. [Online]. Available: https://www.sans.org/reading-room/whitepapers/dlp/mechanisms-effects-code-red-worm-87.

4. (Mar. 2018) The Internet Engineering Task Force (IETF) [Online]. Available: https://www.ietf.org/.

5. (Mar. 2018) bgpdump [Online]. Available: https://bitbucket.org/ripencc/bgpdump/wiki/Home.

6. (Mar. 2018) mRMR feature selection (using mutual information computation). [Online]. Available: https://www.mathworks.com/matlabcentral/fileexchange/14608-mrmr-feature-selection--using-mutual-information-computation-.

7. (Mar. 2018) MRT rooting information export format. [Online]. Available: http://tools.ietf.org/html/draft-ietf-grow-mrt-13.

8. (Mar. 2018) Sans Institute. Nimda worm—why is it different? [Online]. Available: http://www.sans.org/reading-room/whitepapers/malicious/nimda-worm-different-98.

9. (Mar. 2018) RIPE NCC: RIPE Network Coordination Center. [Online]. Available: http://www.ripe.net/data-tools/stats/ris/ris-raw-data.

10. (Mar. 2018) YouTube Hijacking: A RIPE NCC RIS case study [Online]. Available: http://www.ripe.net/internet-coordination/news/industry-developments/youtube-hijacking-a-ripe-ncc-ris-case-study.

11. (Mar. 2018) University of Oregon Route Views project [Online]. Available: http://www.routeviews.org/.

12. (Mar. 2018) Center for Applied Internet Data Analysis. The Spread of the Sapphire/Slammer Worm [Online]. Available: http://www.caida.org/publications/papers/2003/sapphire/.

13. (Mar. 2018) Sans Institute. Malware FAQ: MS-SQL Slammer. [Online]. Available: https://www.sans.org/security-resources/malwarefaq/ms-sql-exploit.

14. T. Ahmed, B. Oreshkin, and M. Coates, "Machine learning approaches to network anomaly detection," in *Proc. USENIX Workshop on Tackling Computer Systems Problems with Machine Learning Techniques*, Cambridge, MA, Apr. 2007, pp. 1–6.

15. N. Al-Rousan and Lj. Trajković, "Machine learning models for classification of BGP anomalies," in *Proc. IEEE Conf. on High Performance Switching and Routing (HPSR)*, Belgrade, Serbia, June 2012, pp. 103–108.

16. N. Al-Rousan, S. Haeri, and Lj. Trajković, "Feature selection for classification of BGP anomalies using Bayesian models," in *Proc. Int. Conf. Mach. Learn. Cybern. (ICMLC)*, Xi'an, China, July 2012, pp. 140–147.

17. K. El-Arini and K. Killourhy, "Bayesian detection of router configuration anomalies," in *Proc. Workshop Mining Network Data*, Philadelphia, PA, USA, Aug. 2005, pp. 221–222.

18. M. Bhuyan, D. Bhattacharyya, and J. Kalita, "Network anomaly detection: methods, systems and tools," *IEEE Commun. Surveys Tut.*, vol. 16, no. 1, pp. 303–336, Mar. 2014.

19. L. Breiman, "Bagging predictors," *Machine Learning*, vol. 24, no. 2, pp. 123–140, Aug. 1996.

20. Y.-W. Chen and C.-J. Lin, "Combining SVMs with various feature selection strategies," *Strategies*, vol. 324, no. 1, pp. 1–10, Nov. 2006.

21. J. Chen, H. Huang, S. Tian, and Y. Qu, "Feature selection for text classification with naive Bayes," *Expert Systems with Applications*, vol. 36, no. 3, pp. 5432–5435, Apr. 2009.

22. M. Ćosović, S. Obradović, and Lj. Trajković, "Classifying anomalous events in BGP datasets," in *Proc. The 29th Annu. IEEE Can. Conf. on Elect. and Comput. Eng. (CCECE)*, Vancouver, Canada, May 2016, pp. 697–700.

23. S. Deshpande, M. Thottan, T. K. Ho, and B. Sikdar, "An online mechanism for BGP instability detection and analysis," *IEEE Trans. Comput.*, vol. 58, no. 11, pp. 1470–1484, Nov. 2009.

24. Q. Ding, Z. Li, P. Batta, and Lj. Trajković, "Detecting BGP anomalies using machine learning techniques," in *Proc. IEEE Int. Conf. Syst., Man, and Cybern.*, Budapest, Hungary, Oct. 2016, pp. 3352–3355.

25. T. Farah, S. Lally, R. Gill, N. Al-Rousan, R. Paul, D. Xu, and Lj. Trajković, "Collection of BCNET BGP traffic," in *Proc. 23rd ITC*, San Francisco, CA, USA, Sept. 2011, pp. 322–323.

26. Q. Gu, Z. Li, and J. Han, "Generalized Fisher score for feature selection," in *Proc. Conf. Uncertainty in Artificial Intelligence*, Barcelona, Spain, July 2011, pp. 266–273.
27. H. Hajji, "Statistical analysis of network traffic for adaptive faults detection," *IEEE Trans. Neural Netw.*, vol. 16, no. 5, pp. 1053–1063, Sept. 2005.
28. G. H. John, R. Kohavi, and K. Pfleger, "Irrelevant features and the subset selection problem," in *Proc. Int. Conf. Machine Learning*, New Brunswick, NJ, USA, July 1994, pp. 121–129.
29. M. N. A. Kumar and H. S. Sheshadri, "On the classification of imbalanced datasets," *Int. J. Comput. Appl.*, vol. 44, no. 8, pp. 1–7, Apr. 2012.
30. J. Kurose and K. W. Ross, *"Computer Networking: A Top-Down Approach (6th edition)."* Addison-Wesley, 2012, pp. 305–431.
31. S. Lally, T. Farah, R. Gill, R. Paul, N. Al-Rousan, and Lj. Trajković, "Collection and characterization of BCNET BGP traffic," in *Proc. 2011 IEEE Pacific Rim Conf. Commun., Comput. and Signal Process.*, Victoria, BC, Canada, Aug. 2011, pp. 830–835.
32. F. Lau, S. H. Rubin, M. H. Smith, and Lj. Trajković, "Distributed denial of service attacks," in *Proc. IEEE Int. Conf. Syst., Man, and Cybern., SMC 2000*, Nashville, TN, USA, Oct. 2000, pp. 2275–2280.
33. J. Li, D. Dou, Z. Wu, S. Kim, and V. Agarwal, "An Internet routing forensics framework for discovering rules of abnormal BGP events," *SIGCOMM Comput. Commun. Rev.*, vol. 35, no. 5, pp. 55–66, Oct. 2005.
34. Y. Li, H. J. Xing, Q. Hua, X.-Z. Wang, P. Batta, S. Haeri, and Lj. Trajković, "Classification of BGP anomalies using decision trees and fuzzy rough sets," in *Proc. IEEE Trans. Syst., Man, Cybern.*, San Diego, CA, USA, Oct. 2014, pp. 1331–1336.
35. R. O. Duda, P. E. Hart, and D. G. Stork, *Pattern Classification*. Hoboken, NJ, USA: Wiley-Interscience Publication, 2001.
36. H. Liu, H. Motoda, Eds., *Computational Methods of Feature Selection*. Boca Raton, FL, USA: Chapman and Hall/CRC Press, 2007.
37. (Mar. 2018) D. Meyer, "BGP communities for data collection," RFC 4384, *IETF*, Feb. 2006. [Online]. Available: http://www.ietf.org/rfc/rfc4384.txt.
38. Z. Pawlak, "Rough sets," *Int. J. Inform. and Comput. Sci.*, vol. 11, no. 5, pp. 341–356, Oct. 1982.
39. C. Patrikakis, M. Masikos, and O. Zouraraki, "Distributed denial of service attacks," *The Internet Protocol*, vol. 7, no. 4, pp. 13–31, Dec. 2004.
40. H. Peng, F. Long, and C. Ding, "Feature selection based on mutual information criteria of max-dependency, max-relevance, and min-redundancy," *IEEE Trans. Pattern Anal. Mach. Intell.*, vol. 27, no. 8, pp. 1226–1238, Aug. 2005.
41. (Mar. 2018) A. C. Popescu, B. J. Premore, and T. Underwood, The anatomy of a leak: AS9121. Renesys Corporation, Manchester, NH, USA. May 2005. [Online]. Available: http://50.31.151.73/meetings/nanog34/presentations/underwood.pdf.
42. J. R. Quinlan, "Induction of decision trees," *Mach. Learn.*, vol. 1, no. 1, pp. 81–106, Mar. 1986.
43. A. M. Radzikowska and E. E. Kerre, "A comparative study of fuzzy rough sets," *Fuzzy Sets and Syst.*, vol. 126, no. 2, pp. 137–155, Mar. 2002.
44. (Mar. 2018) Y. Rekhter and T. Li, "A Border Gateway Protocol 4 (BGP-4)," RFC 1771, *IETF*, Mar. 1995. [Online]. Available: http://tools.ietf.org/rfc/rfc1771.txt.
45. (Mar. 2018) Y. Rekhter, T. Li, and S. Hares, "A Border Gateway Protocol 4 (BGP-4)," RFC 4271, *IETF*, Jan. 2016. [Online]. Available: http://tools.ietf.org/rfc/rfc4271.txt.
46. L. Rokach and O. Maimon, "Top-down induction of decision trees classifiers—a survey," *IEEE Trans. Syst., Man, Cybern., Appl. and Rev.*, vol. 35, no. 4, pp. 476–487, Nov. 2005.
47. M. Thottan and C. Ji, "Anomaly detection in IP networks," *IEEE Trans. Signal Process.*, vol. 51, no. 8, pp. 2191–2204, Aug. 2003.
48. L. Wang, X. Zhao, D. Pei, R. Bush, D. Massey, A. Mankin, S. F. Wu, and L. Zhang, "Observation and analysis of BGP behavior under stress," in *Proc. 2nd ACM SIGCOMM Workshop on Internet Meas.*, New York, NY, USA, 2002, pp. 183–195.

49. J. Wang, X. Chen, and W. Gao, "Online selecting discriminative tracking features using particle filter," in *Proc. Comput. Vision and Pattern Recognition*, San Diego, CA, USA, June 2005, vol. 2, pp. 1037–1042.

50. X.-Z. Wang, L. C. Dong, and J. H. Yan, "Maximum ambiguity based sample selection in fuzzy decision tree induction," *IEEE Trans. Knowl. Data Eng.*, vol. 24, no. 8, pp. 1491–1505, Aug. 2012.

51. D. P. Watson and D. H. Scheidt, "Autonomous systems," *Johns Hopkins APL Technical Digest*, vol. 26, no. 4, pp. 368–376, Oct.–Dec. 2005.

52. D. S. Yeung, D. G. Chen, E. C. C. Tsang, J. W. T. Lee, and X.-Z. Wang, "On the generalization of fuzzy rough sets," *IEEE Trans. Fuzz. Syst.*, vol. 13, no. 3, pp. 343–361, June 2005.

53. J. Zhang, J. Rexford, and J. Feigenbaum, "Learning-based anomaly detection in BGP updates," in *Proc. Workshop Mining Netw. Data*, Philadelphia, PA, USA, Aug. 2005, pp. 219–220.

54. Y. Zhang, Z. M. Mao, and J. Wang, "A firewall for routers: protecting against routing misbehavior," in *Proc. 37th Annu. IEEE/IFIP Int. Conf. on Dependable Syst. and Netw.*, Edinburgh, UK, June 2007, pp. 20–29.

Application of Machine Learning Techniques to Detecting Anomalies in Communication Networks: Classification Algorithms

Zhida Li, Qingye Ding, Soroush Haeri, and Ljiljana Trajković

Abstract In this chapter, we apply various machine learning techniques for classification of known network anomalies. The models are trained and tested on various collected datasets. With the advent of fast computing platforms, many neural network-based algorithms have proved useful in detecting BGP anomalies. Performance of classification algorithms depends on the selected features and their combinations. Various classification techniques and approaches are compared based on accuracy and F-Score.

Keywords Routing anomalies · Border Gateway Protocol · Classification algorithms · Machine learning techniques

1 Introduction

In Chapter "Application of Machine Learning Techniques to Detecting Anomalies in Communication Networks: Datasets and Feature Selection Algorithms", we have introduced Border Gateway Protocol (BGP) datasets used to detect anomalies, feature extractions, and various feature selection algorithms. We describe here machine learning classification techniques used to detect BGP anomalies. We examine the effect of feature selection on performance of BGP anomaly classifiers by evaluating performance of feature selection algorithms introduced in Chapter "Application of Machine Learning Techniques to Detecting Anomalies in Communication Networks: Datasets and Feature Selection Algorithms" in terms of classification accuracy and F-Score.

The readers are advised to first read "Chapter 3: Application of Machine Learning Techniques to Detecting Anomalies in Communication Networks: Datasets and Feature Selection Algorithms."

Z. Li · Q. Ding · S. Haeri · L. Trajković (✉)
Simon Fraser University, Vancouver, BC, Canada
e-mail: zhidal@sfu.ca; qingyed@sfu.ca; shaeri@sfu.ca; ljilja@cs.sfu.ca

© Springer International Publishing AG, part of Springer Nature 2018
A. Dehghantanha et al. (eds.), *Cyber Threat Intelligence*, Advances in Information Security 70, https://doi.org/10.1007/978-3-319-73951-9_4

We apply machine learning techniques to develop classification models for detecting BGP anomalies [6–10]. These models are trained and tested using various datasets that consist features extracted and selected in Chapter "Application of Machine Learning Techniques to Detecting Anomalies in Communication Networks: Datasets and Feature Selection Algorithms". They are used to evaluate the effectiveness of the extracted features. We report on improved classification results emanating from our previous studies (Support Vector Machine (SVM) two-way classification, Naive Bayes (NB) two-way and four-way classifications) and also implement the Long Short-Term Memory (LSTM) machine learning technique.

A survey of various methods, systems, and tools used for detecting network anomalies reviews a variety of existing approaches [12]. The authors have examined recent techniques to detect network anomalies and discussed detection strategy and employed datasets, including performance metrics for evaluating detection method and description of various datasets and their taxonomy. They also identified issues and challenges in developing new anomaly detection methods and systems.

Various machine learning techniques to detect cyber threats have been reported in the literature. One-class SVM classifier with a modified kernel function was employed [36] to detect anomalies in IP records. However, unlike the approach in our studies, the classifier is unable to indicate the specific type of anomalies. Stacked LSTM networks with several fully connected LSTM layers have been used for anomaly detection in time series [27]. The method was applied to medical electrocardiograms, a space shuttle, power demand, and multi-sensor engine data. The analyzed data contain both long-term and short-term temporal dependencies. Another example is the multi-scale LSTM that was used to detect BGP anomalies [14] using accuracy as a performance measure. In the preprocessing phase, data were compressed using various time scales. An optimal size of the sliding window was then used to determine time scale to achieve the best performance of the classifier. Multiple HMM classifiers were employed to detect Hypertext Transfer Protocol (HTTP) payload-based anomalies for various Web applications [8]. Authors first treated payload as a sequence of bytes and then extracted features using a sliding window to reduce the computational complexity. HMM classifiers were then combined to classify network intrusions. It was shown [29] that the naive Bayes classifier performs well for categorizing the Internet traffic emanating from various applications. Weighted ELM [39] deals with unbalanced data by assigning relatively larger weights to the input data arising from a minority class. Signature-based and statistics-based detection methods have been also proposed in [40].

This Chapter is organized as follows. We first introduce machine learning techniques and performance metrics in Sect. 2. Experimental procedures using various classification algorithms are described in Sects. 3–8. The advantages and shortcomings of various classification algorithms are offered in Sect. 9. We conclude with Sect. 10. The list of relevant references is provided at the end of the Chapter.

1.1 Machine Learning Techniques

Machine learning techniques have been employed to develop models for detecting and designing BGP anomaly detection systems. They are the most common approaches for classifying BGP anomalies.

Unsupervised machine learning models have been used to detect anomalies in networks with non-stationary traffic [16]. The one-class neighbor machines [31] and recursive kernel-based online anomaly detection [7] algorithms are effective methods for detecting anomalous network traffic [6].

While unsupervised learning techniques are often used for clustering, supervised learning is employed for anomaly classification when the input data are labeled based on various categories. Well-known supervised learning algorithms include Support Vector Machine (SVM) [11, 38], Long Short-Term Memory (LSTM) [20, 22], Hidden Markov Model (HMM) [11], naive Bayes [28], Decision Tree [33], and Extreme Learning Machine (ELM) [23, 24].

The SVM algorithms often achieve better performance compared to other machine learning algorithms albeit with high computational complexity. LSTM is trained using gradient-based learning algorithms implemented as a recurrent neural network. It outperforms other sequence learning algorithms because of its ability to learn from past experiences long-term dependencies.

No single learning algorithm performs the best for all given classification tasks [37]. Hence, an appropriate algorithm should be selected by evaluating its performance based on various parameters. Statistical methods, data mining, and machine learning have been employed to evaluate and compare various algorithms [17, 19].

2 Classification Algorithms

Classification aims to identify various classes in a dataset. Each element in the classification domain is called a class. A classifier labels the data points as either an anomaly or a regular event. We consider datasets of known network anomalies and test the classifiers' ability to reliably identify anomaly class, which usually contains fewer samples than the regular class in training and test datasets. Classifier models are usually trained using datasets containing limited number of anomalies and are then applied on a test dataset. Performance of a classification model depends on a model's ability to correctly predict classes. Classifiers are evaluated based on various metrics such as accuracy, F-Score, precision, and sensitivity.

Most classification algorithms minimize the number of incorrectly predicted class labels while ignoring the difference between types of misclassified labels by assuming that all misclassifications have equal costs. The assumption that all misclassification types are equally costly is inaccurate in many application domains. In the case of BGP anomaly detection, incorrectly classifying an anomalous sample may be more costly than incorrect classification of a regular sample. As a result, a classifier that is trained using an unbalanced dataset may successfully classify the majority class with a good accuracy while it may be unable to accurately classify the minority class. A dataset is unbalanced when at least one class is represented by a smaller number of training samples compared to other classes. The Slammer and Code Red I anomaly datasets that have been used in this study are unbalanced. In our studies, out of 7,200 samples, Slammer and Code Red I contain 869 and 600 anomalous events, respectively. The Nimda dataset is more balanced containing 3,521 anomalous events. Hence, the majority of samples are regular data.

Various approaches have been proposed to achieve accurate classification results when dealing with unbalanced datasets. Examples include assigning a weight to each class or learning from one class (recognition-based) rather than two classes (discrimination-based) [13]. The weighted SVMs [38] assign distinct weights to data samples so that the training algorithm learns the decision surface according to the relative importance of data points in the training dataset. The fuzzy SVM [26], a version of weighted SVM, applies a fuzzy membership to each input sample and reformulates the SVM so that input points contribute differently to the learning decision surface. In this study, we create the balanced datasets by randomly reducing a portion of regular data points. Each balanced dataset contains the same number of regular and anomalous data samples.

2.1 Performance Metrics

The confusion matrix shown in Table 1 is used to evaluate performance of classification algorithms. True positive (TP) and False negative (FN) are the number of anomalous training data points that are classified as anomaly and regular, respectively. False positive (FP) and True negative (TN) are the number of regular data points that are classified as anomaly and regular, respectively.

Variety of performance measures are calculated to evaluate classification algorithms, such as accuracy and F-Score:

$$\text{accuracy} = \frac{TP + TN}{TP + TN + FP + FN} \tag{1}$$

$$\text{F-Score} = 2 \times \frac{\text{precision} \times \text{sensitivity}}{\text{precision} + \text{sensitivity}}, \tag{2}$$

Table 1 Confusion matrix

	Predicted class	
	Anomaly	Regular
Actual class	(positive)	(negative)
Anomaly (positive)	TP	FN
Regular (negative)	FP	TN

where

$$\text{precision} = \frac{TP}{TP + FP} \tag{3}$$

$$\text{sensitivity(recall)} = \frac{TP}{TP + FN}. \tag{4}$$

As a performance measure, accuracy reflects the true prediction over the entire dataset. It is commonly used in evaluating the classification performance. Accuracy assumes equal cost for misclassification and relatively uniform distributions of classes. It treats the regular data points to be as important as the anomalous points. Hence, it may be an inadequate measure when comparing performance of classifiers [32] and misleading in the case of unbalanced datasets. The F-Score, which considers the false predictions, is important for anomaly detection because it is a harmonic mean of the precision and sensitivity, which measure the discriminating ability of the classifier to identify classified and misclassified anomalies. Precision identifies true anomalies among all data points that are correctly classified as anomalies. Sensitivity measures the ability of the model to identify correctly predicted anomalies.

As an example, consider a dataset that contains 900 regular and 100 anomalous data points. If a classifier identifies these 1,000 data points as regular, its accuracy is 90%, which seems high at the first glance. However, no anomalous data point is correctly classified and, hence, the F-Score is zero. Therefore, the F-Score is often used to compare performance of classification models. It reflects the success of detecting anomalies rather than detecting either anomalies or regular data points. In this study, we use F-Score to compare various classification algorithms.

3 Support Vector Machine (SVM)

Support Vector Machine is a supervised learning algorithm used for classification and regression tasks. Given a set of labeled training samples, the SVM algorithm learns a classification hyperplane (decision boundary) by maximizing the minimum distance between data points belonging to various classes. There are two types of SVM models: hard-margin and soft-margin [15]. The hard-margin SVMs require that each data point is correctly classified while the soft-margin SVMs allow some data points to be misclassified. The hyperplane is acquired by minimizing the loss function [11]:

$$C \sum_{n=1}^{N} \zeta_n + \frac{1}{2} ||w||^2, \tag{5}$$

with constraints: $t_n y(x_n) \geqslant 1 - \zeta_n$, $n = 1, \ldots, N$,

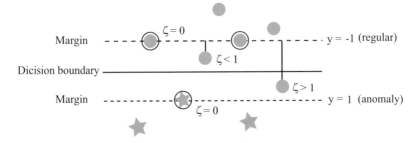

Fig. 1 Illustration of the soft margin SVM [11]. Shown are correctly and incorrectly classified data points. Regular and anomalous data points are denoted by circles and stars, respectively. The circled points are support vectors

where the regularization parameter C controls the trade-off between the slack variable ζ_n, N is the number of data points, and $\frac{1}{2}||w||^2$ is the margin. The regularization parameter $C > 0$ is used to avoid over-fitting problem. The target value is denoted by t_n while $y(x_n)$ and x_n are the training model and data points, respectively. The SVM solves a loss function as an optimization problem (5).

An illustration of the soft margin is shown in Fig. 1 [11]. The solid line indicates the decision boundary while dashed lines indicate the margins. Encircled data points are support vectors. The maximum margin is the perpendicular distance between the decision boundary and the closest support vectors. Data points for which $\zeta = 0$ are correctly classified and are either on the margin or on the correct side of the margin. Data points for which $0 \leq \zeta < 1$ are also correctly classified because they lie inside the margin and on the correct side of the decision boundary. Data points for which $\zeta > 1$ lie on the wrong side of the decision boundary and are misclassified. The outputs 1 and -1 correspond to anomaly and regular data points, respectively. The SVM solution maximizes the margin between the data points and the decision boundary. Data points that have the minimum distance to the decision boundary are called support vectors.

The SVM employs a kernel function to compute a nonlinear separable function to map the feature space into a linear space. The Radial Basis Function (RBF) was chosen because it creates a large function space and outperforms other types of SVM kernels [11]. The RBF kernel k is used to avoid the high dimension of the feature matrix:

$$k(\mathbf{x}, \mathbf{x}') = exp(-||\mathbf{x} - \mathbf{x}'||^2/2\sigma^2). \tag{6}$$

It depends on the Euclidean distance between $\mathbf{x}$ and $\mathbf{x}'$ feature vectors. The datasets are trained using tenfold cross validation to select parameters $(C, 1/2\sigma^2)$ that give the best accuracy.

The SVM algorithm is applied to datasets listed in Table 2. We experiment with the MATLAB SVM functions and the SVM^{light} [4] library modules to train and

Table 2 Training and test datasets

Training dataset	Anomalies	Test dataset
1	Slammer and Nimda	Code Red I
2	Slammer and Code Red I	Nimda
3	Nimda and Code Red I	Slammer
4	Slammer	Nimda and Code Red I
5	Nimda	Slammer and Code Red I
6	Code Red I	Slammer and Nimda
7	Slammer, Nimda, and Code Red I	RIPE or BCNET

test the SVM classifiers. The SVM^{light} library, developed in C language, is an effective tool for classification, regression, and ranking when dealing with large training samples. We adjust the value of parameter C (5), which controls the trade-off between the training error and the margin as well as the cost factor [30].

Feature selection algorithms were implemented in MATLAB and were used to minimize the dimension of the dataset matrix by selecting the ten most relevant features. We used: Fisher, minimum redundancy maximum relevance (mRMR) (mutual information difference (MID), mutual information quotient (MIQ), and mutual information base (MIBASE)), odds ratio (OR), extended/weighted/multi-class odds ratio (EOR/WOR/MOR), and class discriminating measure (CDM). Hence, the dimension of feature matrices that correspond to a 5-day period of collected data is $7,200 \times 10$. Each matrix row corresponds to the top ten selected features within the 1-min interval. In two-way classifications, we target two classes: anomaly (positive) and regular (negative) for each training dataset. While the two-way classification only identifies whether or not a data point is anomaly, the four-way classification detects the specific type of BGP anomaly: Slammer, Nimda, Code Red I, or regular (RIPE and BCNET). SVM classifies each data point x_n, where $n = 1, \ldots, 7,200$, with a training target class t_n either as anomaly $y = 1$ or regular $y = -1$.

In a two-way classification, all anomalies are treated as one class. Validity of the proposed models is tested by applying two-way SVM classification on BGP traffic traces collected from RIPE and BCNET on December 20, 2011. All data points in the regular RIPE and BCNET datasets contain no anomalies and are, hence, labeled as regular traffic, as shown in Table 3. The results are generated using the MATLAB *fitcsvm* support vector classifier. The index of models reflects the dataset used for training and testing. These datasets contain no anomalies (both TP and FN values are zero) and, hence, precision is equal to zero while sensitivity is not defined. Consequently, the F-Score is also not defined and the accuracy reduces to:

$$\text{accuracy} = \frac{TN}{TN + FP}. \tag{7}$$

Table 3 Performance of the two-way SVM classification using unbalanced datasets

| | | Accuracy (%) | | | F-Score (%) |
| | | | Regular | | |
SVM	Feature	Test dataset	RIPE	BCNET	Test dataset
SVM$_1$	37 features	78.65	69.17	57.22	39.51
SVM$_1$	Fisher	81.93	85.67	80.49	41.16
SVM$_1$	MID	85.38	92.63	83.68	45.18
SVM$_1$	MIQ	80.86	86.89	83.75	39.56
SVM$_1$	MIBASE	80.86	87.10	88.47	39.51
SVM$_1$	OR	78.57	70.15	66.74	38.01
SVM$_1$	WOR	**88.03**	89.88	70.90	**47.18**
SVM$_1$	MOR	83.88	83.40	83.75	44.53
SVM$_1$	CDM	84.40	81.36	90.56	44.05
SVM$_2$	37 features	**55.50**	89.89	82.08	**24.29**
SVM$_2$	Fisher	54.22	96.28	**98.33**	16.43
SVM$_2$	MID	53.89	95.88	95.76	11.89
SVM$_2$	MIQ	55.10	96.10	97.57	20.74
SVM$_2$	MIBASE	55.11	92.78	95.83	19.32
SVM$_2$	OR	54.93	93.90	97.64	15.87
SVM$_2$	WOR	54.53	**97.39**	93.26	14.56
SVM$_2$	MOR	55.36	96.74	97.85	20.21
SVM$_2$	CDM	54.67	96.60	97.64	16.65
SVM$_3$	37 features	93.04	73.92	59.24	75.93
SVM$_3$	Fisher	93.31	80.63	57.71	76.51
SVM$_3$	MID	93.35	75.33	59.65	76.30
SVM$_3$	MIQ	93.28	78.99	57.50	76.27
SVM$_3$	MIBASE	**93.40**	79.14	57.85	**76.52**
SVM$_3$	OR	90.44	80.53	79.03	70.32
SVM$_3$	WOR	93.08	77.51	58.19	75.61
SVM$_3$	MOR	92.92	76.79	68.68	75.48
SVM$_3$	CDM	92.93	76.97	68.13	75.54

The best accuracy (93.40%) for two-way classification is achieved by using SVM$_3$ for the Slammer test dataset. The Nimda test data points that are correctly classified as anomalies (true positive) in the two-way classification are shown in Fig. 2 (top) while incorrectly classified anomaly and regular data points are shown in Fig. 2 (bottom).

The SVM models are used to compare results for unbalanced and balanced training datasets. Examples using SVM_3 models are shown in Table 4. For unbalanced training datasets, the features selected by the MIBASE algorithm generate the best F-Score (76.52%). The best F-Scores is achieved by SVM$_b$3 (66.59%) that is trained using balanced datasets and the MID algorithm. Incorrectly classified anomalies (false positive) and regular points (false negative) are shown in Fig. 3.

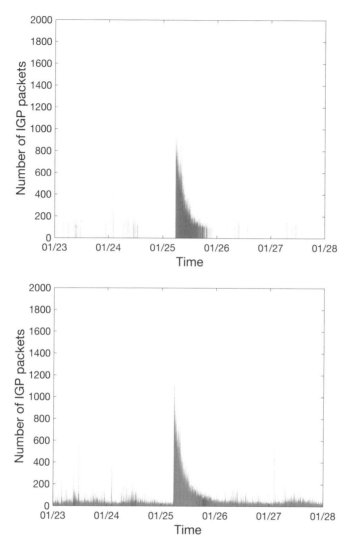

Fig. 2 SVM classifier applied to Slammer traffic collected from January 23 to 27, 2003: Shown in purple are correctly classified anomalies (true positive) while shown in green are incorrectly classified anomalies (false positive) (top). Shown in red are incorrectly classified anomalies (false positive) and regular (false negative) data points while shown in blue are correctly classified anomaly (true positive) and regular (true negative) data points (bottom)

The SVM classifier may be also used to identify multiple classes [21]. For four-way classification, we use four training datasets (Slammer, Nimda, Code Red I, and RIPE) to identify the specific type of BGP data point: Slammer, Nimda, Code Red I, or regular (RIPE or BCNET). Classification of RIPE dataset achieves 91.85% accuracy, as shown in Table 5. The results are generated using the MATLAB *fitcecoc* support vector classifier.

Table 4 Accuracy and F-Score using the SVM$_b$3 models using balanced datasets

Balanced datasets					
Accuracy (%)					F-Score (%)
Model		Test dataset	RIPE	BCNET	Test dataset
SVM$_b$3	37 Features	87.19	63.31	51.11	64.76
SVM$_b$3	Fisher	84.74	62.58	52.01	60.54
SVM$_b$3	MID	**88.33**	66.10	**60.28**	**66.59**
SVM$_b$3	MIQ	87.56	66.69	59.93	65.43
SVM$_b$3	MIBASE	87.40	**66.76**	60.14	65.18
SVM$_b$3	OR	71.94	52.92	52.78	46.16
SVM$_b$3	WOR	87.68	65.61	56.60	65.45
SVM$_b$3	MOR	86.44	64.69	57.43	63.69
SVM$_b$3	CDM	86.67	64.81	57.85	63.99

4 Long Short-Term Memory (LSTM) Neural Network

The LSTM approach employs a special form of the recurrent neural networks (RNNs). Traditional RNNs are designed to store inputs in order to predict the outputs [30]. However, they perform poorly when they need to bridge segments of information with long-time gaps. Unlike the traditional RNNs, LSTM networks are capable of connecting time intervals to form a continuous memory [22]. They were introduced to overcome long-term dependency and vanishing gradient problems [35].

The LSTM module consists of an input layer, a single hidden LSTM layer, and an output layer. The input layer consists of 37 nodes (each node corresponds to one feature) that serve as inputs to the LSTM layer, which consists of LSTM cells called the "memory blocks" [34]. An LSTM cell is composed of: (a) forget gate f_n, (b) input gate i_n, and (c) output gate o_n. The forget gate discards the irrelevant memories according to the cell state, the input gate controls the information that will be updated in the LSTM cell, and the output gate works as a filter to control the output. The logistic sigmoid and network output functions are denoted by σ and tanh, respectively. The output layer has one node that is connected to the output of the LSTM layer. The output is labeled by 1 (anomaly) or -1 (regular). An LSTM module is shown in Fig. 4 [3].

Keras [2], a modular neural network library for the Python language, is designed for deep learning and used as a framework for implementing the LSTM classifier. It uses either TensorFlow or Theano library as the back-end. In this study, we used Keras 2.0.2 with Python 2.7.13 and TensorFlow 1.0.1 [5]. We use all 37 features [18] because LSTM cells select the useful features during the learning process. Keras generates LSTM sequential models with 37-dimensional inputs, 1 hidden layer, and 1-dimensional outputs. Each hidden layer contains 256 LSTM cells. The length of the time sequence is 20, which implies that samples from the current and the 19 most recent time stamps are used to predict the future instance. We utilize the datasets

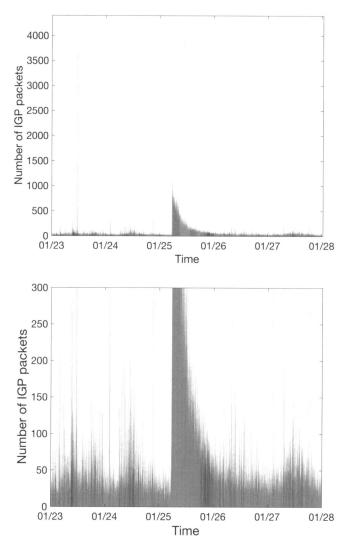

Fig. 3 SVM classifier applied to Slammer traffic collected from January 23 to 27, 2003. Shown in red is incorrectly classified traffic (top) and the detail (bottom)

shown in Table 2 to generate LSTM models. The "Adam" optimizer [25] with the learning rate "lr = 0.001" is used when compiling the LSTM model because of its superior performance when dealing with large datasets and/or high-dimensional parameter spaces.

Results of the LSTM classification are shown in Table 6. When using unbalanced datasets, the highest F-Score (84.62%) is achieved by $LSTM_u 3$ trained by using the combined Nimda and Code Red I datasets. Among balanced datasets, the

Table 5 Accuracy of the four-way SVM classification

| | Accuracy (%) | |
Feature	RIPE	BCNET
37 features	84.47	76.11
Fisher	87.00	**83.13**
MID	91.11	80.07
MIQ	87.26	73.06
MIBASE	87.14	82.64
EOR	87.69	74.38
WOR	88.57	65.35
MOR	88.72	66.39
CDM	**91.85**	72.15

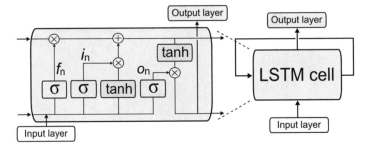

Fig. 4 Repeating module for the LSTM neural network. Shown are the input layer, LSTM layer with one LSTM cell, and output layer

Table 6 Accuracy and F-Score using LSTM models for unbalanced and balanced datasets

| | Unbalanced datasets | | | |
| | Accuracy (%) | | | F-Score (%) |
	Test dataset	RIPE	BCNET	Test dataset
LSTM_u1	95.22	65.49	57.30	83.17
LSTM_u2	53.94	51.53	50.80	11.81
$\mathbf{LSTM}_u\mathbf{3}$	**95.87**	56.74	58.55	**84.62**
	Balanced datasets			
	Accuracy (%)			F-Score (%)
	Test dataset	RIPE	BCNET	Test dataset
LSTM_b1	56.43	60.48	62.78	26.59
$\mathbf{LSTM}_b\mathbf{2}$	56.32	44.27	53.58	**65.96**
$\mathbf{LSTM}_b\mathbf{3}$	**82.98**	55.00	48.20	58.54

LSTM_b2 model achieves the best performance (65.96%). We suspect that the poor performance of LSTM_u2 may be caused by noisy data. LSTM models reported in the previous study [18] were improved by adjusting the length of time sequence and choice of the optimizer.

5 Hidden Markov Model (HMM)

HMMs are statistical tools used to model stochastic processes that consist of two embedded processes: the observable process that maps features and the unobserved hidden Markov process. We assume that the observations are independent and identically distributed (iid). In this survey, HMMs are used for non-parametric supervised classification. We implement the first order HMMs using the MATLAB statistical toolbox. Each HMM model is specified by a tuple $\lambda = (N, M, \alpha, \beta, \pi)$, where:

N: number of hidden states (cross-validated)
M: number of observations
α: transition probability distribution $N \times N$ matrix
β: emission probability distribution $N \times M$ matrix
π: initial state probability distribution matrix.

The proposed HMM classification models consist of three stages:

- *Sequence extracting and mapping*: All features are mapped to an observation vector.
- *Training*: Two HMMs for a two-way classification and four HMMs for a four-way classification are trained to identify the best probability distributions α and β for each class. The HMMs are trained and validated for various numbers of hidden states N.
- *Classification*: Maximum likelihood probability $p(x|\lambda)$ is used to classify the test observation sequences.

In the sequence extraction stage, the BGP feature matrix is mapped to a sequence of observations by selecting feature sets: FS1 (2,5,6,7,9,10,11,13) and FS2 (2,5,6,7,10,11,13). In both cases, the number of observations is chosen to be the maximum number of selected features.

HMMs are trained and validated for various numbers of hidden states. For each HMM, a tenfold cross-validation with the Baum-Welch algorithm [11] is used for training to find the best α (transition) and β (emission) matrices by calculating the largest maximum likelihood probability $p(x|\lambda_{\text{HMM}_x})$. We construct seven two-way HMM models, as shown in Table 7. The name of each HMM model reflects the training dataset and the number of hidden states. Each test observation sequence is classified based on $p(x|\lambda_{\text{HMM}_x})$.

Table 7 HMM models: two-way classification

Training dataset	Number of hidden states						
	2	3	4	5	6	7	8
Slammer, Nimda, and Code Red I	HMM_1	HMM_2	HMM_3	HMM_4	HMM_5	HMM_6	HMM_7

Table 8 Accuracy of the two-way HMM classification

N		Accuracy (%)	
No. of hidden states	Feature set	RIPE	BCNET
2	(2,5,6,7,9,	42.15	50.62
3	10,11,13)	45.21	**62.99**
4		16.11	36.53
5		19.31	27.15
6		16.81	21.11
7		**83.26**	52.01
8		67.50	41.04
N		Accuracy (%)	
No. of hidden states	Feature set	RIPE	BCNET
2	(2,5,6,7,	41.46	50.56
3	10,11,13)	26.60	**59.17**
4		10.14	25.76
5		4.03	28.06
6		16.67	21.11
7		**82.99**	51.94
8		66.87	40.97

We use regular RIPE and BCNET datasets to evaluate performance of various classification models. The FS1 and FS2 are used to create an observation sequence for each HMM. The accuracy (1) is calculated using the highest $p(x|\lambda_{\mathrm{HMM}_x})$ in the numerator while sequences in the denominator share the same number of hidden states. As shown in Table 8, HMMs have higher accuracy using feature set FS1. The regular RIPE and BCNET datasets have the highest accuracy when classified using HMMs with seven and three hidden states, respectively. Similar HMM models were developed for four-way classification and tested on regular RIPE and BCNET datasets.

6 Naive Bayes

The naive Bayes classifiers are among the most efficient machine learning classification techniques. The generative Bayesian models are used as classifiers using labeled datasets. They assume conditional independence among features. Hence,

$$\Pr(\mathbf{X}_k = \mathbf{x}_k, \mathbf{X}_l = \mathbf{x}_l | c_j) = \Pr(\mathbf{X}_k = \mathbf{x}_k | c_j) \Pr(\mathbf{X}_l = \mathbf{x}_l | c_j), \tag{8}$$

where $\mathbf{x}_k$ and $\mathbf{x}_l$ are realizations of feature vectors $\mathbf{X}_k$ and $\mathbf{X}_l$, respectively. In a two-way classification, classes labeled $c_1 = 1$ and $c_2 = -1$ denote anomalous and regular data points, respectively. For a four-way classification, four classes labeled $c_1 = 1$, $c_2 = 2$, $c_3 = 3$, and $c_4 = 4$ refer to Slammer, Nimda, Code Red I, and regular data points, respectively. Even though it is naive to assume that features are independent for a given class (8), for certain applications naive Bayes classifiers perform better compared to other classifiers. They have low complexity, may be trained effectively with smaller datasets, and may be used for online real time detection of anomalies.

The probability distributions of the priors $\Pr(c_j)$ and the likelihoods $\Pr(\mathbf{X}_i = \mathbf{x}_i | c_j)$ are estimated using the training datasets. Posterior of a data point represented as a row vector $\mathbf{x}_i$ is calculated using the Bayes rule:

$$\Pr(c_j | \mathbf{X}_i = \mathbf{x}_i) = \frac{\Pr(\mathbf{X}_i = \mathbf{x}_i | c_j)\Pr(c_j)}{\Pr(\mathbf{X}_i = \mathbf{x}_i)}$$

$$\approx \Pr(\mathbf{X}_i = \mathbf{x}_i | c_j)\Pr(c_j). \tag{9}$$

The naive assumption of independence among features helps calculate the likelihood of a data point as:

$$\Pr(\mathbf{X}_i = \mathbf{x}_i | c_j) = \prod_{k=1}^{K} \Pr(X_{ik} = x_{ik} | c_j), \tag{10}$$

where K denotes the number of features. The probabilities on the right-hand side (10) are calculated using the Gaussian distribution $\mathcal{N}$:

$$\Pr(\mathbf{X}_{ik} = \mathbf{x}_{ik} | c_j, \mu_k, \sigma_k) = \mathcal{N}(X_{ik} = x_{ik} | c_j, \mu_k, \sigma_k), \tag{11}$$

where μ_k and σ_k are the mean and standard deviation of the kth feature, respectively. We assume that priors are equal to the relative frequencies of the training data points for each class c_j. Hence,

$$\Pr(c_j) = \frac{N_j}{N}, \tag{12}$$

where N_j is the number of training data points that belong to the jth class and N is the total number of data points.

The parameters of two-way and four-way classifiers are estimated and validated by a tenfold cross-validation. In a two-way classification, an arbitrary training data point $\mathbf{x}_i$ is classified as anomalous if the posterior $\Pr(c_1 | \mathbf{X}_i = \mathbf{x}_i)$ is larger than $\Pr(c_2 | \mathbf{X}_i = \mathbf{x}_i)$.

We use the MATLAB statistical toolbox to implement naive Bayes classifiers and identify anomaly or regular data points. Datasets listed in Table 2 are used to train the two-way classifiers. The test datasets are Code Red I, Nimda, and Slammer. The combination of Code Red I and Nimda training data points (NB3) achieves the accuracy (92.79%) and F-Score (66.49%), as shown in Table 9. The NB models classify the data points of regular RIPE and regular BCNET datasets with 90.28% and 88.40% accuracies, respectively. The OR and EOR algorithms generate identical results for the two-way classification and thus performance of the EOR algorithm is omitted.

Table 9 Performance of the two-way naive Bayes classification

No.	NB	Feature	Accuracy (%)			F-Score (%)
			Test dataset	RIPE	BCNET	Test dataset
1	NB1	37 features	82.03	82.99	79.03	29.52
2	**NB1**	Fisher	**90.94**	88.13	76.46	36.08
3	NB1	MID	86.75	86.04	83.61	24.64
4	NB1	MIQ	88.86	87.78	75.21	30.38
5	NB1	MIBASE	90.92	87.64	77.92	35.12
6	**NB1**	OR	90.35	83.82	72.57	**37.33**
7	NB1	WOR	86.64	86.88	78.06	18.34
8	NB1	MOR	89.28	86.04	75.56	26.05
9	NB1	CDM	89.53	87.78	75.14	27.50
10	**NB2**	37 features	**62.56**	82.85	86.25	**48.78**
11	NB2	Fisher	57.51	87.01	83.26	27.97
12	**NB2**	MID	57.64	79.58	**88.40**	31.31
13	NB2	MIQ	56.68	84.38	82.15	26.35
14	NB2	MIBASE	57.60	86.88	82.99	28.55
15	NB2	OR	60.38	84.31	84.93	37.31
16	NB2	WOR	53.76	80.69	87.36	18.23
17	NB2	MOR	56.81	88.06	84.10	26.34
18	**NB2**	CDM	56.50	**90.28**	83.26	25.50
19	NB3	37 features	83.58	84.79	81.18	51.12
20	**NB3**	Fisher	**92.79**	87.36	75.97	**66.49**
21	NB3	MID	86.71	87.08	86.32	52.08
22	NB3	MIQ	92.47	88.68	77.15	65.03
23	NB3	MIBASE	92.49	89.31	80.42	62.97
24	NB3	OR	80.63	67.29	59.79	52.47
25	NB3	WOR	88.22	87.22	81.81	50.29
26	NB3	MOR	89.89	88.06	81.39	51.01
27	NB3	CDM	90.89	88.54	77.92	55.43

The Slammer worm test data points that are correctly classified as anomalies (true positives) during the 16 h time interval are shown in Fig. 5 (top). Incorrectly classified (false positives and false negatives) using the NB 3 classifier trained based on the features selected by Fisher in the two-way classification are shown in Fig. 5 (bottom). Most anomalous data points with large number of IGP packets (*volume* feature) are correctly classified.

The four-way naive Bayes model classifies data points as Slammer, Nimda, Code Red I, or Regular. Both regular RIPE and BCNET datasets are tested. Classification results for regular datasets are shown in Table 10. Although it is more difficult to classify four distinct anomalies, the classifier trained based on the features selected by the CDM algorithm achieves 90.14% accuracy. Variants of the OR feature selection algorithm perform well when combined with the naive Bayes classifiers

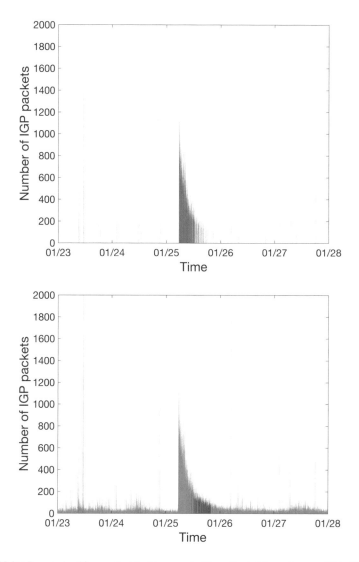

Fig. 5 Naive Bayes classifier applied to Slammer traffic collected from January 23 to 27, 2003: Shown in purple are correctly classified anomalies (true positive) while shown in green are incorrectly classified anomalies (false positive) (top). Shown in red are incorrectly classified anomalies (false positive) and regular (false negative) data points while shown in blue are correctly classified anomaly (true positive) and regular (true negative) data points (bottom)

because feature scores are calculated using the probability distribution that the naive Bayes classifiers use for posterior calculations. Hence, the features selected by the OR variants are expected to have stronger influence on the posteriors calculated by the naive Bayes classifiers [28]. Performance of the naive Bayes classifiers is often inferior to the SVM and HMM classifiers.

Table 10 Accuracy of the four-way naive Bayes classification

No.	Feature	Average accuracy (%)	
		RIPE regular	BCNET
1	37 features	85.90	85.07
2	Fisher	88.75	84.24
3	MID	86.18	82.85
4	MIQ	89.38	84.51
5	MIBASE	88.75	84.24
6	EOR	89.03	90.07
7	WOR	88.40	87.36
8	MOR	88.75	87.71
9	**CDM**	**90.14**	83.54

Table 11 Decision tree algorithm: performance

Training dataset	Test dataset	Accuracy (%)			F-Score (%)
		(Test)	RIPE	BCNET	(Test)
Dataset 1	Code Red I	85.36	89.00	77.22	47.82
Dataset 2	Nimda	58.13	94.19	81.18	26.16
Dataset 3	Slammer	**95.89**	89.42	77.78	**84.34**

7 Decision Tree Algorithm

The decision tree algorithm is one of the most successful supervised learning techniques [33]. A tree is "learned" by splitting the source set into subsets based on an attribute value. This process is repeated on each derived subset using recursive partitioning. The recursion is completed when the subset at a node contains all values of the target variable or when the splitting no longer adds value to the predictions. After a decision tree is learned, each path from the root node (source) to a leaf node is transformed into a decision rule. Therefore, a set of rules is obtained by a trained decision tree that is used for classifying unseen samples. Test accuracies and F-Scores are shown in Table 11. The results are generated using MATLAB *fitctree* from the statistics and machine learning toolbox. The lower accuracy of the training dataset 2 is due to the distributions of anomaly and regular data points in training and test datasets.

8 Extreme Learning Machine Algorithm (ELM)

The Extreme Learning Machine (ELM) [1, 23] is an efficient learning algorithm used with a single hidden layer feed-forward neural network. It randomly selects the weights of the hidden layer and analytically determines the output weights. ELM avoids the iterative tuning of the weights used in traditional neural networks and, hence, it is fast and may be used as an online algorithm.

Fig. 6 Neural network
architecture of the ELM
algorithm

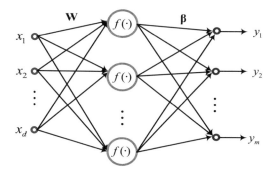

ELM employs weights connecting the input and hidden layers with the bias terms
randomly initialized while the weights connecting the hidden and output layers are
analytically determined. Its learning speed is higher than the traditional gradient
descent-based method. Reported research results indicate that ELM may learn much
faster than SVMs. Incremental and weighted extreme learning machines are variants
of ELM.

A neural network architecture of the ELM algorithm is shown in Fig. 6, where
$[x_1, x_2, \ldots, x_d]$ is the input vector; d is the feature dimension; $f(.)$ is the activation
function; $\mathbf{W}$ is the vector of weights connecting the inputs to hidden units;
$[y_1, y_2, \ldots, y_m]$ is the output vector; and β is the weigh vector connecting the
hidden and the output units.

The three datasets used to verify ELM's performance are shown in Table 2. The
number of hidden units is selected by a 5-fold cross validation for each training
dataset. The best testing accuracy was achieved by choosing 315 hidden units for
each dataset. The input vectors of the training datasets are mapped onto $[-1, 1]$ as:

$$x_i^{(p)} = 2\frac{x_i^{(p)} - x_{i_{min}}}{x_{i_{max}} - x_{i_{min}}} - 1, \tag{13}$$

where $x_i^{(p)}$ is the ith feature of the pth sample while $x_{i_{min}}$ and $x_{i_{max}}$ are the minimum
and maximum values of the ith feature of the training sample, respectively.

The accuracies and F-Scores for the three ELM test datasets with 37 or 17
features are shown in Table 12. Accuracies for RIPE and BCNET datasets are also
included. For each dataset, 100 trials were repeated. The binary Features 14–33
(shown in Chapter 3, Table 6) are removed to form a set of 17 features.

9 Discussion

We have introduced and examined various machine learning techniques for detecting network anomalies. Each approach has its unique advantages and limitations.
Soft-margined SVMs perform well in classification tasks. However, they require

Table 12 Performance of the ELM algorithm using datasets with 37 and 17 features

No. of features	Training dataset	Test dataset	Accuracy (%)			F-Score (%)
			(Test)	RIPE	BCNET	(Test)
37	Dataset 1	Code Red I	80.92	75.81	69.03	36.27
	Dataset 2	Nimda	54.42	96.15	91.88	13.72
	Dataset 3	Slammer	**86.96**	78.57	73.47	**55.31**
17	Dataset 1	Code Red I	80.75	73.43	62.43	39.90
	Dataset 2	Nimda	55.13	94.11	83.75	15.97
	Dataset 3	Slammer	**92.57**	80.57	72.71	**72.52**

relatively long time for training models when dealing with large datasets. Although LSTM algorithms achieve high accuracy and F-Score, their performance is limited to using time sequential input data. HMM and naive Bayes algorithms compute probabilities that events occur and are suitable for detecting multiple classes of anomalies. Decision tree is commonly used in data mining due to its explicit and efficient decision making. ELM is an efficient classifier while its performance is limited due to its simple structure.

10   Conclusion

In this Chapter, we classify anomalies in BGP traffic traces using a number of classification models that employ various feature selection algorithms. We conduct experiments using a number of datasets and various features extracted from data points. We analyze performance of BGP anomaly detection models based on SVM, LSTM, HMM, naive Bayes, Decision Tree, and ELM classifiers. When the testing accuracy of the classifiers is low, feature selection is used to improve their performance. Performance of the classifiers is greatly influenced by the employed datasets. While no single classifier that we have employed performs the best across all used datasets, machine learning proved to be a feasible approach to successfully classify BGP anomalies using various classification models.

Acknowledgements We thank Yan Li, Hong-Jie Xing, Qiang Hua, and Xi-Zhao Wang from Hebei University, Marijana Ćosović from University of East Sarajevo, and Prerna Batta from Simon Fraser University for their helpful contributions in earlier publications related to this project.

References

1. (Jan. 2017) Extreme Learning Machines [Online]. Available: http://www.ntu.edu.sg/home/egbhuang/elm_codes.html.
2. (Mar. 2017) Keras: Deep Learning library for Theano and TensorFlow. [Online]. Available: https://keras.io/.

3. (Mar. 2018) Understanding LSTM Networks [Online]. Available: http://colah.github.io/posts/2015-08-Understanding-LSTMs/.

4. (Mar. 2018) SVM^{light}: Support Vector Machine. [Online]. Available: http://svmlight.joachims.org/.

5. (Mar. 2018) TensorFlow. [Online]. Available: https://www.tensorflow.org/.

6. T. Ahmed, B. Oreshkin, and M. Coates, "Machine learning approaches to network anomaly detection," in *Proc. USENIX Workshop on Tackling Computer Systems Problems with Machine Learning Techniques*, Cambridge, MA, Apr. 2007, pp. 1–6.

7. T. Ahmed, M. Coates, and A. Lakhina, "Multivariate online anomaly detection using kernel recursive least squares," in *Proc. 26th IEEE Int. Conf. Comput. Commun.*, Anchorage, AK, USA, May 2007, pp. 625–633.

8. D. Ariu, R. Tronci, and G. Giacinto, "HMMPayl: an intrusion detection system based on Hidden Markov Models," *Comput. Security*, vol. 30, no. 4, pp. 221–241, 2011.

9. N. Al-Rousan and Lj. Trajković, "Machine learning models for classification of BGP anomalies," in *Proc. IEEE Conf. on High Performance Switching and Routing (HPSR)*, Belgrade, Serbia, June 2012, pp. 103–108.

10. N. Al-Rousan, S. Haeri, and Lj. Trajković, "Feature selection for classification of BGP anomalies using Bayesian models," in *Proc. Int. Conf. Mach. Learn. Cybern. (ICMLC)*, Xi'an, China, July 2012, pp. 140–147.

11. C. M. Bishop, *Pattern Recognition and Machine Learning*. Secaucus, NJ, USA: Springer-Verlag, 2006, pp. 325–358.

12. M. Bhuyan, D. Bhattacharyya, and J. Kalita, "Network anomaly detection: methods, systems and tools," *IEEE Commun. Surveys Tut.*, vol. 16, no. 1, pp. 303–336, Mar. 2014.

13. N. V. Chawla, N. Japkowicz, and A. Kotcz, "Editorial: special issue on learning from imbalanced data sets," *SIGKDD Explor. Newsl.*, vol. 6, no. 1, pp. 1–6, June 2004.

14. M. Cheng, Q. Xu, J. Lv, W. Liu, Q. Li, and J. Wang, "MS-LSTM: a multi-scale LSTM model for BGP anomaly detection," in *Proc. 2016 IEEE 24th Int. Conf. Netw. Protocols, Workshop Mach. Learn. Comput. Netw.*, Singapore, Nov. 2016, pp. 1–6.

15. C. Cortes and V. Vapnik, "Support-vector networks," *Machine Learning*, vol. 20, no. 3, pp. 273–297, 1995.

16. A. Dainotti, A. Pescape, and K. C. Claffy, "Issues and future directions in traffic classification," *IEEE Network*, vol. 26, no. 1, pp. 35–40, Feb. 2012.

17. J. Demšar, "Statistical comparisons of classifiers over multiple data sets," *J. Mach. Learn. Rev.*, vol. 7, pp. 1–30, Jan. 2006.

18. Q. Ding, Z. Li, P. Batta, and Lj. Trajković, "Detecting BGP anomalies using machine learning techniques," in *Proc. IEEE Int. Conf. Syst., Man, and Cybern.*, Budapest, Hungary, Oct. 2016, pp. 3352–3355.

19. T. G. Dietterich, "Approximate statistical tests for comparing supervised classification learning algorithms," *Neural Comput.*, vol. 10, no. 7, pp. 1895–1924, Oct. 1998.

20. D. N. T. How, K. S. M. Sahari, Y. Hu, and C. K. Loo, "Multiple sequence behavior recognition on humanoid robot using long short-term memory (LSTM)," in *Proc. Int. Conf. Robot. Autom. (ICRA)*, Hong Kong, China, Dec. 2014, pp. 109–114.

21. C.-W. Hsu and C.-J. Lin, "A comparison of methods for multiclass support vector machines," *IEEE Trans. Neural Netw.*, vol. 13, no. 2, pp. 415–425, Mar. 2002.

22. S. Hochreiter and J. Schmidhuber, "Long short-term memory," *Neural Comput.*, vol. 9, no. 8, pp. 1735–1780, Oct. 1997.

23. G. B. Huang, Q. Y. Zhu, and C. K. Siew, "Extreme learning machine: theory and applications," *Neurocomputing*, vol. 70, pp. 489–501, Dec. 2006.

24. G. B. Huang, X. J. Ding, and H. M. Zhou, "Optimization method based extreme learning machine for classification," *Neurocomputing*, vol. 74, no. 1–3, pp. 155–163, Dec. 2010.

25. D. P. Kingma and Jimmy Ba, "Adam: A method for sochastic optimization," in *Proc. 3rd Int. Conf. Learn. Representations*, San Diego, USA, Dec. 2014.

26. C. F. Lin and S. D. Wang, "Fuzzy support vector machines," *IEEE Trans. Neural Netw.*, vol. 13, no. 2, pp. 464–471, Feb. 2002.

27. P. Malhotra, L. Vig, G. Shroff, and P. Agarwal, "Long short term memory networks for anomaly detection in time series," in *Proc. Eur. Symp. Artificial Neural Netw., Comput. Intell. Mach. Learn.*, Belgium, Apr. 2015, pp. 89–94.

28. D. Mladenic and M. Grobelnik, "Feature selection for unbalanced class distribution and naive Bayes," in *Proc. Int. Conf. Machine Learning*, Bled, Slovenia, June 1999, pp. 258–267.

29. A. W. Moore and D. Zuev, "Internet traffic classification using Bayesian analysis techniques," in *Proc. Int. Conf. Measurement and Modeling of Comput. Syst.*, Banff, AB, Canada, June 2005, pp. 50–60.

30. K. Morik, P. Brockhausen, and T. Joachims, "Combining statistical learning with a knowledge-based approach - a case study in intensive care monitoring," in *Proc. Int. Conf. on Machine Learning, ICML 1999*, Bled, Slovenia, June 1999, pp. 268–277.

31. A. Munoz and J. Moguerza, "Estimation of high-density regions using one-class neighbor machines," *IEEE Trans. Pattern Anal. Mach. Intell.*, vol. 28, no. 3, pp. 476–480, Mar. 2006.

32. F. Provost, T. Fawcett, and R. Kohavi, "The case against accuracy estimation for comparing induction algorithms," in *Proc. 15th Int. Conf. Mach. Learn.*, Madison, WI, USA, July 1998, pp. 445–453.

33. J. R. Quinlan, "Induction of decision trees," *Mach. Learn.*, vol. 1, no. 1, pp. 81–106, Mar. 1986.

34. H. Sak, A. W. Senior, and F. Beaufays, "Long short-term memory recurrent neural network architectures for large scale acoustic modeling," in *Proc. INTERSPEECH*, Singapore, Sept. 2014, pp. 338–342.

35. R. J. Williams, "Simple statistical gradient-following algorithms for connectionist reinforcement learning," *Mach. Learn.*, vol. 8, no. 3, pp. 229–256, May 1992.

36. C. Wagner, J. Francois, R. State, and T. Engel, "Machine learning approach for IP-flow record anomaly detection," in *Lecture Notes in Computer Science: Proc. 10th Int. IFIP TC 6 Netw. Conf.*, J. Domingo-Pascual, P. Manzoni, S. Palazzo, A. Pont, C. Scoglio, Eds. Springer 2011, vol. 6640, pp. 28–39.
in *Proc. 10th Int. IFIP TC 6 Conf. Netw.*, NETWORKING 2011. Lecture Notes in Computer Science, vol 6640 Apr. 2009 vol. I, pp. 28–39.

37. D. H. Wolpert, "The lack of a priori distinctions between learning algorithms," *Neural Comput.*, vol. 8, no. 7, pp. 1341–1390, Oct. 1996.

38. X. Yang, Q. Song, and A. Cao, "Weighted support vector machine for data classification," in *Proc. IEEE Int. Joint Conf. Neural Netw.*, Montreal, QC, Canada, Aug. 2005, vol. 2, pp. 859–864.

39. W. Zong, G. B. Huang, and Y. Chen, "Weighted extreme learning machine for imbalance learning," *Neurocomputing*, vol. 101, pp. 229–242, Feb. 2013.

40. K. Zhang, A. Yen, X. Zhao, D. Massey, S.F. Wu, L. Zhang, "On detection of anomalous routing dynamics in BGP," in *Lecture Notes in Computer Science: Proc. Int. Conf. Research Netw.*, N. Mitrou, K. Kontovasilis, G. N. Rouskas, I. Iliadis, L. Merakos, Eds. Springer 2004, vol. 3042, pp. 259–270.

Leveraging Machine Learning Techniques for Windows Ransomware Network Traffic Detection

Omar M. K. Alhawi, James Baldwin, and Ali Dehghantanha

Abstract Ransomware has become a significant global threat with the ransomware-as-a-service model enabling easy availability and deployment, and the potential for high revenues creating a viable criminal business model. Individuals, private companies or public service providers e.g. healthcare or utilities companies can all become victims of ransomware attacks and consequently suffer severe disruption and financial loss. Although machine learning algorithms are already being used to detect ransomware, variants are being developed to specifically evade detection when using dynamic machine learning techniques. In this paper we introduce *NetConverse*, a machine learning evaluation study for consistent detection of Windows ransomware network traffic. Using a dataset created from conversation-based network traffic features we achieved a True Positive Rate (TPR) of 97.1% using the Decision Tree (J48) classifier.

Keywords Ransomware · Malware detection · Machine learning · Network traffic · Intrusion detection

1 Introduction

Malicious programs and exploit kits have always been important tools in cyber criminals' toolset [1]. In the last 2 years ransomware has become a significant global threat with the FBI estimating that $1Billion of ransom demands were paid in 2016; this represents a 400% increase from the previous year [2]. In the same

O. M. K. Alhawi · J. Baldwin
School of Computing, Science and Engineering, University of Salford, Manchester, UK
e-mail: O.Alhawi@edu.salford.ac.uk; J.Baldwin1@edu.salford.ac.uk

A. Dehghantanha (✉)
Department of Computer Science, University of Sheffield, Sheffield, UK
e-mail: A.Dehghantanha@sheffield.ac.uk

© Springer International Publishing AG, part of Springer Nature 2018
A. Dehghantanha et al. (eds.), *Cyber Threat Intelligence*, Advances in Information Security 70, https://doi.org/10.1007/978-3-319-73951-9_5

period the U.S. experienced a 300% increase in the number of daily ransomware attacks [3] and the cost of the average ransom demand doubled [4]. At the end of 2015 Symantec logged a record number (100) of new ransomware families [4]. The increase over the 2 year period is attributed to the rise of ransomware-as-a-service (RaaS) model. RaaS provided the cybercriminal with the ability to purchase ransomware creation kits and source code and distribute ransomware with very little technical knowledge [5].

In 2016 Europol reported that ransomware had become the primary concern for European law enforcement agencies with Cryptoware (the class of ransomware that encrypts files in comparison to the decreasingly prevalent locker class) the most prominent malware threat [6]. In July 2016 the No More Ransom project [7] was launched as a partnership between European law enforcement and IT Security companies in an attempt to disrupt ransomware related criminal activities, and help businesses and individuals mitigate against the impact of ransomware. Similarly, commercial software products have been developed to defend networks; Cybereason [8] uses behavioural techniques to protect consumer networks; Darktrace [9] has employed advanced unsupervised machine learning to protect enterprise networks.

Several machine learning techniques and frameworks have been proposed and undertaken for ransomware detection. However, dynamic analysis techniques have limitations in that new ransomware variants can be redesigned in an attempt to decrease the rate of detection by machine learning algorithms [10]. The application of machine learning for dynamic analysis of ransomware has achieved detection rates >96% [11]. Similarly, the application of machine learning for network traffic analysis of Android malware has achieved detection rates >99% [12].

The vast majority of ransomware threats today are designed to target personal computers running the Windows operating system since Windows-based computers make up around 89% of the OS market share of desktop computers [13]. The NetConverse model focuses on the Windows environment and proposes to leverage machine learning techniques for detecting Windows ransomware through analysing network traffic.

The paper is organised as follows: Sect. 2 discusses related works on the topic of machine learning, ransomware detection and network traffic analysis; Sect. 3 describes the research methodology and the three phases that it comprises; Sect. 4 presents the experiment and discusses the results; Sect. 5 presents the conclusion and discusses future works.

2   Related Works

Machine learning techniques have been used for decades for malware detection and analysis [14]. Different detection, analysis and investigation approaches have been proposed to defend against malware, however malicious programs are employing a variety of propagation and evasion techniques to bypass defensive mechanisms

[15]. Malware classification using machine learning has proved very successful in the detection of Android malware [16]. Malware behavioural characteristics such as API calls, filesystem changes and network traffic have been used as features for different classification tasks [17], hence machine learning can be utilised for Ransomware detection as well [18].

Ransomware can be categorized into two main classes, namely Locker ransomware and Crypto ransomware. The Locker ransomware denies access to the computer or device [13], while the Crypto ransomware prevents access to files or data. Previous works for ransomware detection and analysis can be divided into static and dynamic approaches [21]. The static approaches rely on ransomware signature or utilisation of a cryptographic primitive function for detection [22]. On the other hand, the dynamic methods are using dynamic binary instrumentation such as ransomware runtime activities for detection [23].

EldeRan [11], which was a ransomware classifier based on a sample's dynamic features, could achieve a True Positive Rate (TPR) of 96.3% with a low False Positive Rate (FPR) of 1.6%. UNVEIL [24] is another machine learning based system for ransomware detection using a ransomware sample interacting with the underlying O.S. which achieved a True Positive Rate (TPR) of 96.3%, and a zero False Positive Rate (FPR). Network behaviours and Netflow data can also be used for ransomware detection [25].

With NetConverse we are investigating the application of different machine learning classifiers in detecting ransomware samples using features extracted from network traffic conversations; we report accuracy, TPR and FPR as metrics to evaluate the performance of our classification tasks.

3 Methodology

This section presents the data collection, feature extraction and machine learning classifier phases of our experiment. The three phases are outlined in Fig. 1.

In the data collection phase, the network traffic samples are collected for both malicious (ransomware) and benign Windows applications. The feature extraction phase extracts the relevant features and merges them to create our dataset. The final machine learning classifier stage involves the training and testing of several algorithms in the Waikato Environment for Knowledge Analysis 3.8.1 (WEKA) machine learning tool [26] to identify the optimum detection model.

3.1 Data Collection Phase

This experiment focuses on Windows ransomware network traffic, examining the characteristics of the network conversations that were created when a host is infected. The infected host will attempt to connect to a remote attacker network

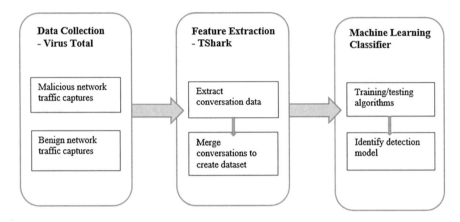

Fig. 1 Workflow showing the three phases for the experiment

address which could be a command and control server, payment or distribution website [27] thus creating a network conversation. Subsequently, the resulting network conversations are captured and compared with the characteristics of the benign applications using different classification techniques.

3.1.1 Malicious Applications

We identified the ransomware families to be included in our experiment by looking at the current tracked families on the Ransomware Tracker website, namely Cerber, Cryptowall, CTB-Locker, Locky, Padcrypt, Paycrypt, Teslacrypt and Torrentlocker. The site provides an overview of the internet infrastructure used by ransomware cyber criminals [27]. Cryptolocker was also included due to its prevalence prior to 2014. By searching for the specific ransomware families in the Virus Total Intelligence platform [28] we could identify portable executable samples that had a corresponding behavioural analysis network traffic capture. For each sample the PCAP file was downloaded and saved with the name of the sample hash value. In total, we collected 210 network traffic captures which are summarised in Table 1.

3.1.2 Benign Applications

Our benign network traffic samples (goodware) were also collected from the Virus Total Intelligence platform [28]. Our search criteria targeted portable executable files that had been submitted at least three times and had 0 detections by antivirus engines; the search results provided 264 goodware samples.

Table 1 Summary of ransomware families

Ransomware family	Class	Sample size
Cerber	Crypto	30
Cryptowall	Crypto	30
Cryptolocker	Crypto	30
CTB-Locker	Locker	30
Locky	Locker	30
Padcrypt	Crypto	1
Paycrypt	Crypto	2
Teslacrypt	Crypto	27
Torrentlocker	Locker	30

Table 2 List of extracted features

Feature name	Type [31, 32]	Description
Protocol	Basic	Protocol type
Address A	Basic	Source IP address
Port A	Basic	Source host port number
Address B	Basic	Destination IP address
Port B	Basic	Destination host port number
Packets	Basic	Total number of packets per conversation
Bytes	Basic	Total number of bytes per conversation
Packets A → B	Connection	The number of packets from source to destination
Bytes A → B	Connection	The number of bytes sent from source to destination
Packets B → A	Connection	The number of packets sent from destination to source
Bytes B → A	Connection	The number of bytes sent from destination to source
Rel Start	Basic	Time relative to start of the conversation (seconds)
Duration	Basic	Duration of the conversation (seconds)

3.2 Feature Selection and Extraction

Feature extraction was achieved using TShark, a terminal based feature of the network protocol analyser Wireshark [29]. The network traffic capture PCAP files can be analysed within Wireshark, but it offers limited export features. TShark provides a more flexible, powerful export feature that can create statistical, calculated data in addition to static feature extraction. We chose to extract several basic, traffic and connection based features using the TShark conversations export option. This aggregated each network capture file into unique conversations based on the 5-tuple [30] protocol, source/destination IP address, source/destination port values; the equivalent statistical values were also extracted. Each export file was merged together to create our initial pre-processed data. Table 2 shows the list of extracted features. Table 3 shows a sample of the dataset before cleaning.

The pre-processed data was analysed to remove any outliers and erroneous records. We removed records with an Address A value of 0.0.0.0 and Port B records with a value of 53 which represented DNS traffic. The Packets, Bytes, Rel.Start

Table 3 Dataset sample

Protocol	Address A	Port A	Address B	Port B	Packets	Bytes	Packets A → B	Bytes A → B	Packets B → A	Bytes B → A	Rel Start	Duration
17	192.168.56.15	59612	91.121.216.96	6892	0	0	1	56	1	56	73.18	0
6	192.168.56.17	58762	2.18.213.64	80	124	16,4942	64	15,590	188	180,532	92.43	118.81
6	192.168.56.26	57258	216.58.214.78	443	2699	3,935,279	1107	100,421	3806	4,035,700	151.63	117.63
6	192.168.56.19	55909	172.217.16.174	443	42	34349	33	11,327	75	45,676	176.14	116.65
6	192.168.56.17	58768	23.37.54.100	80	4	1537	7	1302	11	2839	93.60	107.63
6	192.168.56.14	49278	216.58.214.78	443	2694	3934720	610	62,847	3304	3,997,567	184.56	104.34
6	192.168.56.14	49273	35.161.88.115	443	13	4509	15	1642	28	6151	183.90	61.66
6	192.168.56.17	58767	54.225.100.50	80	4	447	6	1070	10	1517	93.32	61.61

and Duration attributes were also removed to leave us with nine features to use in the experiment. Finally, the IP address value in the 'Address A' and 'Address B' attributes were converted to decimal to more accurately reflect the differences between IP address subnets by the clustering process [33]. Table 4 shows a sample of the final dataset to be used in the experiment.

The WEKA machine learning tool has an option to allocate a percentage split of a dataset for training and test purposes. We chose to manually split our dataset into training and test datasets to ensure each dataset contained records relating to an equal number of malware and goodware samples. Due to the difference in the number of conversations created and subsequently extracted for each sample, the number of instances in each dataset is different; the training dataset contained 75,618 instances and the test dataset contained 48,526 instances. This equates to a percentage split of 60.91% for training, and 39.09% for testing of the NetConverse model. Each dataset was finally converted into Attribute-Relation File Format (.ARFF) for processing within WEKA.

3.3 Machine Learning Classifiers

During this stage of the experiment we identified the machine learning classifier and feature combination that achieved the highest detection rate. Table 5 outlines the 6 machine learning classifiers that we used.

The experiments were performed within a virtual VMWare workstation environment running on Kali Linux 2017.1 and Debian 4.9.25 OS; 4GB memory was allocated from the host. The host laptop was a MacBook Pro with a 2.9 Ghz Intel i7 processer, 16GB DDR3 RAM and MacOS Sierra 10.12.4 OS. The machine learning tool used was WEKA 3.8.1 with a Java Runtime Version of 1.8.0_131. In the experiment, all six classifiers used their default values.

4   Experiments and Results

This section presents the results of the experiment and evaluation of the classifiers that were used to achieve the best detection rate.

The experiment was split into two phases; the first phase ran tenfold cross-validation using all ten extracted attributes; the second ran tenfold cross-validation using 8 extracted attributes (the Packets A → B and Packets B → A attributes were removed at this stage as the corresponding Bytes attributes reflected the overall payload size). In both phases each classifier model was re-evaluated against the supplied test dataset to evaluate its effectiveness.

Table 4 Final dataset sample

Label	Protocol	Address A	Port A	Address B	Port B	Packets A → B	Bytes A → B	Packets B → A	Bytes B → A
Goodware	6	3232236160	55559	1177009456	80	7	854	12	1737
Goodware	6	3232237697	63318	2900408712	443	217	20,075	995	1,132,562
Goodware	17	167772687	123	1074006561	123	1	90	1	90
Goodware	17	167772687	137	167772927	137	24	2640	24	2640
Malware	17	167772687	68	167772674	67	0	0	2	1180
Malware	17	167772687	123	884685931	123	1	90	2	180
Malware	6	167772687	1045	3638213026	80	10	835	19	1468
Malware	6	167772687	1048	876236452	80	5	335	9	990

Table 5 Machine learning classifiers [34, 35]

Classifier	Technique	Pros	Cons
Bayes network	Statistical based	Fast computation and data training	Impractical for large featured datasets
Multilayer perceptron	Perceptron based	Accurate estimation	High processing time
J48	Logic based	Fast and scalable classifier of decision tree	Can be less effective on predicting the value of continuous class attributes
K Nearest Neighbours (IBK)	Instance based	Simple, requires no training	High processing time
Random forest	Logic based	Can improve predictive performance	Output can be hard to analyse
Logistic model tree (LMT)	Logic based	Flexible and accurate	Potentially high bias

Table 6 Evaluation metrics

Metric	Calculation	Value
True positive rate (TPR)	TP/(TP+FN)	Correct classification of predicted malware
False positive rate (FPR)	FP/(FP+TN)	Goodware incorrectly predicted as malware
Precision	TP/(TP+FP)	Rate of relevant results
Recall	TPR	Sensitivity for the most relevant results
F-measure	$2 \times$ (Recall $\times$ Precision)/(Recall + Precision)	Estimate of entire system performance

TP true positive, *FN* false negative, *TN* true negative, *FP* false positive

4.1 Evaluation Measures

We evaluated the performance using the five standard WEKA metrics: true positive rate (TPR), false positive rate (FPR), precision, recall, F-measure. The metrics are summarised in Table 6.

4.2 Malware Experiment and Results

Table 7 summaries the time taken to build each model in each phase of the experiment (with/without feature selection). Only two classifiers (KNN and LMT) experienced an increase in time taken to build the model; the other four classifiers (Bayes Network, Multilayer Perceptron, J48 and Random Forest) experienced a decrease in processing time due to a reduction in the number of attributes to be processed.

Table 7 Comparison of processing time (in seconds)

Classifier	Without feature selection (ten attributes)	Feature selection (eight attributes)
Bayes network	0.72	0.59
Multilayer perceptron	48.9	36.99
J48	0.95	0.18
KNN	0.01	0.03
Random forest	5.46	4.75
LMT	28.5	32.7

Table 8 Comparison without and with feature selection

Classifier	TPR (%)	FPR (%)	Precision	Recall	F-measure
Without feature selection					
Bayes network	94.90	5.10	95.00	94.90	94.90
Multilayer perceptron	94.90	6.50	94.80	94.90	94.90
J48	97.10	1.60	97.30	97.10	97.10
KNN	95.30	4.10	95.50	95.30	95.30
Random forest	96.10	3.70	96.20	96.10	96.10
LMT	96.80	3.90	96.80	96.80	96.80
With feature selection					
Bayes network	95.00	4.70	95.10	95.00	95.00
Multilayer perceptron	95.20	5.50	95.20	95.20	95.20
J48	97.10	1.60	97.30	97.10	97.10
KNN	95.30	4.20	95.50	95.30	95.30
Random forest	95.10	4.10	95.40	95.10	95.20
LMT	96.80	3.90	96.80	96.80	96.80

Table 8 lists the results of our experiment without feature selection (10 attributes) and with feature selection (eight attributes). Only the random forest classifier demonstrated slightly decreased results with a higher FPR (+0.40%) and lower TPR, precision, recall and f-measure values. The Bayes Network and Multilayer Perceptron classifiers demonstrated a very small increase overall (0.10% and 0.30% TPR increase respectively). The KNN and LMT classifier results did not change.

Table 9 summarises the highest performance achieved for each classifier. The results for each performance metric are shown: TPR, FPR, Precision, Recall, F-Measure. The J48 classifier achieved the best performance across all five metrics, with a very low false positive rate (FPR) at 1.60% being an important factor in achieving a high overall system performance (f-measure) value. The J48 classifier achieved the highest accuracy with 97.10% followed by LMT with 96.80%, Random Forest with 96.10%, KNN with 95.30%, Multilayer Perceptron with 95.20% and Bayes Network with 95.00%. It can be clearly seen that the logic based classifiers have outperformed the instance, perceptron and statistical based classifiers due to the discrete nature of the dataset features. The Bayes Network classifier also performs better on smaller datasets [35] whereas the NetConverse datasets contain a large number of instances (75,618 and 48,526).

Table 9 Malware detection evaluation result

Classifier	Technique	TPR (%)	FPR (%)	Precision	Recall	F-measure	Feature selection
J48	Logic based	97.10	1.60	97.30	97.10	97.10	With/without
LMT	Logic based	96.80	3.90	96.80	96.80	96.80	With/without
Random forest	Logic based	96.10	3.70	96.20	96.10	96.10	Without
KNN	Instance based	95.30	4.10	95.50	95.30	95.30	Without
Multilayer perceptron	Perceptron based	95.20	5.50	95.20	95.20	95.20	With
Bayes network	Statistical based	95.00	4.70	95.10	95.00	95.00	With

Table 10 Comparison of results from similar studies

Study	Description	Method	Accuracy (TPR%)
Mobile malware detection [12]	Android malware	Network conversations	99.99
NetConverse	Windows ransomware	Network conversations	97.1
EldeRan [11]	Windows ransomware	Dynamic	96.3
Peershark [36]	P2P Botnets	Network conversations	95.0 (average)

4.3 Result Comparison

As far as the authors are aware there is no directly comparable study, however there are similar machine learning techniques and approaches that we can use to substantiate our results.

In [12] Android malware was analysed using a dataset created by extracting similar, but more statistical network traffic features. This technique achieved a 99.9% TPR with the random forest classifier, in comparison to a value of 97.1% achieved using the J48 classifier in NetConverse. In [11] Windows ransomware was analysed using features obtained via dynamic analysis. A slightly lower TPR of 96.3% was achieved. The final study [36] adopted a statistical network conversation approach to analyse botnet traffic, achieving an average TPR of 95.0% in the detection of 4 different botnet applications (Table 10).

5 Conclusion and Future Works

NetConverse demonstrated an evaluation of different machine learning classifiers to detect Windows ransomware by analysing network traffic conversation data with a high rate of accuracy. Selected classifiers were Bayes network (BN), Decision Tree (J48), K-Nearest Neighbours (IBK), Multi-Layer Perceptron, Random Forest and Logistic Model Tree (LMT).

We trained NetConverse with a set of extracted network traffic features for further evaluation, using a set of different classifiers. In addition, we identified the best classifier based on the TPR value. The importance of this paper relies on the method used for collecting the samples and filtering the network conversations to remove any duplication and non-relevant attributes from our training dataset. Our experiment results (classifiers) show high performance achieved with a high accuracy result.

The experiment results show a 97.1% detection rate accuracy with the decision tree (J48) classifier and 96.8% detection rate accuracy with the LMT classifier. The experiment proves that machine learning classifiers can detect ransomware based on the network traffic behaviour.

This work is a baseline for future research in which researchers can extend and develop a dataset to include other types of malware such as OSX malware [37], IoT malware [38], ransomware [39], cloud environment malware [40, 41] and even Trojans [42] to enhance the detection process by extracting additional attributes. There are several areas of research that could be undertaken, for example: developing real-time ransomware detection using cloud-based machine learning classifiers and outputting detection results for use within other tools or leveraging machine learning to detect ransomware based on end nodes power usage patterns [43].

Acknowledgments We should acknowledge and thank Virus Total for graciously providing us with a private API key for use during our research to prepare the dataset. The authors would like to thank Mr. Ali Feizollah for his assistance with the feature extraction process. This work is partially supported by the European Council 268 International Incoming Fellowship (FP7-PEOPLE-2013-IIF) grant.

References

1. M. Hopkins and A. Dehghantanha, "Exploit Kits: The production line of the Cybercrime economy?," in *2015 2nd International Conference on Information Security and Cyber Forensics, InfoSec 2015*, 2016, pp. 23–27.
2. "Cyber-extortion losses skyrocket, says FBI." [Online]. Available: http://money.cnn.com/2016/04/15/technology/ransomware-cyber-security/. [Accessed: 31-Mar-2017].
3. Federal Bureau of Investigation, "Protecting Your Networks from Ransomware," 2016.
4. D. O'Brien, "Special Report: Ransomware and Businesses 2016," *Symantec Corp*, pp. 1–30, 2016.
5. CERT UK, "Is ransomware still a threat ?," 2016.
6. Europol, *Internet Organised Crime Threat Assessment 2016*. 2016.
7. "The No More Ransom Project." [Online]. Available: https://www.nomoreransom.org/. [Accessed: 31-Mar-2017].
8. "Ransomware Protection - RansomFree by Cybereason." [Online]. Available: https://ransomfree.cybereason.com/. [Accessed: 31-Mar-2017].
9. "Darktrace|Technology." [Online]. Available: https://www.darktrace.com/technology/#machine-learning. [Accessed: 31-Mar-2017].

10. "Cerber Ransomware Now Evades Machine Learning." [Online]. Available: http://www. darkreading.com/vulnerabilities---threats/cerber-ransomware-now-evades-machine-learning/ d/d-id/1328506?_mc=NL_DR_EDT_DR_daily_20170330&cid=NL_DR_EDT_ DR_daily_20170330&elqTrackId=67749c8bfb29467b8ea4140c8f2f3c25&elq= 4474dd7c0c1b440ab1717aa1969e0. [Accessed: 31-Mar-2017].
11. D. Sgandurra, L. Muñoz-González, R. Mohsen, and E. C. Lupu, "Automated Dynamic Analysis of Ransomware: Benefits, Limitations and use for Detection," no. September, 2016.
12. F. A. Narudin, A. Feizollah, N. B. Anuar, and A. Gani, "Evaluation of machine learning classifiers for mobile malware detection," *Soft Comput.*, vol. 20, no. 1, pp. 343–357, 2016.
13. Symantec, "The evolution of ransomware," 2015.
14. A. Feizollah, N. B. Anuar, R. Salleh, and A. W. A. Wahab, "A review on feature selection in mobile malware detection," *Digit. Investig.*, vol. 13, no. March, pp. 22–37, 2015.
15. M. Damshenas, A. Dehghantanha, and R. Mahmoud, "A Survey on Malware propagation, analysis and detection," *Int. J. Cyber-Security Digit. Forensics*, vol. 2, no. 4, pp. 10–29, 2013.
16. N. Milosevic, A. Dehghantanha, and K. K. R. Choo, "Machine learning aided Android malware classification," *Computers and Electrical Engineering*, 2016.
17. M. Damshenas, A. Dehghantanha, K.-K. R. Choo, and R. Mahmud, "M0Droid: An Android Behavioral-Based Malware Detection Model," *J. Inf. Priv. Secur.*, vol. 11, no. 3, pp. 141–157, Jul. 2015.
18. K. K. R. Azmoodeh, Amin; Dehghantanha, Ali; Conti, Mauro; Choo, "Detecting Crypto Ransomware in IoT Networks Based On Energy Consumption Footprint," *J. Ambient Intell. Humaniz. Comput.*, 2017.
19. F. Mercaldo, V. Nardone, and A. Santone, "Ransomware Inside Out," 2016.
20. K. Liao, Z. Zhao, A. Doupe, and G.-J. Ahn, "Behind closed doors: measurement and analysis of CryptoLocker ransoms in Bitcoin," in *2016 APWG Symposium on Electronic Crime Research (eCrime)*, 2016, pp. 1–13.
21. D. D. Hosfelt, "Automated detection and classification of cryptographic algorithms in binary programs through machine learning," 2015.
22. S. Ranshous, S. Shen, D. Koutra, C. Faloutsos, and N. F. Samatova, "Anomaly Detection in Dynamic Networks: A Survey," 2014.
23. Z. Wang, X. Jiang, W. Cui, X. Wang, and M. Grace, "ReFormat: Automatic Reverse Engineering of Encrypted Messages," Springer, Berlin, Heidelberg, 2009, pp. 200–215.
24. A. Kharaz, S. Arshad, C. Mulliner, W. Robertson, and E. Kirda, "UNVEIL: A Large-Scale, Automated Approach to Detecting Ransomware," *Usenix Secur.*, pp. 757–772, 2016.
25. K. Cabaj, P. Gawkowski, K. Grochowski, and D. Osojca, "Network activity analysis of CryptoWall ransomware," pp. 91–11, 2015.
26. "Weka 3 - Data Mining with Open Source Machine Learning Software in Java." [Online]. Available: http://www.cs.waikato.ac.nz/ml/weka/. [Accessed: 31-Mar-2017].
27. "Tracker | Ransomware Tracker," 2016. [Online]. Available: https:// ransomwaretracker.abuse.ch/tracker/. [Accessed: 04-Jan-2017].
28. "VirusTotal - Free Online Virus, Malware and URL Scanner." [Online]. Available: https:// www.virustotal.com/.[Accessed: 31-Mar-2017].
29. G. Combs, "Wireshark · Go Deep.," 2017. [Online]. Available: https://www.wireshark.org/. [Accessed: 29-May-2017].
30. P. Narang, C. Hota, and V. Venkatakrishnan, "PeerShark: flow-clustering and conversation-generation for malicious peer-to-peer traffic identification," *EURASIP J. Inf. Secur.*, vol. 2014, no. 1, p. 15, 2014.
31. A. Buczak and E. Guven, "A survey of data mining and machine learning methods for cyber security intrusion detection," *IEEE Commun. Surv. Tutorials*, vol. PP, no. 99, p. 1, 2015.
32. W. L. W. Lee, S. J. Stolfo, and K. W. Mok, "A data mining framework for building intrusion detection models," *IEEE Symp. Secur. Priv.*, vol. 0, no. c, pp. 120–132, 1999.

33. A. Azodi, M. Gawron, A. Sapegin, F. Cheng, and C. Meinel, "Leveraging event structure for adaptive machine learning on big data landscapes," in *Lecture Notes in Computer Science (including subseries Lecture Notes in Artificial Intelligence and Lecture Notes in Bioinformatics)*, 2015, vol. 9395, pp. 28–40.

34. F. A. Narudin, A. Feizollah, N. B. Anuar, and A. Gani, "Evaluation of machine learning classifiers for mobile malware detection," *Soft Comput.*, pp. 1–15, 2014.

35. S. B. Kotsiantis, "Supervised machine learning: A review of classification techniques," *Informatica*, vol. 31, pp. 249–268, 2007.

36. P. Narang, S. Ray, C. Hota, and V. Venkatakrishnan, "PeerShark: Detecting peer-to-peer botnets by tracking conversations," in *Proceedings - IEEE Symposium on Security and Privacy*, 2014, vol. 2014–Janua, pp. 108–115.

37. Hamed HaddadPajouh, Ali Dehghantanha, Raouf Khayami, and Kim-Kwang Raymond Choo, "Intelligent OS X Malware Threat Detection", Journal of Computer Virology and Hacking Techniques, 2017

38. Amin Azmoudeh, Ali Dehghantanha and Kim-Kwang Raymond Choo, "Robust Malware Detection for Internet Of (Battlefield) Things Devices Using Deep Eigenspace Learning", IEEE Transactions on Sustainable Computing, 2017

39. Sajad Homayoun, Ali Dehghantanha, Marzieh Ahmadzadeh, Sattar Hashemi, Raouf Khayami, "Know Abnormal, Find Evil: Frequent Pattern Mining for Ransomware Threat Hunting and Intelligence", IEEE Transactions on Emerging Topics in Computing, 2017 - DOI: 10.1109/TETC.2017.2756908

40. Yee-Yang Teing, Ali Dehghantanha, Kim-Kwang Raymond Choo, Zaiton Muda, and Mohd Taufik Abdullah, "Greening Cloud-Enabled Big Data Storage Forensics: Syncany as a Case Study," IEEE Transactions on Sustainable Computing, DOI: 10.1109/TSUSC.2017.2687103, 2017.

41. Yee-Yang Teing, Ali Dehghantanha, Kim-Kwang Raymond Choo, "CloudMe Forensics: A Case of Big-Data Investigation," Concurrency and Computation: Practice and Experience, http://onlinelibrary.wiley.com/doi/10.1002/cpe.4277, 2017

42. Dennis Kiwia, Ali Dehghantanha, Kim-Kwang Raymond Choo, Jim Slaughter, "A Cyber Kill Chain Based Taxonomy of Banking Trojans for Evolutionary Computational Intelligence", Journal of Computational Science, 2017

43. Amin Azmoodeh, Ali Dehghantanha, Mauro Conti, Raymond Choo, "Detecting Crypto-Ransomware in IoT Networks Based On Energy Consumption Footprint", Journal of Ambient Intelligence and Humanized Computing, DOI: 10.1007/s12652-017-0558-5, 2017

Leveraging Support Vector Machine for Opcode Density Based Detection of Crypto-Ransomware

James Baldwin and Ali Dehghantanha

Abstract Ransomware is a significant global threat, with easy deployment due to the prevalent ransomware-as-a-service model. Machine learning algorithms incorporating the use of opcode characteristics and Support Vector Machine have been demonstrated to be a successful method for general malware detection. This research focuses on crypto-ransomware and uses static analysis of malicious and benign Portable Executable files to extract 443 opcodes across all samples, representing them as density histograms within the dataset. Using the SMO classifier and PUK kernel in the WEKA machine learning toolset it demonstrates that this methodology can achieve 100% precision when differentiating between ransomware and goodware, and 96.5% when differentiating between five crypto-ransomware families and goodware. Moreover, eight different attribute selection methods are evaluated to achieve significant feature reduction. Using the CorrelationAttributeEval method close to 100% precision can be maintained with a feature reduction of 59.5%. The CFSSubset filter achieves the highest feature reduction of 97.7% however with a slightly lower precision at 94.2%.

Using a ranking method applied across the attribute selection evaluators, the opcodes with the highest predictive importance have been identified as FDIVP, AND, SETLE, XCHG, SETNBE, SETNLE, JB, FILD, JLE, POP, CALL, FSUB, FMUL, MUL, SETBE, FISTP, FSUBRP, INC, FIDIV, FSTSW, JA. The MOV and PUSH opcodes, represented in the dataset with significantly higher density, do not actually have high predictive importance, whereas some rarer opcodes such as SETBE and FIDIV do.

Keywords Malware · Ransomware · Ransomware detection · Ransomware family detection

J. Baldwin
School of Computing, Science and Engineering, University of Salford, Manchester, UK
e-mail: J.Baldwin1@edu.salford.ac.uk

A. Dehghantanha (✉)
Department of Computer Science, University of Sheffield, Sheffield, UK
e-mail: A.Dehghantanha@sheffield.ac.uk

© Springer International Publishing AG, part of Springer Nature 2018
A. Dehghantanha et al. (eds.), *Cyber Threat Intelligence*, Advances in Information Security 70, https://doi.org/10.1007/978-3-319-73951-9_6

1   Introduction

In their December 2016 quarterly threat report [1] McAfee referred to 2016 as the "year of Ransomware; the FBI estimated that $1Billion of ransom demands were paid in 2016 representing a 400% increase from the previous year, and the cost of the average ransom demand doubled [2]. The rise of the ransomware-as-a-service (RaaS) model provided cybercriminals with the ability to distribute ransomware with very little technical knowledge [3] in addition to the potential for huge financial returns for both the distributors, and the developers within the model (In July 2016 Cerber generated US $195,000 revenue for its distributors with a 40% cut of that figure going to the developer) [4].

Europol, in 2017, concluded that ransomware continued to be "one of the most prominent malware threats in terms of the variety and range of its victims and the damage done" [5]. In the recently commissioned 2017 Ransomware Report, 88% of survey respondents who has been affected by ransomware in the previous year had encountered crypto-ransomware [6].

In 2017 ransomware achieved global news coverage due to the WannaCry [7] and subsequent Petya [8] outbreaks. Due to the nature of the WannaCry outbreak many high profile global organisations such as the UK National Health Service, Spanish telecommunications company Telefónica, and logistics company Fed-Ex. were subject to severe disruption [5]. The scale of the infection and subsequent media coverage provoked discussion and reaction down from government level through to security vendors, enterprises and domestic audiences.

Current AV vendors that rely on static detection methods are struggling to contain the threat of ransomware due to the daily deployment of new variants, iterations and families. Recent commercial software products have adopted heuristic detection methods; Darktrace employ advanced unsupervised machine learning for the protection of enterprise networks [9]; MWR have developed RansomFlare "as an effective countermeasure to the increasing threat of ransomware" [10]. Although malware threats and detection techniques are predominantly targeted towards Microsoft Windows systems, machine learning techniques are also applied to other platforms such as OS X [11], Android [12] and IOT (Internet of Things) [13].

Due to its recent significance and effect on the cyber threat landscape [14] this paper focuses on crypto-ransomware affecting Microsoft Windows systems only. It will use static opcode density analysis of crypto-ransomware and benign samples using Support Vector Machine (SVM) supervised machine learning techniques. Malicious and benign programs require a different set of instructions to achieve their function and previous research works have demonstrated opcode characteristics to be an effective predictor for malware. Opcode characteristics can be easily extracted for data input into a machine learning classifier such as SVM which is effective where binary classification is required.

The objective of this paper is to achieve >95% precision when differentiating between ransomware and goodware, and when differentiating between five crypto-ransomware families and goodware. Moreover, eight different attribute selection methods are evaluated to achieve feature reduction. This research will provide scope for further development, and practical or commercial application.

The rest of the paper is organised as follows: Sect. 2 reviews related works on the topic of machine learning, ransomware and malware detection; Sect. 3 describes the research methodology and the four phases that it comprises; Sect. 4 presents the results of the experiment; Sect. 5 presents the conclusion and discusses future works.

2   Related Works and Research Literature

Firdausi et al. demonstrated that the use of machine learning techniques could detect malware effectively and efficiently [15]. They used dynamic analysis reports obtained from an online analysis service, Anubis, to evaluate different machine learning classifiers, with the best performing J48 Decision Tree classifier achieving precision of 97.3%, and a false positive rate (FPR) of 2.4%. In 2011 Rieck et al. proposed a framework for the automatic analysis of malware behaviour using machine learning [16]. They embedded the observed behaviour in a vector space and applied clustering algorithms to achieve significant improvement over previous work in that area. Egele et al. presented a comprehensive overview of the state-of-the-art analysis techniques and tools for use by a malware analyst [17]. They concluded that both static and dynamic analysis tools were required to overcome the evasion techniques that malware authors were using. The following year, after a detailed analysis conducted on the current malware detection systems that included static, dynamic and hybrid malware techniques, Landage and Wankhade concluded that data mining and machine learning was also required to compliment the limitations of existing techniques to achieve better detection [18]. Islam et al. introduced a classification method that integrated static and dynamic to overcome the limitations associated with each technique [19]. They demonstrated the importance of including both old and new malware samples to overcome the evasion techniques employed by malware authors. They achieved a minimum of 5% lower accuracy across all evaluated classifiers when using newer samples only. Similarly, in 2016 another comprehensive review was undertaken of techniques and tools for malware analysis and classification by Gandotra et al. [20]; it included processes for collection, static/dynamic analysis, feature extraction and machine learning classification.

Bilar [21] used static analysis techniques to statistically compare the distribution of opcodes within malware and goodware. He concluded that the infrequently used opcodes were a better indicator of malware compared to the more frequently used opcodes. This statistical research has been cited frequently and is one of most important works relating to opcodes and their ability to be used for malware prediction. Bilar then extended his research to analyse opcode control flows which is now a widely used technique for malware detection. Ding et al. presented a control flow-based method to extract opcode behaviour from executable files to improve on text-based extraction methods and obtain a more accurate representation of the executable file behaviour [23]. The control flow method achieved a 2.3% improvement in accuracy over text-based methods using a KNN classification. Zhao et al. used a similar technique with additional feature filtering to achieve a 97% accuracy with a Random Forest classifier [24].

Cesare et al. proposed a malware classification system using approximate matching of control flowgraphs and a distance metric based on the distance between feature vectors of string-based signatures to achieve high accuracy [25].

Opcode density analysis has been extensively researched and applied to general malware detection. Rad et al. used opcode density histograms to differentiate between malicious and benign PE files with 100% accuracy based on a 100 sample dataset (80 malicious/20 benign) [26]. O'Kane et al. used dynamic analysis techniques to extract the opcodes from runtime traces and introduced SVM classifier filter techniques to perform dimension reduction [27].

Further dimension reduction/feature filtering research has included Lin et al. who proposed a two-stage dimensionality reduction approach combining feature selection and extraction to substantially reduce the dimensionality of features for training and classification [28].

Khammas et al. used static analysis techniques for opcode n-grams and compared several feature selection methods and machine learning classifiers [29]. They concluded that Principal Component Analysis (PCA) feature selection and Support Vector Machines (SVM) classification achieved the highest classification accuracy using a minimum number of features. Park et al. used feature reduction to identify the top-10 opcodes for malware detection and decreased the training time of a supervised learning algorithm by 91% with no loss of accuracy [30]. Lo et al. used feature reduction to identify nine features that could distinguish malware from goodware achieving an accuracy of 99.60% using a Random Forest classifier [31].

There are several techniques that have been researched for the detection of ransomware as a specific family. EldeRan [32], was a ransomware classifier based on a sample's dynamic features; it achieved a True Positive Rate (TPR) of 96.3% with a low False Positive Rate (FPR) of 1.6%. UNVEIL [33] is another machine learning based system that uses a ransomware sample interacting with the underlying O.S. to achieve a True Positive Rate (TPR) of 96.3% and a zero False Positive Rate (FPR). Network related behaviour and Netflow data can also be used for ransomware detection as demonstrated by [34] and [35] in which they extracted conversation-based network traffic features to achieve a precision of 97.3% using the Decision Tree (J48) classifier. In 2016 Ahmadian and Shahriari introduced 2entFox, a framework for ransomware detection based on 20 extracted filesystem and registry events [36]. Using a Bayesian network model, it achieved an F-measure of 93.3%. Most recently in 2017, Homayoun et al. used sequential pattern mining of filesystem, registry and DLL events to achieve 99% accuracy when differentiating between crypto-ransomware and goodware, and 96.5% when differentiating between the 3 different ransomware families [37]. Using a novel approach to detect crypto-ransomware in IOT networks based on power consumption, Azmoodeh et al. achieved a detection rate of 95.65%, and a precision of 89.19% when monitoring connected Android devices [38].

3 Methodology

Our considered methodology comprises four key stages as summarised in Fig. 1.

3.1 Data Collection

The ransomware families used for the experiment were identified from the Ransomware Tracker website [39], an online ransomware resource used by internet service providers (ISPs), computer emergency response teams (CERTs) and law enforcement agencies (LEAs). By studying the current tracked ransomware families focus was given to five crypto families only (Cerber, CryptoWall, Locky, TeslaCrypt, TorrentLocker) with the inclusion of historic samples where available to ensure that variant history and changes to the malicious code were included [19]. The Ransomware tracker website lists known Distribution, Payment and Command and Control hosts associated with each ransomware family; corresponding SHA256 sample references are documented. The SHA256 value for each identified sample was submitted to the Virus Total Intelligence platform [40] to facilitate quick, bulk downloading. The download list was reviewed to ensure that only the PE file format (Portable Executable) was downloaded, and other formats such as DLL (dynamic link library) were omitted. This was done to enable an accurate comparison with the goodware samples which were a similar PE format.

The benign (Goodware) executable samples for the dataset were obtained from the Portable Apps platform [41], a portable software solution that allows popular software to be installed and run from portable storage devices. The Portable Apps platform provides suitable counterpart samples in that the executable files are portable (or standalone), and ensure relevance across multiple OS versions [42]. Using a 'certutil' command run against the 350 benign samples an output file was generated containing the SHA256 values for each sample. The SHA256 values

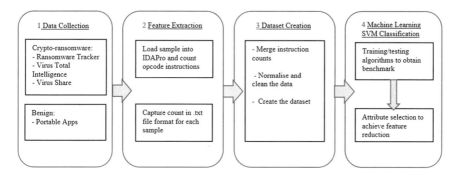

Fig. 1 The four key stages of the research

were submitted in bulk to the VTI platform to determine the detection ratio for
further analysis. Many of the samples were detected as infected by smaller antivirus
vendors but the vendors that offered the highest protection e.g. BitDefender,
F-Secure, Kaspersky, McAfee, Symantec, Trend Micro C [43] identified each of the
goodware samples as clean, therefore the detection from the smaller vendors were
deemed to be false positives, and discounted. Where a detection ratio of 4/total or
higher was registered (regardless of vendor size) the samples were discarded.

3.2   Feature Extraction

As the study focuses on the actual CPU instruction (opcode) and not the data that
is to be processed (operand) the operand value has not been captured during the
feature extraction process. Static analysis was performed using IDAPro with an
InstructionCounter plugin to automate the opcode count process and export the
results to text file format [44]. The InstructionCounter plugin was successfully
installed and run correctly within a reduced-functionality, evaluation version of the
latest IDAPro version 6.95 [45]; it was tested successfully in both a Windows 7
Professional SP1 and Windows 10 Home environments. On loading the sample into
IDAPro the plugin was run and the output captured to a text file that was saved with
a name corresponding to the SHA256 hash file for easy recognition. This process
was repeated for all samples, both malicious and benign. Due to the limitations
with the evaluation version of the latest IDAPro 6.95, only 32-bit PE files could be
loaded—64-bit benign samples files were discarded and not analysed.

Figure 2 shows a sample feature extract using the InstructionCounter plugin.

The columns in the output file represent rank, count, density and, opcode. The
total number of opcodes is also included which provide useful for reference and to
enable recalculation of the density with more numerical precision within the dataset
(see Sect. 3.3.2).

```
0e8e2be2a4e03dcb8bbb71b7d841fc6d32d4772714fd7db4c9c577bdf40e85ea.txt - Notepad        —   □   ×

File  Edit  Format  View  Help
Opcode distribution of file: 0e8e2be2a4e03dcb8bbb71b7d841fc6d32d4772714fd7db4c9c577bdf40e85ea.exe
Total opcodes: 1060398

0001. 522777    49.30%    mov
0002. 100587     9.49%    call
0003. 092192     8.69%    lea
0004. 068179     6.43%    sub
0005. 035504     3.35%    jz
0006. 034083     3.21%    test
0007. 033897     3.20%    jmp
0008. 031512     2.97%    cmp
0009. 025956     2.45%    push
0010. 018663     1.76%    add
```

Fig. 2 Sample InstructionCounter output file with top ten opcodes, count and density

Table 1 Example of MOV Opcode density

Sample	MOV Opcode rank	Total no.	Density%	Total opcodes in sample
Malicious (Cerber)	1	2,368	33	7,215
Benign	1	398,332	33	1,192,874

3.3 Dataset Creation

Each executable sample is represented in the dataset as a density histogram to reflect the percentage density of each opcode occurrence relative to the total number of opcode occurrences. This process removes any variance that is attributed to different application and code lengths. Consider the two samples in Table 1 which relate to the MOV opcode. The malicious and benign samples have a large variation in both the total number of opcodes, and extracted number of MOV opcodes. In both samples, however, MOV has a similar density and therefore are both equally ranked because of this.

3.3.1 Merging the Data

A copy of all the malicious and benign output text files were placed in a single directory and merged into a single text file. The text file was opened in Microsoft Excel and using the 'Text to Columns'/'Sort A to Z'/'Remove Duplicates' features a master list of all the extracted opcodes (443) was obtained. This list was used to subsequently ensure that all records and features could be sorted alphabetically and therefore be correctly ordered.

Using a custom recorded VB Macro each output file was combined with the master opcode list, sorted, transposed and inserted into a master Microsoft Excel worksheet to create a raw representation of the data.

3.3.2 Normalising the Data

Additional processing in Excel was required to finalise the created dataset.

1. Each column was checked for correct alignment and sorting, samples were sorted by opcode count, records analysed and removed if containing duplicate data.

   The cell values were recalculated to increase the decimal place value to eight as the InstructionCounter plugin had only exported to two decimal places. The increase in numerical precision was required as eight decimal places provided a differentiation between no occurrence (i.e. 0 count) and low occurrence (e.g. 5), which in samples of high opcode count were both represented by 0.00.

	A	B	C	D	E	F	G	H	I	J	K	L
1	mov	push	call	cmp	pop	add	lea	jz	jmp	test	sub	xor
2	0.35031	0.130042	0.1246	0.023314	0.071934	0.020267	0.051851	0.024077	0.03578	0.023417	0.007979	0.0:
3	0.213753	0.18011	0.071966	0.062817	0.05701	0.034593	0.035051	0.04589	0.032024	0.035227	0.015414	0.02(
4	0.43864	0.017616	0.098937	0.043622	0.025874	0.025637	0.073195	0.05883	0.03556	0.037643	0.061818	0.00<
5	0.50305	0.025266	0.075659	0.041164	0.030017	0.017788	0.056328	0.041778	0.030734	0.03662	0.020133	0.01(
6	0.211528	0.181965	0.070595	0.061614	0.054506	0.036412	0.034151	0.042616	0.029627	0.034797	0.015605	0.0:
7	0.280236	0.212389	0.117994	0.020649	0.070796	0.00885	0.017699	0.014749	0.103245	0.0059	0.00295	0.06<
8	0.344574	0.13806	0.113272	0.033225	0.083355	0.018063	0.023498	0.033896	0.036169	0.027156	0.007957	0.03:
9	0.347589	0.168669	0.068076	0.042768	0.048054	0.072081	0.020984	0.020343	0.029793	0.019222	0.024027	0.01:
10	0.362844	0.117333	0.108785	0.02724	0.069763	0.024893	0.039931	0.025165	0.031281	0.022335	0.009962	0.03!
11	0.422609	0.093618	0.09872	0.03548	0.057667	0.02889	0.022339	0.026181	0.027454	0.019389	0.011436	0.02!
12	0.291379	0.177653	0.095254	0.037761	0.055566	0.025442	0.051655	0.034969	0.026418	0.037247	0.015222	0.02:
13	0.493001	0.024478	0.094858	0.029717	0.011915	0.0176	0.086941	0.033482	0.031966	0.032142	0.064296	0.00<
14	0.360244	0.120612	0.12741	0.025818	0.06761	0.022205	0.050458	0.021441	0.036766	0.019706	0.009285	0.03:
15	0.341119	0.127007	0.107289	0.033108	0.080335	0.021667	0.03034	0.033023	0.035298	0.029004	0.010726	0.03:
16	0.211874	0.193036	0.076475	0.066477	0.04407	0.033627	0.03623	0.049957	0.032294	0.035754	0.016409	0.02{
17	0.444352	0.035454	0.094401	0.03779	0.019403	0.020256	0.062246	0.041924	0.049955	0.038426	0.014476	0.00(
18	0.216495	0.178139	0.070325	0.066333	0.055018	0.034503	0.03603	0.044292	0.030928	0.033531	0.01628	0.02:
19	0.207111	0.21151	0.10044	0.029692	0.08651	0.070748	0.026393	0.036657	0.018328	0.053886	0.012463	0.02:

Fig. 3 Dataset sample

Table 2 Extracted opcode statistics

Class	Total extracted opcodes	Average no extracted opcodes per sample	Largest no codes
Goodware	70,848,904	308,039	320
Malware	3,418,229	13,147	163
			483 Total

2. An additional "class" column was added where 'good' represented goodware and 'malware' represented malware to provide a response/detection for the machine learning prediction.
3. The dataset values were linearly scaled (0, 1). This was done for two reasons: to avoid attributes in greater numeric ranges dominating those in smaller numeric ranges; to avoid large attribute value calculation errors associated with some kernel functions [46].
4. The final step was to calculate average density for each attribute and sort high to low. Figure 3 shows an example of the final sorted dataset with the attributes highlighted (The 'class' attribute is usually listed at the end of the dataset and is referenced in WEKA using the 'last' parameter. It is not shown in this example).

3.3.3 Opcode Breakdown

Almost 71 million opcodes were extracted from the benign samples with an average of 308,038 codes per sample. This is in contrast to almost 3.5 million codes extracted from the malicious samples, with an average of 13,147 codes per sample (Table 2).

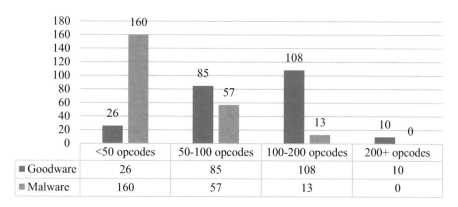

No. of different opcodes used and distribution per class

■ Goodware   ■ Malware

Fig. 4 Number of different Opcodes used and distribution per class

Table 3 Top 20 opcode densities (%)

	Goodware		Malware			Goodware		Malware	
Rank	Opcode	Density (%)	Opcode	Density	Rank	Opcode	Density (%)	Opcode	Density (%)
1	MOV	31.9	MOV	32.9%	11	JNZ	2.5	TEST	2.9
2	PUSH	13.8	PUSH	13.2%	12	XOR	2.2	XOR	2.7
3	CALL	9.6	CALL	6.4%	13	RETN	2.0	JNZ	1.9
4	POP	4.9	ADD	4.5%	14	SUB	1.8	RETN	1.8
5	LEA	4.3	CMP	4.1%	15	INC	1.0	AND	1.6
6	CMP	4.2	SUB	4.0%	16	AND	0.8	OR	1.3
7	JZ	3.5	JZ	3.9%	17	MOVZX	0.7	SHL	1.0
8	JMP	3.4	LEA	3.4%	18	DEC	0.7	INC	0.8
9	ADD	3.2	JMP	3.3%	19	OR	0.6	SAR	0.7
10	TEST	3.2	POP	3.2%	20	JLE	0.3	MOVZX	0.6

Figure 4 also illustrates the opcode distribution for both classes with the malware samples predominantly using <50 different opcodes, in comparison to goodware using between 100 and 200. It can be clearly seen that the structure for the malware samples is much simpler than the goodware samples with a lower overall count for both the number of extracted codes, and number of different opcodes used to perform the instructions.

Table 3 displays the top 20 opcodes for each class. It shows that the MOV opcode has the highest density at over 30% for both malware and goodware, compared to the second highest opcode, PUSH with around 13%. The densities for both classes are quite similar, especially for MOV and PUSH.

3.4 Machine Learning Classification

The final phase involves the training and testing of the SVM classifier in the Waikato Environment for Knowledge Analysis 3.8.1 (WEKA) machine learning toolset [47]. WEKA was selected as the best tool for this experiment as it incorporates several standard machine learning techniques for simple workflow, can output results into a text and statistical format and offers several attribute selection evaluators.

3.4.1 SVM and Kernel Functions

The Support Vector Machine (SVM) is a supervised machine learning technique, especially effective where binary classification is required; it is therefore an effective classifier for malware detection which often has two classes for prediction—malicious (malware) and benign (goodware). An SVM classifies data by constructing a hyperplane to separate data points in one class from those in another class; the best hyperplane therefore should have the largest margin of separation between both classes [48]. Where linear separation is not possible SVM can use kernel functions to transform the data into a higher dimensional feature space e.g. using by a radial hypersphere to achieve separation [49]. The goal of an SVM is therefore to produce a classification model based on a training dataset which is then used to predict the target values of the test dataset [46].

Sequential Minimal Optimization, (or SMO), is an algorithm used to train Support Vector Machines, devised by John Platt in 1998. The SMO can handle large datasets and scales well due to the memory footprint growing linearly with the training set size.

In WEKA, the SMO classifier was run with all the default options including the selection of a 'Logistic' calibration method.

The SMO algorithm in WEKA uses linear, polynomial and Gaussian kernel functions and each kernel choice (Poly, NormalisedPoly, PUK, RBF) was initially tested using default values before further tuning and optimisation was applied.

3.4.2 Feature/Attribute Selection Process

The attribute selection/feature reduction process is performed to enable the classifier to use the lowest number of features while maintaining the highest level of precision. Feature reduction applied to very large datasets can significantly decrease the training time for algorithms and the computational overhead associated with the high number of attributes and instances. Accuracy can also be increased by filtering out the noisy attributes that could have a negative effect on classification.

Attribute selection methods can be grouped into two categories: wrapper methods and filter methods. Wrapper methods can achieve better performance than filter methods due to their ability to be optimised, however they cannot always be used in datasets with a large number of attributes due to the evaluation process requiring a computational overhead and excessively long training times [50].

Within the WEKA toolset there are nine attribute selection evaluators. The WrapperSubsetEval options is not used in this experiment as it was briefly tested and proved unresponsive for the reasons already discussed. The following attribute selection methods were evaluated: CfsSubsetEval, CorrelationAttributeEval, Gain-RatioAttributeEval, InfoGainAttribute, OneRAttributeEval, Principal Component Analysis, ReliefFAttributeEval, SymmetricalUncertAttributeEval.

WEKA has several search methods used by the attribute selection evaluators to perform either feature reduction, or ranking; in this experiment three search methods are employed: (1) 'BestFirst' uses greedy hill climbing (performing evaluation at each iteration) to search the attribute subspace; it can be configured to start with no attributes and search forwards, start with all attributes and search backwards, or search both directions from any point. It has a "backtracking" option which is used to terminate the search when the number of consecutive non-improving nodes is reached; (2) 'GreedyStepwise' performs a greedy search through the attribute subset space and can also be configured to start with no attributes and search forwards, all attributes and search backwards, or search both directions from any point. When the addition or removal of any remaining attributes results in a decrease in evaluation, the search will stop. It can be configured to generate a ranking by recording the order that the attributes are selected. Used in conjunction with the "numToSelect" option (specifies the number of attributes to retain and "threshold" option (threshold at which attributes are discarded) further feature reduction can be achieved; (3) 'Ranker' generates a ranking for each attribute based on their individual evaluations. Used in conjunction with the "numToSelect" option (specifies the number of attributes to retain and "threshold" option (threshold at which attributes are discarded) further feature reduction can be achieved.

3.5 Implementation

The experiment can be separated into four district phases:

1. Pre-processing the dataset
2. Creating the training and test datasets
3. Training and testing the SVM classifier
    Training and testing the attribute selection evaluators
4. Tuning the attribute selection evaluators to achieve further feature reduction

These phases are illustrated in workflow diagram Fig. 5.

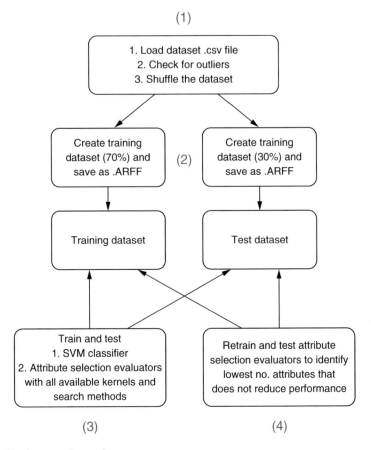

Fig. 5 The four experiment phases

3.5.1 Pre-processing the Dataset (1)

The full dataset CSV file was loaded into the WEKA pre-processing tool to be prepared for the classifier tasks.

Outliers and extreme values are identified and removed in a two-step process.

In step 1 the '*weka.filters.unsupervised.attribute.InterquartileRange*' filter was applied to the loaded dataset to identify outliers and extreme values based on the results of interquartile aggregation.

In step 2 the corresponding '*weka.filters.unsupervised.instance.RemoveWithValues*' filter should be applied to remove the 'outlier' and 'ExtremeValue' attributes labelled as 'yes', however in this instance this step was not applied due to the high number of outliers detected. It was decided to continue with the experiment to see if the classification produced satisfactory results as Interquartile aggregation may not be a suitable method for outlier detection for the type of data in this dataset.

Finally the dataset was shuffled using the filter *weka.filters.unsupervised.instance. Randomize -S 42* to prevent an unequal sample distribution across either training, or test dataset.

3.5.2   Creating the Training and Test Datasets (2)

Following shuffling the dataset was split into a training dataset (70%) and test (evaluation) dataset (30%). The following WEKA filters were applied and after each application the new dataset was saved in the. ARFF (Attribute-Relation File Format) format—a format consisting of a separate header and data section developed for use specifically within the WEKA software:

- *weka.filters.unsupervised.instance.RemovePercentage -P 30.0* (to remove 30% from each class in the dataset)
- *weka.filters.unsupervised.instance.RemovePercentage -P 30.0 -V* (selection inverted to swap the 30% back into the dataset)

The resulting training and test datasets contained 343 and 103 instances respectively.

3.5.3   Training and Testing the SVM Classifier (3.1)

The SVM classification experiment was conducted in multiple phases with each classification run using all available kernel and search methods.

The ten main phases of the classification experiments are summarised in Table 4.

In each of the classification experiments training was performed using tenfold cross validation. Cross-validation is an important technique used to help prevent overfitting by allocating a portion of the training dataset for validation, validating using multiple rounds (the number of rounds is determined by the number of specified folds, in this case 10) and then averaging the prediction results. Using tenfolds has become a standard process for cross-validation and following extensive testing it has been shown that around this number achieves the best estimate of error [51]. All SMO classifier options were set to their default values and the experiment repeated for each of the four available kernel functions (Poly, NormalisedPoly, PUK, RBF).

The test dataset (containing 30%, 103 instances) was supplied to the classifier and each model re-evaluated against the same test set. The evaluation metrics are compared in the following result tables. The highest performing evaluated model is highlighted in green, the lowest in red.

Table 4 The ten main phases of the classifications

Experiment	Options	Kernel Selections	Available Search methods
1. SMO classifier Run against 2 Classes (malware, goodware)	1. Training and evaluation	– Poly – NormalisedPoly – PUK – RBF	–
2. SMO Classifier Run against 6 Classes (5 *malware families, goodware)	1. Training and evaluation	– Poly – NormalisedPoly – PUK – RBF	–
3. CFSSubsetEval	1. Attribute Selection Training and evaluation 2. Feature Reduction Training and evaluation	– Poly – NormalisedPoly – PUK – RBF	BestFirst GreedyStepwise
4. CorrelationAttributeEval	1. Attribute Selection Training and evaluation 2. Feature Reduction Training and evaluation	– Poly – NormalisedPoly – PUK – RBF	Ranker
5. GainRatioAttributeEval	1. Attribute Selection Training and evaluation 2. Feature Reduction Training and evaluation	– Poly – NormalisedPoly – PUK – RBF	Ranker
6. InfoGainAttributeEval	1. Attribute Selection Training and evaluation 2. Feature Reduction Training and evaluation	– Poly – NormalisedPoly – PUK – RBF	Ranker
7. OneRAttributeEval	1. Attribute Selection Training and evaluation 2. Feature Reduction Training and evaluation	– Poly – NormalisedPoly – PUK – RBF	Ranker
8. PrincipalComponents – correlation matrix – covariance matrix	1. Attribute Selection Training and evaluation 2. Feature Reduction Training and evaluation	– Poly – NormalisedPoly – PUK – RBF	Ranker
9. ReliefAttributeEval	1. Attribute Selection Training and evaluation 2. Feature Reduction Training and evaluation	– Poly – NormalisedPoly – PUK – RBF	Ranker
10. SymmetricalUncertAttributeEval	1. Attribute Selection Training and evaluation 2. Feature Reduction Training and evaluation	– Poly – NormalisedPoly – PUK – RBF	Ranker

3.5.4 Training and Testing the Attribute Selection Evaluators

In Phases 3–10 the Attribute Selection evaluators were run using default options and a single parameter changed to discard attributes below a threshold value of 0; this was selected to achieve an initial feature reduction prior to further tuning.

Table 5 Evaluation metrics [52]

Metric	Calculation	Value
True positive rate (TPR)	$TP/(TP+FN)$	Rate of true positives (instances correctly classified as a given class)
False positive rate (FPR)	$FP/(FP+TN)$	Rate of false positives (instances falsely classified as a given class)
Precision	$TP/(TP+FP)$	Proportion of instances that are truly of a class divided by the total instances classified as that class
Recall	TPR	Proportion of instances classified as a given class divided by the actual total in that class (equivalent to TP rate)
F-measure	$2 \times (Recall \times Precision)/$ $(Recall + Precision)$	A combined measure for precision and recall (Estimate of entire system performance)

TP true positive, *FN* false negative, *TN* true negative, *FP* false positive

The dimensionality of the data was therefore reduced by the attribute selection evaluation process before being passed onto the selected classifier, in this case, SMO.

Classifications were performed using all available search methods and kernels (using default, untuned settings) and the results presented.

3.5.5 Evaluation Metrics

The performance of each classification model was evaluated using the five default WEKA metrics as summarised in Table 5 and compared in the later Experiments and Results section.

3.5.6 Machine Specifications

Best practice within malware analysis and malicious executable handling is to use an isolated virtual environment that is detached from its host. This provides the ability to restore the environment to a clean, previous state, to recover from, or clean-up after infection [42, 53].

The feature extraction phase of the experiment was undertaken within an isolated virtual environment on a lab PC with the network cable disconnected to further isolate it from the network. The virtual environment used for data collection and feature extraction was VMWare Workstation due to the ease of configuration, deployment and familiarity as the environment was already configured on the host laptop with a number of suitable VMs already in use for such tasks. Table 6 outlines the environment machine specifications for each stage of the experiment.

Table 6 Machine specifications for each stage of the experiment

Phase	Host	Virtual environment	Application
1. Data collection	Viglen Genie Desktop PC: • Windows 7 Enterprise SP1 • 8GB RAM • Intel Core 2 Quad CPU Q8400@ 2.66 GHz	– VMWorkstation 12 Pro – 12.1.1 build 3770994 – Debian 4.9.6-3 Kali2 (2017-01-30) i686 GNU/Linux 3GB RAM 4 processors – NAT mode (used to share the hosts IP address)	Mozilla Firefox ESR 45.7.0
2. Feature extraction		– VMWorkstation 12 Pro 12.1.1 build 3770994 – Windows 7 Professional SP1 1GB RAM 1 Processor – Host only mode (a private network shared with the host only)	IDA 6.95.160926 (32-bit)
3. Dataset creation	Lenovo IdeaPad 310 • Windows 10 Home • 8GB RAM • Intel Core i5 6200U @2.40 GHz	–	Microsoft Excel 2016 MSO (16.1.7726.1049) 64 bit
4. Machine learning classifier		–	WEKA.version 3.8.1 Java(TM) SE Runtime Environment 1.8.0_112-b15 java.version 1.8.0_112

4   Experiments and Results

4.1   SMO (Two Classes)

In Phase 1 the SMO classifier was trained and tested using the classifier default options to obtain a benchmark set of evaluation metrics for all extracted attributes in the detection model (Table 7). The two classes used were 'malware' and 'goodware'.

With all default options set the PUK kernel (Pearson VII function-based universal kernel) achieved the best results with 100% precision and a 0% False Positive rate (FPR).

The linear and quadratic kernel functions achieved slightly less than the target 95% precision and the RBF Gaussian kernel function only achieving 82.6% precision.

Determining the best kernel function for the dataset can often only be achieved by conducting multiple experiments across all available kernels and parameters, and comparing the chosen evaluation metrics therefore the Poly, NormalisedPoly and RBF kernels were further tuned to achieve higher precision comparable to the PUK kernel results:

– Poly/NormalisedPoly:
   'Complexity' tested using values 0.1, 1.0, 10.0, 100.0; 'exponent using' 1.0, 2.0, 3.0
– RBF kernel:
   'Complexity' tested using values 0.1, 1.0, 10.0, 100.0; 'gamma' using 0.01, 0.1, 1.0, 10.0

Table 8 below summarises the parameter selections that provided the highest precision.

Each kernel, when properly tuned, can achieve 100% precision when re-evaluated against the test dataset.

Table 7 SMO (two classes) evaluation metrics

Model	Kernel	Action	TPR%	FPR%	Precision%	Recall%	F-Measure%	Attributes
1	Poly[a]	Training (tenfold cross-validation)	90.7	9.5	90.7	90.7	90.7	444
1	Poly[a]	Re-evaluation against test set	94.2	5.9	94.4	94.2	94.2	444
2	NormalisedPoly[b]	Training (tenfold cross-validation)	89.8	10.7	90.0	89.8	89.8	444
2	NormalisedPoly[b]	Re-evaluation against test set	94.2	5.9	94.4	94.2	94.2	444
3	PUK	Training (tenfold cross-validation)	86.9	14.0	87.5	86.9	86.8	444
3	PUK	Re-evaluation against test set	100.0	0.0	100.0	100.0	100.0	444
4	RBF	Training (tenfold cross-validation)	80.5	20.2	80.6	80.5	80.4	444
4	RBF	Re-evaluation against test set	82.5	17.4	82.6	82.5	82.5	444

[a] Exponent default value set to 1.0 to achieve linear kernel function
[b] Exponent default value set to 2.0 to achieve quadratic kernel function

Table 8 New parameter selections for tuning the SMO kernels

Kernel	Changed parameters	Action	TPR%	FPR%	Precision%	Recall%	F-Measure%	Attributes
Poly	E = 2 C = 1	Training (tenfold cross-validation)	90.4	9.6	90.4	90.4	90.4	444
Poly	E = 2 C = 1	Re-evaluation against test set	100.0	0.0	100.0	100.0	100.0	444
Poly	E = 1 C = 10	Training (tenfold cross-validation)	90.4	9.6	90.4	90.4	90.4	444
Poly	E = 1 C = 10	Re-evaluation against test set	100.0	0.0	100.0	100.0	100.0	444
NormalisedPoly	E = 2 C = 100	Training (tenfold cross-validation)	89.8	10.5	89.8	89.8	89.8	444
NormalisedPoly	E = 2 C = 100	Re-evaluation against test set	100.0	0.0	100.0	100.0	100.0	444
NormalisedPoly	E = 3 C = 10	Training (tenfold cross-validation)	91.5	8.8	91.6	91.5	91.5	444
NormalisedPoly	E = 3 C = 10	Re-evaluation against test set	100.0	0.0	100.0	100.0	100.0	444
RBF	γ = 1 C = 10	Training (tenfold cross-validation)	84.5	16.4	85.1	84.5	84.4	444
RBF	γ = 1 C = 10	Re-evaluation against test set	100.0	0.0	100.0	100.0	100.0	444

C—The complexity parameter
E—The exponent value
γ—The Gamma value

4.2 SMO (Six Classes)

Phase 2 required a second version of the dataset to be created and labelled with six different classes to represent the benign instances and 5 different ransomware classes (A single dataset with two class attributes could have been used but creating separate datasets reduced the complexity). The steps in 3.5.1 and 3.5.2 were repeated to pre-process the data and create the training and test datasets for use in the 6-class classification model.

The evaluation metrics for this phase of the experiment can be seen in Table 9.

With all default options set the PUK kernel (Pearson VII function-based universal kernel) once again achieved the best results with 96.5% precision and 0.3% False Positive rate (FPR). Table 10 shows the detailed accuracy by each class in the classification. Three classes (Good, TeslaCrypt, Cryptowall) achieved 100% precision and although Cerber achieved a 100% TPR, two Locky samples were incorrectly detected as Cerber resulting in a decrease in precision due to receiving false positives. The confusion matrix for this association can be seen in Table 11. Although all classes were represented in the training dataset, the test dataset did not contain any instances for the Torrentlocker class which highlights an issue in that this class was not represented correctly in the dataset.

4.3 Training and Testing the Attribute Selection Evaluators

In Phases 3–10 the Attribute Selection evaluators were run using default options and a single parameter changed to discard attributes below a threshold value of 0; this was selected to achieve an initial feature reduction prior to further tuning.

Table 9 SMO (six classes) evaluation metrics

Model	Kernel	Action	TPR%	FPR%	Precision%	Recall%	F-Measure%	Attributes
45	Poly[a]	Training (tenfold cross-validation)	70.8	10.2	70.0	70.8	69.8	444
45	Poly[a]	Re-evaluation against test set	87.4	4.1	86.7	87.4	86.7	444
46	NormalisedPoly[b]	Training (tenfold cross-validation)	69.4	14.6	66.9	69.4	66.0	444
46	NormalisedPoly[b]	Re-evaluation against test set	87.4	6.7	86.3	87.4	86.6	444
47	PUK	Training (tenfold cross-validation)	62.7	26.2	60.9	62.7	56.0	444
47	PUK	Re-evaluation against test set	97.1	0.3	96.5	97.1	96.7	444
48	RBF	Training (tenfold cross-validation)	49.3	43.9	35.1	49.3	34.7	444
48	RBF	Re-evaluation against test set	51.5	47.6	46.4	51.5	36.8	444

[a] Exponent default value set to 1.0 to achieve linear kernel function
[b] Exponent default value set to 2.0 to achieve quadratic kernel function

Table 10 Detailed accuracy by class (SMO six classes)

TPR%	FPR%	Precision%	Recall%	F-measure%	Class
100.0	0.0	100.0	100.0	100.0	Good
0.0	0.0	0.0	0.0	0.0	Torrentlocker
100.0	0.0	100.0	100.0	100.0	Teslacrypt
86.7	1.1	92.9	86.7	89.7	Locky
100.0	0.0	100.0	100.0	100.0	Cryptowall
100.0	2.1	75.0	100.0	85.7	Cerber
97.1	0.3	96.5	97.1	96.6	Weighted avg.

Table 11 Confusion matrix with false positives highlighted in red (SMO 6 classes)

a	b	c	d	e	f	<-- classified as
51	0	0	0	0	0	a = good
0	0	0	1	0	0	b = Torrentlocker
0	0	22	0	0	0	c = TeslaCrypt
0	0	0	13	0	2	d = Locky
0	0	0	0	8	0	e = CryptoWall
0	0	0	0	0	6	f = Cerber

The dimensionality of the data was therefore reduced by the attribute selection evaluation process before being passed onto the selected classifier, in this case, SMO.

Classifications were performed using all available search methods and kernels (using default, untuned settings) and the results presented.

4.3.1   CFSSubsetEval

CfsSubsetEval is a Subset evaluator that is used conjunction with an appropriate search option to determine the smallest subset size that has the same consistency as the full attribute set [51]. It assesses the predictive ability of each individual attribute and the degree of redundancy among them; it prefers sets of attributes that are highly-correlated with the class, but have low intercorrelation with each other. The CfsSubsetEval evaluator determined that a subset of 21 attributes had a consistency equal to the full set of 444 attributes.

The highest performing model using the PUK kernel achieved 94.2% precision using 21 attributes (Table 12). The ranked 21 attributes are: SETS, SETNBE, SETNLE, JB, FSUB, XCHG, POP, OR, FUCOMPP, JLE, CMOVS, ROR, FIDIV, SETBE, JA, LEA, FNINIT, CALL, AND, SETLE, FDIVP.

Table 12 CfsSubsetEval evaluation metrics

Model	Search method	Kernel	Action	TPR%	FPR%	Precision%	Recall%	F-Measure%	Attributes
5	BestFirst	Poly	Training (tenfold cross-validation)	87.2	13.7	87.7	87.2	87.1	21
5	BestFirst	Poly	Re-evaluation against test set	87.4	12.7	87.7	87.4	87.3	21
6	GreedyStepwise	Poly	Training (tenfold cross-validation)	87.2	13.6	87.6	87.2	87.1	21
6	GreedyStepwise	Poly	Re-evaluation against test set	87.4	12.7	87.7	87.4	87.3	21
7	BestFirst	NormalisedPoly	Training (tenfold cross-validation)	90.1	10.3	90.2	90.1	90.1	21
7	BestFirst	NormalisedPoly	Re-evaluation against test set	87.4	12.6	87.4	87.4	87.4	21
8	GreedyStepwise	NormalisedPoly	Training (tenfold cross-validation)	90.1	10.3	90.1	90.1	90.1	21
8	GreedyStepwise	NormalisedPoly	Re-evaluation against test set	87.4	12.6	87.4	87.4	87.4	21
9	BestFirst	PUK	Training (tenfold cross-validation)	92.1	8.1	92.2	92.1	92.1	21
9	BestFirst	PUK	Re-evaluation against test set	93.2	6.8	93.2	93.2	93.2	21
10	GreedyStepwise	PUK	Training (tenfold cross-validation)	92.1	8.1	92.2	92.1	92.1	21
10	GreedyStepwise	PUK	Re-evaluation against testset	94.2	5.9	94.2	94.2	94.2	21
11	BestFirst	RBF	Training (tenfold cross-validation)	54.2	51.7	75.4	54.2	39.3	21
11	BestFirst	RBF	Re-evaluation against test set	51.5	49.5	75.3	51.5	36.0	21
12	GreedyStepwise	RBF	Training (tenfold cross-validation)	54.2	51.7	75.4	54.2	39.3	21
12	GreedyStepwise	RBF	Re-evaluation against test set	51.5	49.5	75.3	51.5	36.0	21

4.3.2 CorrelationAttributeEval

CorrelationAttributeEval is another Correlation-based evaluator but it uses ranking to evaluate each attribute and does not apply filtering. This is used in conjunction with the "discard" and "threshold" options to achieve feature reduction.

The CorrelationAttributeEval evaluator uses the ranker search method so only achieved a low initial feature reduction due to the zero-discard threshold setting. It achieved 100% precision with the PUK kernel and this model was selected for further tuning (Table 13).

4.3.3 GainRatioAttributeEval

The GainRatioAttributeEval evaluator measures the gain ratio with respect to the class to evaluate predictor importance of each attribute [52]. Using the zero-discard threshold a feature reduction from 444 to 252 attributes and 99% precision using the PUK kernel was achieved (Table 14).

Table 13 CorrelationAttributeEval evaluation metrics

Model	Search method	Kernel	Action	TPR%	FPR%	Precision%	Recall%	F-Measure%	Attributes
13	Ranker	Poly	Training (tenfold cross-validation)	90.7	9.5	90.7	90.7	90.7	432
13	Ranker	Poly	Re-evaluation against test set	94.2	5.9	94.4	94.2	94.2	432
14	Ranker	NormalisedPoly	Training (tenfold cross-validation)	89.8	10.7	90.0	89.8	89.8	432
14	Ranker	NormalisedPoly	Re-evaluation against test set	94.2	5.9	94.4	94.2	94.2	432
15	Ranker	PUK	Training (tenfold cross-validation)	86.9	14.0	87.5	86.9	86.8	432
15	Ranker	PUK	Re-evaluation against test set	100.0	0.0	100.0	100.0	100.0	432
16	Ranker	RBF	Training (tenfold cross-validation)	80.2	20.5	80.3	80.2	80.1	432
16	Ranker	RBF	Re-evaluation against test set	82.5	17.4	82.6	82.5	82.5	432

Table 14 GainRatioAttributeEval evaluation metrics

Model	Search method	Kernel	Action	TPR%	FPR%	Precision%	Recall%	F-Measure%	Attributes
17	Ranker	Poly	Training (tenfold cross-validation)	91.3	8.9	91.3	91.3	91.3	252
17	Ranker	Poly	Re-evaluation against test set	94.2	5.9	94.4	94.2	94.2	252
18	Ranker	NormalisedPoly	Training (tenfold cross-validation)	91.0	9.3	91.0	91.0	91.0	252
18	Ranker	NormalisedPoly	Re-evaluation against test set	95.1	4.9	95.3	95.1	95.1	252
19	Ranker	PUK	Training (tenfold cross-validation)	90.4	9.7	90.4	90.4	90.4	252
19	Ranker	PUK	Re-evaluation against test set	99.0	1.0	99.0	99.0	99.0	252
20	Ranker	RBF	Training (tenfold cross-validation)	81.0	19.5	81.1	81.0	81.0	252
20	Ranker	RBF	Re-evaluation against test set	82.5	17.4	82.6	82.5	82.5	252

4.3.4 InfoGainAttributeEval

The InfoGainAttribute evaluator measures the information gain with respect to the class to evaluate predictor importance of each attribute [52]. Using the zero-discard threshold the same results as the GainRatioAttributeEval evaluator were achieved i.e. feature reduction from 444 to 252 attributes and 99% precision using the PUK kernel (Table 15).

4.3.5 OneRAttributeEval

OneRAttributeEval evaluates the worth of an attribute by using the OneR classifier, a simple cheap classifier that can obtain high accuracy using of a set of rules that all test one particular attribute to determine the class of an instance and aims to find the attribute with the fewest prediction errors [54].

Using the zero-discard threshold the evaluator initially performed only a single attribute feature reduction by removing the 'class' attribute, however it achieved 100% precision using the PUK kernel (Table 16).

Table 15 InfoGainAttribute evaluation metrics

Model	Search method	Kernel	Action	TPR%	FPR%	Precision%	Recall%	F-Measure%	Attributes
21	Ranker	Poly	Training (tenfold cross-validation)	91.3	8.9	91.3	91.3	91.3	252
21	Ranker	Poly	Re-evaluation against test set	94.2	5.9	94.4	94.2	94.2	252
22	Ranker	NormalisedPoly	Training (tenfold cross-validation)	91.0	9.3	91.0	91.0	91.0	252
22	Ranker	NormalisedPoly	Re-evaluation against test set	95.1	4.9	95.3	95.1	95.1	252
23	Ranker	PUK	Training (tenfold cross-validation)	90.4	9.7	90.4	90.4	90.4	252
23	Ranker	PUK	Re-evaluation against test set	99.0	1.0	99.0	99.0	99.0	252
24	Ranker	RBF	Training (tenfold cross-validation)	81.0	19.5	81.1	81.0	81.0	252
24	Ranker	RBF	Re-evaluation against test set	82.5	17.4	82.6	82.5	82.5	252

Table 16 OneRAttributeEval evaluation metrics

Model	Search method	Kernel	Action	TPR%	FPR%	Precision%	Recall%	F-Measure%	Attributes
25	Ranker	Poly	Training (tenfold cross-validation)	90.7	9.5	90.7	90.7	90.7	443
25	Ranker	Poly	Re-evaluation against test set	94.2	5.9	94.4	94.2	94.2	443
26	Ranker	NormalisedPoly	Training (tenfold cross-validation)	89.8	10.7	90.0	89.8	89.8	443
26	Ranker	NormalisedPoly	Re-evaluation against test set	94.2	5.9	94.4	94.2	94.2	443
27	Ranker	PUK	Training (tenfold cross-validation)	86.9	14.0	87.5	86.9	86.8	443
27	Ranker	PUK	Re-evaluation against test set	100.0	0.0	100.0	100.0	100.0	443
28	Ranker	RBF	Training (tenfold cross-validation)	80.2	20.5	80.3	80.2	80.1	443
28	Ranker	RBF	Re-evaluation against test set	82.5	17.4	82.6	82.5	82.5	443

4.3.6 PrincipalComponents

Principal Component Analysis is a widely-used dimension reduction technique. It is based on the principle of converting a large number of variables into a smaller number of uncorrelated variables; it can reduce training and testing times for SVM classifiers with little decrease in accuracy [55]. The new attributes are then ranked in order of their eigenvalues with a subset of attributes selected by choosing sufficient eigenvectors to account for a specified proportion of the variance, usually 95%. The attributes can then be transformed back to their original space but with a loss of ranking for predictor importance.

The PCA evaluation was performed using both the covariance and correlation (to perform standardisation) matrices which gave very different results.

When run with the default values the covariance matrix achieved significantly higher dimension reduction resulting in just seven attributes, but at the expense of performance. The highest precision using the correlation matrix and PUK kernel achieved just under the target 95% precision with a value of 94.4%, with a reduction in attributes to 87 (Table 17).

Table 17 PCA evaluation metrics

Model	Search method	Kernel	Action	TPR%	FPR%	Precision%	Recall%	F-Measure%	Attributes
29[a]	Ranker	Poly	Training (tenfold cross-validation)	85.4	15.5	85.9	85.4	85.3	87
29[a]	Ranker	Poly	Re-evaluation against test set	90.3	9.8	90.8	90.3	90.3	87
30[a]	Ranker	NormalisedPoly	Training (tenfold cross-validation)	54.2	51.6	63.7	54.2	40.3	87
30[a]	Ranker	NormalisedPoly	Re-evaluation against test set	50.5	50.5	25.5	50.5	33.9	87
31[a]	Ranker	PUK	Training (tenfold cross-validation)	87.2	12.5	87.4	87.2	87.2	87
31[a]	Ranker	PUK	Re-evaluation against test set	94.2	5.9	94.4	94.2	94.2	87
32[a]	Ranker	RBF	Training (tenfold cross-validation)	53.1	53.1	28.2	53.1	36.8	87
32[a]	Ranker	RBF	Re-evaluation against test set	50.5	50.5	25.5	50.5	33.9	87
33[b]	Ranker	Poly	Training (tenfold cross-validation)	72.9	29.6	76.2	72.9	71.5	7
33[b]	Ranker	Poly	Re-evaluation against test set	71.8	28.6	78.5	71.8	70.0	7
34[b]	Ranker	NormalisedPoly	Training (tenfold cross-validation)	54.2	51.6	63.7	54.2	40.3	7
34[b]	Ranker	NormalisedPoly	Re-evaluation against test set	50.5	50.5	25.5	50.5	33.9	7
35[b]	Ranker	PUK	Training (tenfold cross-validation)	85.1	14.3	85.7	85.1	85.1	7
35[b]	Ranker	PUK	Re-evaluation against test set	85.1	14.3	85.7	85.1	85.1	7
36[b]	Ranker	RBF	Training (tenfold cross-validation)	53.1	53.1	28.2	53.1	36.8	7
36[b]	Ranker	RBF	Re-evaluation against test set	50.5	50.5	25.5	50.5	33.9	7

[a] Using the correlation matrix
[b] Using the covariance matrix

Table 18 ReliefFAttributeEval evaluation metrics

Model	Search method	Kernel	Action	TPR%	FPR%	Precision%	Recall%	F-Measure%	Attributes
37	Ranker	Poly	Training (tenfold cross-validation)	91.0	9.2	91.0	91.0	91.0	281
37	Ranker	Poly	Re-evaluation against test set	94.2	5.9	94.4	94.2	94.2	281
38	Ranker	NormalisedPoly	Training (tenfold cross-validation)	90.7	9.8	90.8	90.7	90.6	281
38	Ranker	NormalisedPoly	Re-evaluation against test set	93.2	6.9	93.3	93.2	93.2	281
39	Ranker	PUK	Training (tenfold cross-validation)	90.4	10.2	90.6	90.4	90.3	281
39	Ranker	PUK	Re-evaluation against test set	99.0	1.0	99.0	99.0	99.0	281
40	Ranker	RBF	Training (tenfold cross-validation)	80.8	19.8	80.8	80.8	80.7	281
40	Ranker	RBF	Re-evaluation against test set	82.5	17.4	82.6	82.5	82.5	281

Table 19 SymmetricalUncertAttributeEval evaluation metrics

Desc	Search method	Kernel	Action	TPR%	FPR%	Precision%	Recall%	F-Measure%	Attributes
41	Ranker	Poly	Training (tenfold cross-validation)	91.3	8.9	91.3	91.3	91.3	252
41	Ranker	Poly	Re-evaluation against test set	94.2	5.9	94.4	94.2	94.2	252
42	Ranker	NormalisedPoly	Training (tenfold cross-validation)	91.0	9.3	91.0	91.0	91.0	252
42	Ranker	NormalisedPoly	Re-evaluation against test set	95.1	4.9	95.3	95.1	95.1	252
43	Ranker	PUK	Training (tenfold cross-validation)	90.4	9.7	90.4	90.4	90.4	252
43	Ranker	PUK	Re-evaluation against test set	99.0	1.0	99.0	99.0	99.0	252
44	Ranker	RBF	Training (tenfold cross-validation)	81.0	19.5	81.1	81.0	81.0	252
44	Ranker	RBF	Re-evaluation against test set	82.5	17.4	82.6	82.5	82.5	252

4.3.7   RelieffAttributeEval

ReliefFAttributeEval is instance-based, sampling instances randomly and checking neighbouring instances of the same and different classes. It can operate on both discrete and continuous class data [51].

The ReliefFAttributeEval, an instance-based evaluator achieved 99% precision using the PUK kernel, with a feature reduction to 281 features (Table 18).

4.3.8   SymmetricalUncertAttributeEval

SymmetricalUncertAttributeEval evaluates the worth of an attribute by measuring the symmetrical uncertainty with respect to the class, assigning a value of 0 or 1 to represent irrelevance and relevance respectively [52]. It achieved very high precision, 99% with a feature reduction to 252 features (Table 19).

Table 20 Comparison of feature reduction

Model	Desc	Search method	Kernel	TPR%	FPR%	Precision%	Recall%	F-Measure%	Feature Reduction	Reduction%
3	SMO (Benchmark)	-	PUK	100.0	0.0	100.0	100.0	100.0	-	
10	CFSSubset	GreedyStepwise	PUK	94.2	5.9	94.2	94.2	94.2	21 -> 10	97.7
15	CorrelationAttributeEval	Ranker	PUK	100.0	0.0	100.0	100.0	100.0	432 -> 180	59.5
19	GainRatioAttributeEval	Ranker	PUK	99.0	1.0	99.0	99.0	99.0	252 -> 183	58.8
23	InfoGainAttributeEval	Ranker	PUK	99.0	1.0	99.0	99.0	99.0	252 -> 128	71.2
27	OneRAttributeEval	Ranker	PUK	100.0	0.0	100.0	100.0	100.0	443 -> 332	25.2
31	PrincipalComponents	Ranker	PUK	94.2	5.9	94.4	94.2	94.2	87 -> 55	87.6
39	ReliefFAttributeEval	Ranker	PUK	99.0	1.0	99.0	99.0	99.0	281 -> 77	82.7
43	SymmetricalUncertAttributeEval	Ranker	PUK	99.0	1.0	99.0	99.0	99.0	252 -> 133	70.0

4.4 Tuning the Attribute Selection Evaluators to Achieve Further Feature Reduction (4)

The best performing model from each phase model was tuned by applying a decremental change to the discard threshold within the Ranker or greedy stepwise searches to achieve increased feature reduction, but without a decrease in precision. Once a decrease had been reached, the highest number of attributes required to maintain performance was recorded.

In each of the classification experiments training was performed using tenfold cross validation with each model re-evaluated against the same test set. Table 20 compares the final feature reduction achieved by each tuning process. The CorrelationAttributeEval still achieves 100% precision and 0% TPR with a significantly reduced no. of features (reduced to 180). CFSSubset is the lowest performing evaluator with a 94.2% precision rate but it does provide the highest feature reduction at only 10 features or a 97.7% reduction.

4.5 Important Opcodes

Table 5-16 shows a list of the top 21 ranked Opcodes by each attribute selection evaluator. The top 21 values have been chosen to reflect the value (21) of the initial feature reduction achieved by the CFSSubsetEval method for full comparison. Due to the difficulty in calculating the specific ranked Opcodes by the PCA filter the attributes have been transformed back into their original space resulting in an equal rank being assigned to each attribute. The PCA top 21 Opcodes have included on Table 21 for reference but are not ranked.

Highlighted in Table 5-16 are any occurrences of the common crypto functions used by ransomware: XOR, ROL, ROR, ROT. Although XOR, ROL, ROR have been selected by 4, 6 and 8 attribute filters respectively as predictive features, only ROR appears more than once in the top 21 ranked predictors and does not feature in the top 20 overall ranked predictors.

The CFSSubset Evaluator can provide feature reduction from 443 to 10 attributes but the ROR attribute can be discarded without any decrease in precision.

Table 21 Top 21 ranked opcodes by feature reduction method

Rank	CFSSubset Evaluator	CorrelationAttribute Eval	GainRatioAttribute Eval	InfoGainAttribute Eval	OneRAttribute Eval	ReliefFAttribute Eval	Symmetrical UncertAttribute Eval	Principal Components [a]
1	SETS	JLE	SETLE	FDIVP	FDIVP	POP	FDIVP	SUBPS
2	SETNBE	CALL	FDIVP	XCHG	AND	INC	SETLE	MULPS
3	SETNLE	FILD	SETBE	AND	XCHG	JNZ	FILD	SETNBE
4	JB	POP	SETNBE	JA	SETLE	CMP	FSUBRP	PADDW
5	FSUB	JG	FSUBRP	INC	SETNLE	PUSH	MUL	CVTTSS2SI
6	XCHG	AND	SETNB	SETNLE	JB	CALL	SETNBE	FRNDINT
7	POP	FIDIV	FILD	SETLE	FMUL	ADD	SETBE	XORPD
8	OR	FMUL	ROR	MUL	FSTSW	DEC	AND	FDIVRP
9	FUCOMPP	JL	CALL	FMUL	FADDP	JL	XCHG	ADDPS
10	JLE	DEC	FISTP	STOS	FSUB	JLE	FSUB	FSUBRP
11	CMOVS	SUB	FIDIV	FSUB	FISTP	JNB	FISTP	FUCOM
12	ROR	OR	FNINIT	JB	MUL	AND	JB	PADDD
13	FIDIV	SETNBE	FSTP	JLE	SHLD	RETN	FSTSW	ORPD
14	SETBE	FDIV	BSWAP	RCR	FXCH	XOR	SETNLE	PMINUW
15	JA	FDIVRP	FSTSW	SETZ	SCAS	SUB	JA	COMISS
16	LEA	FISTP	MUL	NOT	FDIV	TEST	STOS	FIADD
17	FNINIT	FMULP	FLD	FSTSW	FABS	JZ	FMUL	PUNPCKLBW
18	CALL	CMC	LODS	FADDP	FILD	JB	SETNB	CMOVBE
19	AND	NEG	FDIV	JS	FSUBRP	STD	JLE	CMOVB
20	SETLE	IMUL	CMOVS	JNZ	SETZ	JNS	FSTP	FXAM
21	FDIVP	LDMXCSR	FSUB	SETNL	FLDZ	OR	SETZ	SUBPS

[a] PrincipalComponents listed are unranked

To achieve an overall ranking for OpCode predictor importance the top 21 attributes selected by the first seven evaluation methods in Table 5-17 have been assigned a weight from 21 to 1, where 21 represents the highest rank, down to 1 for the lowest. The overall ranking is provided in Table 22.

The two opcodes with the highest density, MOV (32.45%) and PUSH (13.49%) do not have good predictive importance due to their prevalence in both ransomware and benign samples. Table 4-16 illustrates that some of the more infrequent Opcodes such as SETBE and FIDIV are better indicators of ransomware. This partly agrees with Bilar's conclusion that less frequent opcodes make better indicators of malware than the most frequent opcodes [21].

5 Conclusion

This research demonstrated that the analysis of CPU instructions (opcodes) can be used to differentiate between crypto-ransomware and goodware with high precision.

As per the results presented in this chapter a high precision (>95%) rate has been achieved for the 2-class model using all four kernel options, the 6-class model with

Table 22 Overall ranking for opcode predictor importance

Overall ranking	Opcode	Description [56]	Histogram density %	Histogram density rank/443
1	FDIVP	Divide, store result and pop the register stack	0.002	140
2	AND	Logical AND	1.201	15
3	SETLE	Set byte if less or equal	0.014	69
4	XCHG	Exchange Register/Memory with Register	0.038	54
5	SETNBE	Set byte if not below or equal	0.001	145
6	SETNLE	Set byte if not less or equal	0.058	45
7	JB	Jump short if below	0.243	28
8	FILD	Load Integer	0.035	56
9	JLE	Jump short if less or equal	0.244	27
10	POP	Pop a Value from the Stack	4.01	5
11	CALL	Call Procedure	7.881	3
12	FSUB	Subtract	0.025	62
13	FMUL	Multiply	0.055	46
14	MUL	Unsigned Multiply	0.024	63
15	SETBE	Set byte if below or equal	0.001	184
16	FISTP	Store Integer	0.008	88
17	FSUBRP	Reverse Subtract	0.002	138
18	INC	Increment by 1	0.857	17
19	FIDIV	Divide	0.006	162
20	FSTSW	Store x87 FPU Status Word	0.008	86
21	JA	Jump short if above	0.133	36

the PUK kernel, and 6 out of 8 feature reduction models (with the remaining two at 94.2%).

It has also been demonstrated that the PUK kernel is the simplest kernel to use for the SMO classifier as it is flexible and self-optimising, achieving 100% precision with no tuning required. The linear, polynomial and Gaussian kernels can also achieve 100% precision when optimised. For all other models (6-class and feature reduction) the PUK kernel achieved the highest precision using the default settings.

By employing the chosen methodology of static analysis, opcode extraction and density histogram representation, a Support Vector Machine can be trained to differentiate between two classes (crypto-ransomware and goodware) with 100% precision when using all kernel selections, and between six classes (five crypto-ransomware families and one goodware) with 96.5% precision (96.7% accuracy) using the PUK kernel. Both levels of precision exceeded the 95% target set in the objectives. Moreover, when differentiating between ransomware and goodware, feature reduction from 443 extracted opcodes down to 180 opcodes can be achieved using the CorrelationAttributeEval filter with no loss of precision. Feature reduction from 443 to 10 opcodes can be achieved using the CFSSubsetEval filter, but with a lower precision of 94.2%.

There is scope to extend and develop this research. The dataset can be extended to include other crypto-ransomware families such as WannaCry or similar advanced "ransomworms" [57] ; a reduced, optimum feature extraction process can be developed by extracting only the groups of opcodes identified by the attribute selection evaluators; dynamic runtime extraction of opcodes with time-based features can be applied to demonstrate real-time application as a crypto-ransomware threat detection method.

Acknowledgements The authors would like to Virus Total for providing access to their Intelligence platform to assist with the dataset creation, and Ransomware Tracker for being an invaluable resource for current ransomware threat detection.

References

1. McAfee Labs, 'McAfee Labs Threats Report', *McAfee Labs Threat. Rep.*, no. December, pp. 1–52, 2016.
2. D. O'Brien, 'Special Report: Ransomware and Businesses 2016', *Symantec Corp*, pp. 1–30, 2016.
3. CERT UK, 'Is ransomware still a threat ?', 2016.
4. Bleeping Computer, 'Criminals earn $195K in July with Cerber Ransomware Affiliate Scheme', 2016. [Online]. Available: https://www.bleepingcomputer.com/news/security/criminals-earn-195k-in-july-with-cerber-ransomware-affiliate-scheme/. [Accessed: 28-Sep-2017].
5. Europol, 'INTERNET ORGANISED CRIME THREAT ASSESSMENT (IOCTA) 2017', 2017.
6. Cybersecurity Insiders, '2017 Ransomware Report', 2017.
7. Symantec Official Blog, 'What you need to know about the WannaCry Ransomware | Symantec Connect Community', 2017. [Online]. Available: https://www.symantec.com/connect/blogs/what-you-need-know-about-wannacry-ransomware. [Accessed: 28-Sep-2017].
8. Symantec Official Blog, 'Petya ransomware outbreak: Here's what you need to know|Symantec Connect Community', 2017. [Online]. Available: https://www.symantec.com/connect/blogs/petya-ransomware-outbreak-here-s-what-you-need-know. [Accessed: 28-Sep-2017].
9. Darktrace, 'Darktrace|Technology', 2016. [Online]. Available: https://www.darktrace.com/technology/#machine-learning. [Accessed: 31-Mar-2017].
10. RansomFlare, 'MWR's ransomware prevention and response service', 2017. [Online]. Available: https://www.mwrinfosecurity.com/work/practice-areas/investigations-and-incident-response/ransomware-prevention-and-response-service. [Accessed: 28-Sep-2017].
11. Hamed Haddad Pajouh, A. Dehghantanha, R. Khayami, and K.-K. R. Choo, 'Intelligent OS X Malware Threat Detection', *J. Comput. Virol. Hacking Tech.*, 2017.
12. N. Milosevic, A. Dehghantanha, and K.-K. R. Choo, 'Machine learning aided Android malware classification', *Comput. Electr. Eng.*, vol. 61, pp. 266–274, Jul. 2017.
13. A. Azmoodeh, A. Dehghantanha, and K. K. R. Choo, 'Robust Malware Detection for Internet Of (Battlefield) Things Devices Using Deep Eigenspace Learning', *IEEE Trans. Sustain. Comput.*, 2017.
14. DARK Reading, 'The Growth And Growth Of Ransomware', *5 Ways The Cyber-Threat Landscape Shifted In 2016*, 2016. [Online]. Available: https://www.darkreading.com/threat-intelligence/5-ways-the-cyber-threat-landscape-shifted-in-2016/d/d-id/1327715?image_number=4. [Accessed: 01-Oct-2017].
15. I. Firdausi, C. Lim, A. Erwin, and a. S. Nugroho, 'Analysis of Machine learning Techniques Used in Behavior-Based Malware Detection', *Adv. Comput. Control Telecommun. Technol. (ACT), 2010 Second Int. Conf.*, pp. 10–12, 2010.

16. K. Rieck, P. Trinius, C. Willems, and T. Holz, 'Automatic Analysis of Malware Behavior Using Machine Learning', *J. Comput. Secur.*, vol. 19, no. 4, pp. 639–668, 2011.
17. M. Egele, T. Scholte, E. Kirda, and C. Kruegel, 'A survey on automated dynamic malware-analysis techniques and tools', *ACM Comput. Surv.*, vol. 44, no. 2, pp. 1–42, 2012.
18. J. Landage and M. Wankhade, 'Malware and Malware Detection Techniques: A Survey', *Int. J. Eng. Res. . . .*, vol. 2, no. 12, pp. 61–68, 2013.
19. R. Islam, R. Tian, L. M. Batten, and S. Versteeg, 'Classification of malware based on integrated static and dynamic features', *J. Netw. Comput. Appl.*, vol. 36, no. 2, pp. 646–656, Mar. 2013.
20. E. Gandotra, D. Bansal, and S. Sofat, 'Tools & Techniques for Malware Analysis and Classification', *Int. J. NEXT-GENERATION Comput.*, vol. 7, no. 3, pp. 176–197, Nov. 2016.
21. D. Bilar, 'Opcodes as predictor for malware', *Int. J. Electron. Secur. Digit. Forensics*, vol. 1, no. 2, p. 156, 2007.
22. D. Bilar and D. Bilar, 'Callgraph properties of executables', *AI Commun.*, vol. 20, no. August, p. 12, 2007.
23. Y. Ding, W. Dai, S. Yan, and Y. Zhang, 'Control flow-based opcode behavior analysis for Malware detection', *Comput. Secur.*, vol. 44, pp. 65–74, Jul. 2014.
24. Z. Zhao, J. Wang, and J. Bai, 'Malware detection method based on the control-flow construct feature of software', *IET Inf. Secur.*, vol. 8, no. 1, pp. 18–24, Jan. 2014.
25. S. Cesare, Y. Xiang, and W. Zhou, 'Control Flow-Based Malware Variant Detection', *IEEE Trans. DEPENDABLE Secur. Comput.*, vol. 11, no. 4, pp. 304–317, 2014.
26. B. B. Rad, M. Masrom, and S. Ibrahim, 'Opcodes Histogram for Classifying Metamorphic Portable Executables Malware', in *2012 INTERNATIONAL CONFERENCE ON E-LEARNING AND E-TECHNOLOGIES IN EDUCATION (ICEEE)*, 2012, pp. 209–213.
27. P. O'Kane, S. Sezer, K. McLaughlin, and E. G. Im, 'SVM Training phase reduction using dataset feature filtering for malware detection', *IEEE Trans. Inf. Forensics Secur.*, vol. 8, no. 3, pp. 500–509, 2013.
28. C.-T. Lin, N.-J. Wang, H. Xia, and C. Eckert, 'Feature Selection and Extraction for Malware Classification', *J. Inf. Sci. Eng.*, vol. 31, no. 3, pp. 965–992, May 2015.
29. B. M. Khammas, A. Monemi, J. S. Bassi, I. Ismail, S. M. Nor, and M. N. Marsono, 'FEATURE SELECTION AND MACHINE LEARNING CLASSIFICATION FOR MALWARE DETECTION', *J. Teknol.*, vol. 77, no. 1, Nov. 2015.
30. E. G. Park, Jeong Been; Han, Kyung Soo; Kim, Tae Gune; Im, 'A Study on Selecting Key Opcodes for Malware Classification and Its Usefulness', *Korean Inst. Inf. Sci. Eng.*, vol. Volume 42, no. Issue 5, pp. 558–565, 2015.
31. C. T. D. Lo, O. Pablo, and C. Carlos, 'Feature Selection and Improving Classification Performance for Malware Detection', in *PROCEEDINGS OF 2016 IEEE INTERNATIONAL CONFERENCES ON BIG DATA AND CLOUD COMPUTING (BDCLOUD 2016) SOCIAL COMPUTING AND NETWORKING (SOCIALCOM 2016) SUSTAINABLE COMPUTING AND COMMUNICATIONS (SUSTAINCOM 2016) (BDCLOUD-SOCIALCOM-SUSTAINCOM 2016)*, 2016, pp. 560–566.
32. D. Sgandurra, L. Muñoz-González, R. Mohsen, and E. C. Lupu, 'Automated Dynamic Analysis of Ransomware: Benefits, Limitations and use for Detection', no. September, 2016.
33. A. Kharaz, S. Arshad, C. Mulliner, W. Robertson, and E. Kirda, 'UNVEIL: A Large-Scale, Automated Approach to Detecting Ransomware', *Usenix Secur.*, pp. 757–772, 2016.
34. K. Cabaj, P. Gawkowski, K. Grochowski, and D. Osojca, 'Network activity analysis of CryptoWall ransomware', pp. 91–11, 2015.
35. J. Baldwin, O. M. K. Alhawi, and A. Dehghantanha, 'Leveraging Machine Learning Techniques for Windows Ransomware Network Traffic Detection', 2017.
36. M. M. Ahmadian and H. R. Shahriari, '2entFOX: A framework for high survivable ransomwares detection', *2016 13th Int. Iran. Soc. Cryptol. Conf. Inf. Secur. Cryptol.*, pp. 79–84, 2016.
37. S. Homayoun, A. Dehghantanha, M. Ahmadzadeh, S. Hashemi, and R. Khayami, 'Know Abnormal, Find Evil: Frequent Pattern Mining for Ransomware Threat Hunting and Intelligence', *IEEE Trans. Emerg. Top. Comput.*, vol. 6750, no. c, pp. 1–1, 2017.

38. K. K. R. Azmoodeh, Amin; Dehghantanha, Ali; Conti, Mauro; Choo, 'Detecting Crypto Ransomware in IoT Networks Based On Energy Consumption Footprint', *J. Ambient Intell. Humaniz. Comput.*, vol. 0, no. 0, p. 0, 2017.
39. Ransomware Tracker, 'Tracker | Ransomware Tracker', 2016. [Online]. Available: https://ransomwaretracker.abuse.ch/tracker/. [Accessed: 04-Jan-2017].
40. VirusTotal, 'Free Online Virus, Malware and URL Scanner'. 2014.
41. PortableApps.com, 'Portable software for USB, portable, and cloud drives', 2017. [Online]. Available: https://portableapps.com/. [Accessed: 06-Sep-2017].
42. C. Rossow *et al.*, 'Prudent practices for designing malware experiments: Status quo and outlook', *Proc. - IEEE Symp. Secur. Priv.*, no. May, pp. 65–79, 2012.
43. AV-TEST, 'Test antivirus software for Windows 10 - June 2017 | AV-TEST', 2017. [Online]. Available: https://www.av-test.org/en/antivirus/business-windows-client/. [Accessed: 06-Sep-2017].
44. The-interweb.com/serendipity, 'InstructionCounter plugin for IDA Pro', 2017. [Online]. Available: http://www.the-interweb.com/serendipity/index.php?/archives/57-InstructionCounter-plugin-for-IDA-Pro.html. [Accessed: 06-Sep-2017].
45. Hex-Rays, 'IDA Support: Evaluation Version', 2017. [Online]. Available: https://www.hex-rays.com/products/ida/support/download_demo.shtml. [Accessed: 06-Sep-2017].
46. C.-J. L. Chih-Wei Hsu, Chih-Chung Chang, 'A Practical Guide to Support Vector Classification', *BJU Int.*, vol. 101, no. 1, pp. 1396–400, 2008.
47. University of Waikato, 'Weka 3 - Data Mining with Open Source Machine Learning Software in Java', 2016. [Online]. Available: http://www.cs.waikato.ac.nz/ml/weka/. [Accessed: 31-Mar-2017].
48. V. N. Vapnik, 'The Nature of Statistical Learning Theory', *Springer*, vol. 8. p. 188, 1995.
49. D. T. Larose, *Discovering knowledge in data: an introduction to data mining*, vol. 1st. 2005.
50. A. G. Karegowda, A. S. Manjunath, and M. A. Jayaram, 'Comparative Study of Attribute Selection Using Gain Ratio and Correlation Based Feature Selection', *Int. J. Inf. Technol. Knowl. Manag.*, vol. 2, no. 2, pp. 271–277, 2010.
51. I. H. Witten and E. Frank, *Data Mining: Practical machine learning tools and techniques*. 2005.
52. R. R. Bouckaert *et al.*, 'WEKA Manual for Version 3-8-1', *Univ. Waikato*, p. 341, 2016.
53. Lenny Zeltser, 'Using VMware for Malware Analysis'. [Online]. Available: https://zeltser.com/vmware-malware-analysis/. [Accessed: 26-Sep-2017].
54. I. H. Witten, E. Frank, and M. a Hall, *Data Mining: Practical Machine Learning Tools and Techniques (Google eBook)*. 2011.
55. X. Xu and X. Wang, 'An Adaptive Network Intrusion Detection Method Based on PCA and Support Vector Machines', in *Advanced Data Mining and Applications*, 2005, pp. 696–703.
56. F. Cloutier, 'x86 Instruction Set Reference', 2014. [Online]. Available: http://www.felixcloutier.com/x86/. [Accessed: 21-Sep-2017].
57. Sergei Shevchenko and Adrian Nish, 'BAE Systems Threat Research Blog: WanaCrypt0r Ransomworm', 2017. [Online]. Available: http://baesystemsai.blogspot.co.uk/2017/05/wanacrypt0r-ransomworm.html. [Accessed: 02-Oct-2017].

BoTShark: A Deep Learning Approach for Botnet Traffic Detection

Sajad Homayoun, Marzieh Ahmadzadeh, Sattar Hashemi, Ali Dehghantanha, and Raouf Khayami

Abstract While botnets have been extensively studied, bot malware is constantly advancing and seeking to exploit new attack vectors and circumvent existing measures. Existing intrusion detection systems are unlikely to be effective countering advanced techniques deployed in recent botnets. This chapter proposes a deep learning-based botnet traffic analyser called Botnet Traffic Shark (BoTShark). BoTShark uses only network transactions and is independent of deep packet inspection technique; thus, avoiding inherent limitations such as the inability to deal with encrypted payloads. This also allows us to identify correlations between original features and extract new features in every layer of an Autoencoder or a Convolutional Neural Networks (CNNs) in a cascading manner. Moreover, we utilise a Softmax classifier as the predictor to detect malicious traffics efficiently.

Keywords Botnet · Intrusion detection · Network flows · Deep learning · Autoencoder · CNNs

S. Homayoun · M. Ahmadzadeh · R. Khayami
Department of Computer Engineering and Information Technology, Shiraz University of Technology, Shiraz, Iran
e-mail: S.Homayoun@sutech.ac.ir; Ahmadzadeh@sutech.ac.ir; Khayami@sutech.ac.ir

S. Hashemi
Department of Computer Engineering, Shiraz University, Shiraz, Iran
e-mail: s_hashemi@shirazu.ac.ir

A. Dehghantanha (✉)
Department of Computer Science, University of Sheffield, Sheffield, UK
e-mail: A.Dehghantanha@sheffield.ac.uk

© Springer International Publishing AG, part of Springer Nature 2018
A. Dehghantanha et al. (eds.), *Cyber Threat Intelligence*, Advances in Information Security 70, https://doi.org/10.1007/978-3-319-73951-9_7

137

1 Introduction

Cybercriminals are becoming the main potential threat to all systems connected to the Internet [1]. Malware attacks are increasing while the total number of unique malwares reached to about 600 million in 2016 tripled from 2013 [2]. A botnet is a network of hosts connected to the Internet that is under control of one or more master machine(s) that coordinates each and every bot malicious activities [3, 4]. Botnets have been heavily used to carry different cyber attacks ranging from information espionage, and click-fraud to malware distribution and Distributed Denial of Services (DDoS) [5]. The owner (master) of a botnet can control the botnet using command and control (C&C) software to manage bot clients.

Botnets are implemented in four main topologies namely Star, Multi-Server, Hierarchical and Peer-to-Peer (P2P) [6, 7]. Star topology facilitates a fast and accurate communication between bot nodes in a simple manner but suffers from a single point of failure when spreads commands across the network [7]. Internet Relay Chat (IRC) based botnets are the best example of star C&C [8]. Multi-Server protocol tackles the problem of single point of failure by using several servers as master nodes [7], but its hierarchical structure requires more setup time but allows sharing of the infrastructure. P2P is the most advanced topology of botnets in which every node may serve as a master or client as needed [9]. Although P2P topology has the most latency of convergence but since hides the presence of master nodes it make it more difficult to trace back botnet operation [10]. Due to the potential power and stealthiness of P2P botnets, it is a favorable option among bot masters C&C channels [11, 12]. In this chapter, botnets with one of a few central servers are considered as centralized topology, while Peer-to-Peer botnets is considered as decentralized topology.

While majority of existing research [10, 13–15] are depending on a single topology for botnet detection, this chapter utilizes deep learning to detect botnet traffics independently of underlying botnet architecture. The main contribution of this research is adopting two deep learning techniques namely *Autoencoders* and *Convolutional Neural Networks (CNNs)* to detect malicious botnet traffics. We propose two detection models based on deep learning to eliminate dependency of detection systems to primary features achieved by NetFlow extractor tools. To the best of our knowledge, this is among very first attempts to employ deep learning in botnet detection, therefore this chapter opens new insights in this field. Our models have the capability of detecting malicious traffics from botnets of two common topologies namely centralized and decentralized botnets. It is worth pointing out that *BoTShark* does not pre-filter any primary extracted features and does not need experts' knowledge in selecting proper features to extract features automatically. In other words, *BoTShark* takes samples with all raw features and generates discriminative features for classifying botnets traffics from normal traffics. *BoTShark* is tested on ISCX Botnet Dataset [16] that is a well-known research dataset in the field of botnet detection.

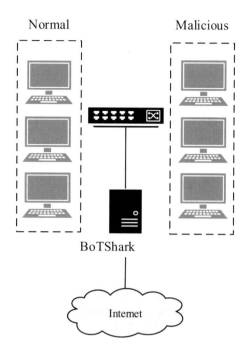

Figure 1 shows the network architecture considered in this chapter. The network includes both malicious and non-malicious hosts, and *BoTShark* works on the traffics generated by systems connected to the Internet.

The remainder of this chapter is organized as follows. Section 2 reviews some related research. Section 3 gives a brief background on deep Autoencoders and CNNs. Section 4 explains dataset and primary features extracted from network flows. We describe *BoTShark* for detecting botnets traffics in Sect. 5 while Sect. 6 evaluates *BoTShark* models. Finally, Sect. 7 concludes the chapter.

2   Related Work

Botnet is becoming a dominant tool for cybercriminals to distribute new malwares between a large scale of infected host or attacking a target by taking the advantage of cooperative characteristic of the network [17]. The growth in botnet sizes is the main motivation of researches on botnet detection [18]. In the past decade, many researchers attempted to propose a model for detecting bot infected hosts [10, 13, 19] or their malicious network traffics [14, 20, 21]. Most bot host detection systems are relying on profile of each host including their behaviour during a period of time [10] e.g. 6 h [22] or 10 min [23]. BotHunter [24] as one of the earliest botnet behaviour detection system attempts to correlate SNORT [25] generated alarms to behaviour of an individual host. However, it works by inspecting payload of packets that is not useful against botnets that benefits cryptography in their connections. BotMiner [13] considers group behaviours of individual bots within the same botnet.

On the other hand, some researches focused on detecting malicious botnet traffics originating from internal hosts inside a LAN based on machine learning techniques to predict new NetFlows [14, 15, 20, 26, 27]. Using of machine learning techniques is more common in detecting botnets malicious traffics. A two-phase system consisting of feature extraction phase and machine learning phase is proposed in [20] to detect botnet C&C traffic of IRC based botnets by creating a Bayesian network classifier with 90% detection rate and 15.4% false positive rate that is high. Some works focused on DNS requests [26] and achieved accuracy of 92.5% in detecting malicious DNS requests. However, relying on DNS requests makes the detection system exclusive to botnets that benefits DNS for finding their C&C servers (most centralized botnets). A system is proposed for detecting P2P traffics by assuming that the traffics generated by normal user fluctuate greatly and is different to P2P bots [15]. The system in [15] achieved 98% of detection rate while the false positive rate is still high (30%).

Working on a set of features is a very common approach in the literature of botnet detection while this approach makes the detection systems dependent on the studied network traffics. The features can be suggested by the experts [14, 20, 26, 27] or can be selected by feature selection algorithms [28, 29]. ISOT [30] and ISCX [16] are two well-known datasets in the literature of botnet detection. Zhao et al. [14] attempted to detect malicious traffics by employing a decision tree using the Reduced Error Pruning algorithm (REPTree) and achieved 98.3% true positive rate in detecting malicious traffics, where the model extracts feature vectors for a time window of 60 s and creates a decision tree to classify malicious and non-malicious traffics. However, a research proved that the model proposed in [14] is biased to the dataset [28]. A new stepwise greedy feature selection algorithm for using in botnet traffic detection proposed in [28] that selects best features to differentiate botnet traffics. However, the algorithm works in a greedy manner and it does not consider different permutation of features. Therefore, it is likely to remove valuable feature information. Recently, an approach for detecting botnet traffics based on NetFlows characteristics is proposed [27] that selects best features according to experts analysis on botnets behaviours, where several datasets of botnet traffics are merged to make a dataset for evaluating proposed model. However, combining different datasets requires considering special methods e.g. overlay methods [31] while the details of combining datasets are not described.

Although there are many papers published on detecting bot infected machines or botnet malicious traffics, few models have the capability of detecting malicious traffics independent of botnets topologies. In other words, almost all proposed methods worked on botnets within the same topologies. For example, a model that is proposed to detect decentralized P2P botnets is unable to detect centralized IRC botnet traffics. This chapter aims at differentiating botnet traffics from benign traffics in both topologies.

3 Background: Deep Learning

Deep Learning is a sub field of machine learning that studies artificial neural networks and related machine learning algorithms that contain more than one hidden layer. Since we are using Autoencoders and CNNs, we give a brief background in the following subsections.

3.1 Autoencoders

Artificial Neural Networks (ANN) is one of the popular machine learning techniques that is used for any condition and has the ability of learning problems structure automatically. The learning method in ANN is usually back-propagation in which the samples are forwarded and the output of network is compared with the desired target. Then the error is calculated according to this difference and the weights are tuned [32].

An Autoencoder is similar to a neural network where the output is regarded as the input and supposes that the hidden layer must reconstruct the initial information with the least possible amount of distortion. Then, Autoencoders are trained to reconstruct their own inputs X instead of being trained to predict Y. An Autoencoder tries to learn a function $h_{(W,b)}(x) \cong x$ by learning an approximation to the identity function. As Fig. 2 shows, an Autoencoder always consists of two parts, the encoder and the decoder, which can be a transition between ϕ and ρ such that $\phi : X \rightarrow F$ and $\rho : F \rightarrow X$ where F is the intermediate representation of sample X. An Autoencoder attempts to minimize reconstruction error based on Eq. (1).

$$argmin_{\phi}, \rho \|X - (\rho \circ \phi)X\|^2 \tag{1}$$

Fig. 2 Stages of an autoencoder that learns the input features in another space

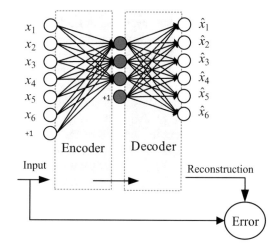

Suppose the dataset only includes a set of unlabeled training examples $X = \{x^{(1)}, x^{(2)}, x^{(3)}, \ldots, x^{(m)}\}$, where $x^{(i)} \in R^d$. The aim of an Autoencoder is to learn a representation (encoding) for a set of data, typically for the purpose of dimensionality reduction. Equation (2) shows the hidden layer while Eq. (3) presents the reconstruction from the hidden unit.

$$z = \sigma_1(W^T X + b) \tag{2}$$

$$X' = \sigma_2(Wz + b') \tag{3}$$

The loss function is as Eq. (4) where W and W^T are the transform matrices.

$$L(X, X') = \|X - X'\|^2 = \|X - \sigma_2(W(\sigma_1(W^T X + b)) + b')\|^2 \tag{4}$$

A simple Autoencoder often ends up learning a low-dimensional representation very similar to PCAs and a subspace is learned for the representation of data. If a nonlinear function is exerted in each layer, the nonlinearity is considered and a submanifold is finally extracted that benefits the separability of data points; then in the new space the discrimination procedure is more effective.

3.2 Convolutional Neural Network (CNN)

CNN owes its inception to a well-known research paper [33]. CNNs are usually applied to image but it is also applicable in spam detection, and topic classification, and studies are growing to use CNNs [34].

A CNN consists of different layers that each layer performs a different function on their inputs. Convolution layer, pooling layer and non-linear layer are three layers that are very common in the literature and are usually stacked sequentially many times based on the application [35].

The convolutional layer contains a filter as a sliding window to generate new feature maps. In other words, each filter will generate a new feature set and the model applies different filters to the inputs. The pooling layer uses a kind of filter to summarize the generated feature maps during the previous layer. As convolution explores the correlation between different features, the pooling layer extracts the existing correlation in any parts of the input. There are a few functions namely max pooling, L2-Norm pooling and average pooling that can be used in pooling layer. Since the operations in the layers of convolution and pooling are linear, a non-linear layer such as tanh is used to make the model efficient for non-linear cases.

Assume $X = \{x_1, \ldots, x_n\}$ as the input vector where x_f is value of feature f. If a filter W with M_F weights is applied to the input vector X then Z_i' is the output of convolution layer and is calculated by Eq. (5) for each $i' \in \{1, \ldots, |X| - M_F + 1\}$ where $|X|$ is size of vector X.

$$Z_{i'} = \sum_{i=1}^{M_F}(X_{i'+i-1}W_{M_F-i+1}) \tag{5}$$

Equation (5) considers applying a filter on the input data and there are usually more than one filter with different weights. So Eq. (5) can be applied individually for each filter. Therefore, using of convolution layer on an input vector creates feature maps as its output.

Now the generated feature maps can be fed as the input of max pooling layer to generate reduced feature maps. Using of max pooling is very common in the literature of CNNs [36]. Max pooling outputs y_i' as the maximum value of the features under the swapping filter and is calculated by Eq. (6).

$$y_{i'} = \max_{i \in \Omega(i')} (x_i) \tag{6}$$

where $\Omega(i')$ is the set of feature values starting with i' feature value located under the swapping filter.

Finally, the non-linearity is applied using tanh according to Eq. (7).

$$\tanh x = \frac{1 - e^{2x}}{1 + e^{2x}} \tag{7}$$

4   Data Collection and Primary Feature Extraction

This chapter uses network traffics from ISCX [16] that is created by using one of the most popular overlay methodology introduced in [31] to combine different datasets. The creators of ISCX claims that their dataset has all three requirements of a validated dataset: generality, realism and representativeness. ISCX dataset includes 44.97% of malicious flows from 16 different botnet flows and contains botnet traffics from both centralized and decentralized topologies as well as normal traffics.

This chapter works on network flows extracted from network traffics that might be in form of packet capture (PCAP) files or live traffics. A NetFlow is a set of fields, namely a record, that gives some information about a connection between source and destination (source/destination address, ports etc.). PCAP consists of an Application Programming Interface (API) for capturing network traffic and store them into a file.

This chapter considers all *TCP* and *UDP* NetFlows into a dataset of NetFlows. There are a few tools for extracting NetFlows from network traffics. Argus [37] is a powerful flow exporter that is popular among researchers and is able to extract features from different aspects: byte-based (extracted features based on bytes in a flow e.g. byte sent/received), time-based (features depend on time e.g. inter-packet arrival time) and packet-based features (e.g. total number of packets in a flow).

Table 1 List of features extracted by Argus

Feature	Description
SrcAddr	Source IP address
DstAddr	Destination IP address
Sport	Source port
Dport	Destination port
Proto	Connection protocol (udp, tcp, icmp, igmp etc.)
Dir	Source → Destination, Source ← Destination, Source ↔ Destination
Dur	Record total duration (time between flow start time and flow end time)
TotPkts	Total transaction packet count
SrcPkts	Source → destination packet count
DstPkts	Destination → source packet count
SIntPkt	Source inter-packet arrival time (mSec)
SIntPktIdl	Source idle inter-packet arrival time (mSec)
DIntPkt	Destination inter-packet arrival time (mSec)
DIntPktIdl	Destination idle inter-packet arrival time (mSec)
TotBytes	Total transaction bytes exchanged between source and destination
SrcBytes	Source → destination transaction bytes
DstBytes	Destination → source transaction bytes
sPktSz	Source active interpacket arrival time (mSec)
dPktSz	Destination active interpacket arrival time (mSec)
sMeanPktSz	Mean of the flow packet size transmitted by the source (initiator)
dMeanPktSz	Mean of the flow packet size transmitted by the destination (target)
sMinPktSz	Minimum packet size for traffic transmitted by the source
dMinPktSz	Minimum packet size for traffic transmitted by the destination
sMaxPktSz	Maximum packet size for traffic transmitted by the source
dMaxPktSz	Maximum packet size for traffic transmitted by the destination
Load	Bits per second
SrcLoad	Source bits per second
DstLoad	Destination bits per second
Rate	Packets per second
SrcRate	Source packets per second
DstRate	Destination packets per second

Argus has the capability of extracting 120 features for each connection. However, some features are not useful in the area of botnet detection because they are all null or zero (for example there are several features special to MPLS networks that basically are not relevant to the considered LAN topology). Table 1 shows extracted features by Argus after removing irrelevant features (primary feature selection).

This chapter does not remove any features from the feature set and works on all features of Table 1 (except SrcAddr, DstAddr, Sport and Dport, because the use of these features became inefficient when data comes from different networks [38]). Since Autoencoders and CNNs need continuous features, two categorical features Dir and Proto are converted to continues aspect e.g. 1 and 2 which could handle in the network. The proposed technique feeds feature vectors for each NetFlow to the learning task. This chapter considers two labels (malicious and non-malicious) for each NetFlow and feeds dataset to *BoTShark*.

5 Proposed BoTShark

We propose *BoTShark* with two deep structures namely *BoTShark-SA* that applies stacked Autoencoders to extract new features for distinguishing malicious and benign network flows and *BoTShark-CNN* which takes the advantage of CNNs to train a classifier for detecting malicious traffics.

5.1 BoTShark-SA: Using Stacked Autoencoders

Figure 3 shows *BoTShark-SA* architecture to learn a classifier that detects malicious NetFlows in a deep structure and to classify new NetFlows as malicious or non-malicious. Since selecting proper features is a big challenge in most machine learning based botnet detection systems [28], *BoTShark-SA* benefits the stacked Autoencoders depicted in Fig. 4. The dataset consists of all unlabeled NetFlows with primary features set $\{f_1, \ldots, f_d\}$ from Sect. 4 is fed to the stacked structure, where d is the dimensionality of data. In the field of deep learning, multiple Autoencoders make an stacked structure to produce the best final denoised output and minimize reconstruction error. This combination learns to extract valuable features in a stepwise manner without employing any particular hand-made feature selection.

Feature Extraction in Fig. 3 extracts efficient features from all given data. As the original number of features are not too much, two layers of Autoencoders are sufficient (see Fig. 4). In the first step of Fig. 4 original feature set is encoded into d_1 features $\{f_1, \ldots, f_{d_1}\}$ to enter the next step. The second Autoencoder receives the output from previous step and extract d_2 features $\{f_1, \ldots, f_{d_2}\}$. The output of layer2 from the second Autoencoder is considered as the final extracted features.

All NetFlows that are now in a new representation, with their corresponding labels provide inputs for training a classifier model to distinguish malicious and non-malicious NetFlows. As the main purpose of deep networks is to extract best features, any classifier can be used in this phase. This chapter input a vector of 27×1 to the first Autoencoder and feed its 20×1 output to the second Autoencoder to extract final ten features (see Fig. 4).

Softmax is a well-known classifier that is using in neural networks [39], it assigns a probability to each class based on the extracted features received from the previous layer to classify the instances. If there are only two classes, *Softmax* acts like a logistic regression which uses a logistic function to assign a probability to instances according to each class. The mentioned function is as Eq. (8).

Fig. 3 BoTShark-SA
architecture to extract
features and train the
classifier

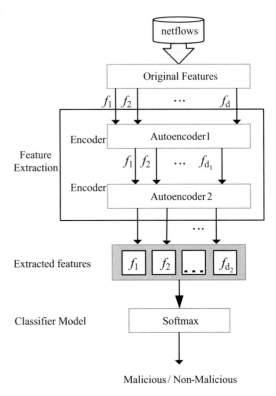

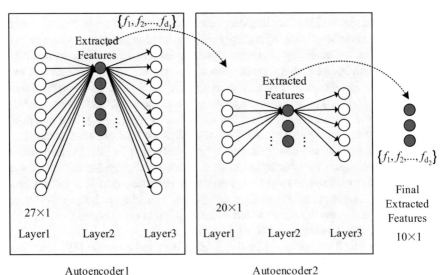

Fig. 4 Stacked Autoencoders that used for extracting features

$$\sigma(z)_j = \frac{e^{z_j}}{\sum_{k=1}^{K} e^{z_k}} ; for j = 1, \ldots, K \qquad (8)$$

where z is considered as the k-dimensional vector of each sample. Although this chapter is involved with two classes (malicious and non-malicious), *Softmax* can handle multiple classes and the proposed method has the ability to expand to more number of classes by *Softmax*.

5.2 SocialBoTShrak-CNN: Using CNNs

Figure 5 depicts our proposed architecture for training a classifier that has the capability of distinguishing malicious traffics. We input a NetFlow as a vector with 27 extracted features to a CNN for training and feeding calculated weights to a fully connected network with a hidden layer to prepare final inputs for *Softmax* to create final classifier.

Fig. 5 BoTShark-CNN architecture to train the classifier

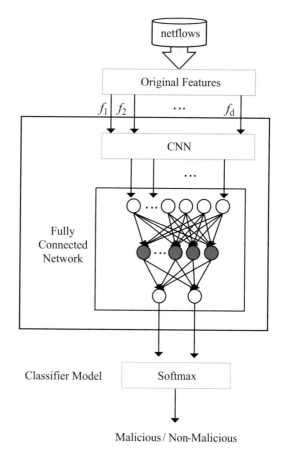

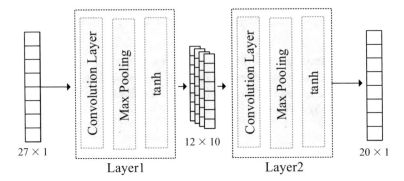

Fig. 6 Implemented architecture for CNNs

We designed a CNN consisting of two layers with three sub-layers of temporal convolution, max pooling and a non-linear function tanh (see Fig. 6). At first all weights are initialized randomly with values between -1 and $+1$ and the structure in Fig. 6 learns appropriate weights automatically for further steps of Fig. 5.

The convolution sub-layer in the first layer of Fig. 6 consists of 10 filters with 4 weights in each filter. This convolution sub-layer turns the 27×1 input vector into 10 feature maps of length 24. These feature maps are then fed to the max pooling sub-layer with filter of width 2 to be converted to 10 feature maps of length 12. After applying tanh sub-layer, we will have feature maps with size of 12×10 given to the second layer. The second layer in its convolution sub-layer applies 5 filters of size 4 that generates 5 feature maps of size 9. Max pooling sub-layer with the filter of size 2 is applied to the feature maps that outputs 5 feature maps of size 4. tanh sub-layer as the final sub-layer is applied to 4×5 feature maps. Finally, these 5 vectors are concatenated to form a 1-D vector of size 20.

We feed our final 20 features to a fully connected neural network with one hidden layer of ten neurons and two outputs in which the neurons apply tanh function. A *Softmax* uses two outputs from the fully connected network to train the final classifier with the capability of detecting malicious network traffics.

6   Evaluation

We are using widely accepted criteria namely True Positive Rate (TPR) and False Positive Rate (FPR) to evaluate our model [40–42]. TPR is reflecting the proportion of positives that are correctly identified and FPR shows the ratio between the number of negative labels wrongly identified as positive. We will also report Receiver Operating Characteristic (ROC) that is a potentially powerful metric for comparison of different classifiers, because it is invariant against skewness of classes in the dataset. In a ROC curve the true positive ratio is plotted in function of the false positive ratio for different thresholds.

We apply *BoTShark* to ISCX botnet dataset to evaluate the performance of the binary classifier in predicting new NetFlows. The proposed technique feeds feature vectors for each NetFlow to the learning task. This chapter considers two labels (malicious and non-malicious) for each NetFlow and feed dataset to *BoTShark*. In this experiment 70% of data is considered as training and the rest 30% for testing the final classifier. *BoTShark-SA* is implemented in Matlab 2015b and *BoTShark-CNN* is implemented using Torch7 framework for deep learning networks and run on a system with 8 GB of RAM and Core i5 of 8 cores of 4 GHz CPU. We set the iteration count of both *BoTShark-SA* and *BoTShark-CNN* to 400 iterations.

Table 2 reflects the performance achieved by lunching *BoTShark* on ISCX dataset. It is demonstrated that *BoTShark-SA* and *BoTShark-CNN* achieved $TPR \geq$ 0.91 on ISCX datasets. *BoTShark* works on all primary features and no feature is filtered by experts. *BoTShark-SA* achieved TPR of 0.91 and its false positive ratio is 0.15 and *BoTShark-CNN* achieved higher detection ratio (0.92).

Figure 7 depicts the ROC diagrams of *BoTShark-SA* and *BoTShark-CNN*. The diagram shows True Positive Rate (X-Axis) against False Positive Rate (Y-Axis) to demonstrate the amount of false positives for achieving a specified true positives. The ROC diagrams of *BoTShark* shows that in false positive ratio $\leq$ 0.05 we will have true positive ratio of about 0.75. However, *BoTShark* achieves higher true positive ratios ($\geq$0.91) by tolerating more false positives (FPR between 0.05 and 0.15).

Table 2 Performance of BoTShark in detecting malicious traffics

	TPR	FPR
BoTShark-SA	0.91	0.13
BoTShark-CNN	0.92	0.15

Fig. 7 ROC diagrams of BoTShark-SA and BoTShark-CNN

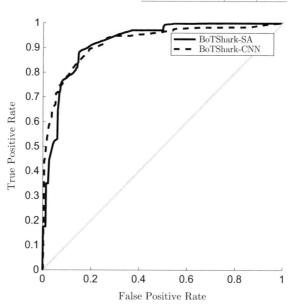

Working directly on the outputs from Argus and extracting features automatically without experts is an advantage of *BoTShark*. In other words, the main advantage of the proposed method is the variety of applications. Since Autoencoders and CNNs are not limited to a special field of data, it can be used for efficient feature extraction in any cases. Then any NetFlow extractor such as Argus [37], YAF [43] and ISCXFlowMeter [44] can be used as the flow exporter.

7 Conclusion

IRC and P2P are two main botnet topologies hence a typical network may include infected hosts from both topologies and new detection systems are required to support both. As deep learning is very efficient in image processing and text mining, this chapter attempted to apply deep learning techniques in the realm of botnet detection by proposing *BoTShark-SA* that uses Autoencoders and *BoTShark-CNN* which uses CNN. *BoTShark* has the ability of detecting botnet traffics from both common topologies of botnets namely centralized and P2P. A *Softmax* classification makes the final predictor of malicious and non-malicious traffics. We achieved *TPR* of 0.91 with FPR of 0.13 in detecting malicious traffics of botnets. Our study also showed that Autoencoders perform better than CNN since as it generates smaller false positives. Applying other deep learning techniques such as Long Short Term Memory (LSTM) can be considered as a future work of this study. Moreover, the approach of this study can be applied for detection of relevant evidences during course of forensics investigation of cloud [45] and IoT [46] botnet traffic as well.

References

1. Nikola Milosevic, Ali Dehghantanha, and Kim-Kwang Raymond Choo. Machine learning aided android malware classification. *Computers & Electrical Engineering*, feb 2017. https://doi.org/10.1016/j.compeleceng.2017.02.013.
2. Malware statistics & trends report, feb 2017. https://www.av-test.org/en/statistics/malware/.
3. Mohsen Damshenas, Ali Dehghantanha, and Ramlan Mahmoud. A survey on malware propagation, analysis, and detection. *International Journal of Cyber-Security and Digital Forensics (IJCSDF)*, 2(4):10–29, 2013.
4. Mohsen Damshenas, Ali Dehghantanha, Kim-Kwang Raymond Choo, and Ramlan Mahmud. M0droid: An android behavioral-based malware detection model. *Journal of Information Privacy and Security*, 11(3):141–157, jul 2015. https://doi.org/10.1080/15536548.2015.1073510.
5. Hamed Haddad Pajouh, Reza Javidan, Raouf Khayami, Dehghantanha Ali, and Kim-Kwang Raymond Choo. A two-layer dimension reduction and two-tier classification model for anomaly-based intrusion detection in IoT backbone networks. *IEEE Transactions on Emerging Topics in Computing*, pages 1–1, 2016. https://doi.org/10.1109/tetc.2016.2633228.
6. Gunter Ollmann. Botnet communication topologies understanding the intricacies of botnet command-and-control, 2009. http://technicalinfo.net/papers/PDF/WP_Botnet_Communications_Primer_(2009-06-04).pdf.

7. Anoop Chowdary Atluri and Vinh Tran. Botnets threat analysis and detection. In *Information Security Practices*, pages 7–28. Springer International Publishing, 2017. https://doi.org/10.1007/978-3-319-48947-6_2.
8. Hossein Rouhani Zeidanloo, Mohammad Jorjor Zadeh Shooshtari, Payam Vahdani Amoli, M. Safari, and Mazdak Zamani. A taxonomy of botnet detection techniques. In *2010 3rd International Conference on Computer Science and Information Technology*. IEEE, jul 2010. https://doi.org/10.1109/iccsit.2010.5563555.
9. C.C. Zou and R. Cunningham. Honeypot-aware advanced botnet construction and maintenance. In *International Conference on Dependable Systems and Networks (DSN06)*. IEEE, 2006. https://doi.org/10.1109/dsn.2006.38.
10. Junjie Zhang, Roberto Perdisci, Wenke Lee, Xiapu Luo, and Unum Sarfraz. Building a scalable system for stealthy p2p-botnet detection. *IEEE Transactions on Information Forensics and Security*, 9(1):27–38, jan 2014. https://doi.org/10.1109/tifs.2013.2290197.
11. Yee-Yang Teing, Ali Dehghantanha, Kim-Kwang Raymond Choo, and Laurence T Yang. Forensic investigation of p2p cloud storage services and backbone for IoT networks: BitTorrent sync as a case study. *Computers & Electrical Engineering*, 58:350–363, feb 2017. https://doi.org/10.1016/j.compeleceng.2016.08.020.
12. Opeyemi Osanaiye, Haibin Cai, Kim-Kwang Raymond Choo, Ali Dehghantanha, Zheng Xu, and Mqhele Dlodlo. Ensemble-based multi-filter feature selection method for DDoS detection in cloud computing. *EURASIP Journal on Wireless Communications and Networking*, 2016 (1), may 2016. https://doi.org/10.1186/s13638-016-0623-3.
13. Guofei Gu, Roberto Perdisci, Junjie Zhang, and Wenke Lee. Botminer: Clustering analysis of network traffic for protocol- and structure-independent botnet detection. In *Proceedings of the 17th Conference on Security Symposium*, SS'08, pages 139–154, Berkeley, CA, USA, 2008. USENIX Association. http://dl.acm.org/citation.cfm?id=1496711.1496721.
14. David Zhao, Issa Traore, Bassam Sayed, Wei Lu, Sherif Saad, Ali Ghorbani, and Dan Garant. Botnet detection based on traffic behavior analysis and flow intervals. *Computers & Security*, 39:2–16, nov 2013. https://doi.org/10.1016/j.cose.2013.04.007.
15. Basil AsSadhan, Jose M. F. Moura, and David Lapsley. Periodic behavior in botnet command and control channels traffic. In *GLOBECOM 2009 - 2009 IEEE Global Telecommunications Conference*. IEEE, nov 2009. https://doi.org/10.1109/glocom.2009.5426172.
16. Unb iscx botnet dataset, jan 2017. http://www.unb.ca/research/iscx/dataset/ISCX-botnet-dataset.html#Botnet%20Data%20set.
17. Sérgio S.C. Silva, Rodrigo M.P. Silva, Raquel C.G. Pinto, and Ronaldo M. Salles. Botnets: A survey. *Computer Networks*, 57(2):378–403, feb 2013. https://doi.org/10.1016/j.comnet.2012.07.021.
18. Igal Zeifman. 2015 bot traffic report: Humans take back the web, bad bots not giving any ground. Report, Incapsula, 9 Dec. 2015 2015. https://www.incapsula.com/blog/bot-traffic-report-2015.html.
19. Brett Stone-Gross, Marco Cova, Lorenzo Cavallaro, Bob Gilbert, Martin Szydlowski, Richard Kemmerer, Christopher Kruegel, and Giovanni Vigna. Your botnet is my botnet: Analysis of a botnet takeover. In *Proceedings of the 16th ACM conference on Computer and communications security - CCS*. ACM Press, 2009. https://doi.org/10.1145/1653662.1653738.
20. Carl Livadas, Robert Walsh, David Lapsley, and W. Strayer. Usilng machine learning technliques to identify botnet traffic. In *Proceedings. 2006 31st IEEE Conference on Local Computer Networks*. IEEE, nov 2006. https://doi.org/10.1109/lcn.2006.322210.
21. Chia Yuan Cho, Domagoj Babic, Eui Chul Richard Shin, and Dawn Song. Inference and analysis of formal models of botnet command and control protocols. In *Proceedings of the 17th ACM conference on Computer and communications security - CCS*. ACM Press, 2010. https://doi.org/10.1145/1866307.1866355.
22. Rouhani S. Zeidanloo HR. *Botnet Detection by Monitoring Common Network Behaviors: Botnet detection by monitoring common network behaviors*. Lambert Academic Publishing, 2012. ISBN 9783848404759.

23. Jing Wang and Ioannis Ch. Paschalidis. Botnet detection based on anomaly and community detection. *IEEE Transactions on Control of Network Systems*, pages 1–1, 2016. https://doi.org/10.1109/tcns.2016.2532804.

24. Guofei Gu, Phillip Porras, Vinod Yegneswaran, and Martin Fong. Bothunter: Detecting malware infection through ids-driven dialog correlation. In *16th USENIX Security Symposium (USENIX Security 07)*, Boston, MA, 2007. USENIX Association. https://www.usenix.org/conference/16th-usenix-security-symposium/bothunter-detecting-malware-infection-through-ids-driven.

25. Snort - network intrusion detection & prevention system, jan 2017. https://www.snort.org/.

26. Hyunsang Choi, Hanwoo Lee, Heejo Lee, and Hyogon Kim. Botnet detection by monitoring group activities in DNS traffic. In *7th IEEE International Conference on Computer and Information Technology (CIT 2007)*. IEEE, oct 2007. https://doi.org/10.1109/cit.2007.90.

27. G. Kirubavathi and R. Anitha. Botnet detection via mining of traffic flow characteristics. *Computers & Electrical Engineering*, 50:91–101, feb 2016. https://doi.org/10.1016/j.compeleceng.2016.01.012.

28. Elaheh Biglar Beigi, Hossein Hadian Jazi, Natalia Stakhanova, and Ali A. Ghorbani. Towards effective feature selection in machine learning-based botnet detection approaches. In *2014 IEEE Conference on Communications and Network Security*. IEEE, oct 2014. https://doi.org/10.1109/cns.2014.6997492.

29. Kuan-Cheng Lin, Wei-Chiang Li, and Jason C. Hung. Detection for different type botnets using feature subset selection. In *Lecture Notes in Electrical Engineering*, pages 523–529. Springer Singapore, 2016. https://doi.org/10.1007/978-981-10-0539-8_52.

30. Isot botnet dataset, jan 2017. http://www.uvic.ca/engineering/ece/isot/datasets/.

31. Adam J. Aviv and Andreas Haeberlen. Challenges in experimenting with botnet detection systems. In *Proceedings of the 4th Conference on Cyber Security Experimentation and Test*, CSET'11, pages 6–6, Berkeley, CA, USA, 2011. USENIX Association. http://dl.acm.org/citation.cfm?id=2027999.2028005.

32. Jeff Heaton. *Artificial Intelligence for Humans*, volume 3. CreateSpace Independent Publishing Platform, 2015. ISBN 1505714346.

33. Y. Lecun, L. Bottou, Y. Bengio, and P. Haffner. Gradient-based learning applied to document recognition. *Proceedings of the IEEE*, 86(11):2278–2324, 1998. https://doi.org/10.1109/5.726791.

34. Alex Krizhevsky, Ilya Sutskever, and Geoffrey E Hinton. Imagenet classification with deep convolutional neural networks. In F. Pereira, C. J. C. Burges, L. Bottou, and K. Q. Weinberger, editors, *Advances in Neural Information Processing Systems 25*, pages 1097–1105. Curran Associates, Inc., 2012.

35. Yann LeCun, Yoshua Bengio, and Geoffrey Hinton. Deep learning. *Nature*, 521(7553):436–444, may 2015. https://doi.org/10.1038/nature14539.

36. Michael Blot, Matthieu Cord, and Nicolas Thome. Max-min convolutional neural networks for image classification. In *2016 IEEE International Conference on Image Processing (ICIP)*. IEEE, sep 2016. https://doi.org/10.1109/icip.2016.7533046.

37. Argus- auditing network activity, jan 2017. http://qosient.com/argus.

38. Huy Hang, Xuetao Wei, M. Faloutsos, and T. Eliassi-Rad. Entelecheia: Detecting p2p botnets in their waiting stage. In *2013 IFIP Networking Conference*, pages 1–9, May 2013.

39. Bishop Christopher. *Pattern Recognition and Machine Learning*. Springer-Verlag New York, 1 edition, 2006.

40. Sajad Homayoun, Ali Dehghantanha, Marzieh Ahmadzadeh, Sattar Hashemi, and Raouf Khayami. Know abnormal, find evil: Frequent pattern mining for ransomware threat hunting and intelligence. *IEEE Transactions on Emerging Topics in Computing*, pages 1–1, 2017 - In Press. https://doi.org/10.1109/tetc.2017.2756908.

41. Mina Sohrabi, Mohammad M. Javidi, and Sattar Hashemi. Detecting intrusion transactions in database systems: a novel approach. *Journal of Intelligent Information Systems*, 42(3):619–644, dec 2013. https://doi.org/10.1007%2Fs10844-013-0286-z.

42. R. Mohammadi, R. Javidan, and M. Conti. Slicots: An sdn-based lightweight countermeasure for tcp syn flooding attacks. *IEEE Transactions on Network and Service Management*, 14(2): 487–497, June 2017. ISSN 1932-4537. https://doi.org/10.1109/TNSM.2017.2701549.
43. Yet another flowmeter, jan 2017. https://tools.netsa.cert.org/yaf/.
44. Gerard Drapper Gil, Arash Habibi Lashkari, Mohammad Mamun, and Ali A. Ghorbani. Characterization of encrypted and vpn traffic using time-related features. In *Proceedings of the 2nd International Conference on Information Systems Security and Privacy ICISSP 2016*, pages 407–414, 2016.
45. Yee-Yang Teing, Ali Dehghantanha, Kim-Kwang Raymond Choo, Tooska Dargahi, and Mauro Conti. Forensic investigation of cooperative storage cloud service: Symform as a case study. *Journal of Forensic Sciences*, 62(3):641–654, nov 2016. https://doi.org/10.1111/1556-4029. 13271.
46. Steve Watson and Ali Dehghantanha. Digital forensics: the missing piece of the internet of things promise. *Computer Fraud & Security*, 2016(6):5–8, jun 2016. https://doi.org/10.1016/s1361-3723(15)30045-2.

A Practical Analysis of the Rise in Mobile Phishing

Brad Wardman, Michael Weideman, Jakub Burgis, Nicole Harris, Blake Butler, and Nate Pratt

Abstract Phishing attacks continue to evolve in order to bypass mitigations applied within the industry. These attacks are also changing due to the attacker's desire for a greater return on investment from their attacks against the common internet user. The digital landscape has been ever-changing since the emergence of mobile technologies. The intersection of the internet and the growing mobile user-base fueled the natural progression of phishers to target mobile-specific users. This research investigates mobile-specific phishing attacks through the dissection of phishing kits used for the attacks, presentation of real world phishing campaigns, and observations about PayPal's insight into mobile web-based phishing numbers.

Keywords Phishing · Abuse reporting · Phishing kits · Mobile attacks

1 Introduction

For years, there has been speculation across the industry that phishing would soon be a solved problem; however, there is evidence that phishing attacks are more prevalent than ever. Phishing is an attack vector used by criminals to lure their victims into divulging personal or financial information through the use of social engineering. Phishing attacks can be distributed through spam email links, email attachments, text messages, phone calls, forum posts, and more [1, 2]. This paper focuses on phishing attacks using fraudulent websites to harvest user information. Phishing attacks can be distributed using a wide net, attempting to attract a broad range of victims or they can be extremely targeted to a few individuals. The latter attacks are referred to as spear phish due to the use of additional personal information about their victim for precise targeting [3].

The Anti-Phishing Working Group (APWG) provides bi-yearly reports on phishing statistics which indicate that phishing continues to grow. The total number

B. Wardman (✉) · M. Weideman · J. Burgis · N. Harris · B. Butler · N. Pratt
PayPal Inc. San Jose, CA

© Springer International Publishing AG, part of Springer Nature 2018
A. Dehghantanha et al. (eds.), *Cyber Threat Intelligence*, Advances in Information Security 70, https://doi.org/10.1007/978-3-319-73951-9_8

of distinct phishing attacks reported to the APWG in Q1 of 2014 was 125,215, Q1 of 2015 was 136,347, and Q1 of 2016 was 289,371 [4–6]. In fact, there was a 250% increase in phishing attacks in Q1 2016 compared to Q4 2015 [6]. PayPal has observed this upward trend within its reporting numbers as well.

The most common response to phishing attacks is to remove the malicious content from the internet as soon as possible as it has been demonstrated that the spamming of phishing content stops shortly after [7]. This process is referred to as "takedown" [8, 9]. The majority of organizations rely on external security companies to provide the service of detecting new phishing attacks and removing the content. Another response to phishing is reporting the websites to the major blacklisting firms such as Google Safe Browsing in order to warn users that a website is likely malicious [10]. Blacklists are used by most web browsers and typically serve a red page containing warnings to the user as a means to prevent them from visiting the page [11]. While these warning pages are an effective method for victim prevention [12] they are limited in that they are only available to the user before they visit the phishing website. There has been research performed on the effectiveness of blacklists to detect phishing websites or URLs. Prior research found that it takes blacklists around 2 h to identify and action 90% of the phishing websites reported to them [13]. There are a number of factors that contribute to a blacklist's ability to identify phishing content, such as the timely reporting of the content, the depth of the queue for scanning content, and the likelihood that the content can be retrieved using traditional methods.

The timeliness of reporting by organizations and security firms is often out of the control of the blacklists as they are reliant on external parties to report the URLs. Nevertheless, the URL queue handling process could be reworked so that trusted contacts sharing potentially abusive content are prioritized over content that is newly introduced to the internet and simply needs to be scanned. There are also limitations to the content retrieval systems or crawlers employed by current blacklists. The development of more robust, adaptive systems could provide increased detection capabilities for the blacklists by scanning from different geolocations, using proper browser language settings, and using content retrieval systems that emulate browsers and devices rather than simple scripted (e.g. curl and wget) commands. These techniques will help to overcome obstacles used by phishers for years such as the use of .htaccess files within phishing kits for denying and allowing certain IP ranges from retrieving the intended content [14, 15]. These access restrictions often cause issues for content retrieval systems, hence preventing them from taking action on the phishing website. Another evolution of website filtering is the use of .htaccess and similar PHP files to check the user-agent being used to retrieve the content. PayPal has recently observed a new trend in phishing websites in the wild ensuring the visitor's user-agent is a mobile device which will be expounded on in this research. According to Cisco, there was a 74% rise in mobile internet traffic as well as a 43% increase in the use of smartphones between 2014 and 2015 [16]. In 2015, Google's Search Chief, Amit Singhal, stated that mobile device searches had exceeded desktop computer searches [17]. With this in mind, it stands to reason that attackers would prioritize targeting mobile users over personal computer users.

This introduces a number of issues for the abuse reporting industry, as they have not typically employed the use of mobile emulators or user-agents as a means to retrieve content targeting mobile users. Furthermore, there are differences between addressing phishing countermeasures for mobile users versus those using a personal computer such as phishing education through the use of warnings.

The research in this paper presents trending data that PayPal is observing in regards to the targeting of mobile users. The first section presents initial research that PayPal performed to better assess the impact phishing is having on direct monetary losses incurred by PayPal. Next, this research will share real-world PayPal numbers on the impact that mobile device usage is having to its phishing numbers. Following the description of the problem, information is shared on phishing kits observed targeting mobile users in the wild. We will then step through an example mobile phishing website reported to PayPal which was not available except through the use of a mobile browser. After presenting these examples, a section presents industry recommendations that could be employed in response to the rise in mobile phishing. The final section concludes the research presented in this paper.

2   Measuring the Impact of Phishing

Previously published research by PayPal proposed an equation for measuring phishing's direct impact to an organization [18]. The equation is as follows:

$$\textbf{\textit{Direct Monetary Loss}} = numSites \times avgVisit \times \%Creds$$
$$\times monetized \times avgLoss$$

where:

- *numSites* is the number of phishing websites per year
- *avgVisit* is the average number of customers visiting each website
- *%Creds* is the percentage of valid credentials acquired by each phishing website
- *monetized* is the number of credentials that undergo attempted monetization
- *avgLoss* is the average amount of loss due to a compromised account

The *numSites* variable is common amongst organizations to collect. The industry is aware that gaps exist for this variable; however, this variable is well documented by members of the industry such as the APWG [4–6]. The *avgVisit* variable, which is important to this paper's research, is the average number of visits that a phishing website observes. This can be achieved by tracking the resources (e.g. graphics, JavaScript files, and CSS files) that phishing websites use from the targeted organization. The *%Creds* variable represents the return rate of legitimate credentials that the phishing website harvests from its visitors. The *monetized* variable is representative of the number of accounts against which have had attempted account takeovers. Finally, *avgLoss* is the measurement of loss per account takeover. This is often institutionally dependent.

Measuring the impact of phishing has proven vital as this research has led to the discovery of mobile phishing abuse through further inspection of the targeted customers. The following section will provide insight into the observations PayPal found when assessing those visiting the phishing websites.

3 Methodology for Visitors to Phishing Websites

PayPal actively monitors phishing attack trends to determine the scope of the problem as well as to better understand the evolution of attack strategies. This is often done through trends observed via customer calls and complaints. PayPal has also found it extremely useful to monitor the trends in phishing by using internal data related to web resource usage. Organizations can analyze data related to phishing websites that are leveraging access to web resources such as images or JavaScript [19]. The current study employs two data sets: a URL data set and a data set of visitor information. The first data set consists of all phishing URLs reported or collected by PayPal over the first half of 2016 (i.e. January through June). The URL data set was collected from internal detection strategies, customer reporting, external security firms, phishing URL aggregation sources, and blacklists. The data set is comprised of over 18K distinct phishing websites, meaning we removed duplicate URLs based on identical hostnames using the same hosting IP on the same day. The second data set is the visitor information collected on phishing websites related to the URLs data set that was collected by PayPal through the execution of JavaScript functions. This means that the phishing URLs in the URL data set were checked against PayPal's internal cookie data in order to identify which URLs had collected visitor information through the execution of PayPal's JavaScript. PayPal had collected data through this source on 24.7% of the total number of observed phishing campaigns. Note that not all phishing campaigns are successful in luring visitors as blacklists and mail filters mitigate a great deal of attacks; therefore, the 24.7% is likely a larger percentage of the total URLs visited.

The initial research into the inspection of targeted customers was tailored towards eliminating sessions in phishing websites that were not traditional internet users or customers. The reasoning for this was to better understand how to remove crawlers (e.g. automated systems for collecting web content) used by security firms, blacklists, and researchers whose visits could inflate the number of actual visitors to phishing websites. A number of filters were applied to the data set, such as IP addresses that visited more than 10 different phishing websites in the first half (i.e. January–June) of 2016, malformed or non-realistic user-agents of visitors, and IP addresses originating within known researcher networks. In addition, phishing websites visited by customers also contained cookies pre-existing from PayPal, allowing PayPal to identify specific customer visits. The initial findings indicated there was a lower than anticipated percentage of customers who visited a phishing website and subsequently had their account taken over. This could be because the customers identified that the website was a scam or, for some other reason, the phishers did not attempt to monetize the collected accounts.

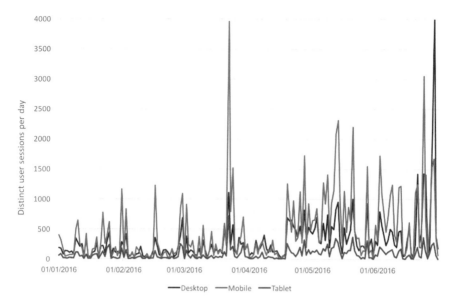

Fig. 1 A comparison of mobile, tablet and desktop users visiting phishing websites in the first half of 2016 (using DD/MM/YYYY format for dates)

The next phase of the research was to identify visits that did not have customer cookies but were still likely to be a legitimate internet user or customer. PayPal started by analyzing the user-agents that remained in the data set after removing known customer cookies as well as removing the sessions that were likely to be blacklists, researchers, or security firms. PayPal found that the user-agent traffic was approximately broken down to 54% mobile, 9% tablet, and 37% desktop. Figure 1 shows the findings plotted each day throughout the first half (or H1) of 2016. There is a observable trend starting in May 2016 until the end of the data set indicating that the number of mobile users visiting phishing websites is rising.

There are two reasons PayPal suspects this rise in mobile browser user-agents started to occur in May 2016. Firstly, it could be that content retrieval systems started using mobile user-agents in their crawlers or are using mobile emulators. The other is that more people are reviewing emails on their mobile devices and viewing more content shared over social media via their mobile devices. For the latter case, when the user clicks the link, the phishing website is presented to them in the mobile browser. This could also be a reason why PayPal did not have cookies on the visitors, as many users on their mobile devices use the PayPal mobile application rather than performing transactions using the mobile browser, in which case pre-existing cookies may not be present. A side observation during the examination of the sessions indicated that the number of HTTP referrer headers referencing mail and webmail providers also increased using the same timescale in Fig. 1 suggesting that many users were being redirected more from their web mailboxes over time.

PayPal also observed a significant number of phishing campaigns distributed via social media in the first half of 2016. In Fig. 1, the large spike in visits towards the end of March 2016 was entirely driven by customers visiting links shared on Twitter, as indicated by the "t.co" URL shortener being present in the HTTP referrer. The "t.co" shortener accounts for 30% of all mobile referrers seen in H1, and is $10\times$ more prevalent than any other.

Further analysis of the data set revealed several trends that can be found in the tables located in the Appendix 1. By classifying each visit by characteristics of the device used, inferred from the user-agent header, the primary devices used to visit phishing sites were Windows 7 (23.44%), iPhone (19.56%), generic 'linux' (8.58%), Windows 10 (6.81%), and Android devices using Chrome browser (6.52%). It is notable to mention that Phantom JS was the 13th most popular device, responsible for 1.14% of unique visits to phishing websites. The use of Phantom JS suggests a crawler capable of executing JavaScript and performing advanced functions that simple content retrieval systems are not capable of. There are additional useful data trends using the geo-location information of the IP addresses visiting phishing websites such as calculating the percentage of phishing websites visited via mobile devices per country. Of the set of countries with more than 1000 phishing site visits, the majority of countries present show more visits via mobile devices than not. Additionally, with the exception of the United States, the countries with the majority of mobile visits have English as either the primary or secondary language.

4   Mobile Phishing Kits in the Wild

A more thorough review of active phishing kits was needed to determine if there are apparent changes in phishing tactics. PayPal decided to analyze a set of six active phishing kits using different organizations as the lure for their victims. The analysis indicates no significant change into the underlying phishing strategy, rather incremental changes to enable tighter access controls by the phisher such as additional commands added to identify and block specific user-agents. Note the highlighted section of the source code in Fig. 2 was observed in a PayPal phishing kit. This JavaScript redirects the visitor to different web resources and experiences based on the user-agent provided by the visitor to the executing JavaScript. For instance, the visitor is redirected to "*rand.php*" if they execute the JavaScript using a mobile user-agent. The "*rand.php*" webpage is employed by the phisher to provide a more mobile friendly experience. Visitors using any other type of user-agent are provided with a typical web browser experience (i.e. redirection to the "*account*" webpage).

There was also a difference in the two experiences between the mechanism of how the phished information was collected and provided to the phisher. Phished information collected by "*rand.php*", resulted in the creation of unique directories per visitor. The directory "*/account*" holds additional directories that are representative of each victim and the names of those directories are based on a string generated by a function in the PHP. The string is computed by taking a substring of five characters from the MD5 hash [20] of a randomly generated number and the IP

Fig. 2 Example source code found in a PayPal phishing kit that directs the visitor to different resources based the user-agent

address of the visitor. For example, a file containing the phished information for a specific visitor would be written to a directory on the phishing webserver located at "*phishing-domain/account/4d876/*". In comparison, the strategy for collecting the phished information from the "*account*" webpage was a standard phishing practice that utilizes functions in a file called "*successfully.php*" to email the collected information of the user to the phisher.

Observations during the analysis of the phishing kits found various obfuscation, blocking, and back door techniques that have been observed in the evolution of phishing kits over the years. For instance, an analysis of a PayPal kit found common source code obfuscation used within the phishing kits to increase the difficulty of analysis by researchers. Another observation is that phishers are employing blocking mechanisms utilizing an array of words that are related to security firms, researchers, and the targeted organizations, as shown in Fig. 3. Also found in Fig. 4 is PHP source code that is blocking requests based on specific IP ranges.

The following section describes a walkthrough of an example mobile phishing campaign that targeted PayPal.

5 Mobile Phishing Campaigns

Mobile specific campaigns are actively being used against PayPal. This section provides a walkthrough of an example phishing campaign that was only retrievable using what the website perceived as a mobile device. PayPal identified a potential phishing redirect website hosted on the subdomain hosting site respectiverespectively.from-ct[.]com registered to DYN Dynamic Network Services, Inc., hosted on 216.146.39.125 AS33517. This site redirected to an unfiltered intermediary redirect site hosted on 82.165.61.207 AS8560, which redirects to the phishing landing page hosted on the unfiltered subdomain hosting site customerde-

```php
<?php
$hostname = gethostbyaddr($_SERVER['REMOTE_ADDR']);
$blocked_words = array
("above","google","softlayer","amazonaws","cyveillance","phishtank","dreamhost","netpilot","calyxinstitute","tor-exit",
"msnbot","p3pwgdsn","netcraft","trendmicro", "ebay", "paypal", "torservers", "messagelabs", "sucuri.net", "crawler");
foreach($blocked_words as $word) {
    if (substr_count($hostname, $word) > 0) {
        header("HTTP/1.0 404 Not Found");
            die("<h1>404 Not Found</h1>The page that you have requested could not be found.");
    }
}
$bannedIP = array("^81.161.59.*", "^66.135.200.*", "^66.102.*.*", "^38.100.*.*", "^107.170.*.*", "^149.20.*.*", "^38.105.*.*",
"^74.125.*.*", "^66.150.14.*", "^54.176.*.*", "^38.100.*.*", "^184.173.*.*", "^66.249.*.*", "^128.242.*.*", "^72.14.192.*",
"^208.65.144.*", "^74.125.*.*", "^209.85.128.*", "^216.239.32.*", "^74.125.*.*", "^207.126.144.*", "^173.194.*.*", "^64.233.160.*",
"^72.14.192.*", "^66.102.*.*", "^64.18.*.*", "^194.52.68.*", "^194.72.238.*", "^62.116.207.*", "^212.50.193.*", "^69.65.*.*",
"^50.7.*.*", "^131.212.*.*", "^46.116.*.* ", "^62.90.*.*", "^89.138.*.*", "^82.166.*.*", "^85.64.*.*", "^85.250.*.*",
"^89.138.*.*", "^93.172.*.*", "^109.186.*.*", "^194.90.*.*", "^212.29.192.*", "^212.29.224.*", "^212.143.*.*", "^212.150.*.*",
"^212.235.*.*", "^217.132.*.*", "^50.97.*.*", "^217.132.*.*", "^209.85.*.*", "^66.205.64.*", "^204.14.48.*", "^64.27.2.*",
"^67.15.*.*", "^202.108.252.*", "^193.47.80.*", "^64.62.136.*", "^66.221.*.*", "^64.62.175.*", "^198.54.*.*", "^192.115.134.*",
"^216.252.167.*", "^193.253.199.*", "^69.61.12.*", "^64.37.103.*", "^38.144.36.*", "^64.124.14.*", "^206.28.72.*", "^209.73.228.*",
"^158.108.*.*", "^168.188.*.*", "^66.207.120.*", "^167.24.*.*", "^192.118.48.*", "^67.209.128.*", "^12.148.209.*", "^12.148.196.*",
"^193.220.178.*", "^68.65.53.71", "^198.25.*.*", "^64.106.213.*", "^91.103.66.*", "^208.91.115.*", "^199.30.228.*");
if(in_array($_SERVER['REMOTE_ADDR'],$bannedIP)) {
    header('HTTP/1.0 404 Not Found');
    exit();
} else {
    foreach($bannedIP as $ip) {
        if(preg_match('/' . $ip . '/',$_SERVER['REMOTE_ADDR'])){
            header('HTTP/1.0 404 Not Found');
            die("<h1>404 Not Found</h1>The page that you have requested could not be found.");
        }
    }
}
```

Fig. 3 Example PHP source code that uses IP ranges and user-agent strings as filtering techniques

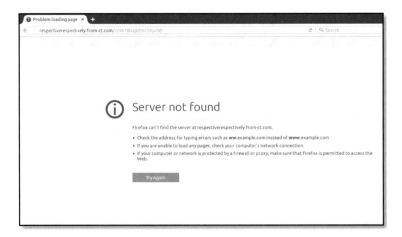

Fig. 4 Page returned upon initial retrieval of phishing URL

skinfo.servehttp[.]com registered to Vitalwerks Internet Solutions, LLC–No-IP.com, 77.68.12.254 AS8560. This URL was reported over 600 times to PayPal.

The hostname respectivelrespectively.from-ct[.]com appeared in 28 of the 600 emails and revealed a weakness in the attack as all 600 URLs in the emails were filtered through the intermediary redirect pages at 82.165.61.207. All those links pointed to the same landing page customerdeskinfo.servehttp[.]com, which was the focus of mitigating this campaign quickly.

First inspection of the URL using a web browser coming from a United States IP address did not display the phishing website. Instead, the content retrieved was a "Server not found" page depicted in Fig. 4. The next step was to change the IP

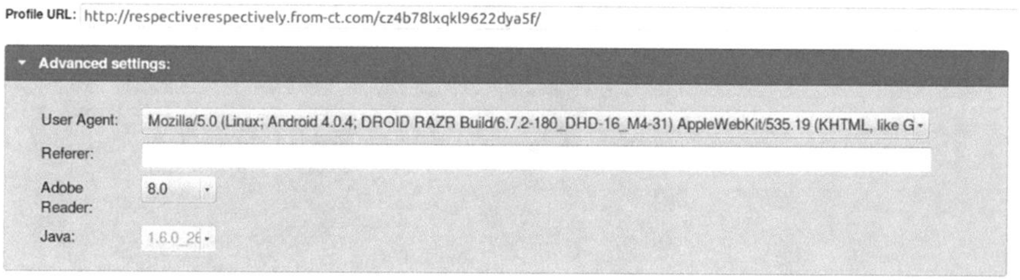

Profile URL: http://respectiverespectively.from-ct.com/cz4b78lxqkl9622dya5f/

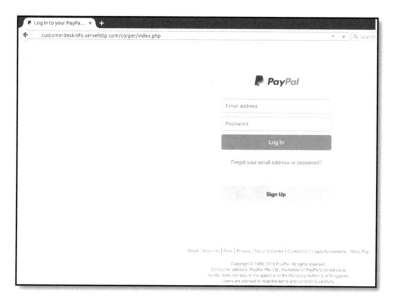

Fig. 5 A screenshot of the phishing URL test being submitted to URLQuery as a Droid Razor browser

Fig. 6 The mobile-friendly phishing content retrieved once a mobile user-agent was employed

address and language setting to the targeted victim country-base. The campaign was being distributed to United Kingdom targets; hence, the IP address and language settings were changed to United Kingdom settings. The content was still not being delivered. Other various proxy services were also used with no success.

The analyst decided to use URLQuery, as seen in Fig. 5, as a means of determining if the data could be captured using a mobile user-agent [21]. The device that was chosen was the Droid Razor browser. Upon submitting the request, URLQuery was sent through a redirect, ultimately getting served the phishing content as observed in Fig. 6. Note that some of the phishing kits analyzed in Sect. 4 do block URLQuery in the *.htaccess* file.

The source code found in Fig. 7 is the filtering mechanism observed in the redirect to the phishing website and is similar to what was found in the phishing kits dissected in Sect. 4. This source code uses JavaScript to determine if the user-agent contains strings that would be present in a mobile browsing experience.

Fig. 7 Source code found for filtering on user agent

```
CODE SNIPPET 1

<html><head>
<script type="text/javascript">
var device = navigator.user    Agent
if (device.match(/Iphone/i)|| device.match(/Ipod/i)||
device.match(/Android/i)|| device.match(/J2ME/i)||
device.match(/BlackBerry/i)||
device.match(/iPhone|iPad|iPod/i)|| device.match(/Opera
Mini/i)||
device.match(/IEMobile/i)|| device.match(/Mobile/i)||
device.match(/Windows Phone/i)|| device.match(/windows
mobile/i)|| device.match(/windows ce/i)||
device.match(/webOS/i)|| device.match(/palm/i)||
device.match(/bada/i)|| device.match(/series60/i)||
device.match(/nokia/i)|| device.match(/symbian/i)||
device.match(/HTC/i))
{
window.location = "./rand.php";
}
else
{
var page = "./random.php";
top.location = page;
}
</script>
</head>
</html>
```

A lasting observation found during the analysis of live mobile phishing websites was the difference in the user experience with regards to the warning page when visiting phishing websites from a web and mobile browsing experience. In some instances, it seems that security measures for mobile browsing has not kept up with current attack vectors. Phishing websites were visited using an actual mobile device and updated Chrome browser as well as using the same updated Chrome browser on a personal computer. The Chrome browser on the personal computer warned the user with a warning page when visiting the phishing website. However, this was not the case when using Chrome on a mobile device to visit the same phishing website. This was a small test and by no means indicates an industry-wide problem, but it does raise the question of what else is being missed. The focus should shift to what the phishers are doing, and where the community is susceptible.

6 Recommended Changes

The implementation of new technologies requires the industry to adapt security controls to protect internet users. The adoption of new security controls is often slow moving, as seems to be the case in regards to mobile-specific phishing attacks. The research presented in this paper demonstrates that phishing kits are available to phishers for targeting mobile users. The research also presents real world examples of the phishing campaigns. The potential damage caused by similar phishing campaigns are backed up with data that PayPal has collected on phishing visitors. The intent is to bring this emerging attack vector to the attention of the industry in the hopes that mitigation technologies will be developed that are capable of thwarting mobile-targeted victims. The remainder of the paper discusses changes to the current processes of organizations, security firms, and blacklists to help them better protect internet users.

The first recommendation is to implement changes to the content retrieval systems or crawlers used to capture the potential phishing content. Minor changes to the user-agents in the request could be implemented in the short term, to give time for more robust, long-term solutions to be put in place. The crawlers could iterate randomly through a list of common mobile device user-agents to help avoid detection and blocking. The suggested longer term solutions would require crawlers that fully emulate mobile devices. This will allow for the crawlers to bypass anti-automation defenses as the emulated devices will be able to perform most actions that any mobile device would be capable of executing.

The next recommendation is to create a distributed system that has access to IP infrastructure located within a diverse number of geolocations. Such a system would make it more difficult to block crawlers from current *.htaccess* files which are typically blocking known IP ranges or only allowing country-specific IP ranges. Simple modifications such as changing the language settings of the crawlers to the country of the IP being used would make the request more realistic. It is important to note that a significant portion of phishing kits are preloaded with *.htaccess* files for blocking most major security firms and blacklists.

The last recommendation is to create a new set of features or protocol for reporting abusive content. The current abuse reports contain lists of URLs, the timestamps observed, and possibly the brand or organization being targeted. The industry should consider additional context around how the content was rendered including details about the browser or device that was able to retrieve the content. Examples of additional fields that would provide more context for others trying to verify the content as being abusive could include user-agent, browser language, operating system, ASN, etc. Such features could be used by content retrieval systems to increase the chances of retrieving the content through programmatic configurations of the crawlers.

7 Conclusion

This research introduces phishing-related data that PayPal uncovered showing a rise in the number of visitors from apparent mobile devices. Deeper investigation into current phishing kits found that some phishers are targeting mobile users specifically with their phishing campaigns. The techniques found in phishing kits to limit access by mobile device visitors causes issues for the security industry, as many of their crawlers are not using mobile device emulators or mobile user-agents in their retrieval strategies. Therefore, many phishing websites are likely not getting labeled as malicious in the blacklists as well as in vendor security products. The security industry requires more robust solutions for scraping potentially malicious content in order to ensure that internet users are adequately protected from malicious websites.

A.1 Appendix

Device type	Unique visits	Unique IP addresses	Most commonly seen user-agent header string
Windows 7	70,577	25,500	Mozilla/5.0 (compatible; MSIE 10.0; Windows NT 6.1; Trident/6.0)
iOS/iphone	58,891	48,610	Mozilla/5.0 (iPhone; CPU iPhone OS 9_3_1 like Mac OS X) AppleWebKit/601.1.46 (KHTML, like Gecko) Version/9.0 Mobile/13E238 Safari/601.1
Linux	25,830	759	Mozilla/5.0 (X11; Linux x86_64) AppleWebKit/537.36 (KHTML, like Gecko) Chrome/28.0.1500.71 Safari/537.36
Windows 10	20,500	13,520	Mozilla/5.0 (Windows NT 10.0; Win64; $\times$64) AppleWebKit/537.36 (KHTML, like Gecko) Chrome/46.0.2486.0 Safari/537.36 Edge/13.10586
Android/Chrome Phone	19,637	19,964	Mozilla/5.0 (Linux; Android 5.0; SM-G900V Build/LRX21T) AppleWebKit/537.36 (KHTML, like Gecko) Chrome/50.0.2661.89 Mobile Safari/537.36
OSX	17,676	7873	Mozilla/5.0 (Macintosh; Intel Mac OS X 10_9_2) AppleWebKit/537.36 (KHTML, like Gecko) Chrome/36.0.1944.0 Safari/537.36
XP/IE6	17,037	138	Mozilla/4.0 (compatible; MSIE 6.0; Windows NT 5.1; SV1; NeosBrowser; .NET CLR 1.1.4322; .NET CLR 2.0.50727)
iOS/iPad	15,780	12,789	Mozilla/5.0 (iPad; CPU OS 9_3_1 like Mac OS X) AppleWebKit/601.1.46 (KHTML, like Gecko) Version/9.0 Mobile/13E238 Safari/601.1
Windows 8	15,012	6379	Mozilla/5.0 (Windows NT 6.3; WOW64) AppleWebKit/537.36 (KHTML, like Gecko) Chrome/48.0.2564.109 Safari/537.36
Windows XP	10,326	3712	Mozilla/5.0 (Windows NT 5.1; rv:9.0.1) Gecko/20100101 Firefox/9.0.1

Country	Percent of visits that are mobile	Unique phishing site visits	Unique IP addresses
United States	30.67	115,114	30,559
United Kingdom	75.01	43,341	28,680
France	11.85	23,646	2438
Germany	4.64	16,931	705
Canada	65.99	13,588	7327
Australia	72.23	13,360	7691
Romania	1.83	11,604	201
Russia	0.73	9650	65
Brazil	9.37	8386	637
Netherlands	16.2	3105	430
Italy	27.19	2953	768
Indonesia	22.03	2782	554
Ireland	73.33	2355	1453
Singapore	68.71	2183	1270
Hong Kong	65.42	1972	1131
Japan	19.63	1717	289
Norway	24.02	1690	353
Poland	2.74	1676	43
India	11.69	1523	170
Spain	57.95	1460	829
Morocco	5.31	1244	55
Serbia	1.29	1242	16
N/A	11.67	1105	58
New Zealand	59.15	1104	582
Switzerland	55.97	1013	346

References

1. Hong, J. (2012), "The State of Phishing Attacks". *Communications of the ACM*. 55, 1 (Jan. 2012), 74-81.
2. RSA Security, Inc. (2009), "Phishing, Vishing, and Smishing: Old Threats Present New Risks". Retrieved November 21st, 2016. https://www.emc.com/collateral/white-papers/h11933-wp-phishing-vishing-smishing.pdf.
3. Halevi, T., Memon, N., and Oded, N. (2015). "Spear-Phishing in the Wild A Real-World Study of Personality, Phishing Self-efficacy and Vulnerability to Spear-Phishing Attacks," *Social Science Research Network*. November 2015.
4. Aaron, Greg (2014), *Phishing Activity Trend Report, 1st Quarter 2015*. Nov. 2016. http://docs.apwg.org/reports/apwg_trends_report_q1_2014.pdf.
5. Aaron, Greg (2015), *Phishing Activity Trend Report, 1st–3rd Quarters 2015*. Nov. 2016. http://docs.apwg.org/reports/apwg_trends_report_q1-q3_2015.pdf.
6. Aaron, Greg (2016), *Phishing Activity Trend Report, 1st Quarter 2016*. Nov. 2016. http://docs.apwg.org/reports/apwg_trends_report_q1_2016.pdf.
7. Moore, T., Clayton, R., and Stern, H. (2009). "Temporal Correlations between Spam and Phishing Websites". *In Proceedings of 2nd USENIX LEET*. Boston, MA.

8. Moore, T., and Clayton, R. (2007). "An empirical analysis of the current state of phishing attack and defence". *In Proceedings of the 2007 Workshop on The Economics of Information Security*. May 2007.
9. Nero, P., Wardman, B., Copes, H., and Warner, G. (2011). "Phishing: Crime that Pays", *APWG eCrime Researchers Summit*, November 2011.
10. Prakash, P., Kumar, M., Kompella, R. R., and Gupta, M. (2010). "PhishNet: Predictive Blacklisting to Detect Phishing Attacks". *In Proceedings of INFOCOM'10*, San Diego, California.
11. Zhang, Y., Egelman, S., Cranor, L., and J. Hong. (2007). "Phinding Phish: Evaluating Anti-Phishing Tools". *In Proceedings of the 14th Annual Network and Distributed System Security Symposium*. San Diego, CA.
12. Egelman, S., Cranor, L.F., and Hong, J. (2008). "You've Been Warned: An Empirical Study of the Effectiveness of Web Browser Phishing Warnings", *Proceedings of the SIGCHI Conference on Human Factors in Computing Systems*, April 2008.
13. Sheng, S., Wardman, B., Warner, G., Cranor, L., Hong, J., & Zhang, C. (2009). "An Empirical Analysis of Phishing Blacklists". *Sixth Conference on Email and Anti-Spam*. Mountain View, CA.
14. Apache. (2016). *Apache HTTP Server Tutorial: .htaccess files–Apache HTTP Server Version 2.4*. Nov. 2016. https://httpd.apache.org/docs/2.4/howto/htaccess.html.
15. Ferguson, E., Weber, J., and Hasan, R. (2012). "Cloud based content fetching: Using cloud infrastructure to obfuscate phishing scam analysis". *Proceedings of 8th World Congress on Services (SERVICES)*. IEEE, 255–261.
16. Cisco. *Cisco Visual Networking Index: Global Mobile Data Traffic Forecast Update, 2015–2020 White Paper—Cisco*. Nov. 2016. http://www.cisco.com/c/en/us/solutions/collateral/service-provider/visual-networking-index-vni/mobile-white-paper-c11-520862.html.
17. Zakrzewski, C. *Mobile Searches Surpass Desktop Searches At Google For The First Time | TechCrunch*. Nov. 2016. https://techcrunch.com/2015/10/08/mobile-searches-surpass-desktop-searches-at-google-for-the-first-time/
18. Wardman, B. (2016). "Assessing the Gap: Measure the Impact of Phishing on an Organization". *12th Annual ADFSL Conference on Digital Forensics, Security, and Law*. Daytona Beach, FL.
19. Wardman, B., Britt, J., and Warner, G. (2014). *New Tackle to Catch a Phisher*. International Journal of Electron Security and Digital Forensics 6,1.
20. Rivest, R. (1992). "RFC 1321 – The MD5 Message-Digest Algorithm. Internet Engineering Task Force. April 1992.
21. URLQuery. urlquery.net–*Free URL scanner*. Nov. 2016. http://urlquery.net/.
22. DynDNS. *DynDNS and Managed DNS | Reliable DNS for your home and business | Dyn*. Nov. 2016. http://dyn.com/dns/.

PDF-Malware Detection: A Survey and Taxonomy of Current Techniques

Michele Elingiusti, Leonardo Aniello, Leonardo Querzoni, and Roberto Baldoni

Abstract Portable Document Format, more commonly known as PDF, has become, in the last 20 years, a standard for document exchange and dissemination due its portable nature and widespread adoption. The flexibility and power of this format are not only leveraged by benign users, but from hackers as well who have been working to exploit various types of vulnerabilities, overcome security restrictions, and then transform the PDF format in one among the leading malicious code spread vectors. Analyzing the content of malicious PDF files to extract the main features that characterize the malware identity and behavior, is a fundamental task for modern threat intelligence platforms that need to learn how to automatically identify new attacks. This paper surveys existing state of the art about systems for the detection of malicious PDF files and organizes them in a taxonomy that separately considers the used approaches and the data analyzed to detect the presence of malicious code.

Keywords Malware detection · Portable document format · Taxonomy

1 Introduction

Portable Document Format, commonly known as PDF, has become, since its introduction in 1993, a *de-facto* standard for document exchange and dissemination. The widespread adoption of this document format is due to both its portable nature and its inherent flexibility. PDF files, in fact, can contain a variety of media (text, pictures), but also embedded files or code that will be interpreted and executed by the reading software. This latter ability makes PDF adaptable to a large amount of extremely different usage requirements.

M. Elingiusti · L. Aniello · L. Querzoni (✉) · R. Baldoni
CIS - Sapienza University of Rome, Rome, Italy
e-mail: elingiusti.1483347@studenti.uniroma1.it; aniello@dis.uniroma1.it;
querzoni@dis.uniroma1.it; baldoni@dis.uniroma1.it

© Springer International Publishing AG, part of Springer Nature 2018   169
A. Dehghantanha et al. (eds.), *Cyber Threat Intelligence*, Advances in Information
Security 70, https://doi.org/10.1007/978-3-319-73951-9_9

Despite the complexity and the number of possibilities this file format offers, end users still treat PDF files as plain, static and immutable documents, without understanding that what the reader software shows them is the result of the execution of a potentially complex program. While end users have become increasingly aware, year after year, about the traps that other document formats may hide (mainly Microsoft Office documents including macros), such awareness struggles to extend toward PDF.

In the last 10 years malicious actors have exploited this lack of awareness, together with the presence of vulnerabilities in mainstream PDF readers, to make PDF become an extremely successful vector for malware diffusion. In 2010 Symantec [20] already reported a large rise in PDF-driven attacks, mainly justifying it with a corresponding rise in the vulnerabilities identified in the Adobe Reader software. More recently, Ke Liu reported [8] about his discovery since December 2015 of more than 150 vulnerabilities in the most common PDF reader software products. This latter news shows how, even today, PDF is an important infection vector that provides a large attack surface.

Malware developers typically use the possibility to supply Javascript to the PDF reader interpretation engine to execute their code. Such code is usually sandboxed[1] for execution, but it may still exploit un-patched vulnerabilities to escape the environment boundaries and execute shellcode at the user level. Complex payloads can be included in the PDF as obfuscated text to evade inspection techniques, or can be downloaded from the Internet as soon as the attacker takes control of the user shell. Malicious PDF files are then delivered through different methods [20]: from drive-by downloads, to targeted attacks or mass mailing approaches.

To counteract such growing phenomenon, the research community produced in the recent past several solutions for detecting malicious PDFs. The most recent and promising ones use a mix of techniques borrowed by standard malware analysis best practices (like static and dynamic code analysis) and adapted to the specificities of the file format to select what features to analyze. The analysis is performed using several different approaches that range from simple string matching through regular expressions to complex classifiers based on machine learning techniques. In this corpus of solutions it is somewhat difficult for the interested reader to identify which approaches are adopted by a given solution and how they are related to competing solutions. Nevertheless, such solutions represent an important building block for threat intelligence platforms that need to automatically analyze incoming data looking for suspicious infection vectors or indicators of compromise. Recently, a survey from Nissim et al. [12] provided an overview of academic contributions on this area, but limited its scope to systems leveraging machine learning approaches.

This work proposes a survey of the existing techniques at the state of the art for the detection of malicious PDF files. The main novelty introduced in this survey lies in its analysis of the most relevant works, which tackles two orthogonal, but strictly

---

[1]This feature is actually reader-dependent. As an example, the Google Chrome PDF reader executes embedded Javascript code within a Google Native Client sandbox.

related aspects: (1) which features are considered and how they derive from the analyzed PDF file, and (2) which techniques are used to analyze such features and detect malicious files. The taxonomy is completed by a global view that considers the combination of these two aspects to correctly contextualize analyzed works and propose possible gaps that could possibly pave the way for new research initiatives. Comparing to [12], we believe that discussing features and analysis techniques as orthogonal topics, helps in shedding further light on available solutions and identifying new directions for additional research.

The text is organized as follows: after this introduction, Sect. 2 provides a basic background on the Portable Document Format and some information about obfuscation techniques that can be used to conceal malicious code in PDF files, with the aim of making the detection process less effective. Section 3 gives an overview of the study we conducted on the state of the art, describes the rationale that drives our taxonomy and details the taxonomy itself. Section 4 puts the pieces together and provides the reader with a unified view with a clear reference to existing works. Finally, Sect. 5 concludes the paper.

2 Background on Malicious PDF Files

This section introduces some basic concepts that are fundamental to understand how PDF malware detection solutions treat the internals of a PDF and how they extract features for further analysis. In addition, we briefly discuss obfuscation techniques that can be adopted by malware developers to hide malicious code with the aim of evading detection.

2.1 The Portable Document Format

The Portable Document Format is the world's leading language for describing the printed page, and the first one equally suitable for paper and online use. It is basically a file format defined in 1993 by Adobe Systems and used until today to exchange and represent documents reliably, independently from the available hardware, software, and operating system. This means that this is a format intended to display content identically in all platforms and media. In 2008 it became an open standard released as ISO 32000-1.

A PDF file may contain a mix of textual and binary data and is composed by different abstraction layers. The layers define the sequential flow by which a PDF viewer application reads the contents and renders them on the screen. According to the PDF Reference [3], the internal structure of a PDF file is made up of the elements depicted in Fig. 1.

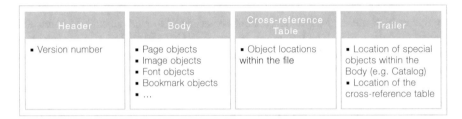

Header	Body	Cross-reference Table	Trailer
• Version number	• Page objects • Image objects • Font objects • Bookmark objects • …	• Object locations within the file	• Location of special objects within the Body (e.g. Catalog) • Location of the cross-reference table

Fig. 1 Internal structure of a PDF file

Metadata All the data that can be extracted by exploring the "raw" PDF file, i.e. from its internal structure, as it is detailed below. *Metadata* include elements such as embedded keywords, "EOF" characters located after the trailer, author field, creation data, etc.

Objects The basic content of a PDF document is represented by a collection of *Objects*. Each object contains a different element that will be used to render the file content, e.g., a page, a picture, a form, a portion of JavaScript code. Objects are the basic building blocks that collectively form the data structure of a PDF document.

An explicit definition is prefixed with a text label "1 0 obj". This kind of object is defined *indirect*, or also *labeled*, as it can be referenced by another object using the first number of its definition, 1 in this example, also known as its *object reference*. Conversely, *direct* objects can not be referenced and do not contain any reference prefix, implying that they will always be embedded in other objects. The syntax used by a container object to refer to an indirect object follows the pattern "1 0 R". PDF only supports eight basic types of objects:

- **Boolean values**
- **Integer and real numbers**
- **Strings**: sequences of bytes. PDF strings have bounded length and can be represented in two distinct formats, namely as a sequence of literal characters enclosed in rounded parentheses, or as hexadecimal dump embedded in angle brackets.
- **Names**: *atomic* symbols *uniquely* defined by a character sequence.
- **Null value**: there exists only one object of type null represented by the corresponding keyword "null". If the null object is specified as the value of a dictionary entry, it means that the entry does not exist. When an object references an indirect object that does not exist within the structure of the PDF, then this indirect reference is interpreted as a null object.
- **Arrays**: one-dimensional ordered collections of PDF objects enclosed in square brackets.
- **Dictionaries**: unordered sets of key-value pairs enclosed between the symbols "⟨⟨" and "⟩⟩", where each pair constitutes a dictionary's entry. Keys must be *name objects* and must be unique within a dictionary. The values may be any kind of PDF object, including nested dictionaries.

- **Streams**: sequences of bytes. Note that, while string objects must be read by a PDF viewer completely in their length, streams can undergo an incremental reading process. Furthermore, stream length is not bounded. This is the reason why large amount of data like images or JavaScript code are represented as streams.

File Structure This layer refers to how objects are organized in a PDF file, and later accessed or updated. A PDF file structure consists of the following four parts:

- **Header**: represents the single first line of the PDF file. It has the format "%PDF-a.b", where a.b denotes the version of the PDF standard specification to which the file conforms.
- **Body**: this is the section which defines the content of the PDF document containing the objects.
- **Cross-reference table**: specifies the byte offset of every object contained in the Body starting from the top of the file.
- **Trailer**: a dictionary consisting of the "trailer" keyword followed by a set of key-value pairs enclosed in double angle brackets. It provides the location of the cross-reference table and of certain special objects within the body of the file, like the root object called *Catalog*. A PDF viewer conforming to the standard should read the file starting from this section in order to locate the cross-reference table and navigate to each object of the physical PDF structure. Within the trailer we can also find other relevant information like the number of revisions made to the document.

Document Structure This layer describes the semantics of the components of the PDF file. This is a hierarchical structure that defines the relationships linking the various objects, i.e., how two objects are connected. Decoupling the document structure from the file structure means that, given a document structure, it is possible to build different equivalent PDF files by simply shuffling the object order in the body. As long as the document structure does not change, the file rendering will not change as well.

At the root of the hierarchy there is the document's *Catalog* dictionary. A few nodes in the Catalog are scalar nodes, but many others are the roots of for higher level objects. There are a lot of objects, but a minimal PDF document will at least contain *Page* objects. Such objects are tied together in a logical structure called *page tree*, whose root is the first page object, which in turn is an indirect object referenced in the Catalog dictionary by using the entry having "/pages" as key.

Content Streams These are PDF stream objects whose data consists of a sequence of instructions describing the appearance of any graphical entity to be rendered on a page. These objects are distinct from the basic types of data objects. The instructions can also refer to other indirect objects which contain information about resources used by the stream.

2.2 PDF Document Obfuscation Techniques

Obfuscation is a well-known approach leveraged by malware coders to hide malicious code from inspection efforts. Code obfuscation is, in general, a legitimate technique that is widely used to protect proprietary code, however it is also one of the best evasion techniques used by malicious coders to fool malware detection systems (especially those based on signature matching) or to make the work of an expert analyst more complex and time consuming. Kittilsen listed several techniques [5] that are usually employed to hide JavaScript code in PDF files.

- **Separating Malicious Code over Multiple Objects**: the code embedded in the PDF document is fragmented among several objects and reassembled upon execution. This technique is made possible by exploiting the reference feature that is relevant to the indirect objects.
- **Applying Filters**: filters are used to compress and encode object streams of a PDF file. The parser of a detection software must be aware of the filter used, otherwise it will not detect the presence of malicious code.
- **White Space Randomization**: randomly placed whitespace characters can be inserted in order to defeat very simple signature matching systems, like the ones based on calculating the *hash sum* of the whole document. This technique can be easily applied to JavaScript code, whose syntax is space-agnostic. Some of the solutions surveyed in the next sections (e.g. [4]) preprocess the code with a normalization phase in order to overcome this kind of obfuscation.
- **Comment Randomization**: similarly to space randomization, comments can be inserted at random to change the code without modifying its functioning.
- **Variable Name Randomization**: variable names are changed in order to overcome signature based detection systems which, for example, during a static analysis, look at the extracted code for suspicious variable names such as "heapspray", "shellcode", "exploit", etc.
- **String Obfuscation**: string manipulation is an obfuscation technique to fool and hinder security analysts and anti-malware software. This can be achieved in different ways. One of the most widely used techniques is to split a string in several substrings, and then merge them back at runtime. String format representation can be easily changed by employing different schemes, like the hexadecimal representation, unicode, base64 etc. An attacker can also use different formats and build hybrid representations. Another commonly used string obfuscation technique is the application of de-obfuscation functions upon strings at runtime, like substitution or XOR. Obfuscated code can be placed in any object and then deobfuscated only at runtime [13]. This kind of approach is extremely powerful against static analysis, while it is potentially subject to detection with dynamic analysis approaches.
- **Function Name Obfuscation**: this technique can be applied by creating pointers to functions using arbitrary names, like "eval"or "unescape".
- **Integer Obfuscation**: numbers can be obfuscated by representing them in a different way, e.g. using a mathematical expression. This technique is often

employed to hide a specific hardcoded memory address or other kind of numbers, such as addresses related to ROP gadgets that are packaged in the code and used to exploit different versions of a reader software.

- **Block Randomization**: this involves modifying the embedded JavaScript code syntax and structure, while preserving its global behavior.
- **Dead code and Pointless code**: as a further element of obfuscation, real code can be augmented with dead code (routines that will never be executed) or pointless blocks (whose results do not impact the execution of the real malicious code).

3 Taxonomy of PDF Malware Detection Approaches

The approaches used in the state of the art to identify malicious PDF files vary widely from solution to solution. However, it is possible to identify a general pattern that, with some specific variations, is commonly adopted:

- feature extraction;
- feature analysis and decision.

In the **feature extraction** phase the PDF file is analyzed to extract various features. Features can be extracted through an analysis of the PDF characteristics, or from the code that the file embeds. In this case standard static or dynamic techniques are leveraged to analyze and characterize the code behavior. Features are then analyzed in the **feature analysis** phase where several metrics of interest can be calculated. A discriminant function is then applied to decide if the input must be classified as malware or benign.

In order to conceptually organize the current state of the art in the field of PDF malware detection, we consider appropriate to apply this two-phases approach as the basis to build a taxonomy. In particular, we propose a taxonomy of the existing works with respect to two different aspects: considered *features*, and *approaches* used to analyze them. These two aspects provide orthogonal information about how the existing solutions tackle the problem of identifying malicious PDF files. In the next two sections we will detail these two taxonomies in more details.

3.1 Features

This section describes which features have been proposed for PDF malware detection, and organizes them in a multi-level taxonomy (see Fig. 2). The first level is the leftmost depicted in Fig. 2 and represents which type of data is extracted from the PDF document. The second level shows the preprocessing techniques used on these data to obtain the actual features used for PDF malware detection; these features are then reported in the third level.

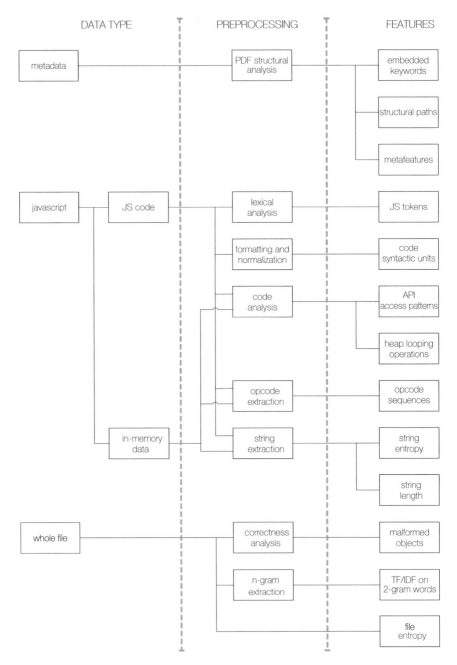

Fig. 2 Taxonomy of features used in literature for PDF malware detection

This section is organized according to the data types identified at the first level: *metadata*, *javascript*, and *whole file*. A final subsection discusses *feature selection* techniques used by some solutions to improve detection performance.

3.1.1 Metadata

Some works focus on the *metadata* of a PDF (see Sect. 2.1) to determine its maliciousness [10, 11, 14, 21, 24]. They all perform *structural analyses* of the documents to extract the features they need.

Embedded Keywords A PDF reader uses the keywords embedded in the document to understand which actions to execute; therefore, the set of keywords embedded in a PDF file can be an effective indicator of its high-level behavior. Pareek et al. [14] propose a fixed reference set of keywords to look for in a document, while PDF Malware Slayer [11] and Slayer Neo [10] identify sets of *most characteristic keywords* by examining the occurrences of keywords in either benign and malicious PDFs included in the training set.

Structural Paths As detailed in Sect. 2.1, the internal structure of a PDF is organized hierarchically in a tree-like fashion. Investigating how objects are arranged in such a structure can unveil valuable clues to recognize malicious documents. Hidost [24] considers the structural paths of leaves in the analyzed documents as features. The obtained feature set is then processed through a technique called *structural path consolidation*(SPC) to merge together similar features. In this way the semantic of the document structure is better preserved because it reduces the dependency of the feature set from the specific dataset.

Metafeatures Other works look at more general characteristics of a PDF, which we refer to as *metafeatures*. We want to stress the fact that metafeatures are different from embedded keywords. Indeed, some works [11] use a set of specific keywords and simply extract them from the structure of the file, because these keywords are closely associated to some known vulnerabilities or malicious behaviors. Conversely, metafeatures are features representing properties of the metadata, like "the count of some keywords", or "the ratio of the number of pages to the size of the whole document", or "the number of uppercase characters in the author field" or other similar properties that parametrize the metadata and the file structure as much as possible. As an example, Slayer Neo [10] considers a number of statistics about the structure of a document, such as its size and the number of contained streams. Similarly, PDFrate [21] gathers many numeric data representing aspects such as the occurrences of specific strings or the length and position of particular sections. Also Pareek [14] considers the frequency of some specific keywords, like /js (i.e., the number of launched javascript) or /JavaScript (i.e., the number of embedded javascript).

Despite systems relying on these kind of features are both efficient and effective, they are possibly subject to two kinds of evasion, namely *mimicry* and *reverse mimicry* attacks. The first attack has been demonstrated in a more systematic way by Smutz and Stavrou [21] and Maiorca et al. [10], and more theoretically by Laskov et al. [6] and Šrndic and Laskov [23]. The second attack has been widely addressed by Maiorca et al. [10].

The peculiarity of these attacks resides in the way they prepare the malicious PDF file. In particular, the *mimicry attack* adds benign metadata-based attributes to malicious samples, while the *reverse mimicry attack* starts instead from a sample classified as benign and renders it malicious in an incremental fashion while trying to avoid that it gets classified as malicious.

3.1.2 JavaScript

The most common attack vector for malicious PDFs derives from embedded *JavaScript* code that can be executed by the PDF reader. Indeed, many surveyed papers consider features derived in different ways from embedded JavaScript code [2, 4, 7, 9, 19, 25, 26]. As Fig. 2 shows, features linked to JavaScript can be extracted from two distinct sources: the *JavaScript code* itself, that is actually executed when the PDF file is opened, and the *in-memory data* that is generated during code execution.

JavaScript code can be extracted from the PDF either statically or dynamically. In the former case, the code is directly extracted from the file, while in the latter the PDF is opened and parsed through a reader software to observe which code is actually executed. The dynamic approach is generally more robust against obfuscation techniques (see Sect. 2.2), but requires a secure sandboxed environment for execution and is, in general, more resource demanding.

In-memory data is generated by the execution of the embedded JavaScript code and can thus be observed only by running the code through dynamic analysis. Features extracted from in-memory analysis can unveil malicious activities such as the preparation of memory areas (e.g. *heap spray*) to use for buffer overflow attacks.

Different preprocessing techniques have been proposed on either JavaScript code and in-memory data to compute the required features: *lexical analysis, formatting and normalization, runtime analysis, code method extraction, opcode extraction* and *string extraction.*

Differently from previous surveys [12], our taxonomy assumes that data can be extracted with either a static or dynamic analysis process. Depending on the sample under analysis, the choice of the right tool for data extraction is either implicit in the taxonomy (i.e., in-memory data can be obtained through dynamic analysis only), or is left to the analyst (i.e., JavaScript code extraction may be performed statically or dynamically, depending on the nature of the analyzed sample.)

Lexical Analysis Examining possibly complex and obfuscated JavaScript code calls for some form of abstraction to get rid of unnecessary details and isolate what is actually relevant for the detection. A lexical analysis of the code can support the automation of such an abstraction process.

Both the approaches proposed by Vatamanu et al. [26], i.e., Hierarchical Bottom-up Clustering and Hash Table Clustering, use PDF fingerprints as features, where a fingerprint is the set of pairs ⟨token, frequency⟩ obtained from a lexical analysis of JavaScript code extracted statically from a document. They consider *JavaScript tokens* identified using a grammar for ECMA Script.

Also PJScan [7] performs lexical analysis on JavaScript code extracted in a static way. It relies on SpiderMonkey[2] to extract JavaScript tokens, and also recognizes further tokens on the base of their length and whether they are invocation of suspicious functions, such as *eval( )* and *unescape( )*.

Formatting and Normalization In case some kind of comparison between JavaScript code fragments is required to decide on the maliciousness of a document, a conversion to some canonical form is usually needed to enable the evaluation of possible similarities or differences.

Karademir et al. [4] use *code syntactic units* as features. As syntactic unit they consider a block or a function in JavaScript code. Code is extracted statically from a document, then it is parsed to identify syntactic units. These are then encapsulated in an XML file with additional metadata, such as the start and end line of each syntactic unit with respect to the original file (*formatting* phase). The *normalization* phase includes three types of transformations aimed at abstracting the actual structure of the unit, i.e., control and assignment statements: (1) renaming of identifiers (to remove any reliance on naming conventions), (2) filtering of non distinguishing elements, such as variable declaration, and (3) replacing elements by their abstract name (e.g., replacing any expression with a unique symbol).

Code Analysis The extracted JavaScript code can be either analyzed or executed in a real or virtual environment, to understand in details which APIs are invoked and with which parameters. The execution environment can be instrumented to capture relevant events and information, depending on the specific features to obtain.

PDF Scrutinizer [19] looks at runtime for operations that add elements to an array to verify whether many identical and large data blocks are inserted, which can be seen as an attempt of heap spraying. It also statically inspects code to find any match with known signatures of malicious vulnerable method calls and parameters.

LuxOR [2] uses PhoneyPDF[3] for executing both static and dynamic analyses to extract all the API references that appear in the considered JavaScript code (i.e., *API access patters*).

---

[2]https://developer.mozilla.org/en-US/docs/Mozilla/Projects/SpiderMonkey.

[3]https://github.com/smthmlk/phoneypdf.

Opcode Extraction A common practice for malicious PDFs is to build the shellcode at runtime by copying the corresponding *sequence of opcodes* in some variables. As a consequence, some PDF Malware detection approaches execute dynamic analysis to identify variables that possibly contain malicious or suspicious opcode sequences.

PDF Scrutinizer [19] employs a dedicated heuristic to properly choose which values to analyse, for example by focussing on the output of *unescape* method invocations, or on strings "with length between reasonable lower and upper bounds" or having many occurrences of the pattern *"%u"*. Indeed, the *unescape* method can be used to decode previously encoded strings where the malicious opcode sequence was stored, and the shellcode is mostly encoded using the *"%u"* pattern.

MDScan [25] chooses the strings where to look for shellcode by observing that such strings are commonly built at runtime, for example by decoding or deciphering other strings. This kind of transformations requires new strings to be allocated, because strings are immutable objects in JavaScript. Hence, MDScan scans memory areas of newly allocated strings.

In a similar way, also MPScan [9] identifies new strings by hooking where they are created, and subsequently examines them to spot shellcodes. Furthermore, it hooks the JavaScript engine of Adobe Reader where opcodes are actually executed, so as to reconstruct the real opcode flow.

String Extraction Besides being analysed to identify sequences of opcodes that may correspond to known shellcodes, strings can be also extracted for other types of analyses, for example for heap spray detection.

MPScan [9] computes the entropy of strings to verify whether they can be used for heap spraying. Indeed, since a memory area to be used for heap spraying mostly contains NOP opcodes, its entropy should smaller compared to any other string.

PDF Scrutinizer [19] looks instead at the length of used strings. Relying on the observation that strings prepared for heap spraying are likely to have significant dimensions, it verifies whether the length is greater than 100000 bytes.

3.1.3 Whole File

In addition to inspecting document metadata or contained/executed JavaScript code, other approaches look at the *PDF file as a whole*. The underlying rationale is that a malicious PDF holds somewhere specific elements designated to run some exploits and deliver a desired payload, which makes the document as a whole contain some distinguishing traits overall. Thus the key idea is analyzing the entire PDF with the aim of catching any feature possibly attributable to malware.

Slayer Neo [10] employs two distinct tools, PeePDF[4] and Origami,[5] to parse PDF documents and observe whether any *malformed object* is found. The presence of malformed objects, streams, actions, code or filters is a valuable information to evaluate the maliciousness of a PDF.

Pareek et al. [15] compute the byte-level *entropy of the entire file* to obtain a representative data to recognize malware. They also extract word-level *2-grams* from the hexadecimal dump of a PDF, and apply a term frequency-inverse document frequency (*TF/IDF*) analysis on the obtained 2-grams.

3.1.4 Feature Selection

Feature extraction is often followed by a technique called *Feature selection* (sometimes also known as *attribute selection*). It is an automatic selection of attributes that are most relevant to the predictive modeling problem under consideration.

What is worth mentioning is that some works address this technique in very different ways. PDFMS [11] and Slayer Neo [10] use a clustering approach in order to reduce the number of features by only selecting those appearing in the larger clusters.

Luxor [2] instead, uses a crafted function to select a set of features, represented by API references, that effectively characterize malicious samples. In particular, it checks the result of the function against a predefined threshold t, where t must be chosen in order to reflect a good tradeoff between classification accuracy and robustness against possible evasion.

Hidost [24] makes a sort of feature selection in order to find the minimum set of features required for a successful machine learning application. Specifically, the huge extracted feature set is analyzed with a technique called *structural path consolidation* (SPC), aiming at merging similar features. In this way, the semantic of the document structure is better preserved by reducing the dependency of the feature set on the specific dataset.

3.2 Detection Approaches

The features extracted according to the techniques described in Sect. 3.1 are then used to determine whether a specific PDF is malicious or not. This section reports on the approaches used in reviewed papers to elaborate available features

---

[4]https://github.com/jesparza/peepdf.

[5]http://esec-lab.sogeti.com/pages/origami.html.

for malware detection. We grouped existing approaches in four macro-classes (see Fig. 3): Statistical analysis, Machine learning classification, Clustering (for family identification) and Signature matching. A subsection is dedicated for each macro-class.

3.2.1 Statistical Analysis

A common way to study a dataset of interest consists in employing well-known *statistical analysis* tools, indeed they allow to easily find trends and relationships that otherwise would remain hidden and unexploited.

Pareek et al. [15] extract the byte-level entropy on the entire file for a set of PDFs including both benign and malicious PDFs, then calculate the confidence interval for the entropy of malevolent documents. A new document to analyse is recognised as malicious if the entropy of its content is within such confidence interval. As underlined by authors, using the entropy only does not lead to acceptable detection accuracy.

3.2.2 Machine Learning Classification

A natural and nowadays really widespread approach to malware detection consists in extracting a set of features from a training set, balanced between benign and malevolent samples, and training a binary classifier to detect new malicious samples with the highest possible accuracy. Several *machine learning classification* techniques are used in literature also for malware detection in PDF files. Often, reviewed papers report evaluation results on employing distinct classification algorithms and discuss which one performs best.

Two-class Support Vector Machines (SVM) are used by PDF Malware Slayer [11], PDFRate [21] and LuxOR [2]. PJScan [7] uses instead a one-class SVM, trained with a set of malicious PDFs only. Decision Tree algorithm is the most widely employed, in fact it is used by Slayer Neo [10], Pareek et al. [14, 15], PDF Malware Slayer [11], Hidost [24] and LuxOR [2]. A Random Forest is an ensemble of decision trees, which usually provides better accuracy than single decision trees. PDF Malware Slayer [11], PDFRate [21] and LuxOR [2] feed their features to a Random Forest. Naive Bayes classifiers are utilized by Pareek et al. [15], PDF Malware Slayer [11] and PDFRate [21]. Pareek et al. [15] also employ other classifiers, i.e., Bayesian Networks, Logistic Regression and Logistic Model Tree (LMT).

3.2.3 Clustering

Within the more general field of malware analysis, it is of high interest grouping together samples that behave more similarly or that share more commonalities among each other. Analyzing new unknown or suspicious samples by understanding

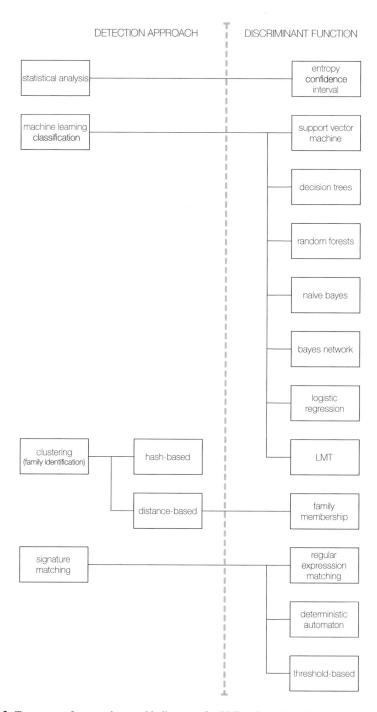

Fig. 3 Taxonomy of approaches used in literature for PDF malware detection

what known malware are most similar is a fundamental task. Indeed, this quickly gives to analysts many relevant information about analyzed samples, e.g., what actions we can expect they execute, and how to neutralize them. A group of similar malware is usually referred to as *malware family*. Given a set of malicious samples, each represented by a feature vector, it is possible to group them on the base of the similarities they have on those features. *Clustering* algorithms are usually employed at this regard, and also some surveyed papers use them.

Vatamanu et al. [26] propose two approaches to cluster malware with the aim of understanding what families can be identified in the considered dataset of malicious PDFs. The first approach is *hash-based* and is called Hash Table Clustering, where for each document of the dataset the hash of the PDF fingerprint is computed, and two PDF files are considered in the same family if their hashes are in the same bucket, i.e., each bucket represents a malware family. Since this approach does not lead to detect malware, the *hash-based* block in Fig. 3 is not linked to any block of the *Discriminant Function* level of the taxonomy. The second approach is *distance-based*, the Hierarchical Bottom-up Clustering, where clusters are built iteratively in a bottom-up fashion, starting from having one cluster for each sample and then gradually merging clusters having higher similarity. Such similarity is measured using a distance metric computed on token frequencies.

Karademir et al. [4] also use a distance-based approach and compute a similarity metric between two samples by using the NiCad clone detection tool [18]. Each sample is represented by its code syntactic units, and if two samples result less than 30% different from each other then they are considered in the same family. Rather than using such clustering methodology only for family identification, they take one step further by realizing a malware detection method based on *family membership*. After a training phase where available malicious PDFs are clustered in families, when a new sample has to be analysed, its similarity is computed with respect to identified families and, if the most similar family results less than 30% different, then the new sample is assigned to that family and hence considered as malicious.

3.2.4 Signature Matching

One of the oldest and still employed approaches for malware detection is *signature matching*. A knowledge base is maintained where distinguishing signatures of known malware are stored. When a new sample has to be analysed, it is verified against these signatures and, if any match is found, the sample is marked as malicious. We recognize three distinct classes of approaches based on signature matching: *regular expression matching*, *deterministic automation* and *threshold-based*.

Regular Expression Matching Rather than relying on a fixed and poorly flexibly signature, approaches based on *regular expression matching* result more powerful and effective in identifying variants of a same malware.

PDF Scrutinizer [19] matches signatures against patterns specified with regular expression. In particular, JavaScript code is checked for occurrences of the signatures, represented by vulnerable method calls and including parameters often used in known exploits. It also employs another kind of regular expression, consisting in the set of words more commonly used by known malicious JavaScript code, such as suspicious variable names (e.g., "shellcode", "heapspray", "exploit"). Vulnerable API methods calls are checked against crafted regular expressions. Furthermore, it executes the code in an emulated environment and uses a basic *endless loop detection* mechanism to recognize situations where a malicious PDF realizes it is being executed in some analysis environment and reacts by not executing its malicious payload.

PDF Scrutinizer [19], MPScan [9] and MDScan [25] use external tools such as Nemu [16] and libemu to perform a pattern matching of extracted opcode sequences against signatures of known shellcodes.

Deterministic Automation When a signature represents specific patterns of opcodes which denote known malicious activities, it can be useful to model such patterns by using finite state machines (FSM). MPScan [9] adopts this approach and relies on a knowledge base of signatures, each of them being an FSM instance modelling a malicious pattern of opcodes.

To verify whether a specific opcode sequence extracted from a PDF matches a particular signature, the correspondent FSM instance is used to check the feasibility to obtain the opcode sequence according to the allowed transitions. If the sequence can be rebuilt exactly and the FSM instance terminates in a final state, then a matching is found and the sequence is considered malicious.

Threshold-Based A particular type of signature can consist in a threshold value, to be used when determining if a document contains malware. Its simplicity of use usually comes at the cost of limited effectiveness in terms of achievable accuracy.

PDF Scrutinizer [19] puts in place a threshold-based mechanism on string lengths. If the length of a variable string value exceeds a predefined threshold, the document is marked as malicious. This is because long strings in a malicious JavaScript code are usually instantiated for the construction of NOP-sleds, to be used in heap spray exploitation.

MPScan [9] selects all the strings longer than a certain threshold, under the assumption that very long strings are likely linked to heap spray activities. The entropy of these long strings is then computed and, because heap spray mostly includes repeated characters, the result should be much lower with respect to normal and harmless strings. Hence, a maximum threshold value (1, in this case) is chosen, to determine whether the string should be considered suspicious.

4 State of the Art Discussion

In the previous sections we described a taxonomy that explores two aspects separately, namely features and detection approaches. For each aspect we detailed several building blocks, grouped in conceptually homogeneous families and organized in a hierarchical structure. This taxonomy helped us in clearly defining how each specific building block is considered by the works that use it. However, considering these building blocks separately does not provide the reader with a global view about how each work in the state of the art analyzes a given set of features.

Figure 4 provides a cross-reference matrix where the two aspects of this taxonomy are represented as different axes. At the intersection of features with detection approaches within this matrix we report references to the systems where that specific combination is used. This global view allows the reader to appreciate two details that are evident. Firstly, some works combine the usage of different detection approaches with several distinct features. This is a common solution to improve the overall detection accuracy of a system. The second detail that is worth noticing is that several systems share similar approaches or work on the same feature sets. This is an important information as it may indicate that these features or approaches have been found to be particularly effective in detecting malware by independent researchers.

We want also to point out how Pareek et al. developed two systems, both introduced in [15], that focus on extracting features from the whole file, with the difference that one is based on entropy measure while the second is n-gram-based.

Furthermore, the two systems introduced by Vatamanu et al.[26] have not been included in the matrix as they mainly propose a method for malware family identification and do not explicitly define a discriminant function to identify benign/malicious input (they assume that all input samples are malicious).

The matrix shows that most detection systems take advantage of machine learning techniques for file classification. What is worth mentioning is how all of them, but [7, 10] and [15], exploit more than just one classification algorithm to train several models and select the ones providing the best accuracy on the available training datasets. By a quick visual inspection of the matrix, it seems that no system has explored, so far, the usage of machine learning classification techniques in combination with *OpCode sequences* as possible features. On the other hand, all the systems that use them employ an instrumented javascript interpreter to keep track of runtime operations and variable values, together with specific dynamic heuristics monitoring the control flow for malicious operations (e.g. shellcode detection using *GetPC* heuristics). In general, three main clusters of works can be spot in the matrix: one characterized by using classifiers on metadata, another one adopting classifiers on the whole file, and a third one applying signature matching on features derived from JavaScript code. The empty parts of this matrix could possibly provide hints for future research directions.

	Metadata — PDF Structural Analysis			JS Code — Lexical Analysis	JS Code — Formatting and Normalization	Javascript — Code Analysis		Javascript — Opcode Extraction	Javascript — String Extraction		Whole File — Correctness Analysis	Whole File — N-Gram Extraction	Whole File
Detection Approaches	Embedded Keywords	Structural Paths	Metafeatures	JS Tokens	Code Syntactinc Units	API Access Patterns	Heap Looping Operations	Opcode Sequences	String Entropy	String Length	Malformed Objects	TF/IDF on 2-Gram Words	File Entropy
Statistical Analysys													
Entropy Confidence Interval													[15]
Machine Learning Classification													
Support Vector Machines	[11]		[21]	[7]		[2]							
Decision Trees	[10,11,14]	[24]	[10,14]			[2]					[10]	[15]	[14]
Random Forests	[11]		[21]			[2]							
Naïve Bayes	[11,14]		[14,21]										[14]
Bayes Networks	[14]		[14]										[14]
Logistic Regression	[14]		[14]										[14]
LMT	[14]		[14]										[14]
Clustering													
Family Membership					[4]								
Signature Matching													
Regular Expression Matching						[19]		[9,19,25]					
Deterministic Automaton								[9]					
Threshold-based							[19]		[9]	[19]			

Fig. 4 Cross-reference matrix

4.1 Related Works

This section briefly reports other solutions that are strictly related to the analysis performed in this survey, but do not fit adequately the proposed taxonomy. This may happen because these works focus on specific solutions that per-se do not constitute a fully fledged malware detection system. In some other cases, it is possible that the proposed work provides a fundamental building block that can be used to build a malware detection system. In any case, we think a survey like this one could not be considered complete without briefly citing these solutions.

NOZZLE Ratanaworabhan et al. [17] presented a runtime heap-spraying detector which examines individual objects in the heap, by interpreting them as code and performing a static analysis on that code to detect malicious intent. In particular the NOZZLE lightweight emulator scans heap objects to identify valid x86 code sequences, disassembles the code and builds a control flow graph. This analysis technique is mainly focussed on the detection of *NOP sleds*. Through the development of an attack surface metric, they try to figure out the likelihood that a random jump on an object allocated in the heap would end up executing a possible shellcode. As we know, in the heap spray technique, any jump that lands in the NOP sled will eventually transfer control to the shellcode. Through the development of a control flow graph made of blocks with disassembled code, NOZZLE calculates the reachability of the various blocks. If one of them contains the shellcode, most likely, by jumping randomly on a different block (containing arbitrary instructions or NOP instructions), it will be eventually reached. The heap spray technique is widely employed within malicious PDF files to give exploits a higher chance of success. For this reason, blocking a part of the attack, the heap spray in this case, would mean stopping the attack itself.

ShellOS Presented by Snow et al. [22], ShellOS is an open source framework that leverages hardware virtualization to better enable the detection of code injection attacks with respect to software-based emulation techniques. It is based on code analysis at runtime. The framework uses hardware virtualization to execute instruction sequences directly on the CPU, significantly improving the speed of code analysis and the execution efficiency. ShellOS kernel runs as a guest OS using *Kernel-based Virtual Machine* (KVM). It communicates with the host operating system by mean of shared memory address space regions, through which it receives the stream of code to analyze and writes back the results

Active Learning Framework Nissim et al. [13] proposed an Active Learning (AL) based framework, specifically designed to efficiently assist anti-virus vendors focussing their analytical efforts aimed at acquiring novel malicious content. The objective is to identify and acquire both new PDF files that are most likely malicious and informative benign PDF documents. These files are used for retraining and enhancing the knowledge bases of both the detection model and anti-virus. The model is built by employing a SVM classifier on the same features used by Šrndić and Laskov [24], namely the structural paths.

Advanced Parsers Carmony et al. [1] highlight how all existing detection techniques rely on the PDF parser to a certain extent. The problem is mainly due to the complexity of the PDF format specification. Parser implementations, built ad-hoc by anti-virus software developers are often limited in functionalities, are less precise than other full-fledged parsers, and are often vulnerable to possible evasion. In order to prove that this problem is actually compelling in the field of malware detection, they implemented a *javascript reference extractor* which directly taps into Adobe Reader, and compared it with publicly available parsers, showing their inability at extracting malicious javascript code from several samples.

5 Conclusions

In this work we presented a comprehensive overview of existing solutions for PDF malware detection. We conveniently organized reviewed solutions along two orthogonal axes: one for the considered features, and one for the approaches used to analyze these features to decide whether a PDF is malicious or benign. By structuring in this way the surveyed solutions, we provided a general taxonomy which can be used by practitioners to identify the best solutions for their needs. Furthermore, the same taxonomy may be of interest for researchers as it hints at clear gaps in the current state of the art that may pave the way for new interesting research directions. More in general, PDF malware analysis represents a fundamental building block for threat intelligence platforms that aim at protecting systems from diverse attacks.

Acknowledgements This present work has been partially supported by a grant of the Italian Presidency of Ministry Council, and by CINI Cybersecurity National Laboratory within the project *FilieraSicura: Securing the Supply Chain of Domestic Critical Infrastructures from Cyber Attacks* (www.filierasicura.it) funded by CISCO Systems Inc. and Leonardo SpA.

References

1. C. Carmony, M. Zhang, X. Hu, A. V. Bhaskar, and H. Yin. Extract me if you can: Abusing pdf parsers in malware detectors. 2016.
2. I. Corona, D. Maiorca, D. Ariu, and G. Giacinto. Lux0r: Detection of malicious pdf-embedded javascript code through discriminant analysis of api references. In *Proceedings of the 2014 Workshop on Artificial Intelligent and Security Workshop*, pages 47–57. ACM, 2014.
3. Document management – portable document format – part 1: Pdf 1.7. Standard, International Organization for Standardization, Geneva, CH, Mar. 2008.
4. S. Karademir, T. Dean, and S. Leblanc. Using clone detection to find malware in acrobat files. In *Proceedings of the 2013 Conference of the Center for Advanced Studies on Collaborative Research*, pages 70–80. IBM Corp., 2013.

5. J. Kittilsen. Detecting malicious pdf documents. Master's thesis, 2011.
6. P. Laskov et al. Practical evasion of a learning-based classifier: A case study. In *Security and Privacy (SP), 2014 IEEE Symposium on*, pages 197–211. IEEE, 2014.
7. P. Laskov and N. Šrndić. Static detection of malicious javascript-bearing pdf documents. In *Proceedings of the 27th Annual Computer Security Applications Conference*, pages 373–382. ACM, 2011.
8. K. Liu. Dig into the attack surface of pdf and gain 100+ cves in 1 year. White paper at Black Hat Asia 2016, 2017.
9. X. Lu, J. Zhuge, R. Wang, Y. Cao, and Y. Chen. De-obfuscation and detection of malicious pdf files with high accuracy. In *System sciences (HICSS), 2013 46th Hawaii international conference on*, pages 4890–4899. IEEE, 2013.
10. D. Maiorca, D. Ariu, I. Corona, and G. Giacinto. A Structural and Content-based Approach for a Precise and Robust Detection of Malicious PDF Files. In *Proceedings of the 1st International Conference on Information Systems Security and Privacy (ICISSP 2015)*, pages 27–36, 2015.
11. D. Maiorca, G. Giacinto, and I. Corona. A Pattern Recognition System for Malicious PDF Files Detection. In P. Perner, editor, *MLDM*, volume 7376 of *Lecture Notes in Computer Science*, pages 510–524. Springer, 2012.
12. N. Nissim, A. Cohen, C. Glezer, and Y. Elovici. Detection of malicious pdf files and directions for enhancements: a state-of-the art survey. *Computers & Security*, 48:246–266, 2015.
13. N. Nissim, A. Cohen, R. Moskovitch, A. Shabtai, M. Edri, O. BarAd, and Y. Elovici. Keeping pace with the creation of new malicious pdf files using an active-learning based detection framework. *Security Informatics*, 5(1):1, 2016.
14. H. Pareek, P. Eswari, and N. S. C. Babu. Malicious PDF Document Detection Based on Feature Extraction and Entropy. *International Journal of Security, Privacy and Trust Management*, 2(5), 2013.
15. H. Pareek, P. Eswari, N. S. C. Babu, and C. Bangalore. Entropy and n-gram analysis of malicious pdf documents. *International Journal of Engineering*, 2(2), 2013.
16. M. Polychronakis, K. G. Anagnostakis, and E. P. Markatos. Comprehensive shellcode detection using runtime heuristics. In *Proceedings of the 26th Annual Computer Security Applications Conference*, ACSAC '10, pages 287–296, New York, NY, USA, 2010. ACM.
17. P. Ratanaworabhan, V. B. Livshits, and B. G. Zorn. Nozzle: A defense against heap-spraying code injection attacks. In *USENIX Security Symposium*, pages 169–186, 2009.
18. C. K. Roy and J. R. Cordy. Nicad: Accurate detection of near-miss intentional clones using flexible pretty-printing and code normalization. In *Proceedings of the 2008 The 16th IEEE International Conference on Program Comprehension*, ICPC '08, pages 172–181, Washington, DC, USA, 2008. IEEE Computer Society.
19. F. Schmitt, J. Gassen, and E. Gerhards-Padilla. Pdf scrutinizer detecting javascript-based attacks in pdf documents. In *Privacy, Security and Trust (PST), 2012 Tenth Annual International Conference on*, pages 104–111. IEEE, 2012.
20. K. Selvaraj and N. F. Gutierrez. The rise of pdf malware. *Symantec Security Response*, 2010.
21. C. Smutz and A. Stavrou. Malicious PDF detection using metadata and structural features. In *Proceedings of the 28th Annual Computer Security Applications Conference*, pages 239–248. ACM, 2012.
22. K. Z. Snow, S. Krishnan, F. Monrose, and N. Provos. Shellos: Enabling fast detection and forensic analysis of code injection attacks. In *USENIX Security Symposium*, pages 183–200, 2011.
23. N. Šrndic and P. Laskov. Detection of malicious pdf files based on hierarchical document structure. In *Proceedings of the 20th Annual Network & Distributed System Security Symposium*, 2013.

24. N. Šrndić and P. Laskov. Hidost: a static machine-learning-based detector of malicious files. *EURASIP Journal on Information Security*, 2016(1):22, 2016.
25. Z. Tzermias, G. Sykiotakis, M. Polychronakis, and E. P. Markatos. Combining static and dynamic analysis for the detection of malicious documents. In *Proceedings of the Fourth European Workshop on System Security*, page 4. ACM, 2011.
26. C. Vatamanu, D. Gavriluţ, and R. Benchea. A practical approach on clustering malicious pdf documents. *Journal in Computer Virology*, 8(4):151–163, 2012.

Adaptive Traffic Fingerprinting for Darknet Threat Intelligence

Hamish Haughey, Gregory Epiphaniou, Haider Al-Khateeb, and Ali Dehghantanha

Abstract Darknet technology such as Tor has been used by various threat actors for organising illegal activities and data exfiltration. As such there is a case for organisations to block such traffic, or to try and identify when it is used and for what purposes. However, anonymity in cyberspace has always been a domain of conflicting interests. While it gives enough power to nefarious actors to masquerade their illegal activities, it is also the corner stone to facilitate freedom of speech and privacy. We present a proof of concept for a novel algorithm that could form the fundamental pillar of a darknet-capable Cyber Threat Intelligence platform. The solution can reduce anonymity of users of Tor, and considers the existing visibility of network traffic before optionally initiating targeted or widespread BGP interception. In combination with server HTTP response manipulation, the algorithm attempts to reduce the candidate data set to eliminate client-side traffic that is most unlikely to be responsible for server-side connections of interest. Our test results show that MITM manipulated server responses lead to expected changes received by the Tor client. Using simulation data generated by shadow, we show that the detection scheme is effective with false positive rate of 0.001, while sensitivity detecting non-targets was 0.016 ± 0.127. Our algorithm could assist collaborating organisations willing to share their threat intelligence or cooperate during investigations.

Keywords Threat intelligence · Traffic finger printing · Darknet · MITM

H. Haughey
University of Northumbria, Newcastle, UK

G. Epiphaniou · H. Al-Khateeb
University of Bedfordshire, Bedfordshire, UK
e-mail: gregory.epiphaniou@beds.ac.uk; haider.alkhateeb@beds.ac.uk

A. Dehghantanha (✉)
Department of Computer Science, University of Sheffield, Sheffield, UK
e-mail: A.Dehghantanha@sheffield.ac.uk

1   Introduction

Threats to individuals and organisations from Cyber attackers have been observed since the early days of computers and the Internet [48]. Threat actors have perpetrated various attacks ranging from relatively innocuous hoaxes to more impact-ful instances of social engineering and reverse engineering to harvest credentials, hold organisations to ransom for their data, or cause actual physical damage to systems [30]. In response to this persistent threat from a wide range of actors with varying motives and methods, a number of ontologies for Cyber Threat Intelligence (CTI) have appeared over the years such as STIX and TAXII [10], OpenIOC [8], SCAP [39], VERIS [46], Cybox [9], and RID and IODEF [25]. Given that so many ontologies exist to address some aspect of exchanging CTI, further work has attempted to taxonomies these systems to understand their dependencies and interoperability [6]. Furthermore, it is widely accepted that a critical part of an organisation's CTI capability requires the sharing of information with trusted peers [2]. This varied selection of offerings highlights the importance of standardisation, as organisations are likely to use a particular solution that may or not be compatible with that in use by another organisation. A gap in the current offerings appears to be in satisfactorily addressing Privacy Enhancing Technology (PET) as a medium for threat actors to perpetrate their nefarious activities undetected.

An example of threat actor behaviour is the use of encrypted channels for data exfiltration [20], and the challenge for organisations in identifying or blocking known bad network locations has increased due to the readiness with which PET is now available. Organisations are then faced with a choice, to allow or disallow traffic originating from, or destined for, such PET on their networks. This choice is further complicated by the open debate on privacy and data protection [13].

It is easily observable that long-standing concerns regarding privacy and anonymity continue to grow among certain groups [17, 35, 47]. This may not come as a surprise, considering the increasing capabilities of some organisations to monitor and report on user behaviour in day to day activities [14].

Fuelling this debate, there have been recent legislations such as the Investigatory Powers Bill in the UK proposed to require Internet Service Providers (ISPs) and Mobile Operators to preserve meta-data on the activities of each Internet user [56]. This has resulted in greater use over time of PET such as The Onion Router (Tor) [15, 55], The Invisible Internet Project (i2p) [24], and Freenet [52], for a wide range of reasons, and no longer limited to cyber-espionage or illegal activities.

Deep Packet Inspection (DPI) is a suitable example of a technique to extend analysis capabilities towards encrypted traffic [61]. For instance, while DPI cannot by default access encrypted streams, it could still facilitate censorship by means of a Denial-of-Service (DoS) attack on PET by analysing IP and TCP headers [61]. Countermeasures in this case focus on obfuscating PET traffic [60, 63]. For example, Tor's obfsproxy [44] is implemented to mock the behaviour of the widely used Transport Layer Security (TLS) protocol, relying on the essential role that

TLS plays in other communications, and the fact that it must be permitted as a key requirement to enable e-commerce in a given region.

There is a known threat to users of PET of powerful adversaries with access to Autonomous Systems (AS) or Internet Exchanges (IX), who are in strong tactical position to view or gain access to large portions of Internet traffic, potentially allowing passive traffic association to take place [51, 57]. While the Tor threat model states that it does not protect against adversaries that can view both sides of a circuit, the Tor path selection algorithm does take steps to reduce the chance of this happening [15, 33] and therefore such an adversary is obviously of concern to the developers and users of the system.

In this work we present a novel algorithm that could act as a fundamental pillar of a Threat Intelligence Platform for use by AS and IX operators either alone, or in collaboration with trusted peers. The algorithm may allow operators to identify encrypted connections engaging in activity that is against their acceptable use policies or terms and conditions of use. The algorithm fingerprints TCP connection meta-data and supplies a fully automated routine to assist with the effective degradation of un-traceability of PET users. The proposed algorithm combines several previously documented techniques. The algorithm can classify network streams according to flow metrics, make use of BGP interception if necessary to increase the attack surface for traffic association, and also manipulate server-side traffic destined for the client. Our initial test results show that MITM manipulated server responses lead to expected changes received by the Tor client. Using simulation data generated by shadow, we show that the detection scheme is effective with false positive rate of 0.001, while sensitivity detecting non-targets was 0.016 ± 0.127. We believe that the algorithm can be further improved or adapted in order to improve detection rates and efficiencies in performance. Our algorithm could assist collaborating organisations willing to share their threat intelligence or cooperate during investigations.

The traffic association methods alone may prove useful to routing providers that wish to engage in intelligence-sharing, by allowing a risk score to be assigned to flows that demonstrate particular behaviour. TCP flow metrics could be combined with other scoring metrics that service providers wish to use, or may highlight candidates for the traffic manipulation or BGP interception components. Such collaboration between providers could lead to improved overall risk-reduction or may prove valuable during forensics investigations.

The remainder of this chapter is structured as follows: Sect. 2 contains background and discussion of existing works describing attack and defence mechanisms relevant to our work. Then, Sect. 3 introduces an adaptive traffic association and BGP interception algorithm (ATABI) against Tor. In Sect. 4 we present our initial experimentation and results and discuss them in Sect. 5. Finally, the chapter is concluded in Sect. 6.

2 Background

It is important for any organisation to have some handle on the common, generic, and opportunistic attacks that they may be subject to. For larger or more risk-averse organisations, there is a case for being aware of more targeted attacks, and applicable Advanced Persistent Threats (APT) [42]. Threat intelligence can be generated from a variety of resources that a typical organisation has access to, such as web server logs, firewall logs, mail logs, antivirus, and host or network intrusion detection systems [38]. The consumption and interpretation of such data can become a challenge due to the large volumes often generated, leading to a case of being unable to see the wood for the trees, or searching for a needles in a haystacks [45]. Often critical to identifying threats is the challenging task of defining the baseline and understanding what normal activity actually looks like [59]. Furthermore, threats are ever evolving, and older threats often tend to become benign as more effective techniques take over, or when law enforcement take down command and control infrastructure [41].

The primary goal of CTI, then, is to inform organisations of what the current threats are so that appropriate actions can be taken, with as much automation as possible [7]. To this end machine learning, big data analytics, and intelligence sharing techniques have become more common in modern Security and Information and Event Management (SIEM) and CTI systems [50]. Primary customers of such technology are always going to be determined by factors such as their risk profile, risk appetite, and of course the size of their security budget [7].

2.1 Analysis of Attack Vectors in Tor

Having a variety of threat intelligence sources increases an organisation's ability to identify threats early on in a typical series of sequential actions leading to data breach. Where PET such as Tor is concerned, the ability to inject relays allows an observer to become a part of the network, and when they are participating as an entrance or exit node, the source or the destination of traffic could be recorded by a threat management platform. Indeed, many attacks against Tor users require visibility of both the entrance and exit traffic [33, 57]. Injection of relays is typically simple to achieve as PET systems are mostly designed to allow anyone to participate as a user or a router of traffic [1, 3, 5, 12, 31, 32, 53, 54, 64]. As such, adversaries can easily initiate rogue routers in order to conduct active traffic analysis by injecting traffic into legitimate communication channels in an attempt to enumerate and analyse underlying traffic [31, 32].

These common and easy-to-deploy attacks may effectively expose anonymous communications, and the current authors assert that they may also give service providers and collaborating organisations the opportunity to record and share observed behaviour originating from specific locations. The more routers that are compromised by the adversary, the greater the probability that circuits will start being built using those routers as entrance and exit nodes. This comes with a financial cost increasing over time with the total number of Tor relays in existence. It is possible with this prerequisite for a Tor exit relay to insert a signal into the traffic that can be detected by an entry relay [32]. This is accomplished by making changes to the Tor application code to control at what point write events are made, which result in output buffers being flushed. By controlling whether either one or three cells[1] are sent in an individual Internet Protocol (IP) packet, it is possible to create a binary signal. If the signal created by the exit relay matches the signal received by the entry relay, then the user will be discovered along with the visited website. The obstacle that must be overcome by an adversary to perpetrate this class of attack is in getting the target to use entry and exit routers belonging to an adversary, or in gaining control of routers belonging to other operators.

Some of the most powerful attacks against PET are those possible if an adversary has access to AS or IX routing infrastructure [18, 21, 33, 34, 51, 57, 62], as this position greatly increases the possibility of observing traffic destined for servers that are participating as relays. More specifically, it has been reported that the probability of an adversary with IX-level access serving ASes appearing on both sides of a circuit is much greater than previously estimated [57]. This is due to traffic between the user and the entry relay, and also between the exit relay and website, passing through several routers existing in multiple ASes and IXes.

Another previous study conducted a real-world analysis of distribution of IXes on Tor entry and exit relay network paths to estimate the probability of the same IX or AS appearing at both ends of a circuit [33]. This involved running *traceroute* analysis from Tor clients to entry nodes, as well as from remote destination websites back to Tor exit nodes. All router points on the discovered route were then associated with an AS and an IX using available IP to AS number reference systems and IX mapping data. It was reported that one specific AS had a 17% chance of routing traffic for both ends of an established circuit, and a specific IX had a 73% chance [33]. This would ultimately allow completely passive analysis and correlation of traffic for large portions of the Tor network, and allow association of website interaction by a Tor user. This class of attack has a high level of sophistication due to the level of access required, and also due to the amount of processing power necessary to analyse the traffic and correlate traffic patterns. Organizations that do have the required access could make use of this capability to perpetrate such attacks themselves or share it with other parties. Changes to the Tor node selection algorithm have been suggested to reduce the feasibility of this attack by taking into account specific ASes and IXes on the paths between relay nodes [33].

It has been suggested that little attention has been given to application-level attacks against low-latency anonymous networks such as Tor [58]. A potential attack was presented in which attackers compromised multiple routers in the Tor network with only one web request to de-anonymise a client. However, there are

---

[1] Individual and equal-sized 512 byte unit of Tor traffic [15].

several other requirements and caveats. Firstly, the target must construct circuits using compromised relays. Secondly, separate relay commands must be set up for each request and it's not clear whether this would work with simultaneous requests such as those over HTTP/1.1. The attack is noted as becoming far less effective if the client is participating in concurrent browsing activity, as this will dilute or completely hide the signal created. Furthermore, certain active circuits can be multiplexed over a single TCP stream with variations of the traffic pattern. Further developments by He et al. [20] identified that HTTP GET requests are typically encapsulated within a single Tor cell. The authors discussed how previous work on fingerprinting in single-hop encrypted connections such as SSH tunnels or openVPN was based on the fact that variations in web asset sizes are useful for allowing association of encrypted traffic to fingerprinted websites. However, since the introduction of HTTP/1.1 and the support for persistent connections handling concurrent requests, such attacks became largely ineffective due to overlapping web asset requests. As a result, attention quickly turned to packet sizes and timing. An important assumption in [20] is that HTTP GET requests exist in a single outbound cell from the client. The proposition is that by delaying these outbound packets by a small period between the client and the entry guard, overlaps between HTTP GET requests and server responses can be removed. This creates much cleaner traffic patterns for analysis and could overcome one of the possible limitations of [58], as already discussed.

2.2 Hidden Services

The nature of Tor hidden services provides a number of challenges in collecting and analysing traffic, because by their very design the service host is intended to remain anonymous [15]. Many hidden services, or "deepnet" sites can be found using publicly available indexes. Such hidden services can then be fingerprinted for traffic analysis by a Tor client, but the wider challenge is in identifying and profiling sites that are not indexed in this way, or accessible by invitation only. There is research into attacks on hidden services in Tor [18, 28, 64], which, as stated, are as much of a problem for the provider of that service as the visiting user due to hidden service operators often wishing to remain anonymous. A brief overview of hidden service operation is provided in Fig. 1. For Tor networks in particular, running a hidden service comes with the greatest risk due to the ease with which an adversary can identify the service host [28]. Three separate attacks namely circuit classification, circuit fingerprinting, and website fingerprinting against Tor hidden services were described in [28] based on the assumption that it is possible to fingerprint the process of connecting to a hidden service. The ability to identify hidden services is significantly greater than association of normal user behaviour due largely to the much smaller number of hosts and typically more static content provided by hidden services compared to the open Internet [28]. Adversarial operators of hidden service

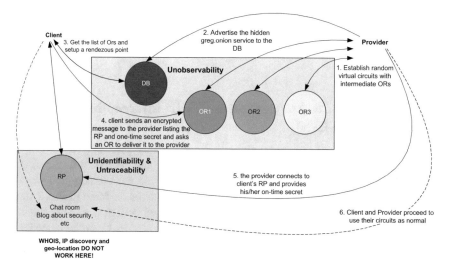

Fig. 1 Hidden services protocol [15]

directories may record the addresses of otherwise unadvertised hidden services to launch application level attacks [40].

There are many ways of covertly tracking a user's behaviour on the Internet such as cookies, server logs, and web beacons. Most PET technology will provide or support fit-for-purpose precautionary measures [43]. However, some attacks, especially against hidden services, may simply take advantage of the human factor. For example, configuration error is a large risk for inexperienced users of the i2p system [11] as well as Tor hidden service hosts. Hidden services can be erroneously hosted on a public-facing interface, or on a server that otherwise also hosts public information and gives away it's identity through private key fingerprints or other unique service information [11]. It is therefore recognised that PET systems are vulnerable to configuration errors.

2.3 Combining Methods

Little research attention has been drawn to the possibility that with sufficient resources, a powerful adversary could combine several documented attacks to further augment degradation of anonymity. Such combined methods are likely to have varying compatibility with each other but the potential end result would be some combination of an increased success rate, and a reduction in number of resources required as part of the attack itself. Considering the range of known attack methods against PET introduced above, we will now present a novel algorithm. Our algorithm combines a number of these previous attacks with a level of automatic adaptation to assist with reduction in un-traceability of Tor users. This can provide a fundamental pillar of a threat intelligence platform capable of identifying threats making use of PET.

3 Adaptive Traffic Association and BGP Interception Algorithm (ATABI)

Normally, the Tor client chooses three relay nodes to route encrypted traffic. Each node in turn then removes a layer of encryption, before the unencrypted traffic leaves the network towards its destination. Therefore, and as depicted in Fig. 2 step 1, server responses destined for the client are unencrypted until they re-enter the tor network, unless the website implements its own TLS encryption. Once the responses reach the exit relay (OR3) they are encrypted within the Tor network (step 2). Responses travelling between the entry relay (OR1) and the client are also encrypted as part of the established Tor circuit (step 3). For simplification, the following description assumes that an entity is interested in generating threat intelligence relating to undesirable use of PET on their infrastructure without being concerned about the potential repercussions of carrying out the methods described. A more pragmatic approach might be to collaborate with other service providers to perform wider passive analysis and reconnaissance, and agreeing about circumstances that collaborating entities are permitted to make BGP announcements for the purposes of association or investigation. Obviously operators could also share the necessary information with their collaborators without the need for BGP updates to gain additional network visibility.

As previously mentioned, the published research does not contain many detailed examples of combining known attacks against Tor, especially given the highly advantageous Man in the Middle (MITM) position provided to an AS- or IX-level entity. For instance, HTTP response traffic can be modified while in-transit with sophisticated regular expression (regex) search and replace methods [29, 36]. We propose that these or similar techniques can be used by an AS- or IX-level entity to manipulate server response traffic sent between websites and Tor exit nodes destined

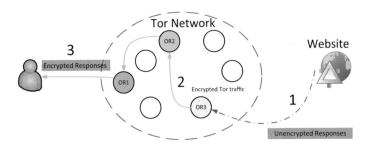

Fig. 2 Server responses in Tor

for the user. This will allow modification of HTTP responses sent back to the browser in order to directly affect or control client behaviour, while removing some of the obstacles to previous attacks such as having to compromise the website itself or for users to have JavaScript enabled in their browser. Obviously this kind of attack is considerably easier on clear text websites as opposed to HTTPS sites employing Secure Socket Layer (SSL) or TLS protocols, as in these cases the adversary would also have to gain visibility of server-side encrypted traffic. There are several known attacks against HTTPS that adversaries may be able to leverage to facilitate this, or they may simply have gained access to the private keys of a root or intermediate certificate authority [16, 37]. The AS or IX operator may instead wish to investigate watermarking techniques to avoid compromising HTTPS. The scope of this study is limited to testing HTTP traffic only assuming that HTTPS is either not enforced, or has been compromised.

Let us assume that an AS or IX operator has identified a website for which they wish to identify the users. If this entity has the capability of instigating a BGP interception attack, then they might begin by enumerating the list of all prefixes hosting Tor relays *that they do not already have visibility of*, or perhaps for locations that they believe to be likely sources of the traffic. With this information and the known prefix of the destination website, a BGP interception attack could be launched against all of these prefixes, thus getting complete visibility of the entry and exit traffic of interest. The challenge is then to associate the website traffic with the encrypted Tor entry traffic.

We present an Algorithm 1 that considers whether or not an adversary already has visibility of their intended targets and performs BGP interception if necessary. The algorithm waits for a trigger condition such as a security alert, indicator of compromise, or manual initiation before saving all required network traffic to disk for analysis. Our algorithm consists of three components: BGP interception, MITM server response manipulation (using MITMProxy [36]), and a detection scheme. The full algorithm can be described as follows (see Fig. 3):

1. The IX-level adversary initiates a BGP interception against the subjects of interest, for instance a destination website. BGP interception can also be performed to gain increased visibility of client to entry-side traffic.
2. The adversary routes unencrypted web server response traffic through a manipulator in order to change the HTTP responses as required, for instance by inserting assets.
3. The traffic then enters the Tor network via the exit relay. From this point back to the client, responses remain encrypted as per the Tor implementation.
4. The adversary performs traffic analysis with the detection scheme on traffic destined for the client at point 2 (unencrypted) and point 4 (encrypted).

The expected outcome is that as routes start to converge, the adversary gains visibility of all traffic destined for that website as well as the proportion of Tor entry node traffic of interest. The MITMproxy configuration forces page responses to include large assets that increase traffic for users that the adversary desires. As mentioned, this attack has a high level of sophistication due to the type of access

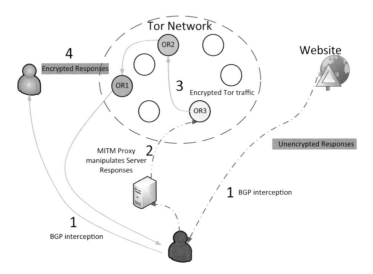

Fig. 3 Adaptive traffic association and BGP interception

required by AS or IX Internet routing systems. However, for entities with that level of access, updating routing to flow through another system running some form of manipulation software would be straightforward. We believe that this is entirely achievable for a service provider or group of collaborating providers.

A number of assumptions based on previous research support the proposed algorithm. Firstly, we assume it is feasible to associate traffic behaviour to individuals if both sides of the connection can be observed [22, 23, 32]. Secondly, BGP routing attacks by an AS or IX operator can allow observation of large or specific proportions of Internet traffic [51, 57]. Finally, HTTPS is not always implemented, or may be vulnerable to a range of attacks, and can be vulnerable to watermarking techniques [16, 37].

3.1 BGP Interception Component

We consider the recently disclosed attack known as RAPTOR (Routing Attacks on Privacy in Tor) [51], which is a further development on previous works such as [57]. Such routing attacks are one example that could place a powerful adversary at great advantage, if they have access to core Internet routing infrastructure. These works describe three main assumptions that can be approached either individually or in combination to increase the exploitability of the system.

First, Internet routing is asymmetric in its nature. In other words, the path that an outgoing packet takes is not necessary the same as that of its reply, and visibility of only one direction of this traffic flow is required to analyse traffic. Therefore the attack surface and likelihood of exposure to an adversary performing a passive traffic association attack are greatly increased.

Second, BGP "churn" over time due to network changes or transient issues such as router failures increases the chances that a regular user of Tor will cross paths with a particular AS or IX, facilitating passive traffic analysis.

Finally, it is possible for an AS operator to make false BGP announcements in order to have traffic intended for another AS route through their own routers in an active attack, which positions themselves on a target circuit.

The active attack comes in two versions, hijack and intercept. The drawback of the hijack is that the traffic never reaches its intended destination and so the client experience will be interrupted, potentially raising the alarm, or causing a new circuit to be built. An interception on the other hand allows the traffic to continue to its destination and the client session remains active. There are three possible scenarios for the interception attack namely: (1) the adversary already monitors a website or exit node and targets a set of known Tor entry relays; (2) the adversary already monitors the client to entry relay side and targets known Tor exit relays (or a destination website); (3) the adversary targets both entry and exit traffic in order to perform general monitoring, data gathering and association. It should be noted that while the impact of a hijack to a user is obvious, there is no mention of the impact on user experience in terms of latency, or packet loss while the new routes propagate and converge during an interception attack.

Once this Man in the Middle position is achieved, the previous authors discussed the strong feasibility of traffic timing attacks, especially given the benefits of asymmetric routing. We propose that this MITM position can be put to further use to provide greater advantage by perpetrating further attacks in combination.

3.2 MITM Component

Manipulating traffic is useful for affecting client behaviour. In a large set of similar candidate connections, the ability to affect those that the entity is interested in and separate them from the rest is obviously a valuable capability. Below, we demonstrate in a simple test that manipulation of server responses prior to entering the Tor network result in the expected client behaviour. We used the MITMProxy application to act as a reverse proxy for Apache HTTPd in order to replace:

```
</body>
```

With:

```
<img src="link_to_large_file" width="1px" /></body>
```

We suggest that an example of a real use case may instead need to simply forward traffic for all non-target destinations as required while pattern matching to manipulate only responses from the target website, and this is possible with MITMProxy filter options. We tested the "--anticache" option and found this to be effective against a caching server (varnish) in front of our test web server.

The output as observed in TORBrowser without MITMProxy was as follows:

```
curl —socks4a 127.0.0.1:9050 http://52.48.17.126/
<html>
<head>
</head>
<body>
<div align="center">
<p>Welcome home!!!</p>
</div>
</body>
</html>
```

And with MITMProxy running with search and replace on the body tag resulted to:

```
curl —socks4a 127.0.0.1:9050 http://52.48.17.126/
<html>
<head>
</head>
<body>
<div align="center">
<p>Welcome home!!!</p>
</div>
<img src="/dsc_0575.jpg" width="1px"/></body>
</html>
```

Note the additional image being included prior to the closing body tag, which is a 3.5 MB JPEG but resized to one by one pixel so as not to be obvious. The image in this test also resided on the web server, but could just as easily be hosted elsewhere. However, hosting assets with another site may require alterations to the detection scheme.

3.3 Detection Scheme

Algorithm 1 includes the detection scheme, which is useful for fingerprinting connections and consists of a reduction function based on a set of filters applied in sequence. The goal is to eliminate client connection streams that are unlikely to be responsible for the observed server-side traffic, based on their meta-data. We propose that this may be useful in assigning a risk score to any client connections that remain after applying the detection scheme. Such scoring may be useful for later interpretation or alerting by Bayesian analysis or machine learning systems. Specifically, server-side sessions are fingerprinted by recording specific metrics including the start and end time of the connection (SCt in Algorithm 1), total number of packets sent to the client (tp), average time distance between successive packets (at), total data sent (td), and total transmission time (tt). Similar metrics have been used in previous studies [22, 23, 32], however we believe our specific generation and treatment of these metrics is novel in its approach.

The same metrics are generated for all other observed connections. Once this fingerprinting is complete, reduction begins by first filtering for only connections that fit within the same time period as the server-side connection (CCt). Thereafter, remaining connections are filtered for similarity using the same metrics already

---

Algorithm 1 Traffic association

1: **function** BGPINTERCEPT(*target*)
2:      Initiate BGP Interception against *target*
3:
4: **function** COMPUTESTATS(*connection*)
5:      $tp =$ Total number of packets in *connection*
6:      $at =$ Average time between packets in *connection*
7:      $td =$ Total data sent in *connection*
8:      $tt =$ Total duration of *connection*
9:      **return** tp, at, td, tt
10:
11: **if** Target website traffic not visible **then** BGPIntercept *website*
12:
13: **if** Suspect clients traffic not visible **then** BGPIntercept *clients*
14:
15: **while** $trigger \neq 1$ **do**
16:      Check for trigger condition
17:
18: **while** $ServerConnection = active$ **do**
19:      Initiate MITM manipulation of server responses
20:      Save all network traffic to disk
21:
22: **for all** ServerConnections **do**
23:      $SCt =$ Timeframe of $ServerConnection$
24:      $SC =$ ComputeStats $serverconnection$
25:      **return** SC
26:
27: **for all** ClientConnections **do**
28:      $CC =$ ComputeStats $clientconnection$
29:      **return** CC
30: **for all** SC **do**
31:      Set initial tolerances
32:      $CCt =$ list of CC where CC packets are in the same time frame as SCt
33:
34:      $CCtp = CCt$ where CCt has similar total number of packets as SC
35:      **if** $CCtp = 0$ **then** Increase tolerance by $\pm1\%$ and repeat
36:      **if** tolerance $\geq$ max tolerance **then** Stop
37:
38:      $CCat = CCtp$ where $CCtp$ has similar average time between packets as SC
39:      **if** $CCat = 0$ **then** Increase tolerance by $\pm1\%$ and repeat
40:      **if** tolerance $\geq$ max tolerance **then** Stop
41:
42:      $CCtd = CCat$ where $CCat$ has similar total data sent as SC
43:      **if** $CCtd = 0$ **then** Increase tolerance by $\pm1\%$ and repeat
44:      **if** tolerance $\geq$ max tolerance **then** Stop
45:
46:      $CCtt = CCtd$ where $CCtd$ has similar total transmission time as SC
47:      **if** $CCtt = 0$ **then** Increase tolerance by $\pm1\%$ and repeat
48:      **if** tolerance $\geq$ max tolerance **then** Stop
49:
50:      **return** $SC, CCtt$

---

discussed in turn, starting by leaving only those with similar total number of packets ($CCtp$), then similar average time between packets ($CCat$), similar total data received ($CCtd$), and finally, similar total transmission time ($CCtt$). Any remaining client connections are returned as possible candidates for the observed server-side connection in question. Moreover, our proposal is that average time distance between individual packets can act as the filter, followed by similar total amount of data sent, and then finally similar total transmission time.

The detection scheme is adaptive in the sense that an initial tolerance is set and if no candidates are found, the filter is performed again after automatically increasing the tolerance. In our initial tests, we selected a base interval of $\pm 1\%$ for increasing tolerances. This proved effective in our tests, but is adaptable and may improved in further work. This occurs for each of the discussed metrics in turn. For example, the check for total packets sent will increase from $\pm 5\%$ by $\pm 1\%$ until at least one candidate is returned, up until a maximum tolerance level. Maximum tolerances were chosen simply to avoid the algorithm continuing indefinitely until candidates are returned that are highly unlikely to be those responsible for the server-side connection of interest. Any candidates found are passed to the next step in the detection scheme. The starting tolerance, incremental amount, and maximum tolerance are all configurable and were chosen by the present authors during testing as they proved to be effective with our data. We anticipate that future research will allow tolerance values to be set automatically by machine learning systems based on measurable factors including network conditions such as latency, packet loss, and jitter.

We will discuss experimental results following initial testing of the detection component of the algorithm, and offer a discussion of current design and performance. We use several key performance indicators (KPI's) used in typical binary classification systems to evaluate the effectiveness of the detection scheme. Our rationale for choosing these KPI's was due to the similarity to clinical studies in which a test is evaluated based on its ability to correctly diagnose members of a population with a condition, while keeping false positives to a minimum. KPI's include sensitivity (se, percentage of target clients correctly identified as candidates for a server-side connection), specificity (sp, percentage of non-target clients who are correctly excluded from the list of candidates), false positive rate (fpr, percentage of non-target clients who are incorrectly included in list of candidates), and false negative rate (fnr, percentage of victim clients who are incorrectly excluded from the list of candidates). For completeness, we also report the positive predictive value (ppv, percentage of included candidates who were truly responsible), and negative predictive value (npv, percentage of excluded clients who were truly not responsible).

4 Experimentation and Results

4.1 Experiment Setup

We used shadow [27] to create simulated networks and generate PCAP data for analysis. Shadow was used due to being readily available, easily accessible, multi-threading capability, simulation of transient network issues, its use of real Tor code, and the fact that it is still actively maintained [49]. Shadow and shadow-plugin-tor were built from the project source code available on github. The tgen plugin was used for the purposes of generating traffic on the network. This plugin makes use of graphml XML files that control the behaviour of a particular client such as which servers to download from, how large a download should be, how many downloads to complete, and how long to pause between each download. The latest stable release of Tor code (0.2.7.6—2015-12-10, at the time of experimentation) was used with shadow-plugin-tor.

In sizing our simulation network, we referred to [19] in which two separate experiments were conducted as follows; First, to test the feasibility of an attack, the authors implemented a small scale experiment consisting of 20 relays, 190 web clients and 10 bulk clients. Secondly, A larger network was also constructed by the authors based on the work of [26] consisting of 400 relays, 3000 clients, and 400 servers. Our approach was similar, implementing small networks for speed of simulations in order to debug any problems, and to develop and test the detection scheme. We then created a larger network resulting in more time-consuming simulation and greater data generation for our testing.

AWS EC2 instances were used for running our simulations. With our time and budgetary constraints in mind, an m4.2xlarge AWS EC2 instance of 8 cores and 32 GB memory was used to run simulations on a network containing 4 authority servers, 400 relays, 1000 clients, and 400 web servers. Generation of the network topology was based on tor metrics and server descriptors for the month of April 2016 (2016-04-30).

The 1000 clients included 989 similar web clients all set to download a 350 KiB file every 60 s, and 10 bulk clients set to download a 5 MiB file repeatedly without pausing. There were also two 50 KiB, 1 MiB, and 5 MiB clients downloading every 60 s. The actual downloaded data is arbitrary and randomly generated by shadow in order to provide simulation data. To simulate increased traffic for a victim (e.g. following a MITM attack) a single default web client as provided by shadow was set to download a 2 MiB file.

Due to the fact that shadow records session information for all clients, servers, and relays, it is straightforward to confirm from simulation output which client was actually responsible for a particular server connection. The process for running a particular test of the detection scheme was automated and involved the following steps:

- Inspect the web client log file for a successful download and take note of the time of the download and name of the destination web server.
- Inspect the web server log file for the correct download (which shadow helpfully confirms in the logs) and take note of the connecting exit relay session tuple (IP and port number).
- Run the algorithm against the given web server PCAP file and record connection tuple information of all clients' PCAP data in order to detect candidates for responsible clients.

The detection scheme is not currently multi-threaded but result generation for detection performance was scripted and split between 16 cores on a c3.4xlarge EC2 instance with 30 GB memory, and with 9000 Input Output Operations Per Second (IOPS).

4.2   Evaluation Criteria

Figure 4 illustrates a linear increase in average runtime of the detection scheme against a single session to identify a specific client amongst a group of 50, 100, 200, 500, and 1000 clients. This is indicative of the one to many relationship between a target connection on a server, and the variable number of potential candidates.

The detection scheme was tested by implementing in python against every client in turn within a particular set of simulation data and the detection performance KPI's were calculated. For a given detection attempt in a network of n clients, the total number of targets t will only ever be 1, with all other clients being non-targets ($nt = n - t$). This is because there is only ever one client that was truly responsible for a specific server-side connection. Using a diagnostic classification matrix, the

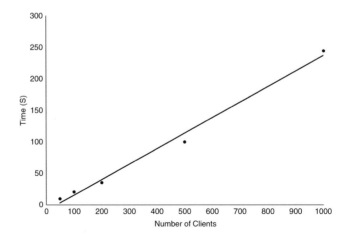

Fig. 4 No. clients vs detection run time (s)

Table 1 Single detection result matrix

	Test result		
Client	Target	Non target	
Target	$(tp = 1)$	$(fn = 0)$	$(t = 1)$
Non target	$(fp = 2)$	$(tn = 197)$	$(nt = 199)$
Total	3	197	$(n = 200)$

Table 2 Detection performance comparison

	Test					
	A	B	C	D	E	Test A victim
se	0.016±0.127	0.558±0.497	0.485±0.500	0.279±0.449	0.008±0.090	1.000
sp	1.000±0.001	0.981±0.014	0.986±0.010	0.993±0.006	1.000±0.000	0.999
fpr	0.000±0.001	0.019±0.014	0.014±0.010	0.007±0.006	0.000±0.000	0.001
fnr	0.984±0.127	0.442±0.497	0.515±0.500	0.721±0.449	0.992±0.090	0.000
ppv	0.012±0.100	0.073±0.186	0.075±0.192	0.065±0.181	0.008±0.090	0.500
npv	0.999±0.000	1.000±0.001	0.999±0.001	0.999±0.000	0.999±0.000	1.000
Victim detected	True	True	False	False	False	True

outcome for a detection attempt contains values for true positives tp, being either 1 or 0; false negatives fn, (being the inverse of tp given that there is only ever one true target); false positives where $0 \leq fp \leq (nt - 1)$; and true negatives tn where $0 \leq tn \leq (n - 1)$ and $tn = nt - fp$. A typical output from our testing is reflected in Table 1.

Performance KPI's are all percentages in the range $0 \leq KPI \leq 1$. Sensitivity se is calculated as $se = \frac{tp}{t}$ and will always be either 1 or 0 as there is only one target. Specificity sp is calculated as $sp = \frac{tn}{nt}$. False positive rate fpr is calculated as $fpr = \frac{fp}{nt}$ or $1 - sp$. False negative rate fnr will always be 0 or 1 and is calculated as $fnr = \frac{fn}{t}$ or $1 - se$. Positive predictive value is $ppv = \frac{tp}{tp+fp}$ and Negative predictive value is $npv = \frac{tn}{fn+tn}$.

4.3 Results

We ran the detection scheme against all clients five times for the largest simulation data, varying the percentages of tolerance in order to identify whether there was an optimised tolerance for the different metrics. Tolerances for each metric began at ±5% in every test and as per the algorithm, increased by ±1% until candidates are returned or until the maximum tolerance is reached. These results are presented in Table 2. The tolerance values tested were (number of packets, average packet time, total data, total time): $52, 32, 2, 1$ (A); $100, 50, 25, 5$ (B); $50, 50, 25, 5$ (C); $50, 50, 10, 5$ (D); $25, 25, 5, 1$ (E).

The results table also includes a column showing detection performance KPI's for the MITM victim during Test (A). The first test (A) used tolerance values tailored to achieve the best detection of the correct MITM victim target. Subsequent tests were performed to quantify detection KPI performance in general, and also tested against the MITM victim. Test (B) allowed a maximum tolerance of ±100% for similar number of packets and resulted in larger numbers of candidates to be included for classification according to the other metrics. Test results show how the performance KPI's are affected by changing the maximum tolerance values of the algorithm. Test (A) clearly performs poorly overall, however is highly successful in terms of true positive and false positive rates. This might be expected as test (A) was designed for detection of the MITM victim.

With these maximum tolerance values set, the correct target was identified only 16 times out of 984 total attempts, while detection performance of the MITM victim client with these tolerance values was very high. Detection of the MITM victim was achieved with a sensitivity of 1 (average for all other detections against non-victims = 0.016±0.127), specificity of 0.999 (average = 1±0.001) and a false positive rate of 0.001 (average = 0±0.001).

Test (B) correctly identified the MITM victim, and also correctly identified other targets with a sensitivity of 0.558±0.497 and false positive rate of 0.019±0.014. Detection performance whilst searching for the victim with these tolerances had a sensitivity of 1 and fpr of 0.003, which indicates an improvement over detection of non-victims.

Tests (C, D, E) all failed to identify the MITM victim and achieved decreasing detection performance KPI's as per Table 2.

5 Discussion

Our tests indicate a poor detection performance for any client while using maximum tolerances for total number of packets, average inter-packet time, and total data sent, and lower maximum tolerance for total connection time (Test (B). While the MITM victim was detected with these tolerances, three false positives were also identified as candidates. With fine tuned tolerances for the MITM victim in Test (A), detection performance for other targets is poor, while the victim detection was successful with just 1 false positive. This suggests that getting the tolerances right is critical to success. Furthermore, with further development and testing, tolerances could be automatically defined based on external factors such as network conditions or factors that the adversary can control, such as the size or number of inserted assets. It may also be worth investigating the splitting of individual connections into sections that can be individually fingerprinted with the same metrics. The relationship between sections when comparing client to server-side traffic may yield improved detection rates thanks to temporal variations in network conditions. We note that the runtime performance of the detection scheme is not currently scalable, and that there are opportunities for further efficiencies to be added. Machine learning in particular is of interest as a solution for eliminating candidates when performing the traffic association element.

A general strength of this algorithm is that it does not require Tor nodes to be injected or compromised. The algorithm is simplified and only requires average and total statistics to be calculated for some individual flow meta data for comparison. By using average data for connections rather than considering all inter-packet timing data for comparison, minor transient network issues such as short-term jitter and packet loss are expected to have a reduced impact on detection, however false positives may be more of a problem when larger data sets are available. Shadow allows for random and transient variables such as bandwidth, computing power, packet loss, and jitter to be simulated in order to mimic real network connections and with these default measures in place, our initial results are positive.

The application layer component of this algorithm relies on visibility of unencrypted traffic between the exit node and the destination, in contrast to watermarking techniques, which operate purely by embedding a signal into the packet timing. Previous attacks such as SWIRL are also blind, meaning that as long as the watermarker and detector both know the watermarking secret, no other data needs to be synchronised between them. Our attack requires that the metadata descriptors of the entry- and exit-side connection be shared with whichever system is performing the algorithm, at less than 150 bytes per connection.

The attack also assumes that the client is only participating in activity on one destination website. Because the onion proxy multiplexes all outgoing connections through a single connection to an entry guard, if several client activities are concurrent then the algorithm will not currently deal with this. However, if we assume that in most cases users of Tor will be browsing one page at any one time, the time slicing of the client side multiplexed connection would in that case only include the relevant data pertaining to the observed exit-side traffic.

We currently make no attempt to remove Tor control cells from the client side connection data. The tolerance level in the algorithm helps to account for this, but a future improvement to the algorithm might wish to take this into account as discussed in [20]. Total data received by the client in a particular window could simply be indicative of client bandwidth limitations. Therefore, for a given time window of the exit-side traffic, there is a risk that other Tor users with similar bandwidth restrictions could appear in the set of candidates, even if they are accessing completely different sites. However this still allows for correlation with the exit-side traffic thanks to the inter-packet timing and total data sent for individual connections. We also note that compared to watermarking techniques, the performance impact of embedding large assets would perhaps be more noticeable in text only applications, image-sparse forums, or bulletin board systems.

5.1 Use Cases

It has previously been presented that a small number of very large ASes are naturally in a position to see at least one end of a circuit due purely to their size [51]. Ten ASes were shown to have visibility of at least 50% of all Tor circuits, with some providers seeing over 90%. This would place these providers in a prime position to generate threat intelligence data points based on traffic analysis, or to initiate BGP updates to hijack or intercept traffic during investigations. The initial threat intelligence gathering could lead to triggering a BGP routing update under certain conditions, such as a security alert. It is worth noting that there are numerous entities and organisations that monitor BGP activity on the internet and report suspected interception incidents [4]. As such, anomalies are generally reported in forums and news sites fairly quickly when they do occur. However, this does not imply that organisations will not carry out such methods anyway, only that they are more likely to be detected, reported and discussed.

We imagine two preliminary use cases for our algorithm during investigations. Firstly, an adversary may have little or no idea of the location of the sources of traffic destined for a particular website. The objective here would be a wide BGP interception attack against all traffic that the adversary does not already have visibility of. This would be a large-scale attack and require significant resource for injecting the HTML into responses and processing the traffic to identify the sources responsible. An alternative to reduce the overhead would be to engage in a number of smaller attacks iterating through multiple source locations. In this case the BGP interception attacks would be targeted at the smaller IP ranges in sequence together with the destination if required. As discussed, another alternative would be if AS or IX operators participate in threat information exchange, or agree terms under which such BGP routing updates are acceptable.

Secondly, the adversary may have a good idea of where the source of traffic is coming from, for instance in a criminal investigation where a suspect is believed to reside in a particular area. In this case, the adversary may be fortunate enough to already have visibility of the required IP ranges thanks to asymmetric routing but if not, then would only have to perpetrate a much smaller BGP interception attack based on the suspect's location.

While our presented algorithm applies to Tor clients accessing public Internet sites, similar techniques could be applied to Tor hidden services. For instance, if an operator was to first identify a remote hidden service, then they could repeatedly make custom requests to it during a widespread BGP interception attack (or working with collaborators) while running the detection scheme. If detection of the hidden service were to prove successful, then BGP interception and detection could be used to identify clients of the hidden service, or the adversary could target the hosting system directly in other ways, leading to further attacks.

5.2 Proposed Defences

To mitigate against the HTML injection component, Tor nodes could consider disallowing port 80/HTTP in their exit policy. This may be strongly advised in any case considering the typical Tor user's privacy concerns as well as the wider industry moving towards HTTPS everywhere, and HTTP Strict Transport Security (HSTS). If blocking port 80 is too problematic for user experience or website functionality, then the only other option is for website operators to correctly implement HTTPS and make use of HSTS. Users that care deeply about their privacy should insist on using HTTPS websites and avoid the use of HTTP sites for accessing or sharing sensitive information. This will still not help if the adversary has the ability to compromise HTTPS, but would make success for the adversary significantly more difficult, or force the use of other methods such as watermarking.

The countermeasures suggested by the authors of RAPTOR [51] would all still apply to the routing component of the current algorithm and therefore deserve a mention. Monitoring was proposed to raise awareness of the possibility of increased traffic visibility due to asymmetric routing, BGP churn, or routing attacks, and to notify clients when a potential degradation of anonymity is identified. BGP and traceroute monitoring were both suggested and tested with successful results reported.

It was also noted that traditional countermeasures that manipulate packet sizes or timing come with a significant latency impact and so would remove one of the main benefits of Tor. A number of alternative countermeasures were proposed, including incorporating traceroute and AS lookups as part of intelligent selection of relays to build circuits that avoid routes crossing the same AS multiple times. However, this may result in lower overall entropy in Tor circuit selection and greater probability of adversaries with large numbers of injected or compromised relays appearing on both ends of a circuit.

Another suggested mitigation was that Tor relays should advertise prefixes of /24 to reduce the capability of BGP hijack or interception attacks. Adversaries could still launch attacks by advertising the same prefix, however the impact of the attack would be more localized to the adversary and more widespread redirection of Internet traffic would not take place. To further mitigate this reduced capability, it was suggested that clients could favour guard relays that are closer in terms of number of AS hops, but that this could reveal probabilistic information about clients, and requires further investigation. The final suggested mitigation requires that the wider Internet moves towards secure inter-domain routing, however this has been slow to get off the ground.

6 Conclusion and Future Work

This work has presented a novel algorithm (ATABI) against the Tor network based on the combination of previously reported HTML injection techniques with BGP routing attacks and a detection scheme. This algorithm could form a fundamental pillar of a PET-capable Cyber Threat Intelligence Management platform. A simplified version of the MITM component was perpetrated against a basic web page to insert a large hidden asset at the bottom of the HTML. This change in the returned HTML was observed in the response received by the Tor client. The suggested detection algorithm yielded positive results in initial tests on data generated by the shadow simulator for Tor. Detection performance of an MITM victim with large tolerances was good with a fpr of 0.003, while average general detection performance of all clients without MITM traffic manipulation was poor with sensitivity of 0.558 ± 0.497 and fpr of 0.019 ± 0.014. By tailoring the tolerances for the MITM victim and running against all clients, general performance was greatly reduced with average sensitivity of 0.016 ± 0.127 and average fnr of 0.984 ± 0.127, while sensitivity when searching for the victim was 1 with a fpr of 0.001.

In future research we intend to evaluate whether temporal patterns manifested throughout the duration of a session can assist detection by splitting sessions and fingerprinting each section. We hope to provide more practical examples of routing attacks facilitating a MITM position and consider other MITM technologies or development of a dedicated lightweight application. With further efficiencies such as multi-threading for an individual attack, performance could be increased to operate with larger data sets. Increased performance may also be achieved by using GPU, or distributed computing. Combining the IX-level advantage with other previous concepts such as watermarking schemes, sending custom requests to hidden services, or delaying GET requests but at the exit side rather than the client side are also of interest. We also plan on performing further simulations and experiments to produce more data in order to further optimise the tolerance levels for each connection metric, and provide more data for potential testing and implementation of machine learning. Given the large number of CTI ontologies available, we would see benefit in developing our algorithm to be platform agnostic. A worthwhile project would be the creation of a PET-capable Cyber Threat Intelligence Management Platform that can interoperate with a wide range of CTI ontologies, with a view to driving standardisation, and with our algorithm as a fundamental pillar.

We believe that this variety of opportunities to perpetrate previously known attacks against PET more effectively in combination with AS- or IX-level access is likely to gain more research attention in the future. This likelihood is augmented especially considering the challenge of attribution in CTI for darknet-based threat activity.

References

1. Michael Backes et al. "(Nothing else) MATor (s): Monitoring the Anonymity of Tor's Path Selection". In: *Proceedings of the 2014 ACM SIGSAC Conference on Computer and Communications Security*. ACM. 2014, pp. 513–524.
2. Sean Barnum. "Standardizing cyber threat intelligence information with the Structured Threat Information eXpression (STIX)". In: *MITRE Corporation* 11 (2012).
3. Todd Baumeister et al. "A Routing Table Insertion (RTI) Attack on Freenet". In: *Cyber Security (CyberSecurity), 2012 International Conference on*. IEEE. 2012, pp. 8–15.
4. BGPMon. *BGPMon* 2016. URL: http://bgpmon.net/ (visited on 10/31/2016).
5. Nikita Borisov et al. "Denial of service or denial of security?" In: *Proceedings of the 14th ACM conference on Computer and communications security*. ACM. 2007, pp. 92–102.
6. Eric W Burger et al. "Taxonomy model for cyber threat intelligence information exchange technologies". In: *Proceedings of the 2014 ACM Workshop on Information Sharing & Collaborative Security*. ACM. 2014, pp. 51–60.
7. Kim-Kwang Raymond Choo. "The cyber threat landscape: Challenges and future research directions". In: *Computers & Security* 30.8 (2011), pp. 719–731.
8. Mandiant Corporation. *The OpenIOC Framework*. 2017. URL: http://www.openioc.org/ (visited on 01/03/2017).
9. The MITRE Corporation. *Cyber Observable eXpression*. 2017. URL: https://cyboxproject. github.io/ (visited on 01/03/2017).
10. The MITRE Corporation. *STIX : Structured Threat Information eXpression*. 2017. URL: https://stixproject.github.io/ (visited on 01/03/2017).
11. Adrian Crenshaw "Darknets and hidden servers: Identifying the true ip/network identity of i2p service hosts". In: *Black Hat* (2011).
12. Norman Danner et al. "Effectiveness and detection of denial-of-service attacks in Tor". In: *ACM Transactions on Information and System Security (TISSEC)* 15.3 (2012), p. 11.
13. Ali Dehghantanha and Katrin Franke. "Privacy-respecting digital investigation". In: *Privacy Security and Trust (PST), 2014 Twelfth Annual International Conference on*. IEEE. 2014, pp. 129–138.
14. Ali Dehghantanha, Nur Izura Udzir, and Ramlan Mahmod. "Towards a pervasive formal privacy language". In: *Advanced Information Networking and Applications Workshops (WAINA), 2010 IEEE 24th International Conference on*. IEEE. 2010, pp. 1085–1091.
15. Roger Dingledine, Nick Mathewson, and Paul Syverson. *Tor: The second-generation onion router* Tech. rep. DTIC Document, 2004.
16. Zakir Durumeric et al. "The matter of heartbleed". In: *Proceedings of the 2014 Conference on Internet Measurement Conference*. ACM. 2014, pp. 475–488.
17. EFF. *The Electronic Frontier Foundation* 2015. URL: https://www.eff.org/ (visited on 10/30/2015).
18. Juan A Elices, Fernando Pérez-González, et al. "Locating Tor hidden services through an interval-based traffic-correlation attack". In: *Communications and Network Security (CNS), 2013 IEEE Conference on*. IEEE. 2013, pp. 385–386.
19. John Geddes, Rob Jansen, and Nicholas Hopper "How low can you go: Balancing performance with anonymity in Tor". In: *Privacy Enhancing Technologies* Springer. 2013, pp. 164–184.
20. Gaofeng He et al. "A novel active website fingerprinting attack against Tor anonymous system". In: *Computer Supported Cooperative Work in Design (CSCWD), Proceedings of the 2014 IEEE 18th International Conference on*. IEEE. 2014, pp. 112–117.
21. Nguyen Phong HOANG, Yasuhito ASANO, and Masatoshi YOSHIKAWA. "Anti-RAPTOR: Anti Routing Attack on Privacy for a Securer and Scalable Tor". In: IEEE. 2015, pp. 147–154.
22. Amir Houmansadr and Nikita Borisov. "SWIRL: A Scalable Watermark to Detect Correlated Network Flows." In: *NDSS* 2011.
23. Amir Houmansadr, Negar Kiyavash, and Nikita Borisov. "RAINBOW: A Robust And Invisible Non-Blind Watermark for Network Flows." In: *NDSS* 2009.

24. i2p Project. *Get i2p* 2015. URL: https://geti2p.net/ (visited on 10/24/2015).
25. Internet Engineering Task Force (IETF). *RFC 6545 Real-time Inter-network Defense (RID)*. 2017. URL: https://tools.ietf.org/html/rfc6545 (visited on 01/03/2017).
26. Rob Jansen and Nicholas Hooper. *Shadow: Running Tor in a box for accurate and efficient experimentation*. Tech. rep. DTIC Document, 2011.
27. Rob Jansen et al. "Methodically Modeling the Tor Network." In: *CSET*. 2012.
28. Albert Kwon. "Circuit fingerprinting attacks: passive deanonymization of tor hidden services". In: *USENIX Security Symposium, 2015 24th Proceedings of*. USENIX. 2015, pp. 286–302.
29. Spider Labs. *Responder* 2015. URL: https://github.com/SpiderLabs/Responder (visited on 10/28/2015).
30. Ralph Langner. "Stuxnet: Dissecting a cyberwarfare weapon". In: *IEEE Security & Privacy* 9.3 (2011), pp. 49–51.
31. Zhen Ling et al. "A new cell-counting-based attack against Tor". In: *IEEE/ACM Transactions on Networking (TON)* 20.4 (2012), pp. 1245–1261.
32. Zhen Ling et al. "Equal-sized cells mean equal-sized packets in Tor?" In: *Communications (ICC), 2011 IEEE International Conference on*. IEEE. 2011, pp. 1–6.
33. Peipeng Liu et al. "Empirical Measurement and Analysis of I2P Routers". In: *Journal of Networks* 9.9 (2014), pp. 2269–2278.
34. Peipeng Liu et al. "IX-Level Adversaries on Entry-and Exit-Transmission Paths in Tor Network". In: *Networking Architecture and Storage (NAS), 2013 IEEE Eighth International Conference on*. IEEE. 2013, pp. 166–172.
35. Gary T Marx. "What's in a Name? Some Reflections on the Sociology of Anonymity". In: *The Information Society* 15.2 (1999), pp. 99–112.
36. MITMProxy. *MITM Proxy Replacements* 2015. URL: https://mitmproxy.org/index.html (visited on 10/28/2015).
37. Bodo Möller, Thai Duong, and Krzysztof Kotowicz. "This POODLE bites: exploiting the SSL 3.0 fallback". In: *Google Sep* (2014).
38. Arsalan Mohsen Nia and Niraj K Jha. "A comprehensive study of security of internet-of-things". In: *IEEE Transactions on Emerging Topics in Computing* (2016).
39. NIST. *Security Content Automation Protocol* 2017. URL: https://scap.nist.gov/index.html (visited on 01/03/2017).
40. Guevara Noubir and Amirali Sanatinia. *Honey Onions: Exposing Snooping Tor HSDir Relays* 2016. URL: https://www.defcon.org/html/defcon-24/dc-24-speaker.shtml#Noubir (visited on 07/10/2016).
41. Opeyemi Osanaiye et al. "Ensemble-based multi-filter feature selection method for DDoS detection in cloud computing". In: *EURASIP Journal on Wireless Communications and Networking* 2016.1 (2016), p. 130.
42. Hamed Haddad Pajouh et al. "A two-layer dimension reduction and two-tier classification model for anomaly-based intrusion detection in IoT backbone networks". In: *IEEE Transactions on Emerging Topics in Computing* (2016).
43. The Tor Project. *The Tor Project: obfsproxy* 2016. URL: https://www.torproject.org/projects/obfsproxy.html.en%5C#Warning (visited on 07/10/2016).
44. The Tor Project. *Want Tor to Really Work?* 2015. URL: https://www.torproject.org/download/download.html.en%5C#Warning (visited on 10/25/2015).
45. Darren Quick and Kim-Kwang Raymond Choo. "Big forensic data reduction: digital forensic images and electronic evidence". In: *Cluster Computing* 19.2 (2016), pp. 723–740.
46. Verizon Security Research and Cyber Intelligence Center *The VERIS Framework* 2017. URL: http://veriscommunity.net/ (visited on 01/03/2017).
47. Schneier B. *Anonymity Won't Kill the Internet* 2006. URL: http://archive.wired.com/politics/security/commentary/securitymatters/2006/1/70000?currentPage=all (visited on 10/18/2015).
48. Kaveh Sharepour Ali Dehghantanha, and Ramlan Mahmod. "A survey on cyber-crime prediction techniques". In: *International Journal of Advancements in Computing Technology* 5.14 (2013), p. 52.

49. Fatemeh Shirazi, Matthias Goehring, and Claudia Diaz. "Tor experimentation tools". In: *Security and Privacy Workshops (SPW), 2015 IEEE*. IEEE. 2015, pp. 206–213.
50. Daniel Sun et al. "Non-intrusive anomaly detection with streaming performance metrics and logs for DevOps in public clouds: a case study in AWS". In: *IEEE Transactions on Emerging Topics in Computing* 4.2 (2016), pp. 278–289.
51. Yixin Sun et al. "RAPTOR: routing attacks on privacy in tor". In: *arXiv preprint arXiv:1503.03940* (2015).
52. The Freenet Project. *The Freenet Project* 2002. URL: https://freenetproject.org/index.html (visited on 10/24/2015).
53. Juan Pablo Timpanaro, Isabelle Chrisment, and Olivier Festor. "Group-Based Characterization for the I2P Anonymous File-Sharing Environment". In: *New Technologies, Mobility and Security (NTMS), 2014 6th International Conference on*. IEEE. 2014, pp. 1–5.
54. Juan Pablo Timpanaro, Isabelle Chrisment, and Olivier Festor. "Monitoring anonymous P2P file-sharing systems". In: *Peer-to-Peer Computing (P2P), 2013 IEEE Thirteenth International Conference on*. IEEE. 2013, pp. 1–2.
55. Tor Project. *Tor Project* 2015. URL: https://www.torproject.org/ (visited on 10/03/2015).
56. GOV UK. *Investigatory powers bill* 2016.
57. Laurent Vanbever et al. "Anonymity on quicksand: Using BGP to compromise Tor". In: *Proceedings of the 13th ACM Workshop on Hot Topics in Networks*. ACM. 2014, p. 14.
58. Xiaogang Wang et al. "A potential HTTP-based application-level attack against Tor". In: *Future Generation Computer Systems* 27.1 (2011), pp. 67–77.
59. Steve Watson and Ali Dehghantanha. "Digital forensics: the missing piece of the Internet of Things promise". In: *Computer Fraud & Security* 2016.6 (2016), pp. 5–8.
60. Zachary Weinberg et al. "StegoTorus: a camouflage proxy for the Tor anonymity system". In: *Proceedings of the 2012 ACM conference on Computer and communications security*. ACM. 2012, pp. 109–120.
61. Philipp Winter and Stefan Lindskog. "How China is blocking Tor". In: *arXiv preprint arXiv:1204.0447* (2012).
62. Philipp Winter and Stefan Lindskog. "How the great firewall of China is blocking tor". In: *Free and Open Communications on the Internet* (2012).
63. Philipp Winter Tobias Pulls, and Juergen Fuss. "ScrambleSuit: A polymorphic network protocol to circumvent censorship". In: *Proceedings of the 12th ACM workshop on Workshop on privacy in the electronic society*. ACM. 2013, pp. 213–224.
64. Lu Zhang et al. "Application-level attack against Tor's hidden service". In: *Pervasive Computing and Applications (ICPCA), 2011 6th International Conference on*. IEEE. 2011, pp. 509–516.

A Model for Android and iOS Applications Risk Calculation: CVSS Analysis and Enhancement Using Case-Control Studies

Milda Petraityte, Ali Dehghantanha, and Gregory Epiphaniou

Abstract Various researchers have shown that the Common Vulnerability Scoring System (CVSS) has many drawbacks and may not provide a precise view of the risks related to software vulnerabilities. However, many threat intelligence platforms and industry-wide standards are relying on CVSS score to evaluate cyber security compliance. This paper suggests several improvements to the calculation of Impact and Exploitability sub-scores within the CVSS, improve its accuracy and help threat intelligence analysts to focus on the key risks associated with their assets. We will apply our suggested improvements against risks associated with several Android and iOS applications and discuss achieved improvements and advantages of our modelling, such as the importance and the impact of time on the overall CVSS score calculation.

Keywords CVSS · Risk management · Risk calculation · Vulnerability · Exploitability

1 Introduction

The problematics of IT risk management often circle vulnerabilities within IT systems and behaviour of people who use those systems [1]. It is, therefore, hard to disagree that "there is no 100% security, there is only risk management" [2]. However, one can only make informed decisions about risks as effectively as informative and accurate are the metrics used for risk evaluation.

M. Petraityte
School of Computing, Science and Engineering, University of Salford, Greater Manchester, UK

A. Dehghantanha (✉)
Department of Computer Science, University of Sheffield, Sheffield, UK
e-mail: A.Dehghantanha@sheffield.ac.uk

G. Epiphaniou
School of Computer Science and Technology, University of Bedfordshire, Bedfordshire, UK
e-mail: gregory.epiphaniou@beds.ac.uk

© Springer International Publishing AG, part of Springer Nature 2018
A. Dehghantanha et al. (eds.), *Cyber Threat Intelligence*, Advances in Information Security 70, https://doi.org/10.1007/978-3-319-73951-9_11

Common Vulnerability Scoring System (CVSS) is used to calculate the severity of vulnerabilities [3] and risks related to IT assets [4]. Industries rely on CVSS as a standard way to capture the principal characteristics of vulnerabilities and produce a numerical score reflecting their severity. CVSS score is currently used to help the organisations to prioritise their vulnerability management process, yet the primary purpose of the CVSS is to detail the technical aspects of the vulnerability [4]. Furthermore, there is an expectation from organisations to use the CVSS calculation if they want to meet the requirements of certifications. For example, Payment Card Industry Data Security Standard (PCI DSS) requires to 'perform quarterly external vulnerability scans using an Approved Scanning Vendor (ASV) approved by the Payment Card Industry Security Standards Council (PCI SSC)' [5]. The ASV requirements clearly state that 'wherever possible, the ASV must use the CVSS base score for the severity level' [6]. The ASV reports need to be configured in such a way that a card vendor could immediately notice non-compliance and fix any issues 'to be considered compliant, a component must not contain any vulnerability that has been assigned a CVSS base score equal to or higher than 4.0.' [6]. The Telecommunication Standardization Sector (ITU-T) base their Recommendations to technical, operating and tariff questions on CVSS too [7, 8]. Previous recommendations have focused solely on CVSS [7], yet the latest report has been dedicated a Common Weakness Scoring System [8], which is largely focused on the methodology of CVSS and adopts a similar calculation [8]. CVSS score is used alongside Common Vulnerabilities and Exposures (CVE) numbers. MITRE considers CVE as the industry standard to systematically register all discovered software vulnerabilities [9]. Before vulnerabilities are registered in a database they are assigned a CVE number and a CVSS score which can be used for software product compatibility testing, within threat intelligence community to build security alerts and within public watch lists such as Open Web Application Security Project (OWASP) to rank and manage risks [9].

However, since the introduction of CVSS there have been numerous complaints and suggestions for improvement of its calculation [3, 4, 10–13]. The CVSS v.2 was recently updated, and several changes were introduced, however, several researchers have shown that this scoring system does not represent the real level of associated risks as well. CVSS exploitability metrics were shown to not correlate strongly with the existence of exploits and have a high false positive rate [4, 11]. Also, grouping vulnerabilities into High, Medium and Low does not represent the distribution of the scores well [14]. Finally, the guidelines of CVSS scoring are not being followed [15]. As a result, the data in National Vulnerability Database (NVD) which contains the latest vulnerabilities with their CVSS scores have poor prediction capability [16].

In addition to the listed issues, neither the documentation of CVSS v2 nor CVSS v3 contains a justification of constant values that have been assigned to the components within the CVSS formula [17, 18]. The changes within the vulnerability ecosystem, such as availability of exploits, patches and updates suggest that vulnerabilities do not retain the same risk score over time. While servility of vulnerabilities is changing over time, CVSS sub-scores are not sensitive to the variation of risk over time. The rapid changes in the Information Security (IS) environment require a significant improvement in CVSS score calculation. As stated in ISO27001 standard any method that is used for risk assessment should ensure that its results are consistent, valid and comparable [19]. Finally, CVSS v2 is not tailored to risks imposed to mobile applications [20].

Mobile devices and their security are quickly becoming a widely recognised issue due to various ways that they can be exploited [21–23]. A wide range of mobile malware forensics and threat hunting models have been developed to fight against growing security issues in mobile devices [22, 24, 25]. For example, investigation of attackers remnants on mobile social networking applications [26, 27], Voice over IP (VoIP) apps [28], mobile cloud storage apps [29], and techniques for mobile malware detection [30],

Mobile device-related vulnerabilities are also different from those of traditional personal computers and laptops [30]. A particular mobile device comes with a pre-installed operating system (OS) which cannot be changed or replaced. Besides, all applications are available via a dedicated application store i.e. Google or Apple app stores. These applications undergo provenance—a process of application implementation scrutiny for security [31, 32] before they become available for download. However, it was shown that manufacturers do not always provide patches promptly or sometimes do not provide them at all [20, 33].

In this paper, we explain how the formula of CVSS should be adjusted to more precisely reflect risks associated with applications vulnerabilities and we explore our model applicability by practicing it on different mobile device vulnerabilities. We discuss the improvements both on impact and exploitability sub-scores, but most importantly we introduce the concept of time which reflects how the risk score changes over time and when there is an environmental change, i.e. when a proof of concept exploit becomes available or when a patch is released.

The structure of this paper is as follow. The first part focuses on the analysis of CVSS score where it is broken down into its components, the Impact and Exploitability sub-scores. This part, also explains the data sets of this research as well as its collection and analysis. In the second part, we discuss the proposed improvements and introduce the new suggested formula and discuss implementation results. The third part covers the conclusions with suggestions for future work and identified limitations of this study.

1.1 Background

Both CVSS v2 and v3 consist of three parts: base score, temporal score and environmental score. The base score is the CVSS score assigned once a vulnerability is evaluated. Both CVSS v2 and v3 consider temporal and environmental metrics as optional, and they are not incorporated into the final CVSS score [17, 34]. Furthermore, temporal score still consists of constant values, yet does not have an explanation of the reasoning behind such values [18].

Table 1 Values of Impact and Exploitability sub-scores of CVSS v2 [17]

Impact		Exploitability	
Confidentiality (C)	Complete (C) Partial (P) None (N)	Access Vector (AV)	Network (N), Adjacent Network (A), Local (L)
Integrity (I)		Access Complexity (AC)	High (H), Medium (M), Low (L)
Availability (A)		Authentication (Au)	None (N), Single (M), Multiple (M)

CVSS calculation is modelled according to the risk formula, where the impact is multiplied by likelihood, whereas CVSS calls it the sub-metrics of impact and exploitability [17]:

$$CVSS = Impact \times Exploitability \tag{1}$$

In formula (1), the impact measures how an exploited vulnerability could affect an asset and exploitability measures the current state of exploit techniques or code availability, moreover, the vulnerability score becomes higher if it is easy to exploit it. Both impact and exploitability scores can be assigned as pre-defined values shown in Table 1.

1.2 Impact Sub-Score

The impact sub-score is evaluated based on the vulnerability effects on the CIA (Confidentiality, Integrity and Availability) triad [17]. For impact sub-score, CVSS v2 used values of Complete (C), Partial (P) or None (N) [17], but CVSS v3 has adopted the values of High (H), Low (L) and None (N) [18]. The impact sub-score of CVSS v2 was obtained using the following formula:

$$Impact = 10.41 \times (1 - (1 - ConfImpact) \times (1 - IntegImpact)$$
$$\times (1 - AvailImpact)) \tag{2}$$

Even though the naming of these values in CVSS v3 have been changed and some clarification was introduced into the new definitions, it has not uprooted the key issue of the evaluation itself.

The evaluation of 'None' means no impact to any of the CIA components, while 'Complete' shows a total compromise of all CIA triad. The definition of 'None' and 'Complete' suggests that the definition of 'Partial' is very broad. It could be that if there is a compromise of a component, but it is not complete, then it automatically falls into the category of 'Partial'.

Table 2 Incidence of impact for Android (left) and iOS (right) NVD datasets, where impact sub-score values demonstrate the combination of possible CIA combinations and their distribution across the data sets. Greyed out areas in the combinations never occurred within the datasets

C	I	A	Absolute #	Incidence%	C	I	A	Absolute #	Incidence%
C	C	C	442	54	C	C	C	187	22.130
C	C	P	0	0	C	C	P	0	0.000
C	C	N	1	0.121	C	C	N	0	0.000
C	P	C	0	0	C	P	C	0	0.000
C	P	P	0	0	C	P	P	0	0.000
C	P	N	0	0	C	P	N	0	0.000
C	N	C	3	0.363	C	N	C	0	0.000
C	N	P	0	0	C	N	P	0	0.000
C	N	N	9	1.09	C	N	N	3	0.355
P	C	C	0	0	P	C	C	0	0.000
P	C	P	0	0	P	C	P	0	0.000
P	C	N	0	0	P	C	N	0	0.000
P	P	C	0	0	P	P	C	0	0.000
P	P	P	62	8	P	P	P	293	34.675
P	P	N	58	7	P	P	N	33	3.905
P	N	C	4	0.484	P	N	C	1	0.118
P	N	P	1	0.121	P	N	P	1	0.118
P	N	N	134	16	P	N	N	173	20.473
N	C	C	6	0.726	N	C	C	3	0.355
N	C	P	0	0	N	C	P	0	0.000
N	C	N	0	0	N	C	N	2	0.237
N	P	C	0	0	N	P	C	0	0.000
N	P	P	17	2	N	P	P	4	0.473
N	P	N	54	7	N	P	N	102	12.071
N	N	C	7	0.847	N	N	C	18	2.130
N	N	P	28	3	N	N	P	25	2.959
N	N	N	0	0	N	N	N	0	0.000

Such evaluation introduces a high possibility that the majority of vulnerabilities will contain an assessment of 'Partial' for all or more than one of the components of their impact sub-score. This definition cannot adequately estimate what is the real impact of a vulnerability as the scale of 'Partial' becomes very broad, namely from minimum to near high. The new definition of 'High' in CVSS v3 includes not only the total compromise of a component but also a significant impact to either of them. However it is still difficult to draw the line and to identify what kind of compromise is a significant one and what could be the one of a lower impact.

The division into the CIA values should make it easier to calculate the Impact score and to introduce more variety, however, this does not seem to work as Table 2 shows a significant amount of greyed-out combinations which are not used within the data set. Tables 3 and 4 shows a condensed version of Table 2 that omits the Availability score for a better display of the statistical score and demonstrates the percentage of frequency in which these combinations are currently being used.

Table 3 Combinations of Confidentiality and Integrity per dataset: Android, obtained from NVD and EDB dataset

C	I	NVD (%)	EDB (%)
C	C	53.00	45.45
C	P	0.00	0.00
C	N	1.08	9.09
P	C	0.00	0.00
P	P	17.00	22.73
P	N	15.70	13.64
N	C	0.16	0.00
N	P	9.00	9.09
N	N	4.18	0.00

Table 4 Combinations of Confidentiality and Integrity per dataset: iOS, obtained from NVD and EDB own dataset

C	I	NVD (%)	EDB (%)
C	C	54	52
C	P	0	0
C	N	1.453	7
P	C	0.0	0
P	P	15	24
P	N	18	10
N	C	0.726	0
N	P	9	7
N	N	4	0

1.3 Exploitability Sub-Score

Exploitability sub-score consists of values detailed in the right column of Table 1 and is calculated according to the following formula [17]:

$$Exploitability = 20 \times Access\ Complexity \times Authentication \times Access\ Vector \quad (3)$$

Both Impact and Exploitability sub-scores consist of constant values and a coefficient that is used to maintain the score between 1 and 10. CVSS v2 constant values are displayed in Table 5. However, CVSS v2 documentation does not provide any justification of why such numbers or coefficients are used for exploitability sub-score calculation [17].

1.4 Research Data Set

Reported Android and iOS software vulnerabilities were collected from following well-known vulnerability databases:

- *National Vulnerability Database (NVD)* [35]: the database contains existing vulnerabilities which are registered and assigned a reference number. 826

Table 5 Constant values in CVSS v2 calculation formula [17]

Access Complexity (AC)	High: 0.35
	Medium: 0.61
	Low: 0.71
Authentication (AU)	Requires no authentication: 0.704
	Requires single instance of authentication: 0.56
	Requires multiple instances of authentication: 0.45
Access Vector (AV)	Requires local access: 0.395
	Local Network accessible: 0.646
	Network accessible: 1
Confidentiality Impact (C)	None: 0
	Partial: 0.275
	Complete: 0.660
Integrity Impact (I)	None: 0
	Partial: 0.275
	Complete: 0660
Availability Impact (A)	None: 0
	Partial: 0.275
	Complete: 0660

vulnerabilities were registered for Android and 845 vulnerabilities were related to iOS as of 23 May 2016.

- *Exploit Database (EDB)* [36]: contains known exploits for existing vulnerabilities which might be listed in NVD. A total of 44 entries found for Android platform, out of which 15 have not been linked to a known CVE hence disregarded. Out of 142 iOS exploits in EDB only 25 entries were associated to a known CVE and used in this research.
- *Vulnerability Lab* [37] is another source that maps the registered vulnerabilities in NVD and EDB and helps to identify additional vulnerabilities.
- *Symantec Connect* [38] database was used to map the vulnerability exploit data with available patches and proof of concept.

The CVSS scores of related vulnerabilities detected from previously mentioned datasets were analysed and compared to understand the distribution of CVSS scores across a scale of 1–10 according to the current CVSS calculation which was discussed previously. CVSS scores range from 1 to 10, where 1 is the lowest vulnerability score, and 10 is the highest, or the vulnerability is most critical. Looking at the comparison of this data in Figs. 1 and 2 it is quite obvious that there are CVSS scores with a particularly high amount of data, while some scores have a visibly low number of data. Wanting to understand the reason behind such distribution the collected dataset spreadsheets, both for Android and iOS, were then used to analyse the CVSS the sub-scores of exploitability and impact, which is explained further in detail.

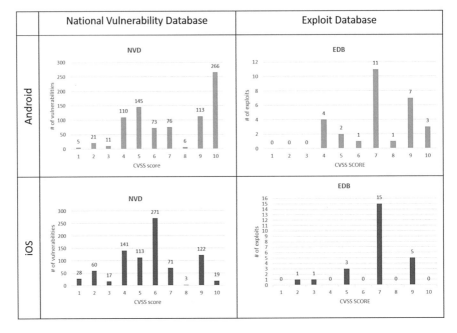

Fig. 1 CVSS score comparison of Android and iOS vulnerabilities across NVD and EDB

Fig. 2 Distribution of CVSS scores in Vulnerability Lab

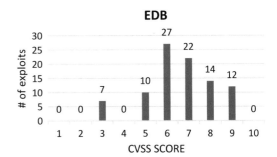

1.5   The CVSS Analysis of Data Set

The analysis of the Impact sub-score data displays two problems. First, Figs. 1 and 2 display the outcome of a vague evaluation definition. Since the definition of Impact values is not informative enough, it is possible that the features of vulnerability are not evaluated consistently. Therefore the 'Partial' score seems to always fit any average impact to either confidentiality, integrity or availability. Second, since the evaluation of vulnerabilities often does not reflect the amount of corresponding exploits available [4, 11], it is possible that the sub-score values simply do not take into consideration the right features of vulnerability which could be better defined, evaluated and therefore measured.

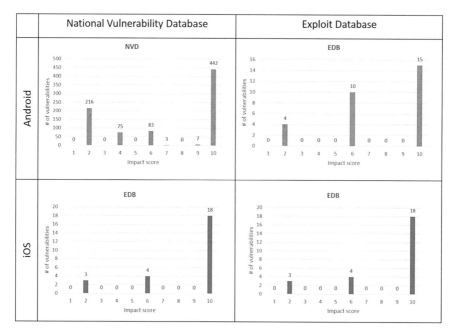

Fig. 3 Impact sub-score distribution across Android and iOS datasets in NVD and EDB

Figure 3 displays how impact score within our dataset is distributed across the scale of 1–10. It is visible that the score mainly consists of three values.

The exploitability sub-score within the dataset was analysed to understand its distribution within the scoring scale of 1-10, the way it was done when analysing the Impact sub-score. The results displayed in Fig. 4 shows that the largest number of vulnerabilities contain an Exploitability score of either 3, or mostly 8 and 10, while other scores are low in number.

2   Proposed Model

In this research we have access to data of existing vulnerabilities and registered exploits, however, this data does not give a drilled down details of a particular use case and how it was remediated if it was at all. It is not possible to know how many devices were affected where a vulnerability was exploited and what happened to it over time. Moreover, the exploit data of mobile devices is very limited, especially for iOS.

The level of variances in this research make it hard to provide comparable results. In such situations, a Randomised Block Design method can be used to compare an individual experiment on several homogenous groups to reduce variances that could impact the study [39]. A comparison is made between two seemingly similar

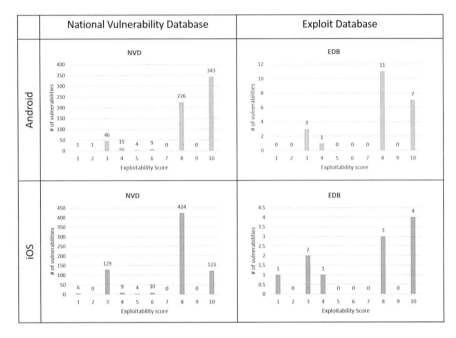

Fig. 4 Exploitability sub-score distribution across Android and iOS datasets in NVD and EDB

object groups or blocks, where the behaviour of one object group has been analysed and understood. The same features of such two object groups allow to predict and suggest the reaction of the other object group. Therefore, in this research, we compare the data of Android and iOS vulnerabilities and exploits with human viruses and diseases.

There was a variety of studies which successfully adopted the same semantics to describe the disease of a computer system as it was long used to describe a disease in a human body [40–42]. In the case of computer systems the system patches and updates is a reaction to any new or existing vulnerability. The concept of changing virus life cycle over time could potentially help to understand how the introduction of time sub-metric makes the score of a vulnerability more accurate [43–45]. Overall, the vulnerability lifecycle may have several critical points that could be approximately matched to a biological virus as shown in Table 6.

Despite the similarities, computer and viruses differ in their survival behaviour. Surviving probability of computer viruses drop sharply over the first two months of their life. Statistically just a small percentage of them cause an outbreak in the computer community, while those viruses that survive still decay over time depending on their type [46]. As for human viruses, some of them (i.e. polio, measles, rubella, etc.) never completely disappear but are dormant due to existing preventive controls (i.e. good hygiene or vaccination), yet when these controls are removed due to any circumstances the viruses infect populations. This behaviour could not be associated with computer viruses since a patch is supposed to provide

Table 6 Comparison of critical points between a biological virus and a vulnerability

Biological virus	Vulnerability
Virus discovery	Vulnerability found
Virus is researched/understood	Proof of concept provided
Infected individuals reported	Exploit is available
Virus treatment discovered	Software patch available
Virus treated	Software update pushed to the mobile devices

appropriate protection for a vulnerability and for this reason it should not be possible to infect the system using the same vulnerability.

For this reason, a more suitable function to mathematically reflect the declining spread of a computer virus would be a mathematical function rather than a line, i.e. constant number. Actuarial science has long used Panjer's Recursion Formula (PRF) to calculate cumulative risks for the insurance purposes [47, 48]. In the insurance industry, collective risk models are used to evaluate processes that produce claims over time [47]. In our case, it resembles to risk score over time where variables are independent and identically distributed events that could impact the change of the risk score [47] such as the development of an exploit or the opposite—a system patch. These events are independent in the sense that they are not necessarily generated by the same subject, one event could occur before another, and one could occur without the existence of the other. One of the techniques to calculate these independent events is using PRF as shown in Fig. 5.

PRF as shown in formula (4) is a sum of the independent variables that re-occur constantly, where N is a random variable with a value of i. In our case N is some exploits for a particular vulnerability and is independent X, that is time over which an exploit or a number of exploits for that particular vulnerability is available.

$$f(x) = \sum_{i=1}^{N} X_i \qquad (4)$$

Using PRF, we assume that every month there is an equal probability for a new critical point to appear, which is in our case an existence of an exploit or a development of a patch. We also make an assumption that if a new critical point appears in the environment of a vulnerability, it does not mean that there will be no more critical points appearing for the same vulnerability in that month. In other words, the appearance of one critical point is independent from the appearance of any other critical point.

Formula (4) could also be an alternative to Monte Carlo simulation [48]. Its key advantage is that the complete aggregate distribution of claims for a given block of

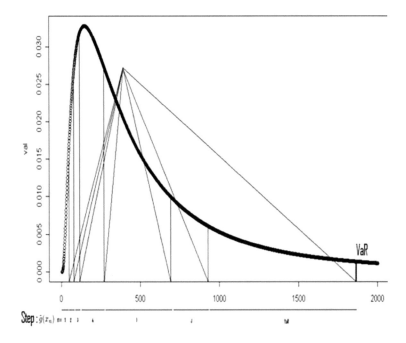

Fig. 5 The graph of Panjer's Recursion Formula, taken from [48]

policies may be quickly calculated and the simulation time decreases nearly 60% [48, 49].

PRF is effective when calculating the recursive events, but it has received criticism in the past that the initialisation of the formula is not clear and could introduce variances. Therefore, Guegan & Hassani [48] have modified the algorithm which mixes Monte Carlo simulation, PRF and kernel smoothing by way of introducing either Binomial or Poisson distributions to the core formula. Poisson distribution is suitable to calculate the total amount of events during a particular time span, while Binomial distribution calculates only positive events during that time. Since we are interested in the amount of total events during the lifetime of vulnerability, therefore the inclusion of Poisson distribution to Panjer's PRF is more suitable to satisfy the requirement of the overall CVSS score calculation (see Formula (5)). Where e is the exponential limit, λ is a mean or an average of critical points per month and κ is the probability of the event:

$$S = \sum_{i-1}^{N} X_i, \text{ where } X = e^{-\lambda}\frac{\lambda^{\kappa}}{\kappa!}, \text{ where } \lambda \in R^+ \text{ and } \kappa \in N \qquad (5)$$

Table 7 Suggested breakdown of Impact sub-score evaluation

CIA Impact	Current constant values	Suggested constant values
Confidentiality Impact (C)	None: 0	None: 0
	Partial: 0.275	Partial-Application: 0.461
		Partial-System: 0.515
	Complete: 0.660	Complete: 0.660
Integrity Impact (I)	None: 0	None: 0
	Partial: 0.275	Partial-Application: 0.461
		Partial-System: 0.515
	Complete: 0.660	Complete: 0.660
Availability Impact (A)	None: 0	None: 0
	Partial: 0.275	Partial-Application: 0.461
		Partial-System: 0.515
	Complete: 0.660	Complete: 0.660

The formula should be the sum of all critical point components that are available as data for each vulnerability. Hence, taking into consideration all the components of exploitability sub-score.

2.1 Results and Discussion

The analysis of the Impact sub-score showed that the CIA evaluation within the Impact sub-score was too broad and too many vulnerabilities could have fallen under an evaluation of 'Partial' impact as it lacked a clear definition. Also, there is a difference in the severity of a vulnerability depending on whether it is an OS vulnerability or the one which exists within a vulnerable application. Therefore, the CIA score evaluation of 'Partial' could be distinguished into two scores, which separate the vulnerabilities apply to applications and OS. For this research, we named the suggested value for application evaluation 'Partial-Application' and the value related to OS 'Partial-System'. The structure together with suggested calculation for each of these values is shown in Table 7. Following the approach of the old CVSS formula the coefficients of 0.461 for the Partial-Application and 0.515 for the Partial-System value were introduced, where coefficient for the vulnerabilities related to OS takes more weight due to their potentially higher impact.

During the implementation of the suggested method, the vulnerabilities within our datasets were separated into either application or OS vulnerabilities. The recommended coefficients were then applied to these vulnerabilities, and a new CVSS Impact sub-score was calculated. After the implementation, another comparison of vulnerability score distribution within the dataset was performed to evaluate how the suggested method changed the values of CVSS score. The result displayed in Fig. 6 shows that only the change of a value within one sub-score of CVSS could

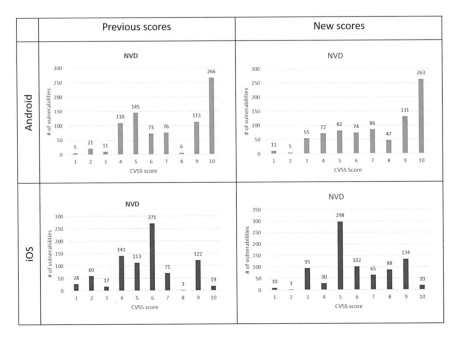

Fig. 6 Recalculated CVSS scores with an improvement of adding additional value to the Impact sub-score

make a significant difference to the overall evaluation of vulnerabilities and their distribution across the scores.

However, the split of the 'Partial' score into application or OS vulnerabilities only improved the definition and use of the 'Partial' value of the Impact sub-score. It is possible that the evaluation of 'Complete' should also be reviewed as part of a future research as there are still proportionally high amounts of vulnerabilities with CIA impact of 'Complete' making more than 50% of the entire mobile vulnerability population for both Android and iOS vulnerabilities. This could be one of the reasons why there are large amounts of vulnerabilities with highest CVSS scores.

To improve the Exploitability sub-score, it is necessary to use the PRF Formula (5). The previous discussion suggests that there could be as many as five critical points of vulnerability (see Table 6). However, not all of this information will be available for all vulnerabilities as a vulnerability may not yet have an exploit or a patch. The amount of these critical points would only improve the accuracy of the overall score, without rendering it invalid.

A test with only one critical point would help to back up the above claim. However, to test the effectiveness of the model, we aimed to test the vulnerabilities with as many critical points as possible. Hence, the experiment was applied on vulnerabilities that have an exploit, i.e. are registered with EDB. As of 26 May 2016 Symantec Connect [38] contained three critical points of registered vulnerability exploits within our dataset: availability of proof of concept (POF), an exploit and a patch.

Formula (5) was used to experiment the collected data set run on vulnerabilities that had one critical point, then two critical points and finally three. The Exploitability score was derived according to the age of the vulnerability counting the months since its registration until June 2016. This score was used for calculation of the CVSS base score.

To be able to calculate the new CVSS scores the suggested model was incorporated into the current CVSS base score calculation. The impact sub-score is recalculated with new CIA values, and PRF was used for calculation of Exploitability as shown in Formula (6).

$$CVSS = (0.6 \times Impact + 0.4 \times Exploitability - 1.5) \times f(Impact) \qquad (6)$$

Having applied Formula (6) to the data set it is possible to demonstrate that the number of critical points does not make an essential difference to the effectiveness of the Formula (6), yet it provides more accuracy to the overall vulnerability score. Fig. 7 displays how a number of critical points improved the accuracy of the calculation and therefore the vulnerability score. However, it does not change the

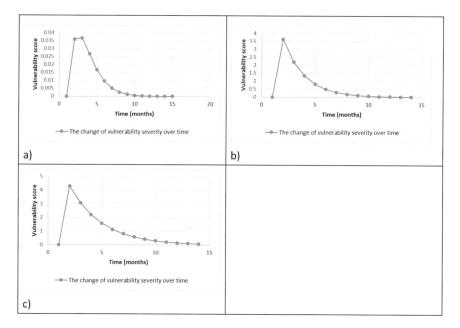

Fig. 7 CVSS exploitability score change according to the new CVSS calculation model. Graphs display the vulnerability score change over two years (in months) when (**a**) there is one critical point, (**b**) two critical points, (**c**) three critical points discovered

overall principle of how the score changes over several months, as displayed in Fig. 7a–c.

The analysis of the present calculation of the CVSS score has exposed some problems. First, the vulnerabilities do not seem to be measured against their true characteristics which result in vague evaluation system of the overall CVSS score. Second, the changing technologies require constant monitoring of whether or not the CVSS result of vulnerability is still relevant. Furthermore, a systematic collection of the data showed that there were large amounts of vulnerabilities that retained repeated values across all of their sub-scores, i.e. a CVSS score of 6.8 will always have an Impact sub-score of 6.4 and Exploitability sub-score of 8.6. The analysis of their breakdown values also appeared to be always the same, most likely due to vague vulnerability evaluation system. This could be one of the reasons why the overall distribution of the CVSS scores across the data set was concentrated at only several scores. Therefore the CVSS calculation does not satisfy the purpose that it was designed for.

The suggested Formula (5) introduces a difficulty in updating the scores of existing vulnerabilities as time goes and a critical point is discovered. This would require a strong collaboration between the administration of National Vulnerability Database and Exploit Database team, which is not being done at the moment. It would also require more sophistication in a website design of NVD, where a 'forecast' calculation could potentially be introduced, showing how vulnerability is expected to decrease over time provided a critical point is not discovered.

3 Conclusions and Future Works

Various researchers have shown that the CVSS score calculation has several drawbacks and does not reflect the real situation of the vulnerability risk. However, a number of industry-wide standards use CVSS score to evaluate cyber security compliance, and there is generally a lot of reliance on the scoring system.

Our suggested model improved calculation and distribution of the CVSS base score. However, the formula should be further improved to entirely replace the constant values within the existing formula with those that are dynamic and true representatives of properties of vulnerabilities. Even though the suggested model improved the way that the mobile device vulnerabilities are calculated, there is potentially an overall limitation in how the nature of vulnerability is perceived and therefore evaluated. It was particularly evident in the way vulnerabilities were evaluated for CIA within the Impact sub-score, where some values were never in use for extracted vulnerabilities. Therefore, a potential future work could focus on investigating what the metrics that would allow an accurate evaluation of vulnerabilities according to the meaningful qualities are. Moreover, development of metrics relevant to specific threats such as malware [50], ransomware [51], Trojans [52], etc. can be considered as an interesting future work.

Another limitation of this research is that we have the data of existing vulnerabilities and registered exploits. However this data does not give a drilled down details of a particular exploit case and how it was remediated if it was at all. Therefore, it is not possible to know how many devices were infected with a virus where a vulnerability was exploited and what happened to it over time. Moreover, the scope of the research is limited to the vulnerabilities related to mobile device software and applications only, and therefore further research should be conducted on different types of data such as vulnerabilities in OSX [53], Internet of Things [54, 55], and Cloud computing [56] to confirm suggested model effectiveness in other domains.

References

1. A. Shameli-Sendi, R. Aghababaei-Barzegar, and M. Cheriet, "Taxonomy of Information Security Risk Assessment (ISRA)," *Comput. Secur.*, vol. 57, pp. 14–30, 2016.
2. W. Ahsford, "Sony data breach: 100m reasons to beef up security," 2011. [Online]. Available: http://www.computerweekly.com/news/1280097348/Sony-data-breach-100m-reasons-to-beef-up-security. [Accessed: 14-May-2016].
3. H. Li, R. Xi, and L. Zhao, "Study on the Distribution of CVSS Environmental Score," pp. 1–4, 2015.
4. L. Allodi and F. Massacci, "Comparing vulnerability severity and exploits using case-control studies," *(Rank B)ACM Trans. Embed. Comput. Syst.*, vol. 9, no. 4, 2013.
5. PCI SSC, "Payment Card Industry (PCI) Card Production: Logical Security Requirements," no. May. 2013.
6. PCI SSC, "Payment Card Industry (PCI) Data Security Standard: Technical and Operational Requirements for Approved Scanning Vendors (ASVs)," *October*, vol. 21, no. October. 2010.
7. ITU-T, "Series X: Data Networks, Open System Communications and Security. Common Vulnerability Scoring System," 2011.
8. ITU-T, "Series X: Data Networks, Open System Communications and Security. Common Weakness Scoring System," 2015.
9. MITRE.ORG, "CVE," 2016. [Online]. Available: https://cve.mitre.org/index.html. [Accessed: 04-Sep-2015].
10. L. Gallon, "On the impact of environmental metrics on CVSS scores," *Proc. - Soc. 2010 2nd IEEE Int. Conf. Soc. Comput. PASSAT 2010 2nd IEEE Int. Conf. Privacy, Secur. Risk Trust*, pp. 987–992, 2010.
11. A. A. Younis and Y. K. Malaiya, "Comparing and Evaluating CVSS Base Metrics and Microsoft Rating System," no. 1, 2015.
12. P. Toomey, "CVSS – Vulnerability Scoring Gone Wrong," 2012. [Online]. Available: http://labs.neohapsis.com/2012/04/25/cvss-vulnerability-scoring-gone-wrong/. [Accessed: 03-Jan-2016].
13. C. Frühwirth and T. Männistö, "Improving CVSS-based vulnerability prioritization and response with context information," *2009 3rd Int. Symp. Empir. Softw. Eng. Meas. ESEM 2009*, pp. 535–544, 2009.
14. P. Toomey, "CVSS – Vulnerability Scoring Gone Wrong | Neohapsis Labs on WordPress.com," 2012. [Online]. Available: https://labs.neohapsis.com/2012/04/25/cvss-vulnerability-scoring-gone-wrong/. [Accessed: 14-May-2016].
15. C. Eiram and B. Martin, "The CVSSv2 Shortcomings, Faults, and Failures Formulation." pp. 1–13, 2013.
16. S. Zhang, X. Ou, and D. Caragea, "Predicting Cyber Risks through National Vulnerability Database," *Inf. Secur. J. A Glob. Perspect.*, vol. 24, no. 4–6, pp. 194–206, Nov. 2015.

17. FIRST, "CVSS v2 Complete Documentation," 2007. [Online]. Available: https://www.first.org/cvss/v2/guide. [Accessed: 16-May-2016].
18. FIRST, "CVSS v3.0 Preview," 2014.
19. British Standard Institution (BSI), "ISO/IEC 27001:2013 - Information technology - Security techniques - Information security management systems Requirements," *Br. Stand. Online*, no. December 2015, 2015.
20. D. R. Thomas, Beresford, Alastair R., and A. Rice, "Security Metrics for the Android Ecosystem," in *Proceedings of the 5th Annual ACM CCS Workshop on Security and Privacy in Smartphones and Mobile Devices*, 2015, pp. 87–98.
21. F. N. Dezfouli, A. Dehghantanha, B. Eterovic-Soric, and K.-K. R. Choo, "Investigating Social Networking applications on smartphones detecting Facebook, Twitter, LinkedIn and Google+ artefacts on Android and iOS platforms," *Aust. J. Forensic Sci.*, 2015.
22. M. Damshenas, A. Dehghantanha, K.-K. R. Choo, and R. Mahmud, "M0Droid: An Android Behavioral-Based Malware Detection Model," *J. Inf. Priv. Secur.*, vol. 11, no. 3, Sep. 2015.
23. A. Dehghantanha, N. I. Udzir, and R. Mahmod, "Towards Data Centric Mobile Security," *IEEE*, no. 7th International Conference on Information Assurance and Security (IAS), pp. 62–67, 2011.
24. N. Milosevic, A. Dehghantanha, and K.-K. R. Choo, "Machine learning aided Android malware classification, Computers & Electrical Engineering." [Online]. Available: https://doi.org/10.1016/j.compeleceng.2017.02.013.
25. M. Petraityte, A. Dehghantanha, and G. Epiphaniou, "Mobile Phone Forensics: An Investigative Framework Based on User Impulsivity and Secure Collaboration Errors," in *Contemporary Digital Forensic Investigations Of Cloud And Mobile Applications*, 2016, pp. 79–89.
26. M. Najwadi Yusoff, A. Dehghantanha, and R. Mahmod, "Forensic Investigation of Social Media and Instant Messaging Services in Firefox OS: Facebook, Twitter, Google+, Telegram, OpenWapp, and Line as Case Studies," in *Contemporary Digital Forensic Investigations Of Cloud And Mobile Applications*, 2016, pp. 41–62.
27. F. Nourozizadeh, A. Dehghantanha, and K.-K. R. Choo, "Investigating Social Networking applications detecting Facebook, Twitter, LinkedIn and Google+ artefacts on Android and iOS platforms," *Aust. J. Forensics Sci.*, 2014.
28. T. Dargahi, A. Dehghantanha, and M. Conti, "Forensics Analysis of Android Mobile VoIP Apps," in *Contemporary Digital Forensic Investigations Of Cloud And Mobile Applications*, 2016, pp. 7–20.
29. M. Amine Chelihi, A. Elutilo, I. Ahmed, C. Papadopoulos, and A. Dehghantanha, "An Android Cloud Storage Apps Forensic Taxonomy," in *Contemporary Digital Forensic Investigations Of Cloud And Mobile Applications*, 2016, pp. 285–305.
30. K. Sharepour, A. Dehghantanha, and R. Mahmod, "Trends in Android Malware Detection.," *J. Digit. Forensics, Secur. Law*, vol. 8, no. 3, pp. 21–40, 2013.
31. I. Mohamed and D. Patel, "Android vs iOS Security: A Comparative Study," *2015 12th Int. Conf. Inf. Technol. - New Gener.*, pp. 725–730, 2015.
32. Google, "Android Security: 2015 Year in Review," 2015.
33. F. Daryabar, A. Dehghantanha, B. Eterovic-Soricc, and K.-K. R. Choo, "Forensic investigation of OneDrive, Box, GoogleDrive and Dropbox applications on Android and iOS devices," *Taylor Fr. Online*, no. 0618 (March), pp. 1–28, 2016.
34. First, "Common Vulnerability Scoring System (CVSS-SIG)." [Online]. Available: https://www.first.org/cvss. [Accessed: 02-Jan-2016].
35. NIST, "National Vulnerability Database," 2016. [Online]. Available: https://nvd.nist.gov/home.cfm. [Accessed: 05-Aug-2015].
36. Offensive Security, "Exploit Database," 2016. [Online]. Available: https://www.exploit-db.com/. [Accessed: 10-Aug-2015].
37. Vulnerability Lab, "Mobile Vulnerabilities," 2016. .
38. Security Focus, "Symantec Connect," 2016.
39. W. C. for S. R. Methods, "Randomized Block Designs," 2006. [Online]. Available: https://www.socialresearchmethods.net/kb/expblock.php.

40. R. Pastor-Satorras, C. Castellano, P. Van Mieghem, and A. Vespignani, "Epidemic processes in complex networks," *Rev. Mod. Phys.*, vol. 87, no. 3, pp. 1–62, 2015.

41. E. Valdano, L. Ferreri, C. Poletto, and V. Colizza, "Analytical computation of the epidemic threshold on temporal networks," *arXiv Prepr.*, vol. 21005, no. 2, p. 19, 2014.

42. G. F. De Arruda, E. Cozzo, P. Tiago, F. A. Rodrigues, and Y. Moreno, "Multiple Transitions and Disease Localization in Multilayer Networks," *Final Draft. Submitt. Publ.*, pp. 1–18, 2016.

43. G. F. Brooks, J. S. Butel, and S. A. Morse, *Medical Microbiology*. 2015.

44. Scitable, "Host Response to the Dengue Virus," *Scitable*, 2014. [Online]. Available: http://www.nature.com/scitable/topicpage/host-response-to-the-dengue-virus-22402106. [Accessed: 14-May-2016].

45. A. Boianelli, V. K. Nguyen, T. Ebensen, K. Schulze, E. Wilk, N. Sharma, S. Stegemann-Koniszewski, D. Bruder, F. R. Toapanta, C. A. Guzmán, M. Meyer-Hermann, and E. A. Hernandez-Vargas, "Modeling Influenza Virus Infection: A Roadmap for Influenza Research," *Viruses*, vol. 7, no. 10, pp. 5274–304, Oct. 2015.

46. R. Pastor-Satorras and A. Vespignani, "Epidemic spreading in scale-free networks," *Phys. Rev. Lett.*, vol. 86, no. 14, pp. 3200–3203, 2001.

47. R. Kaas, M. Goovaerts, J. Dhaene, and M. Denuit, *Modern Actuarial Risk Theory*, vol. 53. 2008.

48. D. Guegan and B. K. Hassani, "A modified Panjer algorithm for operational risk capital calculations," *J. Oper. Risk*, vol. 4, no. 4, pp. 53–72, 2009.

49. L. Spencer and L. Re, "An Overview of the Panjer Method for Deriving the Aggregate Claims Distribution," 2000.

50. Amin Azmoodeh, Ali Dehghantanh**a**, Mauro Conti, Raymond Choo, "Detecting Crypto-Ransomware in IoT Networks Based On Energy Consumption Footprint", Journal of Ambient Intelligence and Humanized Computing, DOI: 10.1007/s12652-017-0558-5, 2017

51. Sajad Homayoun, Ali Dehghantanha, Marzieh Ahmadzadeh, Sattar Hashemi, Raouf Khayami, "Know Abnormal, Find Evil: Frequent Pattern Mining for Ransomware Threat Hunting and Intelligence", IEEE Transactions on Emerging Topics in Computing, 2017 - DOI**:** 10.1109/TETC.2017.2756908

52. Dennis Kiwia, Ali Dehghantanha, Kim-Kwang Raymond Choo, Jim Slaughter, "A Cyber Kill Chain Based Taxonomy of Banking Trojans for Evolutionary Computational Intelligence", Journal of Computational Science, 2017

53. Hamed HaddadPajouh, Ali Dehghantanha, Raouf Khayami, and Kim-Kwang Raymond Choo, "Intelligent OS X Malware Threat Detection", Journal of Computer Virology and Hacking Techniques, 2017

54. Amin Azmoudeh, Ali Dehghantanha and Kim-Kwang Raymond Choo, "Robust Malware Detection for Internet Of (Battlefield) Things Devices Using Deep Eigenspace Learning", IEEE Transactions on Sustainable Computing, 2017

55. Mauro Conti, Ali Dehghantanha, Katrin Franke, Steve Watson, "Internet of Things Security and Forensics: Challenges and Opportunities", Elsevier Future Generation Computer Systems Journal, DoI: https://doi.org/10.1016/j.future.2017.07.060, 201

56. Yee-Yang Teing, Ali Dehghantanha, Kim-Kwang Raymond Choo, Zaiton Muda, and Mohd Taufik Abdullah, "Greening Cloud-Enabled Big Data Storage Forensics: Syncany as a Case Study," IEEE Transactions on Sustainable Computing, DOI: 10.1109/TSUSC.2017.2687103, 2017.

A Honeypot Proxy Framework for Deceiving Attackers with Fabricated Content

Jarko Papalitsas, Sampsa Rauti, Jani Tammi, and Ville Leppänen

Abstract Deception is a promising method for strengthening software security. It differs from many traditional security approaches as it does not directly prevent the attacker's actions but instead aims to learn about the attacker's behavior. In this paper, we discuss the idea of deceiving attackers with fake services and fabricated content in order to find out more about malware's functionality and to hamper cyber intelligence. The effects of false data on the malware's behavior can be studied while at the same time complicating cyber intelligence by feeding fallacious content to the adversary. We also discuss the properties required from a tool generating fabricated entities. We then introduce a design for a honeypot proxy that generates fallacious content for fake services in order to deceive attackers, and test our implementation's accuracy and performance. We conclude that although challenging in many ways, deceiving adversaries with fake services is a promising and feasible approach in order to protect computer systems and analyze malware.

Keywords Deception · Honeypots · Intrusion detection

1 Introduction

Today, cyber attacks and cyber intelligence in computer networks are common and their role will continue to grow in the future. This is because modern infrastructure and society as a whole has become highly dependent on information technology and computer networks.

However, when compared to the real world, in cyberspace it is a difficult task for the attacker to differentiate between legitimate services and fake services. The attacker typically only sees the response received over the network and cannot be

J. Papalitsas · S. Rauti (✉) · J. Tammi · V. Leppänen
Department of Future Technologies, University of Turku, Turku, Finland
e-mail: jastpa@utu.fi; sjprau@utu.fi; jasata@utu.fi; ville.leppanen@utu.fi

© Springer International Publishing AG, part of Springer Nature 2018
A. Dehghantanha et al. (eds.), *Cyber Threat Intelligence*, Advances in Information Security 70, https://doi.org/10.1007/978-3-319-73951-9_12

239

sure about the origin of this response. A piece of malware that has infiltrated the system faces the same problem: is the service or interface it uses really a genuine service?

By effectively and extensively creating deceptive services, the adversary can be deceived. The deceptive resources can also be harnessed to collect information about behavior of the attacker in the system. The malicious activities are thus reversed to produce information in order to reveal the adversary's malicious objectives to the defender. At the same time, fallacious information can be fed to potential cyber spies, which makes cyber intelligence more difficult.

Deception is a promising method to enhance information security, as has been earlier demonstrated with traditional honeypots [5, 31]. It is possible to gather information on how the malware operates by creating *fake services* within a computer or a network and giving fallacious but convincing responses to the malware. More specifically, the responses contain pieces of data, named entities (such as names, locations and dates) referring to real world objects that can be replaced with *fake entities* to deceive the adversary. The approach we take here not only aims for detection via deception [39] but we also deem it worthwhile to learn how a piece of malware reacts to differently crafted responses it receives.

In this paper, we discuss generating fabricated content and present a proxy honeypot for generating fallacious responses. More specifically, it creates messages where the original named entities have been replaced with fake entities. It can also be seen as a framework providing a general reference architecture that can be applied to any TCP-based plain text protocol with relatively small changes. Experiments with an example configuration consisting of plugins we implemented for this proxy show that it is able to recognize entities accurately, does good job in keeping the original confidential information safe and does not produce an unacceptably large performance overhead.

The rest of the paper is organized as follows. Section 2 gives some general background on deception as a security measure. Section 3 discusses properties a fake content generating tool should desirably posses. These properties are used when discussing our implementation and the practical challenges in generating fake content. Section 4 gives a conceptual design for a fake content generator and discusses our practical implementation of a honeypot proxy framework. Section 5 presents experiments measuring the entity recognition accuracy and performance of our proxy implementation. Section 7 reviews related work. Section 6 discusses the strengths and limitations of our approach. Conclusions and plans for future work are presented in Sect. 8.

2   Deceiving Cyber Adversaries

Traditional security measures are not keeping up with today's sophisticated threats such as advanced persistent threats (APT) [9, 37]. For instance, most of these threats are able to successfully evade current anti-virus technology [25]. Since many traditional approaches have lost their effectiveness against advanced attacks, new ways to defend the targeted systems are needed. A promising method to detect and analyze the attacks is using *deception*, that is, giving false cues to the attacker [2, 26].

Conventional security measures usually work directly against the malware's actions with the aim of preventing them. For example, encryption directly prevents the adversary from accessing information. Deception, however, feeds the adversary fallacious information and manipulates his or her thinking so that the defender is ultimately the one who benefits (e.g. by making the malware reveal more information about its functionality).

Being fundamentally different from many other software security approaches in this sense, we believe deception has the ability to compensate for weaknesses of many conventional security schemes. Combining deception with these approaches is therefore advantageous.

Computer deception can be seen as an approach that causes the attackers to choose specific actions that contribute to malware analysis and software security defenses (see e.g. [42]). Computer deception defined like this has several noteworthy properties.

First, it is a *proactive way of detecting and analyzing malware*. Introducing fake services with fallacious responses makes things more difficult for a piece of malicious software or attacker because it receives fake information (we assume the malware or the adversary does not know this, though). We also do not need to be familiar with the exact mechanisms of the attack, because our objective is not to prevent malware from working; this is why deception is also highly effective against zero day exploits. Instead of directly preventing any actions, we are aiming to confuse the adversary with fake entities [32] and collect information about his or her actions (of course, possibly also to raise an alarm and prevent his or her actions at some point).

The second property of deception is that it allows us to *record and analyze the attacker's actions*. It is interesting to monitor what a piece of malware does in the target system. By logging the attacker's behavior, a deceptive honeypot can learn from it—for example, by inferring and modeling the states of a malicious program and using them to react in a correct way to requests the malicious program makes. Analyzing the actions taken by a deceived adversary is also an alternative way to analyze the malware's functionality instead of making use of arduous low-level reverse engineering techniques [33].

Third, what was said above also leads to the possibility of *manipulating the attacker's actions*, at least to some extent [1]. For example, in [8] Cohen and Koike construct an attack graph depicting the processes attacker could use to attack the system. They then manipulate the path the adversary takes this graph by making use of deception.

Fourth, deception also *alleviates the adverse effects cased by harmful programs and curbs the propagation of malware*. In a deceptive environment, the malware cannot make reliable assessments on the changes it has made in the system. The malicious changes may not have any effect or they can be rolled back. We can also try to convince the malware it has successfully propagated while in reality this has not happened.

Finally, deception *causes the adversary to waste his or her resources*. For example, analyzing a fake response from a server requires at least some kind of computational resources. If human scrutiny is required, this naturally wastes the adversary's resources even more effectively.

3   Desirable Properties for a Fake Content Generator

When we want to deceive the adversary with a fake service, there are several desirable properties one would like a tool creating fake responses to have. While these properties are ideal goals in the sense that all of them cannot be perfectly reached in practice, they give a good reference point practical tools can aim for.

First, it is important that the tool *accurately recognizes the entities*. If a tool cannot recognize the original entities that should be replaced with the fakes, this will pretty much deteriorate its other functionality as well.

Second, the tool should be able to *generate convincing fake entities*. The fake entities in responses should look convincing for a piece of malware and when possible, also be believable in human scrutiny. The perpetrator has to trust the fake content and still deem it valuable. The tool should therefore have a good idea what the values of a specific entity in the original service usually look like. At the very least, the tool has to possess a list of possible values of a specific entity or some kind of structural information on the entity.

Third, *keeping the fake content consistent* is important. Of course, a tool that produces deceptive content has to see to it that fake entities stay consistent. We have to remember how we have replaced a specific entity if it appears in the message(s) several times. Some entities can also depend on each other in which case the tool needs a description of this dependence. Consistency has to be maintained not only inside one message but also between several messages. In fact, entity consistency should arguably be persistent so that it exceeds mere sessions. This is because not all attacks are neatly contained in one session [29]. In the most extreme cases like in some APT attacks, the intruders have continued their activity after a break of almost a year (see also [34]). Therefore the generated fake entities, if possible, should not have an expiration date, but rather continue to be used while additional fake entities are created on demand.

Fourth, a good tool is *protocol-independent*. An ideal tool for creating fake entities would do well in recognizing the named entities to be replaced with fakes in any plain text protocol. Of course in practice it is challenging to create a protocol-independent solution that also does very well in entity recognition and creates highly convincing domain-specific entities.

Fifth, *original data should not leak*. In our approach, the original responses possibly containing confidential data are being modified in order to create fake messages. This naturally leads to a risk that the original values of named entities (that we want to replace with fakes) might leak. Therefore our tool has to be careful that this critical data is not revealed to the adversary. Basically, how well this requirement is fulfilled depends on the accuracy of recognizing entities: if the entity recognition is performed well, then the data does not leak because the entities are replaced adequately.

Finally, *the tool should perform efficiently*. Creating fake responses should only cause relatively modest performance penalties compared to the genuine service the tool is mimicking.

In what follows, we present a honeypot proxy framework that strives to provide a good basis for achieving the aforementioned goals for a fake content generator. We demonstrate the use of the tool with the HTTP protocol and discuss the strengths of the tool and the practical challenges it faces.

4   The Design and Implementation of a Fake Content Generator

4.1   A Conceptual Design of a Fake Content Generator

In order to get the understanding what kind of functionality is required for generating fake content, we first discuss a simplified abstract design for a fake content generator. Structurally—and in terms of data processing phases—a tool generating fake entities can conceptually be divided into four separate parts. Figure 1 shows an abstract view of these four main components.

Our approach in this paper is based on the observation that when producing fake responses to deceive the adversary, generating full content from scratch is likely

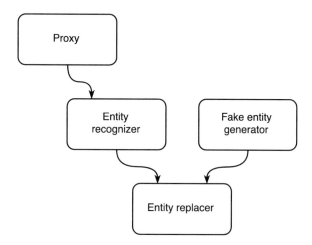

Fig. 1 A conceptual model of the data flow between the four main components

to be much harder than modifying existing content. Therefore the first key part in our tool is *proxy functionality that enables modifying data on the fly* (for example, altering contents of HTTP responses).

Secondly, the tool needs to *recognize the replaceable data*. The ways used to achieve this task can vary. Named-entity recognition (NER) is one possible method of information extraction that aims to detect and classify the named entities in plain text messages into pre-defined set of categories [20]. This approach is fine on natural languages but as our tool will be mainly handling structured data such as LDAP requests or JSON on top of HTTP, there are probably better ways to recognize fields [23]. In this paper, we mainly use regular expressions for entity recognition.

The third part is *generating convincing fake entities* that will replace the original ones in altered responses from the fake service. For consistency reasons, these fake values also have to be memorized.

Lastly, our tool needs to *replace the entities in the original response* with the generated fake values. This step is trivial if the entity recognition has been done accurately.

4.2 The Implementation

To demonstrate generation of fake content on the fly, we implemented a proxy-based honeypot framework, Honeyproxy, with Python. The framework relays TCP data from the client to the remote and back while simultaneously providing hooks for the data in question. The data hooks direct the traffic through a pipeline that is defined by the command line parameters. An abstract class diagram of program structure is shown in Fig. 2.

The pipeline consists of an ordered list of plugins and provides a way to create modular and extensible combinations of functions to analyze, store and modify the data. This way, multiple designs can be independently used and tested. For example, a generic payload parser can be improved by adding or replacing parts with more specific ones. That is, the design of our proxy strives to enable protocol-independence but plugins for some specific protocol can also be added. The proxy only works as a transparent framework in the background.

The interaction between the proxy components is shown in Fig. 3. When the client connects to the proxy, *ProxyListener* assigns a *ClientWorker* for the connection. *ClientWorker* communicates between the client and the remote service after it has been assigned and is also responsible for routing the data through the pipeline composed of plugins.

The pipeline uses a custom dictionary based data structure for passing the information gathered by different plugins. The format includes a few compulsory fields such as `raw` that includes the full document, message or other logical piece of data with headers depending on the application level protocol. The other compulsory field is `content` that includes the content without application level protocol headers ready to be parsed by the content parsers.

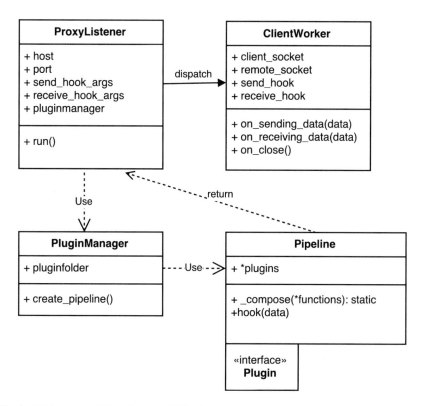

Fig. 2 UML representation of most notable classes

In addition to the compulsory fields, custom fields and objects can be passed by the plugins. Those custom fields are created with the x-* prefix. For example, the *httpsplitter* plugin can pass x-http-headers field with separated HTTP headers from the raw content.

4.3 An Example on the Usage of Honeyproxy

The following example illustrates the usage of the proxy. In this context, *client* refers to the one who is connecting to the service, *remote* to the real service or the server and *proxy* to our implementation of the extensible proxy. In the example, a basic HTTP pipeline will be constructed.

When the remote server is up, our proxy can be started with the command:

```
./honeyproxy.py —receive—pipeline httpsplitter
    typemagic regex replacer printer httpcombiner
```

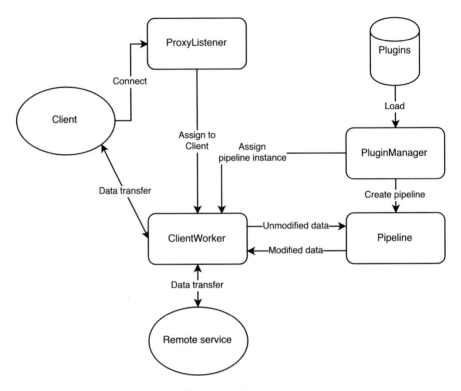

Fig. 3 Interaction diagram between different modules

By default, the proxy assumes that the remote is located in `127.0.0.1:80` and includes several plugins that can be used to construct a pipeline. The data flow in the pipeline constructed next can be seen in Fig. 4. The fields **bolded** in the data flow are the ones the previous plugin has modified or created. In what follows, a more precise description of every plugin in the example pipeline is given.

The `httpsplitter` plugin is responsible for translating the TCP traffic with HTTP into logical documents. This task includes separating and reading the HTTP header, getting the `Content-Length` and filling the content buffer with specified amount of data. After a full document is available and parsed, it will be sent forward. `typemagic` uses libmagic (a library for recognizing magic numbers that identify a file format) [6] to determine the document content type.

When the required preparations for data have been done, more general text parsing plugins can be used. The `regex` and `replace` plugins match specific patterns to find entities and replace all similar entities in the document. For outputting purposes, the `printer` plugin prints all the data it gets at that specific part of pipeline. Lastly, the `httpcombiner` plugin transforms the modified message into a valid HTTP packet, saves it into the `raw` field and returns the data back to the main program of the proxy which then relays the data to the TCP layer for transmission.

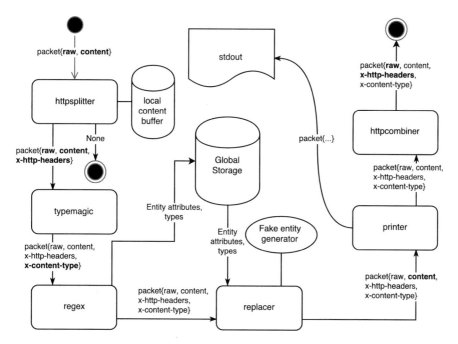

Fig. 4 Data flow through the pipeline

4.4 Recognizing Names Using Regular Expressions

The proxy system is developed to be modular and extensible so that it is able to cover needs of systems with different protocols and content formats. In this subsection and in the following one, we give examples of the implementations of two essential components of the proxy—the entity recognizer and the fake entity generator. These are just example cases because both components can be implemented with different algorithms according to the application area or a specific case.

As one of the central requirements of a system dealing with entities is to recognize the attributes of entities in provided data, we present an example of parsing such data here. In our proxy system, plugins can be made specifically for structured data containing specific fields or a more generic and simultaneously less accurate plugins can be used for these purposes. For example, when dealing with JSON data containing logical blocks of entities, a specialized plugin for this use-case is recommended.

The regular expression plugin `regex` we implemented as an experiment focuses on finding interesting entity attributes using only regular expressions without caring about the format of the data as long as it is in plain text. The current heuristic for finding interesting attributes, person names in our test case, is a naive keyword based system. The parser is supposed to be used on form-style documents without well-defined format. It assumes that after a keyword there is noise or a delimiter separating the real content from the keyword. After recognizing the attribute content, the attribute with its recognized type will be saved into a global storage that is available for all plugins.

It would be possible to replace the recognized attributes outright by substituting the entities matched by the regular expression. However, to boost the recognition recall rate, the matched strings are used to replace every equal string found in the full document. Replacing entity attributes this way will increase the recall rate but lower the precision as the effect of wrongly recognized attributes is multiplied and as such the amount of false positives will rise. This trade-off will decrease the possibility of original information leaking through the proxy while the amount of false positives can raise suspicions of the data being modified on its way to the client.

4.5   Fake Entity Generation

Another essential component in our proxy system is fake entity generator. In our test case, we strive to make entities convincing also for human intruders and for this reason we opted to create a simple fake entity library containing the few entities that are in use in our testing platform. In order to support situation specific fake entity attributes, the API allows the user to specify any number of attributes, which will be used and which will affect all dependent generated attributes. In simplest example, a gender attribute can be defined, and a generated fake person entity will then have an appropriate name, a correct social security number etc.

There are usually more attributes associated with aforementioned person than would usually be required when the fake entity is needed, but because the honey proxy needs to provide consistent content during a session, the generated entity is intended to be stored for further use. As an example, person entities may be needed as a seed for creating a student who has a convincing enrolment year and curriculum in respect to his or her age and so on.

This simple testing implementation does not access recorded traffic to draw information about attribute characteristics. Instead, given the clearly defined entities we deal with, it uses number of dictionaries from which it picks first names, family names, street names and alike. Such approach lacks capabilities to handle generic entities, but is adequate for a specific service.

In the future, however, this somewhat limited implementation can be replaced with a module that can accept entity descriptions, along with detected dependencies, capable of creating content to meet the required criteria. In order to meet demands for more convincing results, number of commonly used entities will still be modelled so that they can be parametrised for suitable generated instances. For example, sampled traffic has likely provided some attribute ranges, such as the age distribution of some specific group of persons, that should be used in fake entity generation.

5 Experiments

In this section, we present a few experiments gauging the entity recognition accuracy and performance of our proxy implementation.

5.1 Recognizing Entity Attributes

In our test-case we try to find person names in HTML documents containing loosely formatted data, without relying too much on the HTML structure. The data being recognized is not guaranteed to be structured in any standard form nor is it formatted as natural language. If we relied more on the HTML structure and attributes such as ids and classes, it could be possible to parse the DOM tree, annotate the fields manually or with selectors and recognize the fields that way.

In Table 1, we can see the results of entity recognition with a regular expression parser when tested with two different web services. The parser had been originally made to with personal information registers in mind, which is why it performs well with the first web page, "Personal information extract". The second test was performed with web different web page, "Personal information form". When we take into account that the parser was not optimized in any way to fit for this second web page having somewhat different way of structuring data, the results are promising. Also noteworthy is the recall value of 1.00, which means that no original data would have leaked through to the adversary.

In addition to these two experiments, the parser was also tested with a very different web service, "E-commerce personal information". In this case it did not recognize the entities and produced a great amount of false positives. This was due to the fact that the parser found a couple of false names that happened to be commonly used words in the web service. This failure, however, was quite expected, since the parser was never designed with this kind of service and data format in mind.

Using more specific information about the data format being used should yield better results. By for example parsing the HTML DOM tree and manually marking the entities with help of CSS selectors is likely to considerably increase the accuracy. However, at the same time it decreases the general nature of the parser and as such increases manual work involved. This is a trade-off we have to accept. Ultimately,

Table 1 Comparing regular expression parser results between a known and an unknown system

	True positives	False positives	Precision	Recall
Personal information extract	8	1	0.89	1.00
Personal information form	4	2	0.67	1.00

it would depend on the exact use case of the proxy whether case-specific accuracy or generality is valued more. In this specific parser implementation, we chose not to depend on the HTML format.

5.2   Performance

We tested the performance impact of Honeyproxy with HTTP traffic. The data was recorded to HAR files using Chromium Debug tools (Inspector) [13] and later unpacked on Google's HAR analyzer [14]. The server, proxy and the client were all running on the same machine simultaneously and communicated by using the loopback interface to minimize the unpredictable and unwanted effects such as lag that could be caused by the network infrastructure. Honeyproxy was using the `httpsplitter`, `typemagic`, `regex`, `replacer` and `httpcombiner` plugins. `printer` was not enabled nor were the debug messages or verbose mode to minimize the impact of I/O blocking.

In Figs. 5 and 6 the web service loading times are compared between plain Nginx (a popular web and proxy server) and with Honeyproxy in between. The actions taken during loading are divided into groups that will be introduced next. Loading is *Blocked* when the browser waits for available TCP connections out of maximum simultaneous connections allowed. *Connect* is the time it takes to establish the connection after one of the connection turns are free for use. After the connection is established, the client *Sends* data to the server. This part mostly depends on the

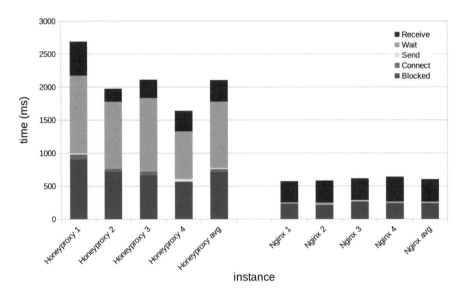

Fig. 5   Sums of load times of Honeyproxy and plain Nginx compared

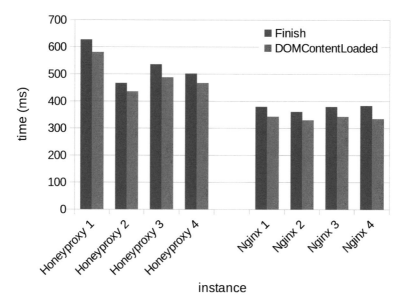

Fig. 6 Real asynchronous loading times of Honeyproxy and plain Nginx compared

connection speed. When the data is received by the server, the server processes the requested data and sends it back. These states are known as *Wait* and *Receive*, accordingly.

Figure 5 presents the total sums of individual components loading. As it can be seen, with Honeyproxy in between, the time spent in *Wait* and *Blocked* states will increase. It should be noted though that the service used in our test environment is only a static version of the real service and as such will be faster to serve than the real dynamic one with a Java or PHP backend. With this in mind, Honeyproxy will always have an overhead over the real service but the real service will also spend time in the *Wait* state. As the overhead by Honeyproxy is not dependent on whether the real service is static or dynamic, the relative difference in case of dynamic backend would be smaller.

The server performance measured in Fig. 6 is the one perceived by the user. The difference between Figs. 5 and 6 is that the first one measures the time all requests take combined and the second one the total time taken by the loading operation. The latter is way faster than the requests combined due to asynchronous requests being sent by the client. Honeyproxy supports these requests by threading the connections thus allowing asynchronous connections.

The overhead by Honeyproxy is easy to see in the time spent in the *Wait* state. In addition to the increase in the *Wait* state, the client spends noticeably more time in the *Blocked* state as it is easy to see in Fig. 7 where the average sums of connections are compared. As said before, when the state is *Blocked*, the request is being queued for free TCP connection. One possible reason for the extended *Blocked* state is that Chromium (version 58.0.3029.110 at the time of testing) has capped the maximum

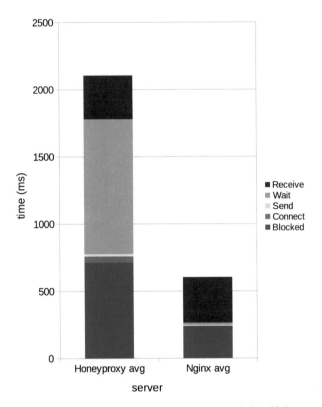

Fig. 7 Average of sums of loading times between Honeyproxy and plain Nginx compared

amount of connections allowed to a single domain to a hard-coded limit of six (see also [38]). As the time spent in the *Wait* state increases, the TCP connections will be occupied longer awaiting for a response from the server. They therefore occupy all six TCP connection turns faster and increase the time spent in the *Blocked* state.

6   Discussion and Limitations

We saw earlier that entity recognition can be quite effective even with relatively simple methods such as regular expressions. Making the tool well aware of the data format in the application protocol comes at the price of lost generality, however.

Differently structured messages are naturally a big challenge for a honeypot proxy. For example, although HTTP is generally quite an easy protocol to modify, it can carry a lot of differently formatted content. This is why many entity recognition methods may be needed. Named Entity Recognition works with natural text, but for the data formats like JSON and XML, a different approach will probably work much better. The structured formats usually include better hints about the content.

For instance, {name: `Jarko`, id: `123456`} tells straight (once the format is known) the type of the object. Named Entity Recognition would not understand the hint and fall back to gazetteer list of names. This is why it would be infeasible to build a proxy that would do an excellent job with all types of HTTP responses (not to mention all plain text protocols). The application level protocol usually defines the structure of the data, after all, so the parser recognizing entities has to be more or less context dependent if we require accurate recognition. Our tool supports this by using a pipeline-based architecture and replaceable plugins.

A little bit more general entity recognizer with a lower success rate is not that big a problem, however, if we allow human help in recognizing entities. After the entity recognition program has performed the recognition process, a human can correct its possible mistakes by annotating the entities present in the message [24]. This approach is very feasible at least in the context of simpler fake services where the messages do not contain a huge amount of entities. Manual annotation is therefore something we plan to take a closer look in the future.

We also discussed creating convincing fake entities. Of course, there is a question who we are trying to convince, what "convincing" means in this case and how to measure it. Without delving into these issues too deeply, we assumed in our example that the fake entities also have to convince human observers. The example implementation was therefore quite application-specific and had a drawback of not being able to handle general entities. We discussed ways to move this component into more general direction, for example by accepting entity descriptions and detected dependencies between entities. The possibility of sampling traffic and learning about the entities from the messages is also worth studying.

A big challenge related to convincing entities, especially in the context of web applications, is the fact that the response often depends on the state of the application [36]. This information is something that may only be in web application's internal session data, and the honeypot therefore has no access to it. We plan to add support for sessions and states of the fake service.

Our proxy honeypot also needs to be made more sophisticated in the sense that it becomes capable of handling message sequences in fake services. This means recording typical message exchanges and then playing them back to adversary with original entities replaced. In other words, the honeypot learns what is the best way to reply in a specific situation based on recorded past interactions. It has to be able to reply as convincingly as possible based on the previous messages.

The issue of consistency also needs to be addressed more comprehensively. While our proxy has the basic functionality of remembering entity values so that the same values can be used in future messages, methods to describe relationships between different entities and preserving consistency between sessions still have to be built.

While there are several aspects and directions that still have limitations and should be further developed, we have provided a honeypot proxy framework design that can be used as a basis for incremental honeypot development. We also demonstrated the use of the tool in the context of specific fake services and showed that the example implementation recognizes entities with high accuracy, does not leak original data and operate with acceptable performance.

7 Related Work

Several methods such as regular expressions and Named Entity Recognition (NER) can used to recognize entities. Regular expressions can easily recognize entities that have a fixed structure such as phone numbers and email addresses. Entities that require contextual understanding are more difficult to recognize this way. For instance, Sekine et al. [28] make use of about 1400 manually created rules in order to detect entities. Named entity recognition tries to recognize named entities and then classify them into groups. Nadeau et al. [21] propose an unsupervised named-entity recognition (NER) system that requires no human intervention.

There are several studies on fake data creation. For example, Whitham [41] proposes a canary file management system that automates fake file generation using content and file statistics drawn from several sources. Weighting of the sources is randomized in order to value to prevent discovery by fake file detection systems. Chow and Golle [7] see the ability to generate believable contextual bogus data as a basic tool in the quest to preserve privacy. They address two types of contextual data, location data and search engine query data, and describe their efforts in faking this content. Rauti et al. survey possible fake entities in computer systems and computer networks in [27].

The idea of replaying computer programs has been studied for many years [3]. Although the context is not exactly the same as in our work, many fake service related approaches have already been proposed and discussed in the existing literature. Cui et al. [10, 11] implement a tool that can replay the messages of both client and server sides of a dialog, having been trained with message sequences that have taken place between them. The approach by Cui et al. is quite general and protocol-independent, and can be applied e.g. to SMTP and FTP protocols.

Newsome et al. define the replay problem more formally and aim to better ensure the replay of application dialog is correct [22]. Small et al. propose an approach that dynamically creates responses to network requests [30]. Their implementation directly learns from raw network traffic. The method presented by Krueger et al. infers a state machine presenting some specific network service and can then replay sessions based on the learned model [17]. Whalen et al. [40] discuss hidden Markov models and specifically a special type of them known as e-machine, which—according to the authors—can derive a protocol solely from network traffic and is well suited for anomaly detection.

It is interesting to note that this kind of advanced methods can also be used by the attackers [18]. In instant messaging applications, for example, a malicious bot can act as a man-in-the-middle, observing and tampering the transmitted messages on the fly. Borders et al. [4] discuss a piece of malware that mimics typical user inputs and tries to merge with normal user activity in hopes of deceiving users.

Farneth et al. [12] propose a mechanism analyzing large amounts of web service requests and responses in order to create emulations for low-interaction honeypots. Gu et al. [15] present a tarpit mechanism in which they hide live targets among phantom addresses. These "white holes" give interactive responses to worms so that the amount of responses in the network segment leaves the worm unable to find potential targets.

Shafique et al. [29] present a replay-based approach for dealing with multi-session attacks such as attacks consisting of an FTP session followed by remote shell login. Lin and Lin [19] present an approach of identifying sensitive information for anonymization purposes. It has been explicitly developed for network traffic dumps and their privacy concerns. The approach works both in TCP/IP and link-layer protocols as well as with transfer protocols (HTTP). While their approach is not perfect (known protocols enjoy 96% accuracy, protocols that do not have a protocol parser have approximately 78% accuracy), this research is definitely interesting in the context of preventing original confidential data from leaking.

8 Conclusions and Future Work

In this paper, we have discussed the task of fake content generation and presented a design and an implementation for a honeypot proxy framework that deceives attackers with fabricated content. The goal is to complicate cyber intelligence by feeding fallacious content to the adversary and also make it possible to study functionality of malware. Experiments with example plugins we implemented for our proxy show it can recognize entities accurately, succeeds well in keeping the original entity values safe and does not produce an unacceptably large performance overhead.

Future work includes extending our honeypot proxy to record and replay message sequences so that we can also take into account the earlier messages. In other words, we extend our scheme so that creating responses and sequences of a fake service based on recorded interaction between clients and services becomes possible.

The tool can also be developed to support manual annotation in entity recognition and to keep the entities consistent in message sequences. Support for sessions and application states should also be added to achieve more convincing entity generation.

More detailed attack scenarios are also a topic worth studying in the future. Compared to basic low interaction honeypots, Honeyproxy delivers high fidelity and ability to respond to unseen attack vectors in expected ways due to the fact that it acts between a real service and clients. The range of attack vectors that can be handled is nearly as large as it would be in a high interaction honeypot—the only perceivable difference being the thoroughness of filtering out sensitive application data and the generation of convincing replacement data.

Three very common attacks vectors listed by The Open Web Application Security Project (OWASP) [35] are Cross Site Scripting (XSS), SQL Injection and Server

Side Includes (SSI) Injection. As they all involve the attacker injecting malicious code or unwanted commands (SSI and SQL injection), we feel that the next logical step forward with our Honeyproxy is to apply filtering to user sent requests. As future research, we would like to determine if malicious content could be reliably intercepted and filtered out without affecting regular web application usage. If reliable detection without false positives can be achieved, it would be interesting to see how we could integrate all this with a honeybridge solution [16], which could intelligently reroute client connections that have turned malicious to either low interaction or high interaction honeypots to play out without damage to the real service. This would also require one-way backend integration between the real service and the honeypots, to maintain the illusion of continuity in terms of content and session.

Creating deceptive fake services is challenging at many points, like when dealing with entity recognition and generating believable fake data. Despite its challenges and inevitable trade-offs we believe deceiving adversaries with fake services is a promising and feasible approach in order to protect computer systems and analyze malware.

Acknowledgements The authors gratefully acknowledge the support of The Scientific Advisory Board for Defence (MATINE). This research is also funded by Tekes—the Finnish Funding Agency for Innovation, DIMECC Oy and CyberTrust research program.

References

1. M.H. Almeshekah and E.G. Spafford. Planning and Integrating Deception into Computer Security Defenses. In *Proceedings of the 2014 workshop on New Security Paradigms Workshop*, pages 127–138. ACM, 2014.
2. M.H. Almeshekah and E.G. Spafford. *Cyber Security Deception*, pages 23–50. Springer International Publishing, 2016.
3. D. Bacon and S. Goldstein. Hardware-assisted replay of multiprocessor programs. *SIGPLAN Not.*, 26(12):194–206, December 1991.
4. K. Borders, Xin Zhao, and A. Prakash. Siren: catching evasive malware. In *2006 IEEE Symposium on Security and Privacy (S P'06)*, pages 6 pp.–85, May 2006.
5. M.L. Bringer, Chelmecki C.A., and Fujinoki H. The honeytank: a scalable approach to collect malicious internet traffic. *I.J. Computer Network and Information Security*, 10:63–75, 2012.
6. BSD. libmagic(3) - Linux man page. https://linux.die.net/man/3/libmagic, 2009.
7. R. Chow and P. Golle. Faking contextual data for fun, profit, and privacy. In *Proceedings of the 8th ACM Workshop on Privacy in the Electronic Society*, WPES '09, pages 105–108. ACM, 2009.
8. F. Cohen and D. Koike. Misleading attackers with deception. In *Proceedings from the Fifth Annual IEEE Information Assurance Workshop*, pages 30–37. IEEE, 2004.
9. E. Cole. *Advanced Persistent Threat: Understanding the Danger and How to Protect Your Organization*. Syngress, 2012.
10. W. Cui, V. Paxson, and N. Weaver. GQ: Realizing a System to Catch Worms in a Quarter Million Places. Technical Report TR-06-004, ICSI, 2006.

11. W. Cui, V. Paxson, N. Weaver, and R.H. Katz. Protocol-independent adaptive replay of application dialog. In *Proceedings of the 13th Annual Network and Distributed System Security Symposium*, 2006.
12. J. Farneth, A. Dhanju, and J.J. Blum. Analysis of embedded web applications for honeypot emulation programs. In *2012 IEEE 16th International Symposium on Consumer Electronics*, pages 1–4, 2012.
13. Google. Chrome DevTools Overview. https://developer.chrome.com/devtools, 2017.
14. Google. HAR Analyzer. https://toolbox.googleapps.com/apps/har_analyzer/, 2017.
15. G. Gu, Z. Chen, P. Porras, and W. Lee. The use of white holes to mislead and defeat importance scanning worms. http://csl.sri.com/papers/whiteholes/whitehole-submission.pdf, 2006.
16. Honeybrid. Honeybrid: Hybrid honeypot framework. http://honeybrid.sourceforge.net/, 2013.
17. T. Krueger, H. Gascon, N. Krämer, and K. Rieck. Learning stateful models for network honeypots. In *Proceedings of the 5th ACM Workshop on Security and Artificial Intelligence*, AISec '12, pages 37–48, New York, NY, USA, 2012. ACM.
18. T. Lauinger, V. Pankakoski, D. Balzarotti, and E. Kirda. Honeybot, your man in the middle for automated social engineering. In *Proceedings of the 3rd USENIX Conference on Large-scale Exploits and Emergent Threats: Botnets, Spyware, Worms, and More*, LEET'10, pages 11–11, Berkeley, CA, USA, 2010. USENIX Association.
19. P.C. Lin and Y.W. Lin. Towards packet anonymization by automatically inferring sensitive application fields. In *2012 14th International Conference on Advanced Communication Technology (ICACT)*, pages 87–92, 2012.
20. D. Nadeau and S. Sekine. A survey of named entity recognition and classification. *Lingvisticae Investigationes*, 30(1):3–26, 2007.
21. D. Nadeau, P.D. Turney, and S. Matwin. Unsupervised named-entity recognition: Generating gazetteers and resolving ambiguity. In *Proceedings of the 19th International Conference on Advances in Artificial Intelligence: Canadian Society for Computational Studies of Intelligence*, AI'06, pages 266–277. Springer-Verlag, 2006.
22. J. Newsome, D. Brumley, J. Franklin, and D. Song. Replayer: Automatic protocol replay by binary analysis. In *Proceedings of the 13th ACM Conference on Computer and Communications Security*, CCS '06, pages 311–321, New York, NY, USA, 2006. ACM.
23. J. Papalitsas, S. Rauti and V. Leppänen. A Comparison of Record and Play Honeypot Designs. In *Proceedings of the 18th International Conference on Computer Systems and Technologies*, CompSysTech'17, pages 133–140, New York, NY, USA, 2017. ACM.
24. T. Poibeau and L. Kosseim. Proper name extraction from non-journalistic texts. *Language and computers*, 37(1):144–157, 2001.
25. Ponemon Institute. The Economic Impact of Advanced Persistent Threats, 2014.
26. N. Rowe. Designing good deceptions in defense of information systems. In *20th Annual Computer Security Applications Conference*, pages 418–427. IEEE, 2004.
27. S. Rauti and V. Leppänen. A survey on fake entities as a method to detect and monitor malicious activity. In *2017 25th Euromicro International Conference on Parallel, Distributed and Network-based Processing (PDP)*, pages 386–390. IEEE, 2017.
28. S. Sekine and C. Nobata. Definition, Dictionaries and Tagger for Extended Named Entity Hierarchy. In *LREC*, pages 1977–1980, 2004.
29. F. Shafique, K. Po, and A. Goel. Correlating Multi-session Attacks via Replay. In *Proceedings of the 2nd Conference on Hot Topics in System Dependability - Volume 2*, HOTDEP'06, pages 3–3. USENIX Association, 2006.
30. S. Small, J. Mason, F. Monrose, N. Provos, and A. Stubblefield. To catch a predator: A natural language approach for eliciting malicious payloads. In *USENIX Security Symposium*, pages 171–184. The USENIX Association, 2008.
31. L. Spitzner. *Honeypots: Tracking Hackers*. Addison-Wesley Longman Publishing Co., Inc., Boston, MA, USA, 2002.
32. L. Spitzner. Honey tokens: The Other Honeypots. http://www.symantec.com/connect/articles/honeytokens-other-honeypot, 2003.

33. J. Stewart. Behavioural malware analysis using sandnets. *Computer Security*, 2006(12):4–6, 2006.

34. C. Stoll. Stalking the wily hacker. *Commun. ACM*, 31(5):484–497, May 1988.

35. University of California San Francisco. Types of attacks for web applications. https://it.ucsf.edu/services/application-and-website-security/types-attacks-web-applications, 2012.

36. N. Vanderavero, X. Brouckaert, O. Bonaventure, and B. Le Charlier. The honeytank: a scalable approach to collect malicious internet traffic. *IJCIS*, 4:185–205, 2008.

37. N. Virvilis and D. Gritzalis. The big four - what we did wrong in advanced persistent threat detection? In *2013 International Conference on Availability, Reliability and Security*, pages 248–254. IEEE, 2013.

38. W3. Server-Sent Events. https://www.w3.org/TR/2012/WD-eventsource-20120426/#notes, 2012.

39. W. Wang, J. Bickford, I. Murynets, R. Subbaraman, A. G. Forte, and G. Singaraju. Catching the wily hacker: A multilayer deception system. In *2012 35th IEEE Sarnoff Symposium*, pages 1–6, May 2012.

40. S. Whalen, M. Bishop, and J.P. Crutchfield. Hidden markov models for automated proto-col learning. In *Security and Privacy in Communication Networks: 6th International ICST Conference, SecureComm 2010*, pages 415–428, Berlin, Heidelberg, 2010. Springer Berlin Heidelberg.

41. B. Whitham. "canary files: Generating fake files to detect critical data loss from complex computer networks". Presented at the Second International Conference on Cyber Security, Cyber Peacefare and Digital Forensic (CyberSec2013), 2013.

42. J. Yuill. *Defensive Computer-security Deception Operations: Processes, Principles and Tech-niques*. PhD thesis, North Carolina State University, 2006.

Investigating the Possibility of Data Leakage in Time of Live VM Migration

Rehana Yasmin, Mohammad Reza Memarian, Shohreh Hosseinzadeh, Mauro Conti, and Ville Leppänen

Abstract Virtual machine migration is a powerful technique used to balance the workload of hosts in environments such as a cloud data center. In that technique, VMs can be transferred from a source host to a destination host due to various reasons such as maintenance of the source host or resource requirements of the VMs. The VM migration can happen in two ways, live and offline migration. In time of live VM migration, VMs get transferred from a source host to a destination host while running. In that situation, the state of the running VM and information such as memory pages get copied from a host and get transferred to the destination by the VM migration system.

There exist security risks toward the migrating VM's data integrity and confidentiality. After a successful VM migration, the source host shall remove the memory pages of the migrated VM. However there should be a mechanism for the owner of the VM to make sure his VM's memory pages and information are removed from the source host's physical memory. On the other hand, the memory portion on the destination host shall be clear from previously used VM's data and possibly malicious codes. In this chapter, we investigate the possibility of misuse of migrating VM's data either in transit or present at source and destination during the VM migration process. Based on the investigations, we give a proposal for a secure live VM migration protocol.

Keywords Live VM migration · Security · Cloud computing · Access control

R. Yasmin (✉) · M. Conti
University of Padua, Department of Mathematics, Padua, Italy
e-mail: conti@math.unipd.it

M. R. Memarian · S. Hosseinzadeh · V. Leppänen
Department of Future Technologies, University of Turku, Turku, Finland
e-mail: moreme@utu.fi; shohos@utu.fi; ville.leppanen@utu.fi

© Springer International Publishing AG, part of Springer Nature 2018
A. Dehghantanha et al. (eds.), *Cyber Threat Intelligence*, Advances in Information
Security 70, https://doi.org/10.1007/978-3-319-73951-9_13

1   Introduction

Virtualization is the technology that enables operation of multiple instances of a system on a single host. Using virtualization technology, system resources can be used in a much more efficient way. The most common method of virtualization is hardware-level virtualization. In the mentioned method, hardware resources are emulated for some execution environment through a software management layer. Those execution environments are called Virtual Machines (VM) whereby the manager software layer is called hypervisor or Virtual Machine Monitor (VMM). The hypervisor emulates the underlying hardware for each VM and manages the resource assignment to each VM. Xen, VMware, and Microsoft Virtual PC are the leading hypervisors which emulate x86-based computers. KVM and VirtualBox, on the other hand, emulate linux environments.

VMs are not pinned to a single host and they can move to run on other hosts in a data center or in a geographically distributed network through migration process. The VM migration process happens either in offline or online manner. Offline VM migration process is simple which requires turning off a VM and transferring the whole VM status as a file from a host to the new host. On the other hand, live VM migration is a bit complex process which is achieved by transmitting a VM's status as data packets across the network from the source host to the destination host while the VM is in use.

In order for a VM to robustly and securely migrate from a source host to a destination host, there are several efficiency and security issues to consider. In terms of efficiency, live VM migration might cause an interrupt in the normal operation of VM in transit by introducing overhead [19]. Furthermore, live migration of VMs negatively impacts other components of the cloud such as anomaly detection systems [17]. From security point of view, confidentiality and integrity of the transmitted VM's data shall be preserved during and after the process of migration. That can be achieved by imposing adequate preventive controls such as proper access control and using a secure transmission channel.

Threat intelligence is referred to the analyzed information about a malicious actor on its intents and capabilities. This information is valuable to an organization in order to adequately take actions. These actions include the tactical choices to impact security, e.g., to detect, defend, or mitigate the risk of threats. These days, organizations rely on cloud technologies to deliver their services to their customers. In this regard, there is a higher need for techniques and procedures for securing clouds, analyzing malware and fighting against cyber crimes in these environments.

In this chapter, we discuss the attacks launched against the VM memory data during live migration in the cloud environment resulting in data leakage. We have also highlighted an area in need of deep investigation which is ignored by the current research work, i.e., a mechanism to ensure the removal of memory data of migrating VM from the source and the provision of clear memory at the destination. Moreover, we discuss a few attacks previously uncovered which may exploit the absence of the above mentioned mechanism and compromise the consistency of the VM memory contents present at either source or destination at the time of live migration. These attacks exploit bugs in hypervisors, message replay, privileged access to the hosts and may carry out malicious actions such as backing up or modifying VM memory contents at source and corrupting VM memory at destination. We then present a few potential solutions for each of the attack scenarios and propose a protocol that utilizes these solutions in order to ensure a secure process of live migration of VMs.

The rest of the chapter is organized as follows: Sect. 2 discusses the necessary background on live VM migration for understanding of some key concepts. Section 3 deals with security threats which may be exploited in order to launch attacks together with the resulting attacks against live VM migration. A threat model is also given. Section 4 covers the secure live VM migration which starts with the description of the security requirements for live migration and then provides the existing work in this area to secure the process of live VM migration. Section 5 describes some of the uncovered threats and areas which need further investigation together with potential research directions for these areas. Section 6 proposes a secure live VM migration protocol, while Sect. 7 concludes the chapter.

2 Background on Live Virtual Machine Migration

In cloud computing environment, virtualization platforms offer dynamic resource management systems in order for administrators to be able to balance the resource usage of hosts. Resource management systems balance the computing capacity among hosts and clusters. That happens by re-arranging VMs on potential hosts that are more suitable for the overall placement of VMs. While the process of VM migration improves service levels, energy consumption decreases. The destination host can be chosen either by a manual check of administrators or automatic recommendation of the migration system itself. When a VM requires a high resource capacity for its operation, the resource management system can suggest a host with sufficient available resources. In cloud environment, live VM migration is effective in situations such as maintenance of hosts, load balancing, resource elasticity requests and over commitment of resources (over commitment refers to the situation where the cumulative amount of resources allocated to VMs on the host is more than the actual available resources). The live VM migration allows a Cloud Service Provider (CSP) to maximize the utilization of resources.

In live migration, a VM is shifted from one VMM to another without halting the guest operating system. This migration usually occurs between two distinct physical machines. The two ways the VM migrates from the host machine to the destination machine are *Managed migration* and *Self migration* [4]. The *managed migration* approach moves the guest OS via migration module (the VMM component that implements live migration functionality) without the participation of guest OS. The *self migration* approach [8] on the other hand is the one in which the guest OS migrates itself without the involvement of VMM.

During live VM migration, the state of the running VM and information such as memory pages get copied from the source host and get transferred to the destination by the VM migration system. The memory of a migrating VM can be moved from the host machine to the destination machine in a number of ways. The important factors which need to be considered while live migrating a VM's memory are *downtime* and *total migration time*. The *downtime* is the period during which the VM service is completely unavailable to clients of the VM and is counted as a service interruption period. In this period, the VM is shutdown and there is no executing instance of the VM. The *total migration time* is the duration in which the live VM migration is initiated on the source host, the VM is resumed on the destination host and the original VM on the source host is finally discarded. Migration of a VM may require transferring tens of gigabytes of data from the source machine to the destination machine. Therefore, it is desirable to minimize the downtime during the migration in order to minimize the service interruption period and to keep the migration transparent to the users. The primary motivation behind live migration of VMs is reducing *downtime*. On the other hand, a reduced total migration time improves load balancing, fault tolerance, and power management capabilities in data centers.

2.1 Memory Migration

In order to provide a trade-off between downtime and total migration time, the memory transfer is generalized in three phases [4]: push phase, stop-and-copy phase, and pull phase.

- **Push phase:** In this phase, the VM keeps running at source host while its memory pages are pushed across the network to the destination host. The memory pages—that are already sent, but modified again at the source during this process, known as *dirty pages*—are sent again to the destination in order to preserve memory consistency.
- **Stop-and-copy phase:** In this phase, the VM at the source host is stopped, memory pages are copied to the destination host and the VM then starts at the destination host (*downtime*).
- **Pull phase:** The new VM at destination, if needs a page which has not been copied from the source host yet (known as page fault), pulls the page across the network from the source host.

Xen [4] and VMware [11] both have the ability to live migrate virtual machines using the tools XenMotion and VMotion respectively. They both have the capability to monitor and manage the migrations for the cloud provider.

2.2   Migration Algorithms

A migration algorithm may integrate all three phases of memory migration, however, the most practical algorithms use either one or two of the phases. The two live VM migration algorithms are pre-copy and post-copy [4].

Pre-copy   The pre-copy algorithm uses an iterative push phase followed by a short stop-and-copy phase. All the memory pages are first copied to the destination in the push phase. After that, only dirty pages are copied to the destination in iterative rounds, i.e., pages transferred during round n are the pages modified during the round $n - 1$. In stop-and-copy phase, only the CPU state and any remaining dirty pages are sent to the destination which brings the destination VM to a fully consistent state. In the pre-copy algorithm, the source host handles the requests to VM services during the live migration process.

Since less pages are to be transferred during the stop-and-copy phase due to the iterative push phase, the VM downtime is reduced. However, it might need to send a large number of pages repeatedly wasting bandwidth, if the pages are modified frequently. Both Xen and VMware use the live migration pre-copy approach.

Post-copy   The post-copy algorithm uses a short stop-and-copy phase followed by a pull phase. In the stop-and-copy phase, the VM is suspended at the source, VM's CPU state is transferred to the destination host and resumed there. The VM is then started at the destination and other memory pages are fetched (pulled) across the network from the source host on their first use. In the post-copy algorithm, the destination host handles the requests to VM services during the live migration process.

The post-copy algorithm results in minimized downtime at the cost of increased total migration time.

2.3   Live VM Migration Process

The migration process using the pre-copy algorithm, first described by Clark et al. [4], consists of the following interactions between the source and destination hosts.

1. **Pre-Migration.** The migration process starts with an active VM on the source host A. The destination host B may be pre-selected in order to speed up the migration process.
2. **Reservation.** It is confirmed that the necessary resources required by the VM at the source host A are available at the destination host B. A VM container of that size is also reserved at B. If the resource reservation fails, the VM simply keeps on running on A.
3. **Iterative Pre-Copy.** During the first iteration, all memory pages of VM at A are transferred to B. Later iterations copy only dirty pages to B.

4. **Stop-and-Copy.** The VM at A is suspended and the CPU state and the remaining inconsistent pages are transferred to B. The network traffic is redirected to B. At the end of this stage, both A and B have suspended consistent copy of the VM. The copy at A is considered the primary copy which can be resumed if the migration process fails.
5. **Commitment.** Host B then sends a commitment to host A that it has successfully received a consistent OS image. Host A now deletes its copy of VM and host B becomes the primary host now.
6. **Activation.** The VM is activated at B now. Post migration code reattaches device drivers to the migrated VM and advertises IP addresses.

3   Security Threat Model

3.1   Threat Model

The valuable asset which needs to be protected is the migrating VM's data. Traditional commodity operating systems are complex having design flaws, implementation bugs and security flaws which facilitate an adversary to gain access to or tamper with the OS running inside a VM, resulting in a malicious OS. Considering the maliciousness of OS, a process running inside an OS may also behave maliciously. A tampered process with high privileges can access VM's private data and tamper with it. Moreover, the adversary can install a rootkit as a VMM below the OS and launch a malicious VMM. Hence OSs, processes running inside OSs, and VMM are all not trusted. The peripheral I/O devices are shared among VMs and hence are exposed to tampering through device drivers. Communication medium is also not trusted allowing anyone to gain access to or modify data in transit.

The owners of other virtual machines are possible adversaries. The owner of the platform is also a potential adversary who can modify or tamper with the software systems installed on the machine including OS images, VMM and applications etc. Other malicious hosts inside the cloud and/or entities outside the cloud may also launch attacks. The goal of both internal and external adversaries is the same: to successfully gain access to or modify the migrating VM's data either via a malicious software system or via an untrusted communication medium.

3.2   Security Threats and Attacks

Oberheide et al. [12] categorized three classes of threats to the migration process as *control plane*, *data plane* and *migration module*. The following is a description of these threats and the resulting attacks against live VM migration in the context of these threats.

3.2.1 Control Plane

Control plane points out the misuse of the communication mechanism adopted by the source and the destination VMMs to initiate and manage live migrations. An attacker able to take control of the communication mechanism among the VMMs is able to launch the following attacks:

- **Outgoing migration control.** An attacker may initiate unauthorized incoming migrations which may ultimately result in the following attacks:
  - Internal attacks. The attacker can migrate a legitimate VM to attacker's machine gaining full control of the guest VM.
  - Denial of service attacks. The attacker can initiate a large number of outgoing migrations of guest VMs to a legitimate host with the intentions of overloading the target host, disrupting its performance, or launching a DoS attack against it. The attacker can also launch a DoS attack against the target VM by forcing it to migrate from host to host, disrupting the services it provides.

- **Incoming migration control.** Similarly, an unauthorized attacker may initiate outgoing migrations, ultimately resulting in the following attacks:
  - Internal attacks. An unauthorized incoming migration will allow an attacker to migrate a VM with a malicious code to a legitimate host, thus enabling the malicious VM to launch attacks against the VMM and other guest VMs running on that host. Moreover, an attacker may live migrate in a legitimate VM to attacker's machine and hence, gain full control over the guest VM.
  - Denial of service attacks. Similar to unauthorized outgoing migrations, the attacker can also initiate a large number of incoming migrations of guest VMs to a legitimate host causing a DoS attack against that host.

- **False resource advertising.** An attacker can exploit the automatic load balancing feature and falsely advertise the resources available, pretending to have plenty of spare resources, thus motivating other VMs to migrate to attacker's VMM. The attacker can then launch both internal attacks and DoS attacks against incoming VMs.

Communication mechanism should be authenticated and tamper resistant employing a proper access control policy describing who can initiate or suspend a live VM migration. The access control lists should be complemented with a firewall to verify the authenticity of the migration source and to allow migrations to legitimate destinations only [16]. Xen implements required access control policy via sHype [22].

3.2.2 Data Plane

Data plane refers to the susceptibility of the transmission channel across which the VM migrations occur. The insecure transmission channel is vulnerable to both passive and active attacks revealing the sensitive information from the migrating VM or at worst compromising the migrating VM. An attacker can place himself in the transmission path using the techniques such as ARP/DHCP spoofing, DNS poisoning, and route hijacking. With such a position, the attacker can launch both types of attacks as follows:

- **Passive attacks.** The attacker can monitor the transmission channel and eavesdrop the data in transit revealing the sensitive data from the migrating VM memory such as encryption keys, passwords and other applications data. Even if the data in transit is encrypted, the attacker may launch snooping attack to uniquely identify the migrating VM and the destination VMMs to launch a later attack against the VM or the destination VMM.
- **Active attacks.** The attacker can launch the most severe attack by manipulating the memory of the migrating VM resulting in the complete compromise of the migrating VM.

The data plane should be secured and protected against both active and passive attacks employing proper cryptographic mechanisms for hiding the contents of the transmission (for instance, encryption/decryption), preserving the integrity of the data (for instance, MAC, digital signatures) and protection against snooping attacks (for instance, padding).

3.2.3 Migration Module

The migration module is the VMM component which implements the necessary migration functionality for the live migration of VMs. The migration modules of the most common commercially available VMMs, for instance XEN, have suffered from different vulnerabilities [12] such as stack overflow, heap overflow and integer overflow. An attacker can exploit these vulnerabilities to take hold of migration functionality. Moreover, the attacker can subvert the VMM through its possibly buggy migration module. Since VMM is the one which controls all VMs running in a host, compromising a VMM would ultimately empower the attacker to compromise all other VMs running on the same host.

The migration modules should be made resilient against attacks by thoroughly inspecting their codes and removing the bugs in them.

3.2.4 Insecure Algorithms and Implementations

Moreover, from the cloud perspective, the information regarding VM migration algorithms used by CSPs are not available publicly. When an attacker has information about migration policies of the CSP such as host thresholds, they can create abusive attacks. Alarifi and Wolthusen [1] presented a method to reverse engineer the migration algorithm of a service provider. When the attackers have information about the migration algorithms, they can strive not to allow their own VMs to migrate as well.

4 Secure Live Migration

4.1 Essential Security Requirements

To ensure the secure live VM migration between two hosts, the above mentioned attacks need to be addressed. Based on the above attacks, the essential security requirements have been listed as follows:

- **Appropriate access control.** Appropriate access control here involves both authentication as well authorization. The source and destination hosts should mutually authenticate each other. No one should be able to impersonate as a VM source or destination. No unauthorized entity should be able to initiate an incoming or outgoing live VM migration or suspend a live VM migration.
- **Confidentiality.** To establish a secure channel between the two ends, the contents of the migrating VM should be hidden so that no one can read or misuse VM data in transit.
- **Integrity of VM data.** The integrity of the VM data should be ensured so that no one could tamper with the in-transit VM data. The state of the VM memory should be preserved before and after migration without the VM memory being polluted.
- **Availability of VM services.** No one should be able to disrupt the services provided by a VM during the live migration of VM.

4.2 Existing Solutions

Even though an increased use of live VM migration has been reported in cloud computing, very little attention has been paid so far to interrogate the security aspects of live migration. So far, the process as well as performance of live migration have been the central point of attention for the researchers in this area. However, the security threats and resulting attacks discussed in Sect. 3.2 require the careful implementation of security properties described in Sect. 4.1 in order to ensure the secure live migration of a VM. The security in live VM migration is recently getting attention. Most of the work in this area is based on Trusted Computing.

4.2.1 Trusted Computing

Trusted Computing (TC) is a technology developed by Trusted Computing Group (TCG) [18]. Trusted computing ensures that a system is secure and it behaves in an expected way. TC incorporates strong security in systems by adding hardware based security via Trusted Platform Module (TPM) in addition to the traditional software based security. TPM is a computer chip that securely stores passwords, certificates and/or encryption keys to authenticate a platform (authentication) as well as platform measurements to ensure the trustworthiness of the platform (attestation). TPM also provides cryptographic functions such as encryption, decryption, signing, random number generation, hashing, asymmetric key generation and migration of keys between TPMs. The TPM is designed in a way that it is extremely difficult to obtain cryptographic data stored in it or to launch a software based attack from malicious code, Trojans, viruses and root kits against it. A variety of applications storing cryptographic material on a TPM can be developed using Trusted Software Stack (TSS), a standard API for accessing the functions of the TPM. Together TPM and TSS provide a strong security level that is applied to a system in order to achieve platform authentication as well as platform attestation. Trusted computing encompasses the following key technology concepts:

- *Endorsement key (EK).* A public and private key pair built into the TPM hardware at manufacture time which cannot be changed.
- *Secure Input/Output.* Thwarts attacks from spyware such as keyloggers and screen scrapers that capture the contents of a display.
- *Memory curtaining.* A hardware-enforced memory isolation scheme providing complete isolation of sensitive areas of memory such that other processes including operating systems cannot read or write to them.
- *Sealed storage.* Seals secure cryptographic data and other critical data by binding it to platform state including software and hardware being used such that only certain combination of software and hardware can unseal the data.
- *Remote attestation.* Encrypted certificates for all software components running on a device are generated and presented as an evidence to remote parties who use a certificate to detect unauthorized changes to a software running on that device.
- *Trusted Third Party (TTP).* An intermediary party between a user and other users for authentication and remote attestation purposes in order to preserve user's anonymity while still providing a "trusted platform".

4.2.2 VM-vTPM Live Migration

In practice, a virtualized platform owns only one hardware TPM which is owned by the VMM [18]. However, from the perspective of virtualization, each VM and VMM must have its own TPM. It leads to the necessity of virtualization of a hardware TPM in order to make its functionality available to each VM running on a single platform with the feeling as it has access to its own private physical TPM. Working on this idea, the design and implementation of a virtual TPM (vTPM) was presented by Berger et al. in [3]. They implemented their designed architecture of vTPM on Xen hypervisor. Their architecture is composed of a vTPM manager and a number of vTPM instances running in either memory or on a cryptoprocessor. Each vTPM instance fully implements the TPM 1.2 specifications of TCG. A VM in need of TPM functionality is assigned a vTPM instance which acts as a hardware TPM for that VM. Only the management VM (Dom0 in Xen) has access to the actual hardware TPM. When a VM starts, a vTPM instance is created for it as a user-space process in the management VM. The management VM runs vTPMs with the help of vTPM manager. The vTPM manager, which runs on the management VM, manages communication between a VM and its associated vTPM instance whereas the management VM coordinates all requests to the hardware TPM.

In addition to providing a perception of separate TPM for each VM, an additional challenge is involved in virtualizing a hardware TPM and that is to provide support for migration of a vTPM instance from the source to the destination platform when the related VM migrates. This is known as VM-vTPM migration. During VM-vTPM migration, the underlying hardware and software platform, i.e., the trusted computing base, changes. Keeping track of this change is challenging in TPM virtualization especially when VM migrates frequently. Berger et al. [3] enabled migration of a vTPM instance by encrypting and packaging TPM state on the source vTPM and decrypting the state on the destination vTPM.

Berger et al.'s Migration Protocol Their proposed protocol initiates migration by creating an empty vTPM instance at the destination for the purpose of migrating TPM state. The destination vTPM then creates a Nonce unique to that particular vTPM migration and transfers it to the source. At the source, the vTPM is locked to that Nonce so that no further changes can be made in it. The vTPM state is then encrypted by a symmetric key generated by the source vTPM. The state includes NVRAM areas, keys, counters, authorization and transport sessions, delegation rows, owner evict keys, and permanent flags and data. An internal migration digest is prepared with the hash of the state data and is embedded in the end of the state information. The source vTPM is then deleted and the encrypted source vTPM state information together with the migration digest is sent to the destination. The symmetric key used to encrypt the vTPM state is encrypted using the *Storage Root Key* (SRK) of the source vTPM parent instance and sent to the destination. The migratable SRK of the vTPM parent instance is also sent to the destination vTPM parent instance using the mechanisms applicable to migratable TPM storage keys. The destination decrypts the encryption key and uses it to recreate the migrating vTPM's state. The migration digest is also recalculated. The vTPM restarts at destination only if the calculated digest matches the received digest. The vTPM protocol supports live VM migration, however, the downtime of the migrating VM in the worst case is increased by the time an outstanding TPM operation takes to complete plus the vTPM migration time. There is no authentication between source and destination.

Danev et al.'s Migration Protocol Danev et al. [6] proposed another TPM based migration protocol which proceeds in three stages:

1. *Authentication:* In authentication stage, the source and destination mutually authenticate each other using their certificates. They both agree upon a session key in order to establish a secure channel for protecting the rest of the transfer process ensuring the confidentiality (through encryption) and integrity (through hashing) using the established session key.
2. *Remote attestation:* In attestation stage, the source sends an attestation request to the destination to ensure the integrity verification of both the source and the destination.
3. *VM-vTPM migration:* In this stage, the destination sends a freshly generated random Nonce to the source. The source locks the VM and vTPM using Nonce to aoivd further changes. The source then transfers encrypted VM and vTPM along with the received Nonce using the previously established session key. The destination checks the integrity of the received VM and vTPM via hash value attached with the received VM and vTPM pair. If integrity check succeeds, the destination imports the VM and vTPM pair and sends an acknowledgment to the source. The source after receiving the acknowledgment, deletes the migrated VM and vTPM pair and informs the destination that the migration is complete. The source and destination then resume their operations.

These both protocols miss the desirable security feature of access control to restrict unauthorized entities to migrate in/out VMs. In these protocols, TPM keys are migrated along with the VM, vTPM pair which might raise security concerns as the security of TPM depends on its non-migratable keys. According to Perez-Botero [14], any changes made to a VM need to be synchronized with the vTPM during the migration which makes live migration more complicated. Thus, synchronization also becomes a requirement in addition to security for a vTPM based live migration protocol which ultimately affects the VM and vTPM resumption timing at destination. Furthermore, ensuring synchronization between the VM state and its vTPM becomes troublesome in those live migration protocols which start VM on the destination before it is stopped at the source. A secure live VM-vTPM migration protocol with the security guarantees is yet to be seen in practice.

4.2.3 Trusted Third Party

According to Aslam et al. [2], the use of virtual TPM increases the size of the Trusted Computing Base (TCB) which is also dynamic in nature and hence causes security concerns. They use TPM without virtualizing the hardware TPM in [2] which results in a small and manageable TCB which is static. In their proposed protocol, a trusted third party PTAA (Platform Trust Assurance Authority) assigns Trust Assurance Levels (TALs) to cloud platforms based on their software and hardware configurations. The PTAA generates a platform trust credential called

TrustToken for every cloud platform. Trust_Token is a PTAA signed certificate which specifies the TAL of the cloud platform for a specific configuration of hardware and software components it possesses. The Trust_Token also includes a TPM created bind key to ensure that a cloud platform can use this token as a proof of its trustworthiness only if it maintains the same configurations for which the PTAA signed the Trust_Token. The TPM allows to use the bind key only if the platform has the same configurations. Their VM machine migration protocol has the following two phases:

1. *Remote attestation:* The source cloud platform P_s and the destination cloud platform P_d exchange their Trust_Tokens in order to perform remote attestation.
2. *VM migration.* The platform P_d sends a Nonce encrypted with the public bind key $PK\text{-}Bind_s$ of P_s which is obtained from the TrustToken of P_s. The platform P_s creates a symmetric key K_m and uses it to encrypt the VM snapshot together with the received Nonce which was decrypted using its private bind key $SK\text{-}Bind_s$. The key K_m is also encrypted using $PK\text{-}Bind_d$ obtained from the TrustToken of P_d. The encrypted key K_m together with the encrypted VM and Nonce are sent to the P_d. The platform P_d first decrypts K_m using $SK\text{-}Bind_d$. Note that the respective bind keys on both sides can only load and work if the TAL values of P_s and P_d remain the same during migration. The platform P_d then decrypts Nonce using K_m and compares it with the sent Nonce in the first step. If both values match, the received VM is decrypted and launched and a signed acknowledgment is sent to P_s, otherwise the migration is stopped.

Their proposed protocol addresses two security issues of platform integrity and confidentiality of VM data in transit by involving a trusted third party. As the hardware and software configuration of a cloud platform might change frequently in cloud environment, their proposed protocol might require a new Trust_Token from PTAA for a cloud platform after every change in its configurations.

4.2.4   Role-Based Migration

Wang et al. [20] proposed a role-based live VM migration protocol which provides the required access control feature using role-based policy which defines who has the right to migrate a virtual machine, and to which hosts this virtual machine can be migrated. Their proposed security framework utilizes the advantages of Intel vPro and TPM hardware platform and contains the following software modules:

- *Attestation Service* provides remote attestation which cryptographically identifies a running hypervisor to a remote hypervisor.
- *Seal Storage* is used by the secure hypervisor to store its private key and role-based policies.
- *Policy Service* parses and manages the role-based policies.
- *Migration Service* is responsible for migration.

- *Secure Hypervisor* utilizes the idea of secure hypervisor, by Dewan et al. [7], to protect the runtime memory of a guest VM's process from the guest OS by hiding process memory into persistent storage from the rest of the OS components.

Their proposed secure live migration protocol works in two steps:

1. *Remote attestation:* First step is the remote attestation of the destination host in order to make sure that the destination host has the required security level. If it does not, the back-end cloud helps the destination to install required security measures.
2. *Secure live migration:* The VM owner initiates a migration request to the migration service module. The migration service module contacts the policy service module to make sure whether this action is allowed to the requesting entity or not. If allowed, it obtains the cryptographic key and certificate from the seal storage module and encrypts the VM state in order to migrate it to the destination.

This work lacks several important details, for instance, the roles of sealed storage and secure hypervisor. The authors mention the use of the sealed TPM keys but do not give details about the purpose of these keys. They also fail to explain the role of the secure hypervisor in their proposed framework.

4.2.5 VLANs

Live VM migration, unlike over the LAN, introduces new challenges over the WAN. Since disk state is also transferred apart from the memory state in WAN migration, a large data is to be transferred over a low bandwidth and high latency WAN. Furthermore, since different routers are involved in WAN migration, the IP address space would be different making seamless transfer of active network connections difficult. Wood et al. [21] presented an architecture, CloudNet, which provides optimized support for live WAN migration of virtual machines. CloudNet addresses the problems linked to WAN migration by virtualizing the network connectivity using layer-2 Virtual Private LAN Service (VPLS) VPN technology [RFC 4761] such that the VM appears to be on the same VLAN. It creates a virtually dedicated path between the two ends providing a secure communication channel. The traffic for a migrating VM is restricted to a particular VLAN which isolates it from other network traffic and thus makes it inaccessible from the public Internet. Their solution provides confidentiality, integrity and authorization at the cost of increased complexity of setting up and maintaining VLANs for each VM and increased administrative costs with the growth of number of VMs.

5   Uncovered Threats with Potential Research Directions

The existing research in this area mainly focused either on the confidentiality of the VM's contents or integrity of the in-transit data. However, there is no mechanism discussed in literature which makes sure that

1. VM's memory pages and information are securely removed from the source host's physical memory once the VM is migrated and resumed at the destination host, and
2. memory assigned to a migrating VM on destination host is clear from previously used VM's data and possibly any malicious codes.

Although confidentiality and integrity of data in transit together build a secure communication channel to avoid data leakage during live migration, the protection of VM data at source and destination during live migration is also crucial. There are many factors which may affect the confidentiality and integrity of VM data at source and destination during live migration. In cloud computing, the major security threats are from the software bugs, system vulnerabilities and careless or malicious employees [23].

5.1   Bugs in VMM

In the process of software development, defects in implementation of a software, known as bugs, are inevitable. Many security breaches start with identifying these bugs and vulnerabilities and taking advantage of them. Therefore, it is significant to prevent the exploitation of these vulnerabilities. In other words, either the bugs should be removed from the software, or the exploitation of them should be made harder. The process of live migration is usually initiated and controlled by the VMM software. Although remote attestation guarantees the tamper proof software components on a platform, it does not provide a guarantee that a software component is bug-free and reliable. A software component might have security related bugs which could be compromised by, for instance, a buffer overflow attack. The most popular and widely deployed VMMs, e.g., Xen and VMware that support live VM migration have bugs in their codes and are vulnerable to practical security attacks launched against their live migration protocols as shown in [12]. Bugs in VMM can be exploited in order to launch attacks against the consistency of the memory of migrating VM.

Possible Research Directions   Obfuscating the VMM could be the one possible solution to make the vulnerabilities harder to be noticed. Obfuscation [5] appertains to scrambling the code in a way that it is more difficult to comprehend and reverse engineer it while preserving the semantics of the code. This means that, even if an attacker succeeds in getting access to the source code, it requires the attacker more time and energy to identify the vulnerabilities in the obfuscated code than in the original source code. With given amount of time, the attacker might be able to understand the code and find the security holes, however, that would be harder and more costly. Obfuscation increases the effort, energy and cost of conducting a successful attack.

The other potential solution to this threat is the use of diversification. Diversification [9], by changing the internal interfaces and structure of the software, generates unique and diversified versions of the software. All these versions are functionally equivalent. As a result, the same attack model is not effective on all these versions, which impedes the risk of massive-scale attacks. Moreover, the malicious software that does not know the diversification secret cannot interact with diversified software component. Thus, the malware becomes ineffective. However, in order to preserve the access of the legitimate applications to the diversified resources/components, the diversification secret is propagated to the trusted applications.

Unlike some other security measures, we do not aim at eliminating the security holes in software by using these techniques; rather we aim at making it more challenging for the adversary to conduct a successful attack. This is achieved by increasing the workload, cost, required time, effort, and failure rate for the attacker to perform its malicious activity.

We believe that these two techniques could successfully protect the VMMs from exploitation of the available bugs and vulnerabilities. In a previous work [10], we have shown different types of attacks that diversification and obfuscation techniques could successfully mitigate, including buffer overflows and code injection.

5.2 Replay of VM Data Messages

During the live migration, whenever a memory page that has already been transferred to the destination host is modified at the source host, it is sent again to the destination host. Frequently updated memory pages are transferred to the destination several times. An attacker who has intercepted a message containing a previous copy of the encrypted memory page, can replay this message to the destination host at a later stage providing an older copy of the memory page. The replayed messages pass authentication check and decrypt successfully, however, compromise the integrity of the VM memory at destination. Oberheide et al. [12] showed a successful man-in-the-middle attack against VM memory migration by manipulating memory of the migrating VM with Xen as a VMM used at both the source and the destination. They successfully modified the memory pages of a test process running inside a guest OS on source host while the memory pages of the guest OS were being transmitted over the network, ultimately polluting the memory of the migrating VM on the destination. This attack together with replay attack allows an attacker to modify pages or add new pages to the migrating VM memory. This attack may become severe if the modified page contains the security related data used by the VM to enforce a security feature, e.g., a private key. However, existing research did not pay attention to the replay attack against migrating memory pages.

Possible Research Directions Replay attack is usually encountered by providing freshness. To ensure freshness, one option is the use of counter. Both the source and the destination manage a counter and agree on the same initial value of the counter. Each memory page from source will be sent with a new counter value that will be verified on destination. The source and the destination both update the counter value. Authentication mechanism will void modifying counter value. Hence, the counter value together with the strong authentication avoid replay attacks as well as man-in-the-middle attack. Another possibility could be attaching timestamp with each page which requires some time synchronization between the source and the destination.

5.3 Privileged Access

A system administrator of the cloud provider needs root privileges at the cloud's machines in order to install and manage the software on them. It enables a malicious system administrator to install any software component on a machine to launch attacks. An example given by Santos et al. [15] states that if Xen is used as a VMM, a system administrator can use Xenaccess [13] (a monitoring library for operating systems running on Xen) to run a user level process in Dom0 (privileged VM in Xen) which provides system administrator a direct access to the VM memory contents. Moreover, the system administrator who has privileged control over the VMM can also access the memory of a customer's VM [15]. A malicious system administrator can modify or keep a backup of the migrating VM memory on the source host or poison the VM memory on the destination host.

Possible Research Directions Rather than a security solution, a security policy may help in controlling privileged access. For instance, appointing more than one person as admins and imposing a policy which keeps more than one admin involved in each privileged access may help. A policy could be that each privileged access by an admin needs permission or authorization from multiple admins or it could be that any privileged access to the system generates a notification to more than one person etc.

5.4 Lack of Access Control

Existing work focused on authentication, confidentiality and integrity of the VM data and almost ignored the necessary access control feature to restrict unauthorized entities to initiate a VM migration. TPM based schemes perform remote attestation, however, they do not check access control. Wang et al.'s live VM migration protocol [20] provides the required access control feature through access control policies, however, it lacks several details about how role-based access control will be implemented. Without proper access control, an adversary can migrate a VM to such a destination host that can corrupt the memory of migrating VM.

Possible Research Directions There have been an extensive research in the area of access control for other systems and several approaches for controlling access in other systems such as web system have been proposed. Those techniques may be explored here. For instance, access control list, a popular solution for access control, could be explored here. A list of access rights could be maintained on the host for a VM, when a VM migrates to a host, defining who is allowed to initiate migration of that VM. Morover, Wang et al.'s live VM migration protocol [17] may be extended by providing detailed control policies.

6   Proposed Secure Live VM Migration Protocol

In order to make sure that live VM migration is secure, there needs to have a secure live VM migration algorithm that protects the VM memory data not only between the source and destination hosts but also at the source and the destination hosts during live migration providing required security properties. In this section, we propose a secure live VM migration protocol keeping in mind the required security considerations.

Day by day more organizations and businesses have started switching to cloud computing for their business applications. One of the main technologies behind cloud computing is virtualization. The security of a cloud cannot be guaranteed unless its virtualization is made secure. Live VM migration is an important operation inside clouds for fault tolerance and load balancing. Ensuring the security of live VM migration is more complex than the security of a switched off VM migration, adding synchronization requirement on top of security requirements. A secure live VM migration protocol also needs to instantly synchronize any changes made in VM pages at source host with the VM pages at the destination host at run time.

Most of the existing solutions for live VM migration are TPM based. TPM based protocols introduce hardware dependency and fail to work with legacy hardware. On the other hand, protocols without TPM handle VM migration security issues individually, either one or another. A protocol which provides one security feature, for instance encryption to hide VM data in transit, but lacks another security feature, for instance data integrity of VM data in transit, is not considered a secure VM migration protocol. Moreover, if a secure VM migration protocol fails to provide synchronization of VM data on both sides during a live migration, it would not be considered a usable protocol. A secure live VM migration protocol must provide all the required security features along with the required synchronization feature.

Furthermore, the current research seems to have completely ignored the need of mechanisms which ensure clearing memory at the destination before migration starts and at the source after migration ends. None of the existing protocols takes the responsibility of ensuring a clear memory portion assigned to an incoming VM on the destination host from previous VM data or malicious codes and secure removal of memory data of outgoing VM. This situation might force the organizations and businesses to get reluctant to switch to cloud due to the potential attacks on their assets. One possible way to ensure memory integrity on both sides may be for the migrated VM to check the state of memory assigned to it on the destination before it starts moving its pages to the destination and dump its memory itself as soon as it is migrated to the new host and check the dump for information.

Keeping in mind the essential security requirements of VM migration and shortcomings of existing solutions, following is a proposal for a secure live VM migration protocol:

- *Access control:* At first step, the access rights should be checked to make sure that if the requesting entity is authorized to perform this operation or not, before the live VM migration is initiated. As discussed previously, access control list mechanism or policy management approach could be suitable for this scenario. Hence, only eligible VMs that are allowed would be allowed to migrate and the illegitimate VMs are denied at first step.
- *Authentication:* If the live migration is initiated by an authorized entity, the source and the destination then mutually authenticate each other to make sure if the VM is going to migrate from a legitimate source to a legitimate destination.
- *Remote attestation:* In remote attestation, both source and destination ensure required security level of each other.
- *Secure live migration:* The live VM migration then performs the following steps:

  1. The VM data is then encrypted by the source to ensure confidentiality.
  2. Counter value or time stamp is attached in order to avoid message replay attack (this step may be performed before encryption if the confidentiality is required).
  3. Authentication information is embedded with the encrypted VM data (authentication information could be the hash of VM data including counter/time stamp).
  4. The encrypted source VM data together with the authentication information and counter is sent to the destination.
  5. On destination, all the security checks are performed and the VM restarts at destination only if the security checks are successful.
  6. The destination will send an acknowledgment to the source if everything goes right.
  7. The source after receiving the acknowledgment, deletes the migrated VM and sends an acknowledgment to the destination that the migration is successfully completed.

7 Conclusion

In this chapter, we first discussed the attacks that are launched against the VM data during live migration in the clouds. In addition to these attacks, we highlighted a few uncovered attacks which may compromise the consistency of the VM memory contents present at the source and/or the destination at the time of live migration. These attacks exploit bugs in hypervisors, message replay, privileged access to the hosts and may carry out malicious actions such as backing up or modifying VM memory contents at source and corrupting VM memory at the destination. These and many other attacks in the cloud environment require new solutions and countermeasures or improvements to the existing solutions. Thence, for each of the studied threat, we presented potential solutions to prevent or mitigate the risk of their occurrences, for instance: obfuscation and diversification techniques could be used to scramble the VM code and change internal interfaces and structure of the software, respectively to make the vulnerabilities in VMM harder to be noticed; freshness, in the form of counter or timestamp, may avoid replay attacks; access control techniques from other systems such as access control lists could be explored for VM migration; root privileges could be controlled by enforcing a security policy rather than a security solution. Using these solutions, we proposed a protocol for secure live migration of VMs.

References

1. Alarifi S, Wolthusen S (2014) Communications and Multimedia Security: 15th IFIP TC 6/TC 11 International Conference, CMS 2014, Aveiro, Portugal, September 25–26, 2014. Proceedings, chap Dynamic Parameter Reconnaissance for Stealthy DoS Attack within Cloud Systems, pp 73–85
2. Aslam M, Gehrmann C, Björkman M (2012) Security and trust preserving VM migrations in public clouds. In: Trust, Security and Privacy in Computing and Communications (TrustCom), 2012 IEEE 11th International Conference on, IEEE, pp 869–876
3. Berger S, Cáceres R, Goldman K A, Perez R, Sailer R, van Doorn L (2006) vTPM: Virtualizing the Trusted Platform Module. In: Proceedings of the 15th Conference on USENIX Security Symposium - Volume 15, USENIX Association, Berkeley, CA, USA, USENIX-SS'06
4. Clark C, Fraser K, Hand S, Hansen J G, Jul E, Limpach C, Pratt I, Warfield A (2005) Live Migration of Virtual Machines. In: Proceedings of the 2Nd Conference on Symposium on Networked Systems Design & Implementation (NSDI'05) - Volume 2, USENIX Association, Berkeley, CA, USA, pp 273–286
5. Collberg C, Nagra J (2009) Surreptitious Software: Obfuscation, Watermarking, and Tamperproofing for Software Protection: Obfuscation, Watermarking, and Tamperproofing for Software Protection. Pearson Education
6. Danev B, Masti R J, Karame G O, Capkun S (2011) Enabling Secure VM-vTPM Migration in Private Clouds. In: Proceedings of the 27th Annual Computer Security Applications Conference, ACM, New York, NY, USA, ACSAC '11, pp 187–196

7. Dewan P, Durham D, Khosravi H, Long M, Nagabhushan G (2008) A Hypervisor-based System for Protecting Software Runtime Memory and Persistent Storage. In: Proceedings of the 2008 Spring Simulation Multiconference, San Diego, CA, USA, SpringSim '08, pp 828–835

8. Hansen J G, Jul E (2004) Self-migration of Operating Systems. In: Proceedings of the 11th Workshop on ACM SIGOPS European Workshop (EW '11), ACM, New York, NY, USA

9. Homescu A, Jackson T, Crane S, Brunthaler S, Larsen P, Franz M (2017) Large-Scale Automated Software Diversity - Program Evolution Redux. IEEE Transactions on Dependable and Secure Computing 14(2):158–171

10. Hosseinzadeh S, Rauti S, Laurén S, Mäkelä JM, Holvitie J, Hyrynsalmi S, Leppänen V (2016) A Survey on Aims and Environments of Diversification and Obfuscation in Software Security. In: Proceedings of the 17th International Conference on Computer Systems and Technologies 2016, ACM, New York, NY, USA, CompSysTech '16, pp 113–120

11. Nelson M, Lim B H, Hutchins G (2005) Fast Transparent Migration for Virtual Machines. In: Proceedings of the Annual Conference on USENIX Annual Technical Conference (ATEC '05), USENIX Association, Berkeley, CA, USA, pp 25–25

12. Oberheide J, Cooke E, Jahanian F (2008) Empirical exploitation of live virtual machine migration. In: Proc. of BlackHat DC convention

13. Payne B, Carbone M, Lee W (2007) Secure and flexible monitoring of virtual machines. In: Computer Security Applications Conference, 2007. ACSAC 2007. Twenty-Third Annual, pp 385–397

14. Perez-Botero D (2011) A Brief Tutorial on Live Virtual Machine Migration From a Security Perspective. [Available Online], URL http://www.cs.princeton.edu/~diegop/data/580_midterm_project.pdf, [Accessed: 29-Apr-2016]

15. Santos N, Gummadi K P, Rodrigues R (2009) Towards trusted cloud computing. In: Proceedings of the 2009 Conference on Hot Topics in Cloud Computing, USENIX Association, Berkeley, CA, USA, HotCloud'09

16. Shetty J, Anala M, Shobha G (2012) A Survey on Techniques of Secure Live Migration of Virtual Machine. International Journal of Computer Applications 39(12):34–39

17. Shirazi N, Simpson S, Marnerides A, Watson M, Mauthe A, Hutchison D (2014) Assessing the impact of intra-cloud live migration on anomaly detection. In: Cloud Networking (CloudNet), 2014 IEEE 3rd International Conference on, pp 52–57

18. Trusted Computing Group | Open Standards for Security Technology (TCG) URL : www.trustedcomputinggroup.org

19. Voorsluys W, Broberg J, Venugopal S, Buyya R (2009) Cost of Virtual Machine Live Migration in Clouds: A Performance Evaluation. In: Proceedings of the 1st International Conference on Cloud Computing, CloudCom '09, pp 254–265

20. Wang W, Zhang Y, Lin B, Wu X, Miao K (2010) Secured and reliable VM migration in personal cloud. In: 2nd International Conference on Computer Engineering and Technology (ICCET), 2010, vol 1, pp V1–705–V1–709

21. Wood T, Ramakrishnan K K, Shenoy P, van der Merwe J (2011) CloudNet: Dynamic Pooling of Cloud Resources by Live WAN Migration of Virtual Machines. In: Proceedings of the 7th ACM SIGPLAN/SIGOPS International Conference on Virtual Execution Environments, ACM, New York, NY, USA, VEE '11, pp 121–132

22. Xen (Xen) Users' Manual Xen v3.3. URL http://bits.xensource.com/Xen/docs/user.pdf

23. Zhang F, Chen H (2013) Security-preserving live migration of virtual machines in the cloud. Journal of Network and Systems Management 21(4):562–587

Forensics Investigation of OpenFlow-Based SDN Platforms

Mudit Kalpesh Pandya, Sajad Homayoun, and Ali Dehghantanha

Abstract Software Defined Networking (SDN) is an increasingly common implementation for virtualization of networking functionalities. Although security of SDNs has been investigated thoroughly in the literature, forensic acquisition and analysis of data remnants for the purposes of constructing digital evidences for threat intelligence did not have much research attention. This chapter at first proposes a practical framework for forensics investigation in Openflow based SDN platforms. Furthermore, due to the sheer amount of data that flows through networks it is important that the proposed framework also implements data reduction techniques not only for facilitating intelligence creation, but also to help with long term storage and mapping of SDN data. The framework is validated through experimenting two use-cases on a virtual SDN running on Mininet. Analysis and comparison of Southbound PCAP files and the memory images of switches enabled successful acquisition of forensic evidential artefacts pertaining to these use cases.

Keywords SDN forensics · Software defined networks · SDN analysis · Openflow forensics

M. K. Pandya
Department of Computer Science, School of Computing, Science and Engineering,
University of Salford, Salford, UK
e-mail: M.Pandya@edu.salford.ac.uk

S. Homayoun
Shiraz University of Technology, Shiraz, Iran
e-mail: S.Homayoun@sutech.ac.ir

A. Dehghantanha (✉)
Department of Computer Science, University of Sheffield, Sheffield, UK
e-mail: A.Dehghantanha@sheffield.ac.uk

© Springer International Publishing AG, part of Springer Nature 2018
A. Dehghantanha et al. (eds.), *Cyber Threat Intelligence*, Advances in Information
Security 70, https://doi.org/10.1007/978-3-319-73951-9_14

1 Introduction

SDN is a network in which there is virtual abstraction of a control layer away from the physical infrastructure layer. This is a relatively new paradigm within networking which diverts away from conventionally designed hardware defined networks in which the network's physical infrastructure retains and limits its configurability. The promise of such programmable SDNs has gained industry wide attention due to its potential for improving upon modern network infrastructure and alleviating many of its drawbacks. Enabling configurability of network functionality will facilitate scalability, storage and flexibility of network architecture to allow for the ever increasing demands placed by world-wide Internet users. As Fig. 1 shows, the framework of SDN usually consists of three planes while it has two types of APIs [31]. The data plane (the lowest-level) performs the flow forwarding operation and deals with flow forwarding devices (switches and routers). The control plane connects all forwarding devices in the data plane and sends forwarding commands to data plane. There may be a variety of network application such as firewalls and access control lists in application plane (the highest-level). Figure 1 also shows two common APIs in SDN namely the northbound interface which allows components of control plane communicate with the higher-level component (application plane) and the southbound interface which enables communication between control plane and data plane.

OpenFlow-based architecture is the most widely used SDN architecture as the southbound API [31]. A forwarding device or OpenFlow switch containing flow

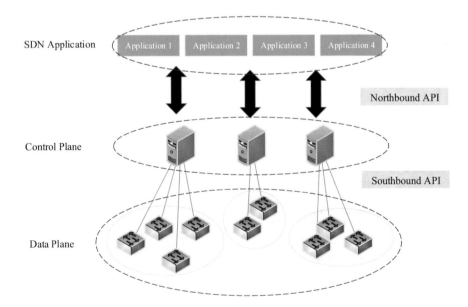

Fig. 1 A typical framework of software-defined networking (SDN) [31]

tables and an abstraction layer uses the OpenFlow protocol to send messages back and forth to the controller. The flow entries within the flow tables determine the policy for processing and forwarding packets [29].

The increasing deployment of SDN made forensic investigation of SDN deployments a growing challenge [2]. In order to facilitate SDN forensics this study proposes a framework for forensic investigation of SDN networks which contains a data reduction module due to the voluminous and widely varied information flowing through SDNs. This chapter follows these objectives:

- Identifying all possible locations within the SDN architecture that may contain evidential data.
- Proposing a framework for forensics investigation and data reduction in SDN platforms. We construct a methodology for acquisition, reduction and analysis of SDN data in a forensically sound manner and demonstrate the framework viability by testing it against three different SDN platforms.

The rest of this chapter is organized as follow: Sect. 2 provides an in-depth research into the literature on digital forensics in particular cloud forensics as the closest example of the type of forensics investigation that will be taking place. Section 3 reviews the specification of a framework for forensics investigation in software defined networks. The proposed framework is introduced in Sect. 4 while Sect. 5 describes the tool developed for southbound forensics. Section 6 designs a testing environment for further evaluation of the framework and Sect. 7 evaluates the framework by designing two practical experiments. Finally, Sect. 8 concludes the chapter.

2   Related Work

Cloud computing is becoming a major implemented use-case for modern day network infrastructure service to provide. Cloud forensics is very closely linked to SDN forensics as evidential data will almost always be transferring across multiple hosts within a cloud via the network [6].

In 2012 a framework for Cloud forensics investigation was described by Martini and Choo [22] which was derived from previous frameworks described by McKemmish [33] and NIST [19]. This framework has been validated through use in various other cloud investigations such as ownCloud [23], Amazon EC2 [46], VMWare [25] and XtreemFS [24], Syncany [45]. and SymForm [43].

Extension and further validation of the framework has been carried out using SkyDrive, Dropbox, Google Drive [8], MEGA [7], SugarSync [38], pCloud [27], SpiderOAK [28], hubiC [10] and ownCloud [23].

Another methodology for cloud forensics investigation on Windows, Mac OS, iOS and Android platforms has been proposed by Chung et al. [5] and applied to investigate Amazon S3, Google Docs and Evernote. A methodology for acquiring remote evidence from a decentralised file synchronisation network was [36] utilised to investigate BitTorrent Sync [37]. A different forensics investigation methodology has been proposed for investigation of any third party or Object Exchange Model (OEM) application including the newer BitTorrent Sync (version 2.0) [44].

A digital forensics adversary model has been proposed and applied towards forensics investigation of mobile devices such as the Android smartwatch [12, 13]. Proposal of a conceptual forensics-by-design framework in which forensics tools and best practices are integrated into the development of cloud systems provided a basis upon which forensics friendly cloud systems may be implemented [32]. A proposal of proactive application level-logging mechanisms which may be helpful during incident response [26, 39] has received criticism for not being truly applicable in real-world scenarios [48]. A different approach involving remote acquisition of evidences through Application Programming Interfaces (APIs) has been outlined by various forensics researchers [15, 17, 23, 25], although it has been suggested that limitations placed by an API's feature sets and also the introduction of possible changes into logged data as a result of remote acquisition Forensic analysis of mobile cloud apps has also been carried out. Examples include forensics investigation of social networking apps [11] and data storage apps [9].

Various challenges exist when carrying out cloud forensics that have been well documented. Opinions of digital forensics investigators vary with regards to perception of what the main challenges are [40], however, lack of data control, inability to access evidences due to decentralization and laws preventing access to the data from different parts of the world, difficulty in automating forensic analysis on cloud platforms due to cloud architecture and lack of available tools for analysis, volume of data to be analysed and insufficient time to carry out thorough analysis all present some of the major obstacles to successfully executing forensic investigations on Cloud [3, 14, 30, 41].

Among all such challenges, physical inaccessibility of evidences due to decentralized nature of the cloud as well as potential legal barriers to obtaining evidences though potentially located due to jurisdiction differences, are obstacles that could be overcome in an SDN based cloud system through initial forensic analysis of the SDN as opposed to direct analysis of cloud clusters.

3   Framework Specification and Design

In order to design a correct forensics investigation framework, it is necessary to first determine all possible locations within a SDN in which potential forensic evidences may be obtained. A software defined network consists of a controller connected to the network infrastructure (switches and routers) via a southbound interface. It is also connected to various applications that are involved in consuming or configuring the network via a northbound interface. There may also be connections between SDN controllers via westbound and eastbound interfaces [16].

At first glance the most thorough approach to ensure that all potential evidences of a network is obtained would be to capture all traffic travelling across every single interface as well as acquiring artefacts from the northbound applications and complete memory images of all SDN controllers and all routers and switches. Although such a forensics investigation would leave no stone unturned, it would involve analysis of very large volumes of data, much of which would be duplicated across multiple interfaces. The large amount of time involved in carrying such a thorough SDN forensics investigation out would cause a wasteful, unnecessary over-allocation of investigative resources. It is also contrary to the ideals of the framework being designed, as such an approach lacks consideration of data reduction, which should be integral to the investigative approach even in the preliminary stages prior to evidential artefact acquisition.

Whilst the SDN controller is responsible for governing all functionalities within a SDN, it is the switches and routers within the infrastructure or data layer of the network that actually carry out the respective functions that enable different network operations. Therefore, all network activities will ultimately have to be relational, either directly or indirectly, to whatever data transfer occurs across the southbound interface of the Software Defined Network. Hence, it should be possible to obtain all necessary evidential forensic artefacts by acquisition of all network traffic data that flows across only the southbound interface of the SDN, it being pivotally instrumental for all other network activity. This approach is more direct, less time-consuming to carry out and should result in the acquired data being less voluminous and more relevant.

The data that is acquired from the southbound interface network traffic should reference all other data from network traffic across all other interfaces within a SDN. It may not, however, be thorough enough in and of itself to provide sufficient information to stand successfully in a case of law in court. There could be further information contained within the memory images of switches that is also referenced by the southbound network traffic that would provide further elaboration and clarity to any evidential information acquired from the southbound network traffic. As such in addition to the southbound network traffic data, acquisition and analysis of the memory images of SDN switches should also be incorporated into a SDN forensics investigation methodology.

Depending on the size of the network even an investigation involving acquisition of just the southbound traffic data and the SDN switches' memory images could result in far too much data than is possible to adequately analyse in a practical manner within realistic time frames provided to forensic investigators. As a result further data reduction on acquired data must be an integral step in any SDN Forensics Framework

The Semantic Web is a systematically classified set of data relationships catered towards machine readability. This is achieved through the use of ontologies which formalise the naming of relationships and entities within a particular domain of discourse [42]. Successful representation of knowledge can be achieved primarily through the use of ontologies due to their ability to provide a clear vision of relationships among structured data. In the absence of such ontologies, representing and understanding data relationships within a specific domain becomes difficult. If the naming of entities and relationships within the specified domain is clearly established further processing of data for knowledge discovery becomes more straightforward [35]. It is for these reasons that the data acquired from the forensics investigation should be mapped into an ontology in order to simplify processing of data for reduction in volume and variety.

A further approach towards data reduction could potentially be obtained via mining of the ontologically mapped data. Data mining is a means of analysing data with the objective of extracting useful information from it. Relationships, associations and quantities within the data may be discovered as a preliminary step through which the forensics investigator could narrow down the searchlight by concentrating efforts on analysing data from locations that are found to have a stronger likelihood of containing relevant evidences as per the resulting discoveries found through the data mining process. For example, it could be discovered that data obtained from a certain packet type flowing through a SDN is related to data obtained from the switches' memory that always show a certain activity, such as sending emails, on a host machine.

4 Framework Development and Implementation

Figure 2 shows our proposed framework that is designed based on Martini and Choo's Digital Forensics Framework for Cloud [22]. Following appropriate preparation procedures and having obtained authorization to acquire evidences from the SDN southbound network packet captures and the SDN switches' memory images, collection of those southbound network traces should take place. Thereafter, the evidences must be preserved and protected in a forensically sound manner prior to examination and analysis. The results of the analysis are then to be investigated and any resulting theories on attributions must be established prior to presenting evidences. With SDN forensics it is always possible that certain evidences cannot be found directly from switches' memory and network packets but are referred to within those evidences and are actually located elsewhere on the network, for example a host's machine. The analysis and results phases therefore may lead back to the start of the framework flow with new locations within the SDN in which forensic evidences need to be acquired.

Various ontologies for forensics have been proposed. Among them are the Digital Evidences Semantic Ontology (DESO) [4], an attempt to automate event and social network evidence extraction [47] and a method for intelligent network forensics analysis [35]. Of these the DESO is relevant ontology our investigation to this particular due to it's simplicity stemming from a fewer number of entity classifications which aids greatly in achieving reduction of data variety.

DESO consists of three classes: artefact location, artefact reference and artefact type identifier. The artefact location has a "asProvenanceReference" relationship to artefact reference and a "isArtefactType" relationship to artefact type identifier.

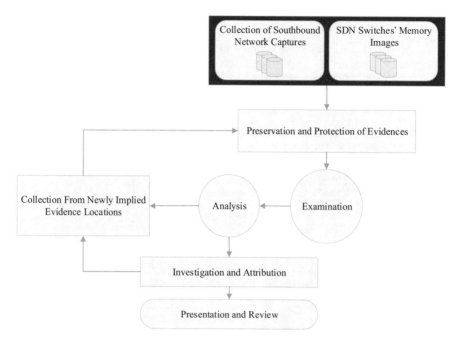

Fig. 2 Proposed framework for forensics in Software Defined Networks (SDN)

Artefact type identifier has a "isFoundAt" relationship to artefact location. The implementation of this particular ontology in SDN Forensics for data reduction occurs through alteration of three classes to "packet location" which shows the origin of the packet file, "packet type", which represents the protocol of the packet, and "packet reference" which is a reference to the case being investigated. Once the data is mapped to the ontology, it is then in a format which may be mined. Mining of the mapped data is advantageous due to the potential value that subsequent knowledge gained may bring to the forensics investigation.

5 SDN Southbound Forensics Tool

SDN forensics is a relatively new focus within the digital forensics research community, partly due to the fact that SDN is an emerging paradigm [21]. For this reason, as part of this research, a prototype for a SDN forensics tool called *SDN Southbound Forensics* which is a python3.5.1 application was written. The application is contained within a file named *sdn_southbound_forensics.py* and requires the host machine to have Python3.5.1 and the forensics tool named *bulk extractor* installed in order to run. *sdn_southbound_forensics.py* consists of two classes of GUI class for showing graphical user interface and Forensics class to capture and analyze the data.

Fig. 3 Initial GUI screen of SDN Southbound Forensics Tool

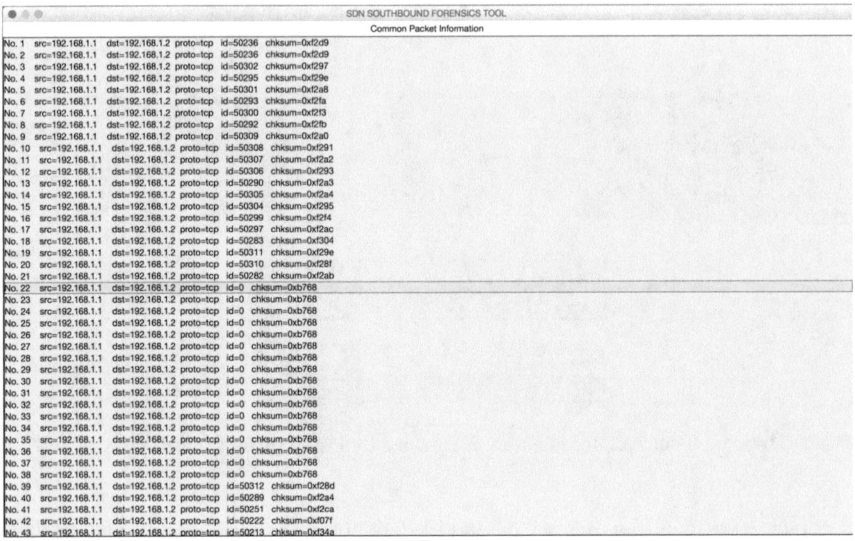

Fig. 4 Common packets shown by the tool

After lunching *sdn_southbound_forensics.py*, the *SDN Southbound Forensics Tool* GUI will appear to the user (Fig. 3). Figure 4 presents the common packet information screen that shows a list of common packets between the switch's memory image and the southbound packet capture file. The source and destination IP addresses, the packet protocol, packet identification and checksum information is shown in Fig. 4. Double clicking on one of the entries will open a more detailed outlook on comparison between packets (Fig. 5).

More details regarding information from different packet layers are shown by scrolling down in the page (Fig. 6). Comparisons can be made between the two packets and potential evidences can be preserved. Clicking on the "Save and Preserve Evidence" button will save the packet information into a directory folder named "SDNEvidence" followed by a timestamp at which the evidence was acquired and saved. The *MD5* hashes of the saved files are also stored in a *.zip* file. This will all be contained within the same directory as the southbound packet capture file used for the investigation.

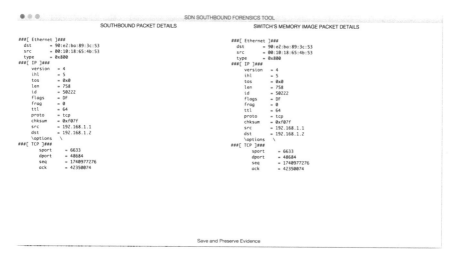

Fig. 5 Detailed common packet information

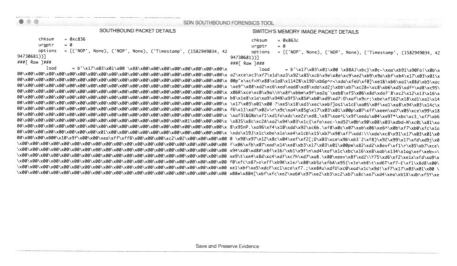

Fig. 6 Scrolled down look on more detailed common packet information screen

6 Testing Environment Setup

To determine whether the proposed SDN Forensics Framework is a suitable for
SDN forensic investigation, it is tested within a simulated environment. Simulating
a software defined network can either be done through a virtual network simulator
or by actually implementing an SDN controller and a northbound interface into a

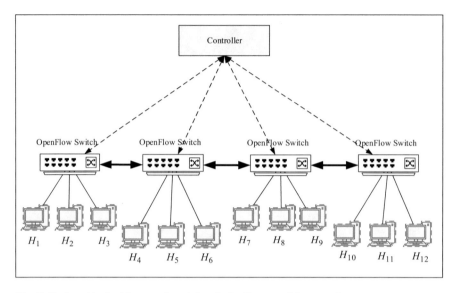

Fig. 7 Designed testbed for experimental analysis of proposed framework

physical network's switches and routers. The mininet virtual environment has been used for the purposes of SDN simulation as a well-known SDN simulator [18]. The simulated environment consists of four switches each connected to three hosts as shown in Fig. 7. In order to verify the validity of the framework it should be tested across a variety of SDN controllers and use case scenarios. Due to their prevalence in a variety of studies within the literature, OpenDaylight [34], Project Floodlight [1] and Ryu [20] are the three types of SDN controllers that have been selected for this study. The first step in running experiments is to install the three SDN controllers being investigated onto the computer carrying out the experiment. In this case all experimentation was carried out on a Mac OS X Yosemite computer. Then we installed OpenDaylight, Floodlight and Ryu to prepare our testbed. A virtual machine was set up using VirtualBox in which an Ubuntu Desktop 16.04 Xenial image was loaded. Figure 7 is implemented in mininet for lunching our case-studies. It is notable that in order to extract memory images of switches from mininet the Linux Memory Extractor (LiMe)[1] module needs to be installed. LiMe allows full memory capture of volatile memory from Linux and Linux-based devices. It also has the capability of capturing memory of android devices.

---

[1] https://github.com/504ensicsLabs/LiME/tree/master/doc.

7   Evaluation and Discussion

To determine whether the proposed SDN Forensics Framework is a valid approach towards SDN forensic investigations, a specific measure for success must be defined. Success of the framework is to be proven through actual experimental use in a simulated forensics investigation. We designed two different use cases to evaluate our proposed framework:

- Use Case 1: The first use case simply involved pinging all hosts on the network. This was achieved simply by the mininet Command Line Interface (CLI) using the pingall command. All 12 hosts were sent ICMP messages to one another. Packet information was picked up using Wireshark and dumped into a PCAP file. Linux Memory Extractor (LiME) was used to extract the memory images of the four switches for analysis as well. This experiment acted as an initial test to establish whether relevant forensics artefacts showing the ICMP processing can be extracted from within the southbound network packet capture and the switches' memory images.
- Use Case 2: The second use case involved running web services with different web pages on hosts H_2, H_5, H_7 and H_{12}, ensuring that at least one host per switch will act as a server (see Fig. 8). A PHP server is started on each one of these hosts, which provides web services that are accessed remotely by various hosts. In this case the web pages were accessed using Firefox on host H_1. Various tests were present on the web pages in which various user activity will need to be carried out. The first test involved clicking a link to another web page hosted on

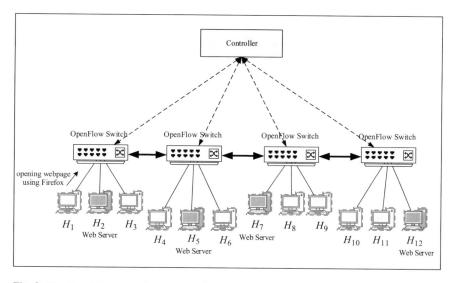

Fig. 8 Use Case 2, testing web activities of users

a different host to the initial web page. Thereafter, a test involving an image as a link was conducted, followed by another test involving the running of a video and the submission of a web form. The web form submission was carried out both with ordinary login details for an already existing user as well as three different types of SQL injection attacks. The attacks which were carried out are as follows:

$' OR '' = '';-$
$' OR 1 = 1; --$
$'; DROP TABLE Users; --$

As with Use Case 1 packet information was picked up using Wireshark and dumped into a PCAP file. Linux Memory Extractor (LiME) was used to extract the memory images of the four switches for analysis as well (*Collection of Southbound Network Captures* and *SDN Switches' Memory Images* in Fig. 2). After lunching Use Case 1, we saw there was no problem discovering information for ICMP about all the pings happening between hosts (*Examination, Analysis* and *Investigation* from Fig. 2). It should be noted that the source and destination IP addresses for the hosts are written explicitly with openflow 1.0 but in openflow 1.3 they are embedded within the OpenFlow data segment. This difference shows that wireshark will portray different versions of OpenFlow packets differently. This was true across all controllers.

Results from experimenting Use Case 2 on three SDN environments such as OpenDaylight, Project Floodlight and Ryu show that all relevant evidences could be recovered with the OpenDaylight controller but not so with the other two controllers. However the limited evidence that we did manage to recover from Project Floodlight and Ryu could provide clues as to the locations of further evidences so could still be used as a basis to theorise an SDN Forensics Framework. If suspected evidence has not been completely discovered in southbound PCAPs and switchs' memories, it may be contained on the hosts, then forensic analysis of the hosts that are suspected based on evidence gained from the PCAPs and switch memories should be carried out. Cross-comparison of evidential artefacts gained from the southbound packet capture information and the switches' memory images may be carried out using a forensics tool that has been developed as part of this research. Installation and usage information for this particular tool is described in the next section.

The framework tested through running multiple use cases across a simulated Software Defined Networking Environment using mininet. Forensic artefacts extracted included southbound network packet capture (pcap) files and the memory images of SDN switches. A tool built using python was used to compare and contrast network packet information such that the related information is displayed to the forensics investigator for successful cross-referencing. This helps in identifying trends and patterns within the acquired data in order to help classify data relationally. Data reduction has been achieved both by reduction at intake by specifying only two locations in which acquisition within an SDN should take place as well as through the use of ontological mapping via a custom ontology. The ontology was based upon the DESO ontology [4].

In light of the results of the experimentation it can be suggested that the complexity of the data that has been extracted is a factor that needs to be thought about. As found in the results, data found relating to packet information may not always be in an appropriate format for easy interpretation even when using tools such as Wireshark. This will have to be looked into in future investigations in which not just the volume and variety but also the nature of data acquired from digital forensics investigations of SDN Platforms needs to be addressed.

The resultant framework created was based upon the findings of the experimentation using [22] Digital Forensics Framework as a basis. A custom ontology based on DESO [4] has been specified as a means for achieving data reduction as part of the proposed framework. Whilst it was found that the OpenDaylight controller successfully yielded positive results for the verification of the proposed framework, further experimentation is necessary in future investigations to conclusively establish the accuracy of the framework when applied to various other SDN controllers as Floodlight and Ryu did not provide the same level of confidence in the framework as OpenDaylight.

Data reduction was found to be achievable through the specified acquisition locations along the southbound interface of SDNs by ensuring that the amount of data necessary to acquire is kept at a minimum. An approach involving ontological mapping using a custom ontology extended from Digital Evidences Semantic Ontology (DESO) has also been put forward as a means of further reducing volume and variety of data. In addition to the volume and variety of data to be reduced, complexity is another factor which must be considered for reduction processes. Data mining of the acquired forensic evidence could also be an option for further data reduction as it may help pinpoint specific locations for focusing forensic extraction efforts by using information gained from any patterns or associations found from the mining process.

8 Conclusion

This chapter followed three main objectives. (1) We carried out a thorough taxonomy of SDN architecture to determine all possible areas that are potential providers of SDN data. The southbound API was identified as the best possible location for obtaining all necessary evidential data that will be correlated across the entire SDN. (2) We constructed a methodology for the acquisition, reduction and analysis of SDN data in a forensically sound manner and demonstrate its viability on a sample of three particular SDN Platforms. (3) This chapter proposed a framework for forensics investigation and data reduction in SDN Platforms based on the conclusions drawn from the experimentation of the proposed forensically sound methodology. We also considered data reduction in SDN Platforms.

It was found that the OpenDaylight controller successfully yielded positive results while other SDN controllers as Floodlight and Ryu did not provide the same level of confidence in the framework. Moreover, a Python-based tool was built to facilitate SDN forensics investigation of southbound traffics.

References

1. Alekseev I, Nikitinskiy M (2015) Eventbus module for distributed openflow controllers. In: 2015 17th Conference of Open Innovations Association (FRUCT), Institute of Electrical and Electronics Engineers (IEEE), DOI 10.1109/fruct.2015.7117963, URL https://doi.org/10.1109%2Ffruct.2015.7117963

2. Bates A, Butler K, Haeberlen A, Sherr M, Zhou W (2014) Let SDN be your eyes: Secure forensics in data center networks. In: Proceedings 2014 Workshop on Security of Emerging Networking Technologies, Internet Society, DOI 10.14722/sent.2014.23002, URL https://doi.org/10.14722%2Fsent.2014.23002

3. Birk D, Wegener C (2011) Technical issues of forensic investigations in cloud computing environments. In: 2011 Sixth IEEE International Workshop on Systematic Approaches to Digital Forensic Engineering, Institute of Electrical and Electronics Engineers (IEEE), DOI 10.1109/sadfe.2011.17, URL https://doi.org/10.1109%2Fsadfe.2011.17

4. Brady O, Overill R, Keppens J (2015) DESO: Addressing volume and variety in large-scale criminal cases. Digital Investigation 15:72–82, DOI 10.1016/j.diin.2015.10.002, URL https://doi.org/10.1016%2Fj.diin.2015.10.002

5. Chung H, Park J, Lee S, Kang C (2012) Digital forensic investigation of cloud storage services. Digital Investigation 9(2):81–95, DOI 10.1016/j.diin.2012.05.015, URL https://doi.org/10.1016%2Fj.diin.2012.05.015

6. Daryabar F, Dehghantanha A, Udzir NI, Sani NFBM, bin Shamsuddin S (2013) A review on impacts of cloud computing and digital forensics. International Journal of Cyber-Security and Digital Forensics 2(2):77–94

7. Daryabar F, Dehghantanha A, Choo KKR (2016) Cloud storage forensics: Mega as a case study. Australian Journal of Forensic Sciences pp 1–14

8. Daryabar F, Dehghantanha A, Eterovic-Soric B, Choo KKR (2016) Forensic investigation of OneDrive, box, GoogleDrive and dropbox applications on android and iOS devices. Australian Journal of Forensic Sciences 48(6):615–642, DOI 10.1080/00450618.2015.1110620, URL https://doi.org/10.1080%2F00450618.2015.1110620

9. Daryabar F, Dehghantanha A, Eterovic-Soric B, Choo KKR (2016) Forensic investigation of OneDrive, box, GoogleDrive and dropbox applications on android and iOS devices. Australian Journal of Forensic Sciences 48(6):615–642, DOI 10.1080/00450618.2015.1110620, URL https://doi.org/10.1080%2F00450618.2015.1110620

10. Dehghantanha A, Dargahi T (2017) Chapter 14 - residual cloud forensics: Cloudme and 360yunpan as case studies. In: Choo KKR, Dehghantanha A (eds) Contemporary Digital Forensic Investigations of Cloud and Mobile Applications, Syngress, pp 247–283, DOI http://dx.doi.org/10.1016/B978-0-12-805303-4.00014-9, URL http://www.sciencedirect.com/science/article/pii/B9780128053034000149

11. Dezfouli FN, Dehghantanha A, Eterovic-Soric B, Choo KKR (2015) Investigating social networking applications on smartphones detecting facebook, twitter, linkedin and google+ artefacts on android and ios platforms. Australian Journal of Forensic Sciences 48(4):469–488, DOI 10.1080/00450618.2015.1066854, URL https://doi.org/10.1080%2F00450618.2015.1066854

12. Do Q, Martini B, Choo KKR (2015) A forensically sound adversary model for mobile devices. PLOS ONE 10(9):e0138,449, DOI 10.1371/journal.pone.0138449, URL https://doi.org/10.1371%2Fjournal.pone.0138449

13. Do Q, Martini B, Choo KKR (2016) Is the data on your wearable device secure? an android wear smartwatch case study. Software: Practice and Experience 47(3):391–403, DOI 10.1002/spe.2414, URL https://doi.org/10.1002%2Fspe.2414

14. Fahdi MA, Clarke N, Furnell S (2013) Challenges to digital forensics: A survey of researchers: practitioners attitudes and opinions. In: 2013 Information Security for South Africa, Institute of Electrical and Electronics Engineers (IEEE), DOI 10.1109/issa.2013.6641058, URL https://doi.org/10.1109%2Fissa.2013.6641058

15. Gebhardt T, Reiser HP (2013) Network forensics for cloud computing. In: IFIP International Conference on Distributed Applications and Interoperable Systems, Springer, pp 29–42

16. Jarraya Y, Madi T, Debbabi M (2014) A survey and a layered taxonomy of software-defined networking. IEEE Communications Surveys & Tutorials 16(4):1955–1980, DOI 10.1109/comst.2014.2320094, URL https://doi.org/10.1109%2Fcomst.2014.2320094

17. Josiah D, T SA (2013) Design and implementation of frost: Digital forensic tools for the openstack cloud computing platform. Digital Investigation 10:S87–S95

18. Kaur K, Singh J, Ghumman NS (2014) Mininet as software defined networking testing platform. In: International Conference on Communication, Computing & Systems (ICCCS

19. Kent K, Chevalier S, Grance T, Dang H (2006) Guide to integrating forensic techniques into incident response. Tech. rep., DOI 10.6028/nist.sp.800-86, URL https://doi.org/10.6028%2Fnist.sp.800-86

20. Khondoker R, Zaalouk A, Marx R, Bayarou K (2014) Feature-based comparison and selection of software defined networking (SDN) controllers. In: 2014 World Congress on Computer Applications and Information Systems (WCCAIS), Institute of Electrical and Electronics Engineers (IEEE), DOI 10.1109/wccais.2014.6916572, URL https://doi.org/10.1109%2Fwccais.2014.6916572

21. Kreutz D, Ramos FMV, Verissimo PE, Rothenberg CE, Azodolmolky S, Uhlig S (2015) Software-defined networking: a comprehensive survey. In: Proceedings of the IEEE, 103(1):14–76, DOI 10.1109/JPROC.2014.2371999, URL https://doi.org/10.1109/JPROC.2014.2371999

22. Martini B, Choo KKR (2012) An integrated conceptual digital forensic framework for cloud computing. Digital Investigation 9(2):71–80, DOI 10.1016/j.diin.2012.07.001, URL https://doi.org/10.1016%2Fj.diin.2012.07.001

23. Martini B, Choo KKR (2013) Cloud storage forensics: ownCloud as a case study. Digital Investigation 10(4):287–299, DOI 10.1016/j.diin.2013.08.005, URL https://doi.org/10.1016%2Fj.diin.2013.08.005

24. Martini B, Choo KKR (2014) Distributed filesystem forensics: XtreemFS as a case study. Digital Investigation 11(4):295–313, DOI 10.1016/j.diin.2014.08.002, URL https://doi.org/10.1016%2Fj.diin.2014.08.002

25. Martini B, Choo KKR (2014) Remote programmatic vCloud forensics: A six-step collection process and a proof of concept. In: 2014 IEEE 13th International Conference on Trust, Security and Privacy in Computing and Communications, Institute of Electrical and Electronics Engineers (IEEE), DOI 10.1109/trustcom.2014.124, URL https://doi.org/10.1109%2Ftrustcom.2014.124

26. Marty R (2011) Cloud application logging for forensics. In: Proceedings of the 2011 ACM Symposium on Applied Computing, ACM, pp 178–184

27. Mohtasebi S, Dehghantanha A, Choo KK (2017) Chapter 12 - investigating storage as a service cloud platform: pcloud as a case study. In: Choo KKR, Dehghantanha A (eds) Contemporary Digital Forensic Investigations of Cloud and Mobile Applications, Syngress, pp 185–204, DOI http://dx.doi.org/10.1016/B978-0-12-805303-4.00013-7, URL http://www.sciencedirect.com/science/article/pii/B9780128053034000137

28. Mohtasebi S, Dehghantanha A, Choo KK (2017) Chapter 13 - cloud storage forensics: Analysis of data remnants on spideroak, justcloud, and pcloud. In: Choo KKR, Dehghantanha A (eds) Contemporary Digital Forensic Investigations of Cloud and Mobile Applications, Syngress, pp 205–246, DOI http://dx.doi.org/10.1016/B978-0-12-805303-4.00013-7, URL http://www.sciencedirect.com/science/article/pii/B9780128053034000137

29. Nunes BAA, Mendonca M, Nguyen XN, Obraczka K, Turletti T (2014) A survey of software-defined networking: Past, present, and future of programmable networks. IEEE Communications Surveys & Tutorials 16(3):1617–1634, DOI 10.1109/surv.2014.012214.00180, URL https://doi.org/10.1109%2Fsurv.2014.012214.00180

30. Pichan A, Lazarescu M, Soh ST (2015) Cloud forensics: Technical challenges, solutions and comparative analysis. Digital Investigation 13:38–57

31. Qi H, Li K (2016) Software Defined Networking Applications in Distributed Datacenters. Springer International Publishing, DOI 10.1007/978-3-319-33135-5, URL https://doi.org/10.1007%2F978-3-319-33135-5
32. Rahman NHA, Cahyani NDW, Choo KKR (2016) Cloud incident handling and forensic-by-design: cloud storage as a case study. Concurrency and Computation: Practice and Experience DOI 10.1002/cpe.3868, URL https://doi.org/10.1002%2Fcpe.3868
33. Rodney M (1999) What is forensic computing? Australian Institute of Criminology Canberra
34. Röpke C, Holz T (2015) SDN rootkits: Subverting network operating systems of software-defined networks. In: Research in Attacks, Intrusions, and Defenses, Springer Nature, pp 339–356, DOI 10.1007/978-3-319-26362-5_16, URL https://doi.org/10.1007%2F978-3-319-26362-5_16
35. Saad S, Traore I (2010) Method ontology for intelligent network forensics analysis. In: 2010 Eighth International Conference on Privacy, Security and Trust, Institute of Electrical and Electronics Engineers (IEEE), DOI 10.1109/pst.2010.5593235, URL https://doi.org/10.1109%2Fpst.2010.5593235
36. Scanlon M, Farina J, Kechadi MT (2014) BitTorrent sync: Network investigation methodology. In: 2014 Ninth International Conference on Availability, Reliability and Security, Institute of Electrical and Electronics Engineers (IEEE), DOI 10.1109/ares.2014.11, URL https://doi.org/10.1109%2Fares.2014.11
37. Scanlon M, Farina J, Khac NAL, Kechadi T (2014) Leveraging decentralization to extend the digital evidence acquisition window: Case study on bittorrent sync. Journal of Digital Forensics, Security and Law 9(2):85–99
38. Shariati M, Dehghantanha A, Choo KKR (2015) SugarSync forensic analysis. Australian Journal of Forensic Sciences 48(1):95–117, DOI 10.1080/00450618.2015.1021379, URL https://doi.org/10.1080%2F00450618.2015.1021379
39. Shields C, Frieder O, Maloof M (2011) A system for the proactive, continuous, and efficient collection of digital forensic evidence. Digital Investigation 8:S3–S13, DOI 10.1016/j.diin.2011.05.002, URL https://doi.org/10.1016%2Fj.diin.2011.05.002
40. Sibiya G, Venter HS, Fogwill T (2015) Digital forensics in the cloud: The state of the art. In: 2015 IST-Africa Conference, Institute of Electrical and Electronics Engineers (IEEE), DOI 10.1109/istafrica.2015.7190540, URL https://doi.org/10.1109%2Fistafrica.2015.7190540
41. Simou S, Kalloniatis C, Kavakli E, Gritzalis S (2014) Cloud forensics: identifying the major issues and challenges. In: International Conference on Advanced Information Systems Engineering, Springer, pp 271–284
42. Staab S, Studer R (eds) (2009) Handbook on Ontologies. Springer Nature, DOI 10.1007/978-3-540-92673-3, URL https://doi.org/10.1007%2F978-3-540-92673-3
43. Teing YY, Dehghantanha A, Choo KKR, Dargahi T, Conti M (2016) Forensic investigation of cooperative storage cloud service: Symform as a case study. Journal of Forensic Sciences DOI 10.1111/1556-4029.13271, URL https://doi.org/10.1111%2F1556-4029.13271
44. Teing YY, Dehghantanha A, Choo KKR, Yang LT (2016) Forensic investigation of p2p cloud storage services and backbone for IoT networks: BitTorrent sync as a case study. Computers & Electrical Engineering DOI 10.1016/j.compeleceng.2016.08.020, URL https://doi.org/10.1016%2Fj.compeleceng.2016.08.020
45. Teing YY, Ali D, Choo K, Abdullah MT, Muda Z (2017) Greening cloud-enabled big data storage forensics: Syncany as a case study. IEEE Transactions on Sustainable Computing DOI 10.1109/tsusc.2017.2687103, URL https://doi.org/10.1109%2Ftsusc.2017.2687103
46. Thethi N, Keane A (2014) Digital forensics investigations in the cloud. In: Advance Computing Conference (IACC), 2014 IEEE International, IEEE, pp 1475–1480
47. Turnbull B, Randhawa S (2015) Automated event and social network extraction from digital evidence sources with ontological mapping. Digital Investigation 13:94–106, DOI 10.1016/j.diin.2015.04.004, URL https://doi.org/10.1016%2Fj.diin.2015.04.004
48. Zawoad S, Hasan R (2013) Cloud forensics: a meta-study of challenges, approaches, and open problems. arXiv preprint arXiv:13026312

Mobile Forensics: A Bibliometric Analysis

James Gill, Ihechi Okere, Hamed HaddadPajouh, and Ali Dehghantanha

Abstract In the past few years mobile devices have advanced in a variety of ways such as internal power source capacity, internal memory storage, and CPU capabilities thereby increasing computing capacity while still maintaining a portable size for the owners of mobile devices, this essentially turning it into a portable data storage device where people store their personal information. These changes in the nature and sage of the mobile devices have led to their increased importance in areas such as legal implications in police or company investigations. In this paper we will conduct a bibliometric analysis of the subject of mobile forensics which will enable us to examine the degree to which this new development can become potential evidence, the advances investigators have made over time on the subject, the possible future technologies that could influence more changes in the field of mobile forensics and its impact, covering also the difference between mobile forensics and computer forensics.

Keywords Mobile forensics · Mobile analysis · Bibliometric analysis

J. Gill · I. Okere
Department of Computer Science, School of Computing, Science and Engineering,
University of Salford, Greater Manchester, UK
e-mail: J.Gill2@edu.salford.ac.uk; I.Okere@edu.salford.ac.uk

H. HaddadPajouh
Department of Information Technology and Computer Engineering,
Shiraz University of Technology, Shiraz, Iran
e-mail: hp@sutech.ac.ir

A. Dehghantanha (✉)
Department of Computer Science, University of Sheffield, Sheffield, UK
e-mail: A.Dehghantanha@sheffield.ac.uk

© Springer International Publishing AG, part of Springer Nature 2018
A. Dehghantanha et al. (eds.), *Cyber Threat Intelligence*, Advances in Information
Security 70, https://doi.org/10.1007/978-3-319-73951-9_15

1 Introduction

Mobile forensics is the technique of using a set of tools in order to gain access to digital information stored on a mobile devices [1] such as a smartphone, Tablet or even a digital camera to be used as evidence in an investigation [2].

This can be anything from images, call logs, GPS data, and audio/visual recording along with any deleted information on the device [3]. This has given rise to a complication due to the development of mobile devices with considerable storage size and internet capabilities along with a myriad of other abilities when compared to mobile devices from just a few years ago [4]. We are currently moving from the Internet society to a mobile society where more and more access to information is done by previously dumb phones [5].

There is a difficulty when trying to retrieve information from a mobile device due to the vast variety of available devices [6] as the process of finding an appropriate forensic tools is very difficult [7]. Despite the aforementioned research conducted on mobile forensics being quite extensive, no bibliometric analysis can be traced to the topic using reports on the research impacts and trends of such investigations.

In order to show the growth and impact of mobile forensics, this paper proposition is to provide an assessment of research into mobile forensics between 2005 and 2016 using keywords and major academic databases. The bibliometric methods are now firmly established as scientific specialties and are an integral part of research evaluation methodology especially within the scientific and applied fields[8]. This method parameters have become a vital role of the modern academic assessment [9]. The results of such analysis also help in decision making when a research is to be funded [10]. This paper will look at the distribution and trends of the bibliometric data in order to know the impact and influence of mobile forensics around the world. Figure 1 shows the statistics of Mobile Forensic publications by the top 10 countries in the world.

2 Methodology

The purpose of bibliometric data is to review and quantify the impact of a scientific field. The field of bibliometric studies publication patterns by using quantitative analysis and statistics [11]. In this paper, searching the correct bibliometric information involved multiple search options such as using keywords like "mobile forensics" and "mobile analysis" in order to retrieve the most relevant information. The keywords themselves allow us to search database collections such as IEEE Xplore Digital Library and Web of Science to find the relevant data for this paper, which involved using the websites of each stated database. This involved using keywords to search a database for relevant information, as an example using the keyword Mobile Analysis within the Web of Science displays 121,643 results (Fig. 2).

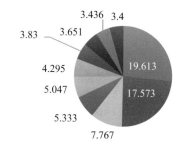

Mobile Forensics

■ Peoples R China	■ USA	▣ South Korea	■ Germany
▣ India	▣ Japan	■ England	■ Spain
■ Italy	■ Taiwan		

Fig. 1 Publications by Countries

Fig. 2 Data collection process

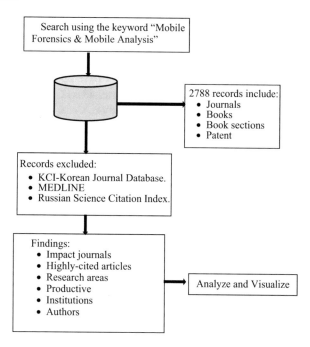

Search using the keyword "Mobile Forensics & Mobile Analysis"

2788 records include:
- Journals
- Books
- Book sections
- Patent

Records excluded:
- KCI-Korean Journal Database.
- MEDLINE
- Russian Science Citation Index.

Findings:
- Impact journals
- Highly-cited articles
- Research areas
- Productive
- Institutions
- Authors

Analyze and Visualize

In order to break down and remove unwanted information, certain search criteria were employed, for example, by using a search criteria such as a time frame, 2005–2016, limiting how far back the database could search for the information, we were able to focus our research area, within Web of Science when searching for mobile analysis using the time frame, a result of 76,351 was produced as compared to the earlier result of 121,643, by using such search criteria as this in conjunction with others, languages, research domains, research areas as well as giving the information a viewing order such as the highest to lowest times cited along us to easily see the most impactful documents which is at the heart of bibliometric.

2.1 Web of Science

There is a variety of databases available for us to use in order to collect the information necessary for this paper, such as IEEE Xplore digital library, Scopus Centre for Science and Technology Studies (CWTS), The Institute for Research Information and Quality Assurance (IFQ) and Web of Science. We first investigated different databases to find one that was most suitable for our needs. We first eliminated Google Scholar as our database of choice due to it not being well accepted or at the very least scrutinized by many in the academic field and Google Scholar was released as a beta product in November of 2004. Since then, Google Scholar scrutinized and questioned by many in academia and the library field [12] and the worry of manipulated data, In order to alert the research community over how easily one can manipulate the data and bibliometric indicators [13]. The elimination of IEEE Xplore was due to multiple accounts of Scopus, the Web of Science (WoS) and Google Scholar being the main three databases when considering bibliometric data and we have already removed Google Scholar as an option, it seems that the two most extensive databases are Web of Science and Scopus. Besides searching the literature, these two databases used to rank journals in terms of their productivity and the total citations received to indicate the journals impact, prestige or influence [14]. There are three major bibliometric databases investigated as follows: Google Scholar, Scopus and the Web of Science [15].

This left us only with Scopus and Web of Science as the two main databases we could choose from [16]. It is due to multiple factors, including its scholarly citations, The Web of Science, an online database of bibliographic information produced by Thomson Reuters draws its real value from the scholarly citation index at its core [17]. The tools and content of the Web of Science are trusted by a vast amount of institution s worldwide The Web of Science s content and tools are trusted by nearly 7000 of the world's leading scholarly institutions responsible for scientific policy making. [18] and for its ability to refine search options within its own database, this allowed us, when using keywords to search for relevant information for this paper, to narrow the search results with a multitude of options such as documentation type, language, times cited, research domains, countries, authors and so on. All these capabilities made the Web of Science database an extremely effective tool in searching for relevant information quickly in a format of our choosing.

3   Finding in Publications Distribution

This section will be broken down into numerous sub-topics: productivity, research areas, institutions, authors, impact journals, highly-cited articles, and keyword

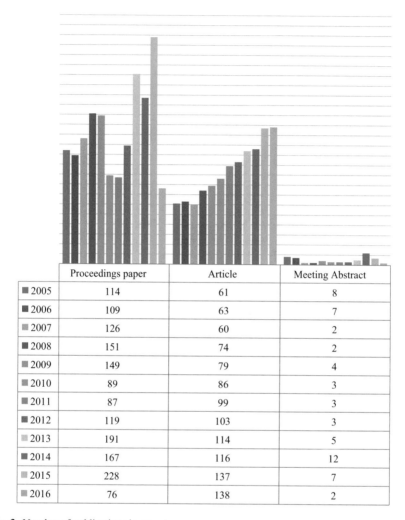

	Proceedings paper	Article	Meeting Abstract
■ 2005	114	61	8
■ 2006	109	63	7
▨ 2007	126	60	2
■ 2008	151	74	2
■ 2009	149	79	4
■ 2010	89	86	3
■ 2011	87	99	3
■ 2012	119	103	3
▨ 2013	191	114	5
■ 2014	167	116	12
▨ 2015	228	137	7
▨ 2016	76	138	2

Fig. 3 Number of publications in recent years

frequency. These findings are important due to showing the publication rates with bibliometric data. In addition, this method is also able to reveal research that helps to create new knowledge and to guarantee this inquiry into mobile forensics is more in-depth. Fig. 3 provided is to show the number of publications between the years 2005-2016.

Figure 3 shows numerous publications taken from various fields of study that are related to mobile forensics. It shows three categories, Conference paper, Article and Meeting abstract. The Conference paper has the highest proportion of the publications with a 57.60% of the publications. This is then followed by the articles proportion of the publications with 40.53%. This is then finally followed by the meeting abstract portion of the publications with 1.89 %, the lowest percentage of all the publications. Looking at Fig. 3, in 2016, publications of proceeding papers

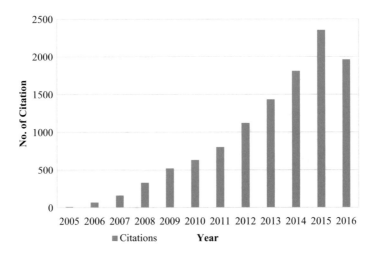

Fig. 4 Citation distribution

have declined quite significantly. This is possibly due to the revision process of proceeding papers, in some cases taking up to a year of feedback and alterations. Following this cycle, it is likely that proceeding papers publications would be on the increase in the following year 2017. Furthermore, the likely increase to proceeding papers publications will have an increasing effect on citations.

As stated earlier, citation analysis is used to evaluate the prevalence of the publications based on data extracted from the citation index. It also supplies information about researchers to other researchers using shared references, providing a holistic view of the topic being researched. Fig. 4 illustrates the citations accumulated by the publications in the last 11 years. This demonstrates the number of publications influences on the number of citations. The longer a publication stays within a database the longer that publications have to amass citations.

The medium number of citation collected by the publications is 935 annually during the period of 2005–2016. Distinct peaks occur in 2014 and 2015. This is conceivably due to an increase in research into mobile forensics/analysis, such as a new type mobile malware or mobile device. Researchers citing other researchers causing an increase in citations. Concluding that the number of citations for the 11 years will also include co-citations.

3.1 Productivity

This section will analyze articles by continents, to help ascertain which is the most productive in the field. Productivity in the bibliometric analysis is taken into consideration because it is a factor that enables the researcher to ascertain which

Table 1 Africa mobile forensics articles

List of continents	No. of articles	No. of articles (%)
South Africa	14	0.53
Egypt	11	0.42
Cameroon	4	0.15
Ghana	3	0.11
Kenya	3	0.11
Algeria	2	0.08
Nigeria	2	0.08
Senegal	2	0.08
Tunisia	2	0.08

continents are leading in a particular branch of the research. Another important way it helps researchers is that it increases research productivity by building on the works of the identified leaders. As such, it weeds out least impactful works, and as a result, helps researchers have a better focus on how to advance the research with recent technologies and the new and best methods.

To create a clearer picture, the results of the mobile forensics publications search were analyzed by their originating continents. The results were further broken down into countries. Showing each country's number of publications and the percentage of their contributions to the research subject.

Tables 1, 2, 3, 4 and 5 shows that publication rate on subject of mobile forensics in five continent. Asia is the leading continent in mobile forensics research with a total of 1321 publications and a massive 50.08% of the total publications. The top four countries in Asia having above 100 publications in mobile forensics realm. The bulk of it coming from the top country which is The People s Republic of China s 545 which is 20.66% of the world's publications, having more than double of what the second in that continent, India, could muster up. The second most productive continent is Europe with 980 publications. Germany lead in the continent with 149 and they are closely followed by England with 106. Both of them, together with Spain occupy the top 3 positions in the continent having published above 100 publications each. The third-ranked continent is North America. It is clear that the USA is the leading researcher in that continent. In addition to being the top publishers in that continent, they are the second highest in the world. Coming in with 488 publications, which is 18.50% of the world's publications on mobile forensics just behind China by 2.16%. The only other North American country who made a sizeable contribution to the list is Canada, having only 93 publications on the subject. According to Tables 1, 2, 3, 4, and 5, Chinese and the Americans stand head and shoulders above the other countries.

One key observation here is the gap in quantity between the USA and other countries when taken independently. It may be due to the heavy government investments in research and development. The United States federal government invests almost 140 billion on research and development every year [19].

Table 2 Asia mobile
forensics articles

List of continents	No. of articles	No. of articles (%)
Peoples R China	545	20.66
Australia	72	2.73
India	141	5.35
Japan	120	4.55
Taiwan	95	3.60
Malaysia	60	2.27
Singapore	41	1.55
Iran	31	1.18
Pakistan	20	0.76
Indonesia	15	0.57
Saudi Arabia	15	0.57
Thailand	14	0.53
U Arab Emirates	4	0.15
Jordan	3	0.11

Table 3 North-America
mobile forensics articles

List of continents	No. of articles	No. of articles (%)
USA	488	18.50
Canada	93	3.53
Mexico	18	0.68
Cuba	2	0.08

Table 4 South-America
mobile forensics articles

List of continents	No. of articles	No. of articles (%)
Brazil	42	1.59
Chile	4	0.15

3.2 Research Areas

This section highlights the direction of the research into other disciplines. As a discipline evolves it tends to borrow practices and scientific method from related and even some unrelated disciplines. It is also critical in the measurement of the research scope based on publications and citations frequency. Knowing the frequency is vital because it shows the trend of the research over a given time period. An analysis by research areas on the results gotten from the WoS database showed several publications linked with other discipline as can be seen in Table 6.

A quick glance at Table 6 would show that the highest publications come from engineering, computer science and telecommunications which is understandable. However, with disciplines like imaging science photographic technology, it could imply that mobile forensics is getting more important in crime scene investigations. While the disciplines like automated control systems, and transportation show the breadth in the usage of mobile device forensics.

Table 5 Europe mobile forensics articles

List of continents	No. of articles	No. of articles (%)
Austria	61	2.31
Ireland	18	0.68
Czech Republic	13	0.49
Denmark	11	0.42
New Zealand	11	0.42
Germany	149	5.65
England	106	4.02
Spain	102	3.87
Italy	96	3.64
France	80	3.03
Austria	37	1.40
Switzerland	35	1.33
Sweden	33	1.25
Greece	29	1.10
Romania	29	1.10
Poland	27	1.02
Netherlands	26	0.99
Turkey	26	0.99
Belgium	22	0.83
Portugal	22	0.83
Norway	20	0.76
Hungary	11	0.42
Russia	11	0.42
Cyprus	4	0.15
Wales	4	0.15
Croatia	2	0.08
Israel	2	0.08
Luxembourg	2	0.08

3.3 Institutions

This section breaks down the number of publications with respect to the institutions they were published from. The aim of the section is also to find out which institutions have been actively publishing on the subject. Table 7 below shows the top 20 institutions, their publications and the country of the institutions. The data from the table reaffirms the observation from Table 6 that The People's Republic of China is the leading researcher in the field. The Table 7 below shows a representation of the most active institutions. The results come as no surprise when the information from Table 6 is considered. With Asia having the most active institutions on the list, and China contributing the most. Reaffirming the observation from Table 7.

Table 6 Research areas

Research areas	Publications	Publications (%)
Engineering	1117	42.34
Computer Science	1051	39.84
Telecommunications	709	26.88
Automation Control Systems	153	5.80
Robotics	136	5.16
Business Economics	116	4.40
Chemistry	101	3.83
Transportation	85	3.22
Materials Science	73	2.77
Operations Research Management Science	62	2.35
Physics	61	2.31
Education Educational Research	59	2.24
Science Technology Other Topics	56	2.12
Health Care Sciences Services	50	1.90
Optics	49	1.86
Information Science Library Science	46	1.74
Instruments Instrumentation	44	1.67
Environmental Sciences Ecology	43	1.63
Imaging Science Photographic Technology	43	1.63
Biochemistry Molecular Biology	40	1.52
Communication	39	1.48

3.4   Impact Journals

This section will discuss the listing of impact journals under the computer science area. This category will be influential because it shows the most leading publications and the highest citations received. From this information, researchers are able to bolster their work by publishing in high-quality journals.

Table 8 displays 10 journal publications with the highest number of publications. It shows the most significant number of publications belongs to the Lecture Notes in Computer Science proceeded by Applied Mechanics and Materials and Proceedings of SPIE publications. The publication series of Lecture Notes in Computer Science has the most significant number of publications. This is due to providing publishing services to areas such as education, computer science, and information technology research.

Table 9 shows that Lecture Notes in Computer Science, accumulated a total of 68,000 citations, secondly IEEE Transactions on Communications with 53,045 citations and thirdly Lecture Notes on Artificial Intelligence with 20,713.

Then according to Table 9 and the quality of the journal a correlation can be seen, a high-quality journal will attract researchers for citations, which will then, in turn, attract more researchers through the increase of citations.

Table 7 Institutions

Institutions	Publications	Publications (%)	Country
Beijing University Posts Telecomm	51	1.93	China
Chinese Acad Sci	25	0.95	China
Korea University	22	0.83	South Korea
Sungkyunkwan University	20	0.76	South Korea
Beijing Jiao tong University	19	0.72	China
Nanyang Technological University	19	0.72	Singapore
Seoul Natl University	19	0.72	South Korea
Purdue University	17	0.64	USA
Korea Adv Inst Sci Technology	15	0.57	South Korea
Tsinghua University	15	0.57	China
Columbia University	13	0.49	USA
Natl University Singapore	13	0.49	Singapore
University Illinois	13	0.49	USA
Georgia Inst Technology	12	0.46	USA
Han-yang University	12	0.46	South Korea
Shanghai Jiao Tong University	12	0.46	China
Natl Cheng Kung University	11	0.42	China
Politecn Milan	11	0.42	Italy
University Carlos Iii Madrid	11	0.42	Spain

Table 8 Top 10 most cited journals

Journal titles with the highest number of publications	IF	Q	P	Most cited journals	C
Lecture Notes in Computer Science	0.402	Q4	36,143	Lecture Notes in Computer Science	68,000
Lecture Notes in Artificial Intelligence	0.302	Q4	7064	IEEE Transactions on Communications	53,045
Wireless Personal Communications	0.701	Q3	4344	Lecture Notes on Artificial Intelligence	20,713
IEEE Transactions on Communications	2.925	Q1	4220	Computer Communications	19,640
IEICE Transactions on Communications	0.226	Q4	4058	IEICE Transactions on Communications	10,064
Computer Communications	2.099	Q1	2588	Wireless Personal Communications	9322
Journal of Network and Computer Applications	2.331	Q1	1297	Journal of Network and Computer Applications	8479
Telecommunications Policy	0.982	Q3	734	Telecommunications Policy	5567
Digital Investigations	1.211	Q3	734	Digital Investigations	2547
International Journal of Mobile Communications	0.765	Q3	309	International Journal of Mobile Communications	1588

Table 9 Highly citied articles

Titles	Times cited	Year published
SURF: Speeded Up Robust Features	1628	2006
Machine Learning for High-speed Corner Detection	482	2006
Differential Privacy	385	2006
Calibrating Noise to Sensitivity in Private Data Analysis	326	2006
Overview and Recent Advances in Partial Least Squares	290	2006
Bandit Based Monte-Carlo Planning	283	2006
Practical Identify	249	2006
Information Retrieval in Folksonomies: Search and Ranking	228	2006
Sampling Strategies for Bag-of-Features Image Classification	198	2006

3.5 Highly Cited Articles

This section discusses the amount of citations accumulated by the journals. This section will evaluate the research quality and the influence it has upon related fields.

Table 9 displays nine of the highest cited articles from the previously mentioned Lecture Notes in Computer Science publication. It will display the top cited article, SURF: Speeded Up Robust Features, has accumulated 1628 citations and was published in the year 2006, 10 years ago, strongly supporting the idea that the longer a publication has been in the database, the higher the accumulated citations will be. This, in turn, made the article itself a high-quality publication attracting more and more researchers.

4 Conclusion and Future Works

Although numerous studies and research has supplied multiple mobile forensic possibilities, but as mobile devices become more integrated into daily life such as banking and social networking, along with the production of new devices, there will always be the difficulty of mobile forensics keeping pace [20, 21].

With the exponential growth and development of mobile devices, mobile forensics has not been far behind. Mobile devices in recent years hold vital and copious amounts of information when compared to just a few years ago [22]. Banking, E-mails, GPS, and social networking are just a few parts of information that can be stored on a mobile device [27]. This has, in turn, caused a rise in the need and abilities of mobile forensics, as more and more sophisticated attack techniques such as malware [23, 24] and ransomware are targeting major mobile operating systems such as Android [25] and iOS.

In this paper, the bibliometric method was used to analyze mobile forensic trends from 2005 until 2016. In this study, we presented a variety of criteria including, impact journals, highly-cited articles, research areas, productivity, institutions and authors. Using these criteria, it helped to unearth global trends linked to mobile forensic publications. In the past 11 years, it has been shown that the number of publications related to mobile forensics had steadily grown.

We compiled and analyzed the articles published between 2005 and 2016. First, these were categorized into continents. Asia is the greatest producer of publications in research, followed by Europe. This trend can also be seen in the institutions and authors, with the Asian continent holding a majority of the publication positions, including majority of the top positions. The Asian continent also hold a majority position with institutions, including the top 7 positions, followed by the United States of America.

Developing biblimometric analysis of other types of malware such as IoT malware [26], OSX malware [27], and ransomware [28] is an interesting future work of this study. Moreover, using bibliometric analysis to detect current and future research trends in IoT security and forensics [29], ransomware analysis [30], and cloud security and forensics [31] would pave the way for future researchers in the field.

References

1. F. Daryabar, A. Dehghantanha, B. Eterovic-Soric, and K.-K. R. Choo, "Forensic investigation of OneDrive, Box, GoogleDrive and Dropbox applications on Android and iOS devices," *Aust. J. Forensic Sci.*, vol. 48, no. 6, pp. 615–642, 2016.
2. G. Grispos, T. Storer, and W. B. Glisson, "A comparison of forensic evidence recovery techniques for a windows mobile smart phone," *Digit. Investig.*, vol. 8, no. 1, pp. 23–36, 2011.
3. B. C. Ogazi-Onyemaechi, A. Dehghantanha, K. R. R. Choo, and others, "Performance of android forensics data recovery tools," 2016.
4. F. Norouzizadeh Dezfouli, A. Dehghantanha, B. Eterovic-Soric, and K.-K. R. Choo, "Investigating Social Networking applications on smartphones detecting Facebook, Twitter, LinkedIn and Google+ artefacts on Android and iOS platforms," *Aust. J. Forensic Sci.*, vol. 48, no. 4, pp. 469–488, 2016.
5. M. Becher, F. C. Freiling, J. Hoffmann, T. Holz, S. Uellenbeck, and C. Wolf, "Mobile security catching up? Revealing the nuts and bolts of the security of mobile devices," in *Proceedings - IEEE Symposium on Security and Privacy*, 2011, pp. 96–111.
6. M. Petraityte, A. Dehghantanha, and others, "Mobile phone forensics: an investigative framework based on user impulsivity and secure collaboration errors," 2016.
7. M. Yates, "Practical investigations of digital forensics tools for mobile devices," *2010 Inf. Secur. Curric. Dev. Conf.*, pp. 156–162, 2010.
8. O. Ellegaard and J. A. Wallin, "The bibliometric analysis of scholarly production: How great is the impact?," *Scientometrics*, vol. 105, no. 3, pp. 1809–1831, 2015.
9. A. F. Choudhri, A. Siddiqui, N. R. Khan, and H. L. Cohen, "Understanding Bibliometric Parameters and Analysis," *RadioGraphics*, vol. 35, no. 3, pp. 736–746, 2015.
10. M. Olensky, M. Schmidt, and N. J. van Eck, "Evaluation of the citation matching algorithms of CWTS and iFQ in comparison to the Web of science," *J. Assoc. Inf. Sci. Technol.*, vol. 67, no. 10, pp. 2550–2564, Oct. 2016.
11. M. K. McBurney and P. L. Novak, "What is bibliometrics and why should you care?," *Proc. IEEE Int. Prof. Commun. Conf.*, pp. 108–114, 2002.
12. J. L. Howland, T. C. Wright, R. A. Boughan, and B. C. Roberts, "How Scholarly Is Google Scholar? A Comparison to Library Databases," *Coll. Res. Libr.*, vol. 70, no. 3, pp. 227–234, 2009.

13. E. Lopez-Cozar, Delgado, N. Robinson-Garcia, and D. Torres-Salinas, "Manipulating Google Scholar Citations and Google Scholar Metrics: simple, easy and tempting," 2012.

14. A. Aghaei Chadegani *et al.*, "A comparison between two main academic literature collections: Web of science and scopus databases," *Asian Soc. Sci.*, vol. 9, no. 5, pp. 18–26, 2013.

15. A. W. Harzing and S. Alakangas, "Google Scholar, Scopus and the Web of Science: a longitudinal and cross-disciplinary comparison," *Scientometrics*, vol. 106, no. 2, pp. 787–804, 2016.

16. H. Pasula, B. Marthi, B. Milch, S. Russell, and I. Shpitser, "Identity uncertainty and citation matching," *Adv. Neural Inf. Process. Syst.*, pp. 1425–1432, 2003.

17. M. E. Mcveigh, "Citation Indexes and the Web of Science," *Encycl. Libr. Inf. Sci. Third Ed.*, no. August 2013, pp. 37–41, 2009.

18. T. Reuters, "WEB OF SCIENCE, Citation Report, Thomson Reuters," *Thomson Reuters*, 2014.

19. A. A. for the A. of Science., "Historical Trends in Federal R&D | AAAS - The World's Largest General Scientific Society," *Historical Trends in Federal R&D*, 2016. [Online]. Available: https://www.aaas.org/page/historical-trends-federal-rd.

20. Tooska Dargahi, Ali Dehghantanha, and Mauro Conti, "Forensics Analysis of Android Mobile VoIP Apps," in *Contemporary Digital Forensic Investigations Of Cloud And Mobile Applications*, Elsevier, pp. 7–20.

21. M. N. Yusoff, R. Mahmod, A. Dehghantanha, and M. T. Abdullah, "An approach for forensic investigation in Firefox OS," in *Cyber Security, Cyber Warfare and Digital Forensic (CyberSec), 2014 Third International Conference on*, 2014, pp. 22–26.

22. A. Dehghantanha and K. Franke, "Privacy-respecting digital investigation," in *Privacy, Security and Trust (PST), 2014 Twelfth Annual International Conference on*, 2014, pp. 129–138.

23. M. Damshenas, A. Dehghantanha, K.-K. R. Choo, and R. Mahmud, "M0Droid: An Android Behavioral-Based Malware Detection Model," *J. Inf. Priv. Secur.*, vol. 11, no. 3, pp. 141–157, Jul. 2015.

24. K. Shaerpour, A. Dehghantanha, and R. Mahmod, "Trends In Android Malware Detection," *J. Digit. Forensics Secur. Law*, vol. 8, no. 3, pp. 21–40, Sep. 2013.

25. N. Milosevic, A. Dehghantanha, and K.-K. R. Choo, "Machine learning aided Android malware classification," *Comput. Electr. Eng.*

26. Amin Azmoudeh, Ali Dehghantanha and Kim-Kwang Raymond Choo, "Robust Malware Detection for Internet Of (Battlefield) Things Devices Using Deep Eigenspace Learning", IEEE Transactions on Sustainable Computing, 2017,

27. Hamed HaddadPajouh, Ali Dehghantanha, Raouf Khayami, and Kim-Kwang Raymond Choo, "Intelligent OS X Malware Threat Detection", Journal of Computer Virology and Hacking Techniques, 2017

28. Sajad Homayoun, Ali Dehghantanha, Marzieh Ahmadzadeh, Sattar Hashemi, Raouf Khayami, "Know Abnormal, Find Evil: Frequent Pattern Mining for Ransomware Threat Hunting and Intelligence", IEEE Transactions on Emerging Topics in Computing, 2017 - DOI: 10.1109/TETC.2017.2756908

29. Mauro Conti, Ali Dehghantanha, Katrin Franke, Steve Watson, "Internet of Things Security and Forensics: Challenges and Opportunities", Future Generation Computer Systems Journal, DoI: https://doi.org/10.1016/j.future.2017.07.060, 2017

30. Amin Azmoodeh, Ali Dehghantanha, Mauro Conti, Raymond Choo, "Detecting Crypto-Ransomware in IoT Networks Based On Energy Consumption Footprint", Journal of Ambient Intelligence and Humanized Computing, DOI: 10.1007/s12652-017-0558-5, 2017

31. Yee-Yang Teing, Ali Dehghantanha, Kim-Kwang Raymond Choo, Zaiton Muda, and Mohd Taufik Abdullah, "Greening Cloud-Enabled Big Data Storage Forensics: Syncany as a Case Study," IEEE Transactions on Sustainable Computing, DOI: 10.1109/TSUSC.2017.2687103, 2017.

Emerging from the Cloud: A Bibliometric Analysis of Cloud Forensics Studies

James Baldwin, Omar M. K. Alhawi, Simone Shaughnessy, Alex Akinbi, and Ali Dehghantanha

Abstract Emergence of cloud computing technologies have changed the way we store, retrieve, and archive our data. With the promise of unlimited, reliable and always-available storage, a lot of private and confidential data are now stored on different cloud platforms. Being such a gold mine of data, cloud platforms are among the most valuable targets for attackers. Therefore, many forensics investigators have tried to develop tools, tactics and procedures to collect, preserve, analyse and report evidences of attackers' activities on different cloud platforms. Despite the number of published articles there isn't a bibliometric study that presents cloud forensics research trends. This paper aims to address this problem by providing a comprehensive assessment of cloud forensics research trends between 2009 and 2016. Moreover, we provide a classification of cloud forensics process to detect the most profound research areas and highlight remaining challenges.

Keywords Cloud forensics · Cloud computing · Cloud analysis · Cloud investigation · Digital forensics

1 Introduction

Cloud Computing is an emerging technology that has seen a rapid adoption by enterprises and individual consumers. Gartner forecasted that the cloud computing market will hit US$250 billion by 2017 as cloud adoption increases in organizations

J. Baldwin · O. M. K. Alhawi · S. Shaughnessy · A. Akinbi
School of Computing, Science and Engineering, University of Salford, Manchester, UK
e-mail: J.Baldwin1@edu.salford.ac.uk; O.Alhawi@edu.salford.ac.uk;
S.Shaughnessy@edu.salford.ac.uk; O.A.Akinbi@salford.ac.uk

A. Dehghantanha (✉)
Department of Computer Science, University of Sheffield, Sheffield, UK
e-mail: A.Dehghantanha@sheffield.ac.uk

© Springer International Publishing AG, part of Springer Nature 2018
A. Dehghantanha et al. (eds.), *Cyber Threat Intelligence*, Advances in Information Security 70, https://doi.org/10.1007/978-3-319-73951-9_16

[1]. Cisco have also forecasted that annual global cloud IP traffic will reach 14.1 ZB (14.1 billion TB) by the end of 2020, up from 3.9 ZB in 2015 [2].

The National Institute of Standards and Technology (NIST) considers three cloud service models [3]: Software as a Service (SaaS), Platform as a Service (PaaS) and Infrastructure as a Service (IaaS). In the SaaS model an Application Service Provider (ASP) provides various applications over the Internet which eliminates the need for software and IT infrastructure (servers/databases etc) maintenance for the ASP customers [4]. The applications are accessed using a client browser interface. Google Apps, Yahoo Mail and CRM applications are all instances of SaaS. In the PaaS model, cloud infrastructure is owned and maintained by the provider; the customer is then able to deploy and configure applications into a provider managed framework and infrastructure [5]. Examples of PaaS are Google App Engine, Apprenda and Heroku. In the IaaS model resources are provided to the customer as virtualised resources e.g. Virtual Machines (VMs). Whereas the customer has full control over the operating system, the provider maintains control over the physical hardware. This allows for services to be scaled and billed in line with customer resource requirements [6]. Amazon Web Services (AWS), Microsoft Azure and Google Compute Engine (GCE) are examples of IaaS models.

Furthermore, NIST suggests four cloud deployment models, namely private cloud, community cloud, public cloud, and hybrid cloud. With public clouds, services are available through a public cloud service provider (Microsoft, Amazon, etc) who host the cloud infrastructure, and customers don't have any control over the located infrastructure. Private clouds are dedicated to organizations (as opposed to the public) and host specific business relevant applications. Community clouds are shared between organisations with similar requirements and business objectives; they are maintained by all participating members of the community. The final model, hybrid cloud, consist of two or more of the public, private and community models [7].

According to the 2016 State of the Cloud Survey in which 1060 technical professionals representing a broad cross section of organizations were questioned [8], there has been an increase (from 2015) in the number of organisations utilizing the services of cloud providers. This change is illustrated in Fig. 1.

Actual statistical figures of how many crimes have been committed in the cloud are unclear as Cloud Service Providers (CSPs) often ask clients not to disclose any information to the public in relation to cyber incidents [9]. As more organisations move away from traditional 'in house' computing and adopt cloud technology to provide the infrastructure to run their businesses, there are more opportunities and vulnerabilities for attackers in such a rapidly changing environment. According to DarkReading [10] the number of cybercrime incidents reported in the UK has surpassed traditional crime within this current year. With the crime rate increasing, the need for forensic investigations within the cloud has also increased.

The term "cloud forensics" (a cross-discipline of cloud computing and digital forensics [11]) was first introduced in 2011 [11] to recognize the rapidly emerging need for digital investigation in cloud computing environments. According to the 2016 State of the Cloud Survey [8] there is a lack of forensic tools that are tailored

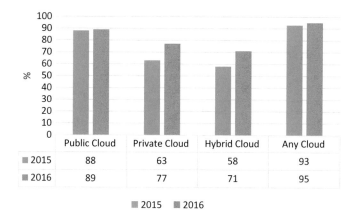

	Public Cloud	Private Cloud	Hybrid Cloud	Any Cloud
▪ 2015	88	63	58	93
▪ 2016	89	77	71	95

▪ 2015 ▪ 2016

Fig. 1 Survey respondents adopting cloud—2016 vs. 2015 [8]

for cloud systems. Approximately 58% of respondents agreed that digital forensic process automation is needed to tackle future challenges including cloud forensics [12]. Current forensic tools appear unsuited to process cloud data as the physical inaccessibility of the evidence and lack of control over the system make evidence acquisition a challenging task [13]. Table 1 illustrates a summary of mostly used tools to conduct cloud forensics [14].

Variety of investigation frameworks have been suggested for cloud forensics [25, 26]. Moreover, researchers tried to identify residual evidences of users' interactions with different cloud platforms such as DropBox [27], MEGA [28], GoogleDrive [29], SugarSync [30], pCloud [31, 32], CloudMe [33], SpiderOak [32] and hubiC [34] on Windows, Linux and mobile devices. There were several attempts to extract server-side evidences of different cloud platforms such as Syncany [35], BitTorrent Sync [36], SymForm [37] as well. While there was a lot of focus on technological and procedural development in cloud forensics [38], to the best of authors' knowledge, a bibliometric analysis of this emerging technology does not exist. As such, this paper aims to provide a comprehensive bibliometric analysis of cloud forensics studies and to demonstrate research trends by highlighting the substantial research contributions. We discuss publication statistics, citation distributions and statistics, regional and institutional productivity, research areas, impact journals, and keywords frequency. By identifying research gaps and challenges in the forensic process this paper will open the way for future research within cloud forensics.

This paper is organised as follows: Sect. 2 describes the research methodology; Sect. 3 presents the results and discusses cloud forensics studies; Sect. 4 introduces the challenges and future trends; Sect. 5 is the conclusion to the study.

Table 1 A summary of mostly used tools to conduct cloud forensics [14]

Utilized tools	General/cloud-based tools	Functionality
FTK remote agent [15]	General	Remote drive and memory image acquisition; remote mounting
Encase remote agent [16]	General	Remote drive image acquisition
Snort [17]	General	Network traffic monitoring and packet logging
FROST [18]	Cloud-based	Digital forensics tools for the OpenStack cloud platform
OWADE [19]	Cloud-based	Reconstruction of browsing history and online credentials
CloudTrail [20]	Cloud-based	Logging in the AWS cloud
Wireshark [21]	General	Network traffic capture and analysis
Sleuthkit [22]	General	Forensic image analysis and data recovery
FTK imager [15]	General	Acquisition of memory and disk images
X-Ways [23]	General	Acquisition of live systems (Windows and Linux)
Encase e-discovery suite [24]	General	Drive image acquisition and offline examination

2 Methodology

Bibliometrics is a method which allows us to verify the relevance, appropriateness and research impacts of a research area/subject based on citation metrics [39]. According to Eugene Garfield [40] the citation index has a quantitative value which helps to define the significance of an article. This in turn helps to measure the 'influence' or 'impact factor which is based on two elements: the number of citations in the current year to items published in the previous 2 years, and the number of substantive articles and reviews published in the same 2 years [41].

We chose to use Web of Science (WoS) as our primary database researching about published articles on 'cloud forensics' as a reliable single source for publications. There are other databases available to search such as Google Scholar and Scopus however WoS provides a more comprehensive and accurate image of the scholarly impact of author [42].

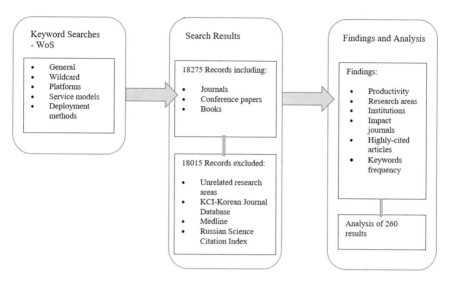

Fig. 2 The data collection process

Table 2 Publication categories

Category	No. publications	% Publications
Book	190	73.08
Journal	70	26.92

As illustrated in Fig. 2 the first step in the data collection process was to use key word searches against the WoS database. We used various general search terms including 'cloud forensic*', forensic* (where * denotes a wildcard character in the search term) and 'cloud investigation' in addition to specific search terms to include platforms, service models and deployment methods. The initial 18,275 results were then refined by excluding other databases such as KCI-Korean Journal Database, Medline and Russian Science Citation. Finally, we refined the results by removing unrelated publications providing a final total of 260 publications directly related to the cloud forensics research area.

Analysis of our results were performed using a combination of the WoS results analysis tools and spreadsheet processing to obtain further detail such as clearly defined geographical region and keyword frequency statistics; they are presented and discussed in Sect. 3.

3   Results and Discussion

Table 2 categorizes related publications based on their source to journals and books (which contain conference proceedings as well). The book category has the highest proportion of publications at 73.08%. This is more than double the journal category which totals 26.92%.

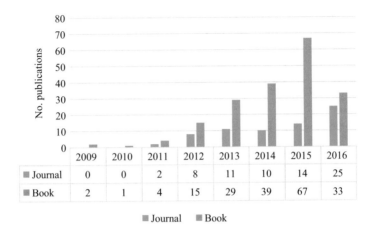

	2009	2010	2011	2012	2013	2014	2015	2016
■ Journal	0	0	2	8	11	10	14	25
■ Book	2	1	4	15	29	39	67	33

■ Journal   ■ Book

Fig. 3 Number of publications

The publication frequency of both categories is illustrated in Fig. 3.

Between 2011 and 2015 there has been a significant increase in the number of book chapters. In 2011 the introduction of the term "cloud forensics" [11] and the release of both the UK [43] and US [44] cloud computing strategies may have contributed to an increased global focus on cloud computing. This year (2011) also represented the beginning of funding into cloud forensics research with a single (1) publication funded by the National Science Foundation Cyber Trust. From 2011 to 2016 the number of funded articles then increased to 8 with an overall 28 publications funded over this period.

WoS provides a citation map feature that allows the researcher to have a holistic view of related research which reflects how researchers embed their work within related and earlier publications [45, 46]. Figure 4 shows the annual citation distribution over the period 2009–2016. This 7-year period represents the start of research into cloud forensics and the average number of citations over the period is 87.75. In 2011 there was only 1 citation while there were 6 citations in 2012 with significant growth in 2013 (650%), 2014 (305%) and 2015 (172%).

Figure 5 represents the total number of available cloud forensic publications and the number of citations for each year in the period of 2009–2016. The earlier an article is published the more citations it received [47]. The top 3 cited publications in this study were published in 2012 which corresponds to the first significant annual citation increase as discussed earlier.

3.1 Productivity

This section will discuss productivity based on the publication output from the 6 geographical regions identified in this study. It can show whether there are any significant geographic trends that correlate to institutional and author research contribution.

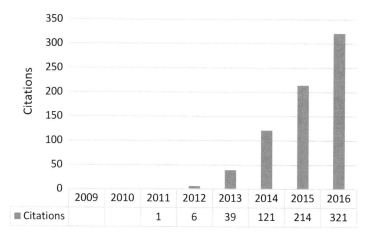

Fig. 4 Citation distributions

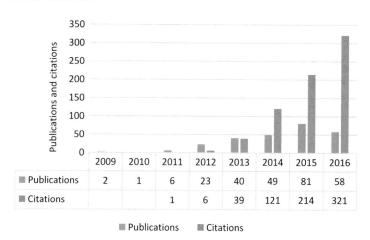

Fig. 5 Publications and citations

Table 3 lists the productivity ordered by regional and country contribution. It shows that Asia is the major contributor to cloud forensics publications with a total of 36.92% of all publications. It is closely followed by Europe with 28.85%. The North American, African, Australian and Middle Eastern regions total 34.23% combined. Asia and Europe are therefore the most productive regions both contributing to almost two-thirds of all publications.

Within Asian India and China are clear research-leaders with a combined 26.92% of overall global publications. 72.92% of all publications produced by 9 countries in Asia. The second highest contributor, Europe, has 2 clear research leaders with England and Ireland contributing 14.23% of all global publications and 49.33% of

Table 3 Productivity by region

List of regions	No. of articles	(%)	List of regions	No. of articles	(%)
Asia	**96**	**36.92**	Scotland	2	0.77
India	40	15.38	Croatia	1	0.38
Peoples R China	30	11.54	Poland	1	0.38
Taiwan	7	2.69	Serbia	1	0.38
Japan	5	1.92	Slovenia	1	0.38
South Korea	4	1.54	Spain	1	0.38
Bangladesh	3	1.15	Switzerland	1	0.38
Malaysia	3	1.15	Wales	1	0.38
Pakistan	3	1.15	**North America**	**46**	**17.69**
Sri Lanka	1	0.38	USA	42	16.15
Europe	**75**	**28.85**	Canada	4	1.54
England	21	8.08	**Africa**	**22**	**8.46**
Ireland	16	6.15	South Africa	19	7.31
Italy	7	2.69	Ghana	1	0.38
Greece	6	2.31	Morocco	1	0.38
Germany	5	1.92	Tunisia	1	0.38
Romania	5	1.92	**Australia**	**17**	**6.54**
France	2	0.77	Australia	17	6.54
Netherlands	2	0.77	**Middle East**	**4**	**1.54**
Norway	2	0.77	U Arab Emirates	4	1.54

Table 4 Productivity by leading regional countries

Country	Region	No. countries in region	Publications (%)	Contribution to region %
USA	North America	2	16.15	91.30
India	Asia	9	15.38	41.67
Peoples R China	Asia	9	11.54	31.25
England	Europe	17	8.08	28.00
Australia	Australia	1	6.54	100.00
South Africa	Africa	4	7.31	86.36
Ireland	Europe	17	6.15	21.33
U Arab Emirates	Middle East	1	1.54	100.00

the publications from the 17 countries in that region. North America is a single leader in the USA with 16.15% overall and 91.30% regional contribution out of just the 2 representative countries. The USA, India and China are the overall top 3 countries with a combined total of 43.08% of all publications. Table 4 shows the major contributing countries within each region.

Table 5 Research areas

Research areas	Publications	%
Computer Science	130	50.00
Computer Science; Engineering	56	21.54
Computer Science; Telecommunications	22	8.46
Engineering; Telecommunications	12	4.62
Computer Science; Engineering; Telecommunications	8	3.08
Engineering	6	2.31
Computer Science; Engineering; Information Science & Library Science; Government & Law; Telecommunications	3	1.15
Telecommunications	3	1.15
Automation & Control Systems; Computer Science	2	0.77
Computer Science; International Relations	2	0.77
Government & Law	2	0.77
Automation & Control Systems; Computer Science; Engineering	1	0.38
Automation & Control Systems; Engineering	1	0.38
Automation & Control Systems; Engineering; Materials Science	1	0.38
Computer Science; Criminology & Penology	1	0.38
Computer Science; Education & Educational Research	1	0.38
Computer Science; Engineering; Operations Research & Management Science	1	0.38
Computer Science; Medical Informatics	1	0.38
Computer Science; Operations Research & Management Science	1	0.38
Computer Science; Physics	1	0.38
Criminology & Penology	1	0.38
Engineering; Materials Science	1	0.38
Engineering; Medical Informatics	1	0.38

3.2   Research Areas

The WoS database contains 150 different scientific research areas that can be categorised depending on the focus and reach of the research across multiple sectors. As seen in Table 5 they can be a combination of single and multi-disciplined research. Table 5 illustrates that 50% of all publications are attributed to the single-disciplined Computer Science research area. The second and third highest research areas are the multi-disciplined Computer Science & Engineering (21.54%), and Computer Science and Telecommunications (8.46%). Within this study the most influential publications in the top 3 research areas are "Acquiring Forensic Evidence from Infrastructure-As-A-Service Cloud Computing: Exploring and Evaluating Tools, Trust, And Techniques", "Cloud Computing-Based Forensic Analysis for Collaborative Network Security Management System" and "A Cloud Computing Platform for Large-Scale Forensic Computing".

Table 6 Research areas in isolation

Research areas	No. publications	%
Computer Science	230	88.46
Engineering	91	35.00
Telecommunications	48	18.46
Automation Control Systems	5	1.92
Government Law	5	1.92
Information Science Library Science	3	1.15
Criminology Penology	2	0.77
International Relations	2	0.77
Materials Science	2	0.77
Medical Informatics	2	0.77
Operations Research Management Science	2	0.77
Education Educational Research	1	0.39
Legal Medicine	1	0.39
Physics	1	0.39
Science Technology Other Topics	1	0.39

Table 6 displays each research area in isolation and illustrates that the research Computer Science research contains majority of the published articles, featuring 88.46% of all publications. Engineering and Telecommunications area feature 35% and 18.46% of all publications respectively.

3.3 Institutions

This section discusses the number of publications attributed to different institutions to determine which institutions are prevalent within cloud forensics research.

Table 7 lists the institutions with at least three relevant publications. Combined they are credited for 44.83% of all publications. The University of Pretoria (South Africa), University of South Australia (Australia) and University College Dublin (Ireland) are the 3 leading institutions with 5.38%, 5% and 4.62% of total publications respectively. The list features 7 institutions from Asia, 6 from Europe, 2 from North America and 1 each from Africa, Australia and The Middle east. The single country with the highest number of institutions is India with 3 institutions.

3.4 Impact Journals

This section discusses the impact journals from the cloud forensics research. The findings from this section will help the researcher identify the best publication to promote their papers.

Table 7 List of Institutions

Institution	Publications	Publications %	Country
University of Pretoria	14	5.38	South Africa
University of South Australia	13	5.00	Australia
University College Dublin	12	4.62	Ireland
Birla Institute of Technology and Science	10	3.85	India
Tsinghua University	6	2.31	Peoples R China
University of The Aegean	6	2.31	Greece
University of Alabama at Birmingham	6	2.31	USA
Military Technical Academy	5	1.92	Romania
University of New Orleans	4	1.54	USA
University of Plymouth	4	1.54	England
Central Police University	3	1.15	Taiwan
Cisco Systems Inc	3	1.15	India
G.H. Raisoni College of Engineering	3	1.15	India
Khalifa University	3	1.15	U Arab Emirates
Ministry of Public Security	3	1.15	Peoples R China
Nanjing University	3	1.15	Peoples R China
National University of Sciences and Technology	3	1.15	Pakistan
University of Derby	3	1.15	England
University of Naples Federico II	3	1.15	Italy

Table 8 Impact journals

Journal title	P	C	CY	CI	H	IF	Q	%
ACM Computing Surveys	357	5561	695.12	15.58	33	5.243	1	0.86
Future Generation Computer Systems the International Journal of Grid Computing and EScience	611	6431	803.88	10.53	28	2.430	1	0.86
IEEE Transactions on Dependable and Secure Computing	387	2459	307.38	6.35	21	1.592	1	0.86
Digital Investigation	322	1319	164.88	4.1	17	1.211	2	10.78
Computer	2113	7213	801.44	3.41	33	1.115	2	1.29
Tsinghua Science and Technology	228	379	75.8	1.66	8	1.063	4	1.72
Journal of Internet Technology	835	1249	156.12	1.5	10	0.533	4	0.86
Computer Law Security Review	492	478	95.6	0.97	10	0.373	3	0.86

P No. Publications, *C* No. citations, *CY* Average citations per year, *CI* Average citations per item, *H* h-index, *IF* Impact factor, *Q* Quartile in category

Table 8 lists the journal titles identified within this study and their citation and publication data for the period 2009–2016. Although Digital Investigation is the journal with the highest number of publications, it has a relatively low impact factor (1.211)

Table 9 Top source titles

Source titles	No. publications	%
Digital Investigation	27	10.39
Lecture Notes in Computer Science	11	4.23
IFIP Advances in Information and Communication Technology	11	4.23
Proceedings of The International Conference on Cloud Security Management	7	2.69
Advances in Digital Forensics XI	4	1.54
Communications in Computer and Information Science	4	1.54
Computers Security	4	1.54
Lecture Notes of the Institute for Computer Sciences Social Informatics and Telecommunications Engineering	4	1.54
Proceedings 10th International Conference on Availability Reliability and Security Ares 2015	4	1.54
Tsinghua Science and Technology	4	1.54
2013 Eighth International Workshop on Systematic Approaches to Digital Forensic Engineering SADFE	3	1.15
Advances in Digital Forensics VIII	3	1.15
Computer	3	1.15
Digital Forensics and Cyber Crime ICDF2C 2012	3	1.15
IEEE Cloud Computing	3	1.15
IEEE International Advance Computing Conference	3	1.15
Information Security for South Africa	3	1.15
International Workshop on Systematic Approaches to Digital Forensic Engineering SADFE	3	1.15
Procedia Computer Science	3	1.15
Proceedings of 2016 11th International Conference on Availability Reliability and Security Ares 2016	3	1.15
Proceedings of the 3rd International Conference on Cloud Security and Management ICCSM 2015	3	1.15
Proceedings of The International Conference on Information Warfare and Security	3	1.15

The Computer Surveys journal published by the Association for Computing Machinery (ACM) has the highest impact factor (5.243) and the highest average number of citations per paper (15.58). It also has the highest h-index which is a measure of predicting future scientific achievement proposed [48].Within the Computer Science, Theory & Methods citation reports category it is ranked 2 out of 105 whereas between the years 2002-2011 it was ranked at no. 1.

Table 9 lists the journals and books that have published at least three relevant articles.

The Digital Investigation journal is a clear leader with 10.39% of all publications. Digital Investigation is an international journal in digital forensics & incident response promoting innovations and advancement in the field.

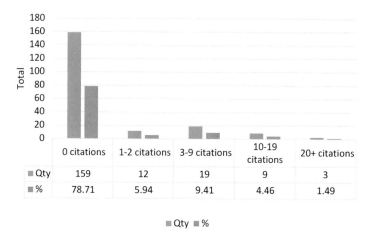

	0 citations	1-2 citations	3-9 citations	10-19 citations	20+ citations
■ Qty	159	12	19	9	3
■ %	78.71	5.94	9.41	4.46	1.49

■ Qty ■ %

Fig. 6 No. citations

3.5   Highly-Cited Articles

This section discusses the most highly-cited articles within both journal and book publications. Figure 6 shows that 78.71% of all publications in this study do not yet have any citations. Only 5.94% of the 260 publications have greater than 10 citations.

Table 10 lists the articles that have received more than 10 citations between 2009 and 2016.

It also includes details of the publication (journal or book series), published year and research area.

The Computer Science research area comprises 89% of this list and the journal Digital Investigation is responsible for 57.89% all published articles. The top 3 cited articles were all published in 2012 which reinforces the idea that the earlier a work is published, the more it will be cited. The top 3 articles are high quality forensics procedural-based research papers [38] that are acknowledged by future authors due to their originality and value [49].

3.6   Keywords Frequency

This section discusses the use of author keywords and how it enables researchers to identify specific research [50]. The publications within this study contained 1172 keywords across 260 publications; 35 did not contain any keywords. The largest number of keywords for publications is 17; the average number of keywords is 4.52. The top author keywords and their relationship to their occurrence within the title are provided in Table 11.

Table 10 Highly-cited articles

Title	Times cited	Publication	Year	Research areas
Acquiring Forensic Evidence from Infrastructure-As-A-Service Cloud Computing: Exploring and Evaluating Tools, Trust, And Techniques	44	Digital Investigation	2012	Computer Science
An Integrated Conceptual Digital Forensic Framework for Cloud Computing	43	Digital Investigation	2012	Computer Science
Digital Forensic Investigation of Cloud Storage Services	37	Digital Investigation	2012	Computer Science
Cloud Forensics Definitions and Critical Criteria for Cloud Forensic Capability: An Overview of Survey Results	31	Digital Investigation	2013	Computer Science
Dropbox Analysis: Data Remnants on User Machines	28	Digital Investigation	2013	Computer Science
Cloud Storage Forensics: OwnCloud as A Case Study	26	Digital Investigation	2013	Computer Science
Efficient Audit Service Outsourcing for Data Integrity in Clouds	25	Journal of Systems and Software	2012	Computer Science
Design and Implementation of Frost: Digital Forensic Tools for The Openstack Cloud Computing Platform	25	Digital Investigation	2013	Computer Science
Digital Droplets: Microsoft Skydrive Forensic Data Remnants	25	Future Generation Computer Systems - The International Journal of Grid Computing and EScience	2013	Computer Science
Forensic Collection of Cloud Storage Data: Does the Act of Collection Result in Changes to The Data or Its Metadata?	23	Digital Investigation	2013	Computer Science
Google Drive: Forensic Analysis of Data Remnants	21	Journal of Network and Computer Applications	2014	Computer Science
Cloud Computing-Based Forensic Analysis for Collaborative Network Security Management System	20	Tsinghua Science and Technology	2013	Computer Science; Engineering
Cloud Computing and Its Implications for Cybercrime Investigations in Australia	18	Computer Law & Security Review	2013	Government & Law

(continued)

Table 10 (continued)

Title	Times cited	Publication	Year	Research areas
Impacts of Increasing Volume of Digital Forensic Data: A Survey and Future Research Challenges	15	Digital Investigation	2014	Computer Science
A Survey of Information Security Incident Handling in The Cloud	14	Computers & Security	2015	Computer Science
Amazon Cloud Drive Forensic Analysis	12	Digital Investigation	2013	Computer Science
Distributed Filesystem Forensics: XtreemFS as A Case Study	11	Digital Investigation	2014	Computer Science
A Forensically Sound Adversary Model for Mobile Devices	11	Plos One	2015	Science & Technology - Other Topics
Overcast: Forensic Discovery in Cloud Environments	10	IMF 2009: 5th International Conference on IT Security Incident Management and IT Forensic	2009	Computer Science

Table 11 Relationship between title and author keywords

Titles	Frequency	Keywords	Frequency
Cloud	187	Cloud computing	104
Forensic	178	Digital forensics	78
Forensics	81	Cloud forensics	66
Digital	68	Computer forensics	20
Digital forensic	58	Security	19
Cloud computing	48	Digital evidence	12
Analysis	42	Cloud storage	11
Cloud forensic	34	Cloud	10
Data	34	Forensics	10
Digital forensics	33	Digital investigation	10
Cloud forensics	26	Big data	7
Model	23	Network forensics	7
Evidence	21	Evidence	6
Security	19	Privacy	6
Challenges	15	Cybercrime	6
Forensic analysis	13	Cloud forensics challenges	6
Log	13	Virtualization	6
Forensic investigation	12	Digital	5

The top 3 author keywords are "cloud computing", "digital forensics" and "cloud forensics". Within this study the top 3 author keywords have been included together in 19 publications; at least 2 of the top 3 keywords have featured in 46 publications. The mostly used keywords paper titles are "cloud", "forensic" and "forensics" with 187, 178 and 81 occurrences respectively. The author keyword "forensic" is included in just 4 publications but features highly in titles. Two examples of this are the publications "Cloud Manufacturing: Security, Privacy and Forensic Concerns" and "An Integrated Conceptual Digital Forensic Framework for Cloud Computing".

4   Challenges and Future Trends

This section discusses the limitations that a forensic investigator may face during examination within a cloud environment. Moreover, issues relating to data sovereignty, data confidentiality, and inadequacy of existing legislative and regulatory frameworks are elaborated [51].

4.1   Evidence Identification

Identification is the reporting of any malicious activity in the cloud such as illegal file storage or file deletion. The identification phase is initiated as a result of a complaint made by an individual or by a CSP authority that reports any misuse of the cloud [52]. The distributed nature of cloud computing makes evidence identification a difficult task. The first evidence collection issue that an investigator will encounter is of the system status and log files. Whereas this is not possible to collect in either a SaaS or PaaS model, it is possible in an IaaS cloud model where access is provided through a Virtual Machine (VM); within this model the VM behaves almost the same as an Actual Machine [53].

Data loss from volatile storage is the next issue facing a forensic investigator as all the client's data is volatile due to the high dependence on cloud computing. Also, due to the nature of cloud computing storage policies any evidence or stored data in the volatile storage will be removed, or deleted, if the criminal restarts or forces a power down of the computer.

Client-side evidence identification is another necessary step in computer forensic investigations that is usually not possible, especially in SaaS and PaaS models. In both models there are always some vital parts of evidence data that can be found on the client side interface (e.g. web browser temp data) [54]. Thus, the fragile and volatile nature of cloud environments require more attention and specialist techniques to ensure that the evidence data can be properly evaluated and isolated.

4.2   Legal Issues in the Cloud

Special care should be taken in from the outset to ensure that privacy of users are not violated during investigation of any criminal case [55]. Crimes involving cloud computing typically involve an accumulation or retention of data on a digital device (such as a mobile phone) that must be identified, preserved, analysed, and presented in a court of law [56]. Cloud data distribution within numerous data centres around the world creates jurisdictional issues relating to locating and seizing elusive evidential data [57]. Because of the nature of cloud computing, investigations require a co-operation between government agencies and law enforcement investigations from different countries, in addition to a collaboration of cloud service providers.

4.3   Data Collection and Preservation

Data collection in a computer forensic investigation is a significantly vital task and requires a physical acquisition for any forensic investigation. For example, within digital forensics the process of taking custody of any storage device (including hard disk) and then taking a bit-by-bit image for this device is one of the procedures that must be performed. This becomes a key issue in cloud computing as this step of the process is not possible due to the shared nature of the cloud environment. The investigator may have to contact the CSP for physical acquisition of data because these resources are distributed between numerous data centers, as previously discussed. Moreover, resources can be shared simultaneously among multiple cloud clients and can be constantly in use. The privacy of other client's data is therefore another issue faced in the seizure of physical evidence [58].

The data collection phase of cloud forensics should also consider the storage capacity for collecting evidence [59]. The amount of extracted data and the collected evidence would be greater than non-cloud digital forensics because of the wider nature of the cloud. The preservation of the evidence in a forensic investigation is vital to prove that an offence has been committed and how it relates to evidence can make it inadmissible. Another issue in evidence collection and preservation is the chain of custody which is the chronological documentation that shows how evidence was collected, preserved and analyzed [59]. Again, due to the cloud nature this attribute can violate digital forensic rules. To solve this challenge having a multifactor authentication method can prevent the perpetrator from claiming stolen authentication credentials [54].

4.4 *Analysis and Presentation*

Data analysis is another phase involving the analysis of collected data from different resource layers. In cloud computing this step has significant challenges because of the utilization of the intensive computation and massive data within cloud computing. This becomes an additional issue for cloud forensics investigation mainly due to the limitations in processing and examining vast amounts of data [60]. During forensics presentation, the judge or jury members may not fully understand the validity of evidence collected from the cloud, or comprehend what they are being told, or shown.

4.5 *Future Trends*

When considering the challenges that cloud computing environments offer there are several areas of future research that could be undertaken, for example: the evidence collection process and data volatility in SaaS and PaaS cloud models; chain of custody and privacy considerations for the seizure of physical evidence; jurisdiction and multi-agency/provider collaboration within cloud environments.

5 Conclusion

Cloud computing and the internet are interrelated and that makes them increasingly vulnerable to security threats. Digital forensic practitioners must extend their expertise and toolsets to conduct cloud examination. Moreover, cloud-based entities, CSPs and cloud customers must consider including built-in forensic capabilities to their platforms. In this paper the bibliometric methods were used to analyse cloud forensic research trends from 2009 until 2016. We presented criteria including publication statistics, citation distributions and statistics, regional and institutional productivity, research areas, impact journals, and keywords frequency. These criteria helped to uncover the global trends and significant areas in cloud forensic research. It is noticeable that the number of publications relating to cloud forensics has increased with an average annual growth rate of 218%. Asia had the largest number of publication in academic research followed by Europe and North America respectively. This paper findings provide researchers with better understanding of emerging trends in cloud forensic and help them to identify key areas for future research in this field. Future works may include conducting bibliometric analysis in areas of IoT security and forensics [61], OSX [62], mobile [63] and IoT [64] malware analysis, Trojans [65] ransomware [66] investigation.

References

1. "Forecast: IT Services, 2011-2017, 4Q13 Update." [Online]. Available: https://www.gartner.com/doc/2637515/forecast-it-services–q. [Accessed: 09-Dec-2016].
2. Cisco Public, "Cisco Global Cloud Index: Forecast and Methodology, 2015–2020," 2016.
3. P. Mell and T. Grance, "The NIST Final Version of NIST Cloud Computing Definition Published," *Nist Spec. Publ.*, vol. 145, p. 7, 2011.
4. S. Bhardwaj, L. Jain, and S. Jain, "An Approach for Investigating Perspective of Cloud Software-as-a-Service (SaaS)," *Int. J. Comput. Appl.*, vol. 10, no. 2, pp. 975–8887, 2010.
5. P. Mell and T. Grance, "The NIST Definition of Cloud Computing Recommendations of the National Institute of Standards and Technology," *Natl. Inst. Stand. Technol. Inf. Technol. Lab.*, vol. 145, p. 7, 2011.
6. J. Dykstra and A. T. Sherman, "Acquiring forensic evidence from infrastructure-as-a-service cloud computing: Exploring and evaluating tools, trust, and techniques," *Digit. Investig.*, vol. 9, no. S, pp. S90–S98, Aug. 2012.
7. N. Gupta, B. Tech, B. Chauhan, T. Anand, and C. Dewan, "Cloud Computing: Comparison with Previous Technique and Research Challenges," *Int. J. Comput. Appl.*, vol. 85, no. 8, pp. 975–8887, 2014.
8. K. Weins, "Cloud Computing Trends: 2016 State of the Cloud Survey," 2016.
9. A. Hutchings, R. G. Smith, and L. James, "Criminals in the Cloud: Crime, Security Threats, and Prevention Measures," in *Cybercrime Risks and Responses*, London: Palgrave Macmillan UK, 2015, pp. 146–162.
10. "Cybercrime Now Surpasses Traditional Crime In UK." [Online]. Available: http://www.darkreading.com/threat-intelligence/cybercrime-now-surpasses-traditional-crime-in-uk/d/d-id/1326208. [Accessed: 12-Dec-2016].
11. K. Ruan, J. Carthy, T. Kechadi, and M. Crosbie, "Cloud forensics," *Advances in Digital Forensics VII, IFIP Advances in Information and Communication Technology*, vol. 361. pp. 35–46, 2011.
12. M. Al Fahdi, N. L. Clarke, and S. M. Furnell, "Challenges to digital forensics: A survey of researchers & practitioners attitudes and opinions," in *2013 Information Security for South Africa - Proceedings of the ISSA 2013 Conference*, 2013.
13. A. T. Dykstra, Josiah; Sherman, "UNDERSTANDING ISSUES IN CLOUD FORENSICS: TWO HYPOTHETICAL CASE STUDIES - ProQuest," *Proc. Conf. Digit. Forensics, Secur. Law*, no. 45, pp. 1–10, 2011.
14. S. Alqahtany, N. Clarke, S. Furnell, and C. Reich, "A forensic acquisition and analysis system for IaaS," *Clust. Comput. J. NETWORKS Softw. TOOLS Appl.*, vol. 19, no. 1, pp. 439–453, Mar. 2016.
15. "Forensic Toolkit (FTK)." [Online]. Available: http://accessdata.com/products-services/forensic-toolkit-ftk. [Accessed: 13-Jul-2017].
16. "EnCase Endpoint Investigator - Remote Digital Investigation Solution." [Online]. Available: https://www.guidancesoftware.com/encase-endpoint-investigator. [Accessed: 13-Jul-2017].
17. "Snort - Network Intrusion Detection & Prevention System." [Online]. Available: https://www.snort.org/. [Accessed: 13-Jul-2017].
18. J. Dykstra and A. T. Sherman, "Design and implementation of FROST: Digital forensic tools for the OpenStack cloud computing platform," in *Digital Investigation*, 2013, vol. 10, no. SUPPL.
19. E. Bursztein, I. Fontarensky, M. Martin, and J.-M. Picod, "Beyond files recovery OWADE cloud-based forensic." BlackHat, 2011.
20. Amazon Web Services, "AWS CloudTrail : User Guide," 2016.
21. G. Combs, "Wireshark · Go Deep.," 2017. [Online]. Available: https://www.wireshark.org/. [Accessed: 29-May-2017].
22. "The Sleuth Kit." [Online]. Available: http://www.sleuthkit.org/sleuthkit/. [Accessed: 13-Jul-2017].

23. "Software for Computer Forensics, Data Recovery, and IT Security." [Online]. Available: http://www.x-ways.net/. [Accessed: 13-Jul-2017].
24. "EnCase eDiscovery- Litigation Hold Management & Digital Forensics." [Online]. Available: https://www.guidancesoftware.com/encase-ediscovery. [Accessed: 13-Jul-2017].
25. B. Martini and K.-K. R. Choo, "An integrated conceptual digital forensic framework for cloud computing," *Digit. Investig.*, vol. 9, no. 2, pp. 71–80, Nov. 2012.
26. N. H. Ab Rahman, N. D. W. Cahyani, and K. K. R. Choo, "Cloud incident handling and forensic-by-design: Cloud storage as a case study," *Concurrency Computation* , 2016.
27. D. Quick and K.-K. R. Choo, "Dropbox analysis: Data remnants on user machines," *Digit. Investig.*, vol. 10, no. 1, pp. 3–18, Jun. 2013.
28. F. Daryabar, A. Dehghantanha, and K.-K. R. Choo, "Cloud storage forensics: MEGA as a case study," *Aust. J. Forensic Sci.*, vol. 618, no. July, pp. 1–14, 2016.
29. F. Daryabar *et al.*, "Forensic investigation of OneDrive, Box, GoogleDrive and Dropbox applications on Android and iOS devices," *Aust. J. Forensic Sci.*, vol. 48, no. 1, pp. 1–28, 2016.
30. R. Shariati, Mohammad; Dehghantanha, Ali; Choo, "SugarSync Forensic Analysis," *Res. Artic.*, p. 28, 2014.
31. T. Dargahi, A. Dehghantanha, and M. Conti, "Chapter 12 – Investigating Storage as a Service Cloud Platform: pCloud as a Case Study," in *Contemporary Digital Forensic Investigations of Cloud and Mobile Applications*, 2017, pp. 185–204.
32. S. H. Mohtasebi, A. Dehghantanha, and K.-K. R. Choo, "Chapter 13 – Cloud Storage Forensics: Analysis of Data Remnants on SpiderOak, JustCloud, and pCloud," in *Contemporary Digital Forensic Investigations of Cloud and Mobile Applications*, 2017, pp. 205–246.
33. A. Dehghantanha and T. Dargahi, "Chapter 14 – Residual Cloud Forensics: CloudMe and 360Yunpan as Case Studies," in *Contemporary Digital Forensic Investigations of Cloud and Mobile Applications*, 2017, pp. 247–283.
34. B. Blakeley, C. Cooney, A. Dehghantanha, and R. Aspin, "Cloud Storage Forensic: hubiC as a Case-Study," in *2015 IEEE 7TH INTERNATIONAL CONFERENCE ON CLOUD COMPUTING TECHNOLOGY AND SCIENCE (CLOUDCOM)*, 2015, pp. 536–541.
35. Y.-Y. Teing, D. Ali, K. Choo, M. T. Abdullah, and Z. Muda, "Greening Cloud-Enabled Big Data Storage Forensics: Syncany as a Case Study," *IEEE Trans. Sustain. Comput.*, pp. 1–1, 2017.
36. Y.-Y. Teing, A. Dehghantanha, K.-K. R. Choo, and L. T. Yang, "Forensic investigation of P2P cloud storage services and backbone for IoT networks: BitTorrent Sync as a case study," *Comput. Electr. Eng.*, 2016.
37. Y.-Y. Teing, A. Dehghantanha, K.-K. R. Choo, T. Dargahi, and M. Conti, "Forensic Investigation of Cooperative Storage Cloud Service: Symform as a Case Study," *J. Forensic Sci.*, Nov. 2016.
38. S. A. Almulla, Y. Iraqi, and A. Jones, "A State-of-the-Art Review of Cloud Forensics," *J. Digit. Forensics, Secur. Law*, vol. 9, no. 4, pp. 7–28, 2014.
39. G. E. Derrick, A. Haynes, S. Chapman, and W. D. Hall, "The Association between Four Citation Metrics and Peer Rankings of Research Influence of Australian Researchers in Six Fields of Public Health," *PLoS One*, vol. 6, no. 4, 2011.
40. E. Garfield, "The History and Meaning of the Journal Impact Factor," *J. Am. Med. Assoc.*, vol. 19104, no. 1, pp. 90–93, 2006.
41. "A New Dimension in Documentation through Association of Ideas." [Online]. Available: http://www.garfield.library.upenn.edu/papers/science_v122v3159p108y1955.html. [Accessed: 09-Dec-2016].
42. L. I. Meho and K. Yang, "Impact of data sources on citation counts and rankings of LIS faculty: Web of science versus scopus and google scholar," *J. Am. Soc. Inf. Sci. Technol.*, vol. 58, no. 13, pp. 2105–2125, 2007.
43. G. Ict and S. March, "Government Cloud Strategy," no. March, 2011.
44. M. Metheny, "Federal Cloud Computing," *Fed. Cloud Comput.*, pp. 71–102, 2013.
45. H. Small, "Visualizing science by citation mapping," *J. Am. Soc. Inf. Sci.*, vol. 50, no. 9, pp. 799–813, 1999.

46. M. F. A. Razak, N. B. Anuar, R. Salleh, and A. Firdaus, "The rise of malware: Bibliometric analysis of malware study," *Journal of Network and Computer Applications*, vol. 75. pp. 58–76, 2016.
47. L. Bornmann and H.-D. Daniel, *What do citation counts measure? A review of studies on citing behavior*, vol. 64, no. 1. 2008.
48. J. E. Hirsch, "Does the H index have predictive power?," *Proc. Natl. Acad. Sci. U. S. A.*, vol. 104, no. 49, pp. 19193–8, 2007.
49. E. Garfield, "Can Citation Indexing be Automated?," *Stat. Assoc . Methods Mech. Doc.*, vol. 269, pp. 84–90, 1964.
50. X. Wu, X. Chen, F. B. Zhan, and S. Hong, "Global research trends in landslides during 1991???2014: a bibliometric analysis," *Landslides*, vol. 12, no. 6, pp. 1215–1226, 2015.
51. K. Choo, "Cloud computing: challenges and future directions," *Trends Issues Crime Crim. Justice*, no. 400, pp. 1–6, 2010.
52. J. J. Shah and L. G. Malik, "Cloud Forensics: Issues and Challenges," in *2013 Sixth International Conference on Emerging Trends in Engineering and Technology (ICETET 2013)*, 2013, pp. 138–139.
53. D. Birk and C. Wegener, "Technical Issues of Forensic Investigations in Cloud Computing Environments," *2011 Sixth IEEE Int. Work. Syst. Approaches to Digit. Forensic Eng.*, pp. 1–10, 2011.
54. M. Damshenas, A. Dehghantanha, R. Mahmoud, and S. Bin Shamsuddin, "Forensics investigation challenges in cloud computing environments," in *Proceedings 2012 International Conference on Cyber Security, Cyber Warfare and Digital Forensic, CyberSec 2012*, 2012, pp. 190–194.
55. N. Raza, "Challenges to network forensics in cloud computing," in *Proceedings - 2015 Conference on Information Assurance and Cyber Security, CIACS 2015*, 2016, pp. 22–29.
56. A. Butler and K. Choo, "IT standards and guides do not adequately prepare IT practitioners to appear as expert witnesses: An Australian perspective," *Secur. J.*, pp. 1–20, 2013.
57. D. Quick, B. Martini, and K.-K. R. Choo, "Cloud Storage Forensics," *Cloud Storage Forensics*, no. October, pp. 13–21, 2014.
58. S. Ahmed and M. Y. A. Raja, "Tackling cloud security issues and forensics model," in *7th International Symposium on High-Capacity Optical Networks and Enabling Technologies, HONET 2010*, 2010, pp. 190–195.
59. G. Grispos, T. Storer, and W. Glisson, "Calm before the storm: the challenges of cloud computing in digital forensics," *Int. J. Digit. Crime Forensics*, vol. 4, no. 2, pp. 28–48, 2012.
60. D. Reilly, C. Wren, and T. Berry, "Cloud computing: Forensic challenges for law enforcement," *Internet Technol. Secur. Trans. (ICITST), 2010 Int. Conf.*, pp. 1–7, 2010.
61. Mauro Conti, Ali Dehghantanha, Katrin Franke, Steve Watson, "Internet of Things Security and Forensics: Challenges and Opportunities", Future Generation Computer Systems Journal, DoI: https://doi.org/10.1016/j.future.2017.07.060, 2017
62. Hamed HaddadPajouh, Ali Dehghantanha, Raouf Khayami, and Kim-Kwang Raymond Choo, "Intelligent OS X Malware Threat Detection", Journal of Computer Virology and Hacking Techniques, 2017
63. Amin Azmoodeh, Ali Dehghantanha, Mauro Conti, Raymond Choo, "Detecting Crypto-Ransomware in IoT Networks Based On Energy Consumption Footprint", Journal of Ambient Intelligence and Humanized Computing, DOI: 10.1007/s12652-017-0558-5, 2017
64. Amin Azmoudeh, Ali Dehghantanha and Kim-Kwang Raymond Choo, "Robust Malware Detection for Internet Of (Battlefield) Things Devices Using Deep Eigenspace Learning", IEEE Transactions on Sustainable Computing, 2017
65. Dennis Kiwia, Ali Dehghantanha, Kim-Kwang Raymond Choo, Jim Slaughter, "A Cyber Kill Chain Based Taxonomy of Banking Trojans for Evolutionary Computational Intelligence", Journal of Computational Science, 2017
66. Sajad Homayoun, Ali Dehghantanha, Marzieh Ahmadzadeh, Sattar Hashemi, Raouf Khayami, "Know Abnormal, Find Evil: Frequent Pattern Mining for Ransomware Threat Hunting and Intelligence", IEEE Transactions on Emerging Topics in Computing, 2017 - DOI: 10.1109/TETC.2017.2756908

Index

© Springer International Publishing AG, part of Springer Nature 2018
A. Dehghantanha et al. (eds.), *Cyber Threat Intelligence*, Advances in Information
Security 70, https://doi.org/10.1007/978-3-319-73951-9